And the Beat Goes On

And the Beat Goes On

An Introduction to Popular Music in America, 1840 to Today

Michael Campbell

Schirmer Books
New York

Schirmer Books
1633 Broadway
New York, NY 10019

Library of Congress Catalog Card Number: 95-31768

Printed in the United States of America

printing number
    4 5 6 7 8 9 10

Library of Congress Cataloging-in-Publication Data

Campbell, Michael, 1945–
    And the beat goes on : an introduction to popular music in America
1840 to today / Michael Campbell.
        p.   cm.
    Includes bibliographical references (p.   ) and index.
    ISBN 0-02-870165-8
    1. Popular music–United States–History and criticism.
I. Title.
ML3477.C36   1995
781.64′0973–dc20   95-31768
                                                        CIP
                                                        MN

This paper meets the requirements of ANSI/NISO Z39.48-1992 (Permanence of Paper).
All photographs courtesy Frank Driggs Collection unless otherwise noted.

Dedication

To Jimmy Wells, Donald Bailey, and Hugh Walker,
three fine Baltimore jazz musicians
who gave me–by instruction and example–an essential part
of my musical education.

Contents

Prelude

As this is written, popular music is so much a part of life in America that we perhaps take it for granted. It is available to us almost anytime and anywhere we want. Its biggest stars, like Elvis and Madonna, are such celebrities—in Elvis's case, even in death—that one name identifies them. It is difficult to imagine a time when popular music did not have such a pervasive presence.

Yet only forty years ago, Elvis was a truck driver, the British hadn't invaded, transistor radios and portable playback equipment were not available, and the multitrack recording studio was still an audio engineer's fantasy. In 1914, forty years earlier, George Gershwin was still learning to play the piano and Louis Armstrong had just started playing the cornet (a cousin of the trumpet). Commercial radio was almost a decade away, talking films almost two, and network television more than three. Most of the great Tin Pan Alley songs had yet to be written, almost all of the great musicals had yet to be staged, and all of the great jazz performances had yet to be recorded. In 1874 there was no ragtime, no vaudeville, no sound recording, and no popular music industry. In 1834, the idea of a distinct popular music tradition had just begun to take shape.

It is difficult to overstate the difference between popular music then and now. Early in the nineteenth century, there was music that was popular, but no popular music as we know it. Most of the secular music that was popular in the United States came from Europe or was composed by European musicians working in America. There was virtually no identifiably American popular music, no well-established tradition of American popular song or dance music.

Today popular music is a global, multibillion dollar industry whose products are available at the push of a button. In its many forms—country, jazz, rock, blues, popular song, musical theater—it has been America's most distinctive and impressive cultural achievement and its most popular export. Economically, culturally, technologically, and musically, the differences between popular music then and now are so pronounced that they seem to be from different worlds.

Nevertheless, a clear evolutionary path runs through the popular music of the last 150 years. Before then, music that was popular was solely European in fact or inspiration. A distinctive popular tradition emerged only through cross-pollination of established European styles with white and African-American folk music. African-American music has been the primary catalyst in the evolutionary process. Change has come about mainly through the infusion of African elements into the prevailing popular style. Each major period of change has produced a mainstream style that shows more extensive African influence. From the largely indirect, almost tangential influence evident in the minstrel show, popular music has evolved to the fully integrated styles of today.

Progress along the evolutionary path has moved in a zigzag pattern, not a forward march. Periodic interactions between Americans of European and African descent thoroughly redefined the prevailing popular style, creating a new music distinctly different from the one it replaced. After a short period of change and consolidation—about fifteen years—the most commercially important branches of the new style reached a plateau. At this point the new style was, for all intents and purposes, fully evolved. After the formation of a new style, the dominant trend was a partial return to the musical values in place prior to the period of change. The evolution of popular music has been a case of two steps forward, one step back: revolution followed by retreat.

THE REVOLUTIONS OF POPULAR MUSIC

There have been three revolutions in the history of American popular music. All three started on the fringes of popular taste, as "low-class music" not suitable for respectable people. Before long, however, outside was on the inside, and new had supplanted old. Each new style would take little more than a decade to become commercially and musically dominant.

Prior to the first revolution, most popular music came from—or, on some occasions through—Western Europe. Even the popular music created in the United States was firmly based on European models. The popular songs of the day had much in common with the more accessible music of European classical masters Beethoven, Schubert, Rossini, and Bellini. Differences between "popular" and "classical" were, more than anything, a matter of craft and complexity. All spoke the same musical language with much the same accent.

The creation of the minstrel show in the early 1840s touched off the first revolution. Minstrel songs were a vigorous everyman's music. They gave expression to particularly American attitudes that had emerged in the 1820s and 1830s. In both words and music, they contrasted sharply with the slow and sentimental songs fashionable in genteel parlors.

This first revolution established an American musical vernacular. No one would confuse "Dixie" or "Oh! Susanna" (both minstrel songs) with European music. This musical vernacular quickly caught on. By the Civil War, dozens of minstrel-show songs were on everyone's lips. For the rest of the century, they coexisted with parlor songs. Although not as numerous as parlor songs, minstrel songs, especially those of Stephen Foster, were more popular. Several remain among the most memorable songs composed in nineteenth-century America.

The modern era in popular music began in the 1910s, when dancing the fox-trot to syncopated music became the rage. This second revolution gave American popular music a distinctive sound identity. In its rhythms, melodies, instrumentation, and ways of singing and playing, it was original and unprecedented. The fox-trot songs and dance music of the twenties sounded like no other music. It was a unique, recognizably American synthesis.

The third revolution came in the mid-1950s, when rock 'n' roll exploded on the national consciousness. It gave an increasingly bland pop music a much needed wake-up call. Although ignored or reviled at first by the establishment, it soon came to dominate popular music. After the British invasion of the mid-1960s, most popular music had a rock beat. Rock bands and soul groups typically topped the charts, ousting the stars of an earlier generation.

The rock revolution of the fifties and sixties was just as radical as those that preceded it. The first revolution had given popular music a different accent. The second had created a discrete dialect, with its own intonation and vocabulary. The third revolution went even further: It gave popular music its own language. For rock was a new musical language, a mixture formed from two dissimilar musical traditions.

All three revolutions grew out of the interaction of African-American musics with the prevailing popular style. The impact of African-derived music became more pronounced with each revolution. In the first, there was little direct interaction between the two. African-American music served mostly as a model. The second came about primarily through the interpretation of European music by African-Americans and the subsequent reinterpretation of this new music by whites. In the third, there was substantial intermixing of African-based styles with pop and country music. This produced a new style that drew heavily on several sources, African-American and European-based.

We might characterize the three revolutions in this way. The first revolution resulted from the *inspiration* of African-American music. The second revolution resulted from the *influence* of African-American music. The third revolution resulted from the *integration* of African-American and white musical styles.

What makes these three revolutions so important is their comprehensiveness. All invigorated popular music with a new dance-inspired beat. All expanded its sound world, introducing new instruments, instrument combinations, and ways of singing and playing. All redefined popular song, not only its form, but also its performance style, even its essence. Many other musical developments have influenced the evolution of popular music, but none have transformed commercially dominant styles so radically. As such, they demarcate the major epochs in the history of popular music.

ORGANIZATION OF THE TEXT

In keeping with the emphasis on popular music *as music*, the organization of this book takes its cue from these revolutions. The first of its four parts examines the elements and sources of popular style in some detail. The remainder of the book falls into three parts. Each covers the popular music of an extended timespan: 1840s to 1920s, 1910s to 1960s, and 1950s to the 1980s. Discussions of the popular mainstream—the most commercially prominent styles of an era—form the main thread through the narrative.

Both the individual chapters and the survey as a whole sketch the history of popular music rather than paint its portrait. The broad outlines are there but not the myriad details that flesh them out. This is in keeping with the introductory intent of the book. Those readers seeking a more comprehensive view of a genre are encouraged to consult the bibliography.

More than anything else, this book is about musical style. The survey that follows is an introduction to the styles of popular music and their interrelationship. It pursues four lines of inquiry:

1. Those qualities that most clearly define a style—for example, what differentiates blues from ragtime or rock

2. The interaction among styles and the influence of one style on another—for example, the interaction of blues with popular song in the teens and twenties

3. The transformation of the mainstream—i.e., commercially dominant—style over the history of American popular music

4. The stylistic evolution of genres within a timespan—for example, jazz from the twenties through the fifties.

Taken together, these four lines of inquiry help us explore the broad range of popular music in America. They encourage the perception of popular music as an extended, diverse, yet quite inbred family, spread over several generations. Individuality, influence and interconnection, essence and evolution: all are integral to an understanding of popular music and its development.

The broader the frame of reference, the easier it is to bring both the uniqueness of a style and its relationship with other styles into focus. An example: It is impossible to trace the origins of the rock of the fifties and sixties or fully appreciate its originality without being familiar with pop, country, a variety of folk styles, several shades of blues, Afro-Cuban music, even jazz. A familiarity with the elements of style helps a listener work toward *musical* understanding of popular music in all its richness.

The organization and context of the survey reflect the primary goals of the book. Their purpose is to help the reader/listener become more aware of the heritage of popular music: to appreciate its diversity; to perceive the underlying kinship of its many styles; to sense its evolutionary momentum. It seeks to impart an understanding of the music of the past and provide a frame of reference for the music of today. If this book does its job well and its readers do theirs, then they will listen to *all* popular music with greater acuity, insight, perspective, and discrimination.

ACKNOWLEDGMENTS

I have many people to thank for the writing of this book. The students at Western Illinois University who have taken the popular music survey course from which the book developed have helped me shape the structure of the manuscript, and have enlightened me with papers ranging from the popular music of Burma to a style profile of death metal. My colleagues in the music department at Western–Bruce Prueter, Hugo Magliocco, John Murphy, Jim Caldwell (who offered a most helpful insight on the Beatles) and John Vana–have taught the course from earlier drafts of the manuscript and have advised me on its strengths and weaknesses.

Many thanks also to my sons, Aaron and Raphael, who have served as unpaid consultants on alternative rock and rap, respectively; and to Sheila McGrath, who has run her expert eye over every word of the manuscript.

Anyone familiar with Jan LaRue's *Guidelines for Style Analysis* will recognize its profound impact on my discussions of recorded performances as well as the overall design of the book. I am deeply indebted to him not only for his ideas, but also for his guidance over the last twenty years. I am glad to take his ideas and methods in this perhaps unanticipated direction.

I am most grateful to the editorial staff at Schirmer Books, in particular former editor Maribeth Anderson Payne, who offered me a contract; Robert Axelrod, who suggested many useful revisions; and especially current senior editor Richard Carlin, who has applied cleaver and scalpel to the manuscript to make the book much better than it would otherwise have been, and whose prodding has helped bring the project to completion.

A NOTE ON LISTENING EXAMPLES

Throughout the text, the term "Listening Example" designates a recording that illuminates a key point in the discussion. Most of these recordings are included in the set of five CDs or cassettes that accompanies this book. CD and cassette icons with track numbers appear in the margin where these selections are cited. Some Listening Examples are selections that cannot be included in the recording set for copyright reasons. The letter D appears in a circle next to these examples, referring the reader to the Discography at the end of the book, where information on widely available sources for these recordings is given.

M. C.

PART I

BACKGROUND

CHAPTER ONE

Perspectives on Popular Music

Popular music is an integral part of life in America. It can surround us from the moment we wake up to the moment we drift off to sleep. It's present while we eat, travel, work, and play. We hear it as theme or background music for films and televisions shows. Jingles help sell us drinks, fast food, cars, and a host of other products. And diluted versions of hit songs soothe us in elevators, dentists' offices, restaurants, and grocery stores.

popular music

Precisely because popular music is so much a part of daily life, we may take its identity and importance for granted. So, asking questions like "What is popular music?" and "Why is popular music important?" may seem unnecessary, because the answers are apparently all around us. But this is not the case; both questions elicit several meaningful answers. We can use them as the basis of a brief inquiry into the nature and significance of popular music. Then we can raise the questions again, answering them from a primarily musical point of view.

WHAT IS POPULAR MUSIC?

What is popular music? The obvious answer is: music that is popular, or at least music created with commercial success in mind. But it's not so simple. The answer prompts additional questions that complicate the issue. How do we measure popularity? Is all music that is popular considered "popular music"? Is there music that is not popular (commercially successful) that is popular music?

MEASURES OF POPULARITY

Like assessing athletic performance, measuring popularity in music begins with numbers. In both cases, there are plenty of statistics: Number 1 hits and gold and platinum records; batting averages, yards gained, assists, and turnovers. Bing Crosby, the most popular singer of the first half of the century, sold over 300 million records, including over 28 million copies of "White Christmas," the best-selling single of all time. The Beatles rang up even more impressive numbers. During their short career, they had more Number 1 albums (fifteen) and spent more weeks at the top of the charts (119) than any other artist or group.

Statistics also document prevailing taste. For instance, record album sales show the ascendancy of rock after the midsixties British invasion. Around 1960, album sales reflected adult taste, with the majority of the top-selling albums consisting of film or musical sound tracks or recordings by pre-rock style singers. After 1965, however, rock albums dominated the charts. Frank Sinatra's record sales graphically illustrate this change: Sinatra had twenty-eight top-ten albums between 1958 and 1967, but none after 1967, until his duet albums in the 1990s. This trend clearly indicated that, by 1970, rock was no longer simply music for teens.

THE BOUNDARIES OF POPULAR MUSIC

classical
music

folk music

In this century, there have been three broad categories of music in the United States: popular music; classical music; and folk music. They differ from each other in intent as well as musical result. Popular music strives for popularity and, with it, commercial success. Ideally, classical composers pursue art for art's sake. Folk music, created anonymously and passed down orally from generation to generation, entertains the group in which it developed, without much thought toward commercial gain or composing for the ages. These three musical traditions are like the three primary colors. It's easy to distinguish among typical examples of classical, popular, or folk music. Few would confuse a Beethoven symphony with a hard-rocking Rolling Stones's song or an Appalachian folk melody. But the boundaries between popular, classical, and folk are often as amorphous as the shift from one color to the next.

When does folk become pop? There is a rich repertory of American folk songs. But when the Kingston Trio started the sixties folk revival by singing

Candide. *Friedman-Abeles, photographers; courtesy Performing Arts Research Center, New York Public Library at Lincoln Center.*

songs from this repertory, selling millions of records in the process, were they folk or pop performers? Did Bob Dylan transform himself into a popular singer when he began performing his own songs instead of folk songs? When does musical theater cross the line from popular to classical? Is Leonard Bernstein's *Candide* classical (it won a Grammy in 1991 as best classical album) and *West Side Story* pop (it was the Number 1 album for over a year)?

Blues in the first third of the century presents an even more complex mosaic. Many different kinds of music–from the country blues of performers like Robert Johnson, the popular blues of Bessie Smith, instrumental blues performed by Louis Armstrong ("West End Blues"), to the famous *Rhapsody in Blue* by George Gershwin–were all categorized as "blues," despite their many differences. But which is folk, pop, or even classical? Is Bessie Smith a pop singer because she was a paid entertainer, even though her singing style has much more in common with country–blues singers than almost all of the contemporary popular singers? Has Louis Armstrong transcended pop both in intent and substance and given us one of the first examples of jazz as "America's classical music"?

These examples point out how important commercial success is to our conception of popular music. It is hard to imagine "St. Louis Blues," *West Side Story,* or the Kingston Trio recordings as anything but popular music precisely because they were so popular even though each approaches the boundary between popular and folk or classical music. But commercial success is certainly not the sole determinant. In 1958, at the height of the Cold War, pianist Van Cliburn returned from Moscow to a hero's welcome after

Mance Lipscomb, Texas blues singer. Photograph by Chris Strachwitz, courtesy Arhoolie Records.

winning the Tchaikovsky Competition. Not surprisingly, his recording of Tchaikovsky's first piano concerto was the best-selling album of any kind for seven weeks of that year. A recent album by three outstanding tenors, Luciano Pavarotti, José Carreras, and Placido Domingo, has enjoyed comparable commercial success. It has been on *Billboard*'s classical album chart for over two years and has sold over a million units, a figure many rock bands fail to achieve.

Neither, however, is a recording of popular music, although both are recordings of popular classical music. Popular music is more than music that is popular. There are musical and cultural, as well as commercial, reasons for identifying a performance as popular music, as we'll discover soon. For now, we will turn our attention to the other side of the coin—music that is not popular.

Whether commercially less-successful music is "popular music" again raises the question of intent. An act may set out to create a career in popular music and fail, through a shortfall of musical imagination, skill, business sense, or perseverance. Its music is certainly popular music although it's not "popular."

But commercial success is not everyone's primary goal. In the late thirties and early forties, jazz was a popular music. The best white swing bands charted hit after hit; fans flocked to ballrooms to Lindy hop and jitterbug to songs like "In the Mood." But after World War II, a small nucleus of jazz musicians—Charlie Parker, Dizzy Gillespie, and a few others—created bebop, a complex jazz style strictly for listening. The desire to create a revolutionary new music drove these musicians much more than financial gain.

Musicians may also spurn popular acclaim to preserve an existing tradition. The music of Eddie Palmieri, a critically acclaimed salsa pianist/com-

Bop stars Max Roach (drums), Dizzy Gillespie (trumpet), and Charlie Parker (saxophone) at Massey Hall, Toronto, Canada, May 1953.

poser, expresses a dilemma that many Latin musicians face. Palmieri had to decide whether to remain true to the Afro-Cuban roots of salsa (and its limited market) or seek a broader audience by mixing Latin music with other popular styles. Palmieri has chosen to remain close to his roots, although he is certainly capable of crossing over into a jazz or pop market.

Bebop and salsa are clearly nonpopular styles. Yet, both bop and salsa are nodes in a network of styles that also includes popular music, which suggests that musical as well as commercial criteria should determine what is or is not popular music. Before exploring this idea further, we need to consider another aspect of popular music, its cultural identity.

AMERICA AND POPULAR MUSIC

The subtitle of this book is "An Introduction to Popular Music in America (1840 to Today)" rather than "An Introduction to American Popular Music" because a significant percentage of the music discussed in the book comes from outside the United States, including British rock, and Brazilian bossa nova.

Yet almost all of this music has developed from, or has been strongly influenced by, American music. British guitarists Eric Clapton and Jimmy Page listened intensely to American bluesmen, and British bands like the Beatles and Rolling Stones began their careers by covering rock 'n' roll songs by Chuck Berry and Buddy Holly, to name just two. Jamaicans tuned their radios to American stations, and turned their native mento into ska and reggae by absorbing American rhythm and blues. Brazilian bossa nova musicians acknowledged the impact of jazz on their music by recording frequently with American jazz musicians like Stan Getz. Virtually all of the fundamental premises of popular music—its forms, most of its rhythms, its instrumentation (particularly the rhythm section), and its expressive vocabulary—have American roots.

In a nice symmetry, the roots of American popular music are international. This new music grew out of the interaction of three distinct musical traditions: the art music of central Europe (classical music); the folk music of the British Isles; and west African music. (West African music reached the United States from two sources: directly, via the slaves brought to the United States; and indirectly, via the Caribbean.) Precisely because of this cross-pollination, any recognizably American popular music is different from the traditions that fed it. From nineteenth-century minstrel music through ragtime, blues, the fox-trot song, country, jazz and swing, and rock, to the spectrum of contemporary styles, popular music has drawn on these traditions in varying proportions.

cross-pollination

American popular music owes much of its identity to a specific feature of the musical cross-pollination: an African-inspired rhythmic conception. More than any other quality, it distinguishes American popular music from other encounters of African and European musical traditions. The most basic expression of this African-inspired rhythmic conception has been the backbeat. It has been a rhythmic feature and the rhythmic reference of all commercially important popular styles since about 1920. It is a common element between styles that seemingly have little in common: for example, "Surrey with a Fringe on Top," from Rodgers and Hammerstein's *Oklahoma!* and Wynonie Harris's "Good Rockin' Tonight," both from the forties, share this rhythmic base. It also links popular styles across generations. We can hear it in the fox-trot songs of the jazz age and the hip-hop, hard country, and heavy metal of today.

Musical cross-pollination also gives popular music its evolutionary thrust. The audience for country music grew in the thirties and forties as the music began to absorb noncountry influences: a pop rhythm section, blues-tinged vocals (especially the recordings of Jimmie Rodgers and Hank Williams); and the heavy backbeat of honky-tonk music. Country music returned the favor in the fifties and sixties by providing the model for a new type of popular song. Yesterday's fringe music may well be tomorrow's mainstream.

THE IMPORTANCE OF POPULAR MUSIC

We can turn our attention now from "What is popular music?" to "Why is popular music important?" Like the first question, the second also inspires several responses. Perhaps we can rephrase the question so that it reads: "In what ways is popular music important?" American popular music can be important in at least three ways: culturally (because it is American and reveals some dimension of our cultural experience); commercially (because it is part of our world by virtue of its commercial success); and artistically (because it is music of artistic worth and influence).

There are at least three ways in which popular music has been culturally important. First, it tells us about ourselves. In words and music, it mirrors the prevailing attitudes and values of any generation as well as those of its diverse audiences. Second, it speaks both to us and for us. It can communicate ideas and feelings with great power, in a way not possible with words, simply because it is music. Third, it has been an agent of social change. Its impact has been especially telling in the reshaping of racial and sexual attitudes. All enrich our understanding of American society.

From a commercial perspective, popular music also becomes important because it *is* popular. This is not to downplay the significant economic impact of the popular-music industry. However, over time, the most *popular* popular music is important primarily because it is well known. Its familiarity gives it significance: a popular song becomes a shared experience for its audience. From the songs of Stephen Foster—"Oh! Susanna," "Camptown Races"—that are still part of our culture, to the top hits, jingles, and theme music of today, the most popular songs are the musical equivalent of celebrities: meaningful because so many recognize them.

ASSESSING ARTISTIC VALUE

It is impossible to discuss popular music meaningfully without considering cultural and commercial importance. However, this is primarily a book about musical style, so it is the artistic dimension of popular music that is of particular interest.

Artistic importance is trickier to assess than popularity because it's difficult to quantify: there are no statistics for greatness. Separating great from not-so-great is an imperfect art for any kind of music. The history of music criticism is littered with egregious errors in judgment. The functional purpose of much popular music further complicates the issue. And three unique qualities of popular music—its popularity, rapid style change, and its racially mixed roots—make the task even more difficult.

Much popular music supports other kinds of activities. It might be physical movement: dancing or exercising. It might help sell products or identify television shows and movies. It might serve as background music at work, during meals, or simply relaxing. These and other functions make specific demands on the music. Dance music must have a beat, whether it's the gentle "businessman's bounce" or the jackhammer rhythms of almost any Green Day song. Advertising jingles and theme music for television shows should have easily recognized melodic snatches that embed themselves in our subconscious through frequent repetition. Background music must soothe, not challenge, its listeners. Even ostensibly nonfunctional music, like songs intended for Top 40 radio, cater to the demands of the medium: Such songs should grab the casual listener.

nonfunctional music

The distinction between functional and nonfunctional music exists in other musical traditions. In European art music, the line is usually sharply drawn. A Johann Strauss waltz is functional music, even though audiences may listen to it in concert; a Stravinsky ballet is not, even though it's music for dance. In classical music, there is a clearer consensus as to the relative artistic worth of functional and nonfunctional music. In any history of European art music (at least since the advent of the public concert in the late eighteenth century), music strictly for listening occupies center stage. Functional music, no matter how beautiful, is considered less profound.

functional music

By contrast, the popular tradition does not have a well-established hierarchy of esthetic experience, with concert music at the top. It's not clear that popular music strictly for listening is the highest form of popular music. Compare an infectiously funky James Brown song with a beautifully crafted Joni Mitchell melody. Is the James Brown song less successful artistically simply because it demands some kind of physical movement? Even jazz, called by many "America's art music," typically asks for more than just the attention of its audience. Toe-tapping is an appropriate, even welcome, physical response to the elegant swing of the Modern Jazz Quartet.

There are other qualities, also unique to popular music, that make it more difficult to determine artistic value. One is the pervasive use of popularity as the primary measure of importance in popular music. By its very nature, popular music is popular, or aspires to be. Almost by definition, popularity is a—even *the*—significant measure of importance. In his excellent history of early rock, Carl Belz identifies Elvis Presley as "the most important individual rock artist to emerge during the music's early development between 1954 and 1956." The reason: "his extraordinary popularity." Belz then lists three "firsts" to support his assertion: Elvis was the first to have a career in the movies; to record a series of million-selling records; and to penetrate foreign markets. There's no mention of Elvis's musical impact.

The conflict between popularity and artistry as a measure of the importance of an artist has posed a dilemma for commentators on popular music. Charlie Gillett's observations about Chuck Berry bring the problem into focus:

> If importance in popular music were measured in terms of imaginativeness, creativeness, wit, the ability to translate a variety of experiences and feelings into musical form, and long-term influence and reputation, Chuck Berry would be described as the major figure of rock 'n' roll. At the time of his greatest popularity,

Crowds gather at the opening of Elvis's first movie, Love Me Tender, *Paramount Theater, New York, November 14, 1956.*

1955-59, there were several other singers who had more hits, were more often copied, and commanded higher fees for personal performances. But Chuck Berry had the greatest long-term effect on his audience, shown in the immense influence his music had on the Beatles, Bob Dylan, the Rolling Stones, and other singers and musicians who began making records in the mid-sixties. . . .

Artistic worth is also difficult to assess because styles change so rapidly in popular music. Artists who seem innovative and influential at the time of their greatest popularity may turn out to be less so with the passage of time. Popular music's rich racially mixed heritage also creates musical difficulties in the perception of artistic value. The several dissimilar musical traditions that have fed into popular music have their own expressive vocabularies. There are no precedents for a Marvin Gaye, a Loretta Lynn, an Ethel Merman, or a Michael Jackson outside of the popular-music tradition. Popular music prizes individuality of expression rather than adherence to a common standard. Most of its stars have a distinctive, easily recognizable sound. As a result, the popular tradition lacks a well-defined esthetic, a single preferred way of making music.

In popular music it is possible to communicate meaningfully in a broad spectrum of styles. They can be so different that they are mutually exclusive: imagine Bing Crosby singing "Satisfaction" or Mick Jagger singing "White

Christmas." Each style develops its own expressive vocabulary, which may not have much in common with another style. What's appropriate for country music is inappropriate for Broadway, and vice versa. Still, precisely because popular music is a melting pot, some expressive elements carry over from one style to another, although they assume a different form when they blend with other styles: Jimi Hendrix transformed electric blues into rock's first virtuoso guitar style; at about the same time, George Benson took the blues in another direction, merging rhythm and blues with jazz into the most popular jazz-guitar style of the seventies.

Just as a stylistic network in popular music links even the most disparate styles, shared values create an expressive continuum. It is the musical equivalent of those "Do you know...?" conversations at a party: two people haven't met, but the first person knows someone who knows someone else who is a friend of the second person. Two styles may be so far apart on the continuum that they seem unrelated, as the Crosby-Jagger comparison suggests. But Crosby was a crooner. So was Frank Sinatra, who listened to and learned from Billie Holiday, who claimed that her biggest influences were Bessie Smith and Louis Armstrong. Bessie Smith sang the blues with much the same raw emotion as country and urban bluesmen, like Robert Johnson and Howlin' Wolf, who influenced Mick Jagger. The circle is complete.

Cross-pollination, the quality that has driven the evolution of popular music, also seems to be a common thread through the classic music of any style or generation. Most of the great artists of any era have forged a highly personal style from several sources. Stephen Foster's plantation melodies, perhaps his most original contribution to popular song, blend minstrel and parlor-song styles. Scott Joplin's piano rags draw on European art music as well as syncopated rhythms; so do Jerome Kern's elegantly crafted melodies. Bob Dylan merged folk, country, and rock; Ray Charles brought blues, country, and gospel together . . . the list is extensive. Popular music is pragmatic and egalitarian. Any combination of styles can conceivably work as long as it moves people. What seems to matter most is the originality, integrity, and power of the synthesis.

Popular music has a unique artistic heritage. In its century and a half of existence, its great musicians—composers, songwriters, and performers—have created a rich legacy, unlike any other in substance and range. It reaches back to the songs of Stephen Foster and the marches of John Philip Sousa. And it continues to grow as contemporary giants composer/lyricist Stephen Sondheim, jazzman Wynton Marsalis, producer/arranger/composer Quincy Jones, Paul Simon, Prince, Willie Nelson, Bruce Springsteen, and many others add to it.

Let's return to the two questions that began this chapter: What is popular music?; and, Why is it important? The primary purpose of this book is to help readers discover popular music as a musical legacy, to encounter it in all its variety, and to understand it more fully. Certainly, popular music is indivisible from its context. Full appreciation depends on knowing the circumstances of its creation, the environment in which it developed, and the audience for whom it was intended. But the focus is on musical matters. The discussions that comprise most of this book present the styles of popular music: their musical characteristics; their origins; their development; their interaction with other styles; their influence; and their artistic expressions.

Terms to Know

classical music	cross-pollination	folk music
functional music	nonfunctional music	popular music

Study Questions

1. Without consulting the chapter, quickly write out a definition of popular music, based on your encounters with it.

2. Think of two instances in your musical experience in which the boundary between popular music and nonpopular styles was not clear. What are they, and why is the boundary not clear?

3. Select three popular music performances that you especially like. Write down the main reasons that you like each performance. Be as specific as possible.

4. In what ways is popular music an international style?

5. Can you think of two examples of popular music styles that show cross-pollination of influences? What are the influences that are drawn on? How can they be identified?

6. Think of a distinctive popular vocalist. Describe what makes his/her vocal style distinctive?

7. Identify the following selections as either functional or nonfunctional music. For each choice, write out your reasons: an advertising jingle; rap song; symphony; movie soundtrack; Rolling Stones song; banjo tune.

CHAPTER TWO

The Elements of Popular Music

Imagine that you're driving along toward a city far from home. You turn on the radio and start scanning the dial. You reject the first station; you're not into easy-listening music. You stay a little while on the second. It's a country station, and they're playing Randy Travis, whom you like.

But you decide you're not in the mood for country after all when you hear the next song. So you check the left side of the dial to try to locate an alternative music station from a local college. As it happens, you find one, but they're playing a song by a thrash metal band. You don't care for slash-and-burn guitar playing, so you try another station. You've found an oldies station, and they're in the middle of a Motown tribute. So you sing along with Marvin Gaye, ready with an answer when he asks "What's Goin' On?"

The process by which you chose a station was a form of musical style analysis. You listened to each song long enough to decide whether you liked it. There were aspects of the music that you responded to, one way or the other. You don't like syrupy strings, but you do like Randy Travis's twang. In both cases, you listened, observed, and evaluated: thumbs up or down.

This is selective listening. You focus on a specific aspect of a song and react to it. Sometimes it's easy: there are features of a song that may jump out at you. You immediately recognize the extreme distortion of a metal band, the relentless beat of dance music or disco, or the machine-gun verbal delivery of a rapper. There are others that may become apparent only with repeated listening. It may take you a few times through the words to pick out the form of a Paul Simon song. And it may take four or five tries to identify the role of each instrument within the rhythm section of a funk band. All these features tell you something about the style of a song. The purpose of this chapter is to give you the tools and a framework to do a similar kind of analytic listening in a comprehensive and systematic way. We begin by considering the properties of musical sound.

beat

THE PROPERTIES OF MUSICAL SOUND

Most musical sounds have four properties: *timbre, intensity, pitch,* and *duration. Timbre* is the color of a musical sound, that quality which distin-

timbre
intensity
pitch
duration

13

guishes the tone of a saxophone from that of a piano. *Intensity* refers to the loudness of a musical sound. We hear sound as wave vibrations. When a sound vibrates at a specific frequency, then it has definite *pitch*. We identify rapidly vibrating sounds as high pitches, slower vibrations as low. *Duration* measures how long a musical sound lasts.

Example 2.1 features five short excerpts that highlight the four properties of musical sound. The first is a series of sounds, unvarying in all four properties. The second varies the timbre of every fourth note, the third varies intensity, the fourth varies pitch, and the fifth varies duration.

We should include one qualifier. Every musical sound evidences the four properties of musical sound. However, not all musical sounds have *definite* pitch. Many percussion instruments produce sounds without specific pitch. Some, like those from the various drums of a drum set, do not vibrate at a specific frequency long enough for us to identify it as a definite pitch. Others, like the cymbals on the drum set, vibrate at several frequencies simultaneously, so that we are again unable to distinguish a specific frequency. Still, we sense high and low in both cases, as we can hear in the next pair of examples. Example 2.2 gives short excerpts that feature the drums and cymbals of the standard drum set, played in sequence from smallest to the largest. In each case, we can notice a drop in pitch—the last is lower than the first—even though we can not identify specific pitches.

Electronically generated or modified sounds are the other major source of indefinite pitch sounds in popular music. With the rapid advance of technology, the range of possible sound is almost unlimited. At times, electronically modified sounds straddle the boundary between definite and indefinite pitch. The distortion so familiar to heavy-metal aficionados is the addition of white noise—a mass of frequencies sounding simultaneously—to the basic electric guitar sound; extreme distortion tends to obscure the actual pitch of a note.

THE ELEMENTS OF POPULAR MUSIC

instrumen-
tation

dynamics

melody

harmony

texture

form

The elements of popular music include *instrumentation, performing style, dynamics, rhythm, melody, harmony, texture,* and *form. Instrumentation* refers to the range of timbres in a performance. In its largest application, instrumentation embraces both instruments and voices. Resources may be as modest as a single singer or instrumentalist or as grand as the combination of symphony orchestra, rock band, solo vocalists, and chorus.

Performing style refers to how the instruments are played or how the voice is used. Particularly in popular music, *how* performers sing or play is as significant as whether they sing or what they play. Frank Sinatra, James Brown, Bob Dylan, and Michael Jackson are all male singers, but their voices are so different it's as if they're completely different "instruments." Similarly, George Benson and Eddie Van Halen both play electric guitar, but they produce distinctly different sounds using their instruments.

Dynamics refer to gradations of intensity: the volume level(s) of a performance and the changes between loud and soft. Changes can be abrupt, gradual, or nonexistent: a typical Ramones's song is two minutes of unrelenting loudness. A more subtle use of dynamics is *inflection,* the note-to-note dynamic shading of a singer or instrumentalist. Inflection occurs when a performer stresses a syllable or note to highlight its verbal or musical importance.

Rhythm is concerned with duration: it involves any aspect of the music considered as a function of time. There is a rhythm in any element: the rise and fall of a melody, the addition or subtraction of instruments, or the OOM-pah-pah of a waltz accompaniment. Our rhythmic impression of a performance takes all of these matters into account.

Melody and *harmony* refer to two different (but intertwined) ways of organizing pitch. Musical pitches combine in two distinct ways: in a series, or simultaneously. A group of pitches heard as a series is a melodic *line.* A group of pitches heard—or understood—as a simultaneous event is a *chord.* The difference between chord and line often lies with the manner of perception, rather than the musical event itself. Indeed, it's sometimes possible to hear the same musical event as both harmony and melody. The opening phrase of the American national anthem illustrates this point. We can listen to the first six pitches of "The Star Spangled Banner" ("Oh say can you see") as a series, observing such features as the pattern of rise and fall (down, then up), the distance between pitches (skips instead of steps), and the rhythm. When we hear it this way, we are listening to it as a melody. But we can also hear the six pitches as an *arpeggio.* From this vantage point, the first phrase is a single event—the chord—heard in succession instead of all at once.

In a performance, each voice or instrument is a *part.* Texture describes the various relationships among parts: their number; how independent they are of one another; how closely they are spaced; and what role each fills. There are two dimensions of texture that we will explore. One is melodic texture, the distribution of melodic interest. Which part or parts offer the most melodic interest, and which parts are of lesser interest? The other is rhythmic texture that considers the relationship of the parts of the song to the beat: do they confirm it, contradict it, ignore it?

Form is the organization of music in time. Form emerges from the interaction of all the elements. Form in musical time is essentially different from form in space. Unlike most of the visual arts, where the form of an object can be apprehended in a single glance, music reveals its form progressively, over the duration of the performance. Decisive changes in one or more elements—pauses in the melody, a switch in instrumentation, higher or lower dynamics, a different accompaniment, melodic rhythm, or beat pattern—outline the sections within a performance. More gradual changes, or the absence of change, regulate the activity within and between sections.

The elements of music—instrumentation, performing style, dynamics, rhythm, melody, harmony, texture, and form—apply to all music. (Or most of them: a few musics of the world use just voice and drum, so do not have harmony in any sense.) However, we are most interested in two applications: how they operate in popular music, and how their use in popular styles resembles or differs from their use in the styles from which popular music emerged: European classical music, Anglo-American folk music, and African folk music, in its various New World transformations. We will examine each element in more detail with these questions in mind.

Margin terms: inflection

melody line

arpeggio

part

INSTRUMENTATION

The instruments of popular music fall easily into five groups. At the center is the rhythm section. Other commonly used families of instruments include winds, strings, percussion, and electronic instruments.

Jelly Roll Morton's Red Hot Peppers, 1926, showing early jazz rhythm section: drums, acoustic bass, piano, and banjo, in addition to lead instruments, trombone, cornet, and clarinet.

The rhythm section, a fixture in popular music since the twenties, is a heterogeneous group of instruments that includes at least one chord instrument, one bass instrument, and one percussion instrument. It is complete unto itself, as jazz piano trios and rock power trios have demonstrated for almost half a century. The chord instruments are of two types: strummed and keyboard. Strummed instruments include banjo and guitar, both acoustic and electric. Keyboard instruments include piano, organ, electric piano, and synthesizer. Bass instruments include tuba (brass bass), string bass, electric bass, and synthesizer bass. The main percussion instrument is the drum set. Occasionally, other percussion instruments, especially the conga drum, have augmented the rhythm section or substituted for the drum set. More recently, synthesized drum sounds have replaced human drummers.

Most of the wind instruments commonly used in popular music have arrived via the military band. These include the trumpet, trombone, flute, clarinet, and saxophone. Trumpet and trombone are brass instruments with cup-shaped mouthpieces. Clarinet and flute are considered woodwinds, although the modern flute is usually made of metal. The saxophone is a hybrid: it has a metal body like a brass instrument, plus a mouthpiece and keys something like those of a clarinet. Of these five instruments, the trumpet, trombone, and saxophone have been the most widely used over the last sixty years.

Stringed instruments can be bowed or plucked. In addition to banjo, guitar, and string and electric bass, the most commonly used string instruments have been the violin and the steel guitar. In popular music, the violin has had a multiple personality: it is the classical violin in dance, theater, and film orchestras and background music, a fiddle in country music, and occasionally a jazz instrument as well. The steel guitar, a big part of the sound of progressive country music since the thirties, has also found occasional use in rock.

Percussion instruments fall into two groups: pitched and unpitched. In the first group are instruments like the vibraphone and marimba, both occasionally present in various kinds of popular music. In the latter are the drum set, Latin drums, especially the conga drum, and various other instruments in which sound is made by striking or rattling something, including maracas, claves, and cowbells.

There are three families of electronic instruments. One is amplified acoustic instruments, such as the early electric guitar. Closely related are acoustic-like instruments, for example, solid-body electric guitars and basses, that require amplification to produce an audible sound. The third kind are "true" electronic instruments, in which the sound begins as an electrical signal. These include electronic organs and synthesizers.

Popular music *sounds* different from other kinds of music because: its instruments are different, or played in a different way; these instruments feature a widespread application of electrical technology; and its instrumental combinations are unique. Continuing evolution in all three areas has created an unparalleled range of timbres. Popular music today sounds much different from the popular music of the turn of the century partly because of its much broader timbral palette.

In particular, the impact of electrical technology on the sound of popular music has been substantial and decisive. At the turn of the century, a typical popular-music performance featured an unamplified singer with piano or theater orchestra accompaniment. Today, a typical popular-music performance features a singer singing into a microphone, perhaps with the sound modified as well as amplified, accompanied by an all-electric band, also heavily amplified. Technology has completely transformed the sound world of popular music, creating a new array of sonorities and escalating sound levels to previously unscalable heights. A listener from 1900 would not recognize it.

INSTRUMENT CHOICE

There are five sources of the unparalleled instrumental variety of popular music: the instruments inherited from popular music's many sources; significant adaptation of existing instruments; the creation of new instruments specifically for use in popular music; the application of electrical technology for sound modification; and the use of "found" instruments.

Popular music developed from several different kinds of music; all added their instruments to the mix. Most nineteenth-century popular music used the same instruments as classical music. These included the piano and guitar, plus many of the instruments of the orchestra and band—especially trumpet, trombone, clarinet, tuba, violin, and drums and cymbals.

As new styles have been incorporated into popular music, their instruments have enriched its sound world. From African-American music it got the handclap of the backbeat (often transferred to other instruments), plus new ways of playing existing instruments. Anglo-American folk music and country music added banjo (actually a white adaptation of an African instrument recreated by slaves in America), fiddle, and steel guitar. Latin music added an array of percussion instruments: conga drum, bongos, timbales, claves, and more. Newly created instruments like the Hammond organ and the vibraphone found a home in popular music.

The sound of popular music has also been shaped by instruments designed for use in popular music. Most of the instruments used in contemporary popular music were invented principally, even exclusively, for that purpose. These include not only the drum set, but also an almost unlimited array of electronic instruments: electric guitar, electric bass, various electronic keyboards, even synthesized drums and wind instruments.

Electronics can also drastically modify the sound of existing instruments. Sometimes amplification results in such a dramatic timbral change and leads to such significant changes in the design and setup of the instrument that it in effect becomes a new instrument. This happened with the solid-body guitar in rock and the amplified string bass in jazz. Signal processing can also reshape the basic timbre of an instrument, as guitarist Jimi Hendrix proved so convincingly.

At the other end of the technology spectrum are "found" instruments: instruments created from materials close at hand but intended for other uses or for no use at all. Most of these are percussion instruments and most now exist in a more refined, commercial form after becoming well-established. These include not only the handclap mentioned previously, but a tap dancer's feet; the bones of the early minstrel show; a host of Afro-Cuban percussion instruments—claves, cowbell, gourd, and the like; the pans of calypso, originally steel drums used to store oil; and the turntable, used by rap DJs for scratching.

INSTRUMENTAL COMBINATIONS

The sound blends produced by the characteristic performing units of popular music are just as distinctive as the instruments themselves. Certain combinations of instruments not only identify a performance as popular music but pinpoint the style. The pared-down lineup of a rock power trio, the array of plucked and bowed string instruments—fiddle, banjo, mandolin, guitar, and bass—of a bluegrass band, the three-man front line—clarinet, trumpet, and trombone—of a New Orleans jazz band: all immediately identify style by instrumentation.

Despite obvious differences in instrumentation, there is a common thread running through the vast majority of popular music groups. It is the prominent role of percussion instruments. The crucial role of percussion in defining the sounds of popular music is most evident in the early years of a style. It was the addition of percussion instruments and percussively played instruments that gave the syncopated dance bands of the teens and twenties their modern sound. In the thirties and forties, it was the addition of drums, despite the resistance of country traditionalists, that clearly distinguished country music from its roots in "old-time music." It was the preeminence of percussion and percussive sounds that helped differentiate rock 'n' roll from other kinds of popular music.

Appropriately enough, the nucleus of most groups within the popular tradition is the rhythm section. Its instrumentation has changed over the years, but its basic role—to supply the rhythmic and harmonic foundation of a performance—remains the same.

Small groups may consist only of a rhythm section and perhaps a singer. Others, slightly larger, add some kind of melody instrument, most commonly a saxophone. Bands may further enrich their sound by adding instruments in any of several areas: extra percussion, additional rhythm-section instruments (especially guitar and keyboard), more horns, and backup vocals.

Groups cross a line when there are enough of any particular instrument or instrument-family to form a section. A section comprised of melody instruments—horns or strings—usually requires at least three of the same instrument, one for each note of a three-note chord. Four is even better.

Big-band pianist Count Basie, Strand Theater, New York, 1942.

The best-known and most enduring large group in popular music has been the big band. Big bands contain at least four sections: rhythm, saxophones, trumpets, and trombones. Some also include strings or additional brass. Other large groups include the theater orchestras that accompany musicals and stage shows.

Since the advent of powerful amplification and synthesizers, the size of groups has diminished without a dramatic decrease in sound. A synthesizer programmed to produce string or brass sounds can replace an entire section. One performer can then do the work of four or more.

PERFORMING STYLES

The instruments and instrument mixes of popular music are just part of its unparalleled timbral variety. Just as important is the diversity of performing styles.

In 1960, these singers had or participated in Number 1 hit singles or albums:

- Elvis Presley, the king of rock and roll, the white man with the African-American sound
- Ray Charles, who, having merged blues and gospel, brought his unique style to pop and country
- Marty Robbins, a popular country singer who was part of the mainstreaming of Nashville in the late fifties
- Chubby Checker, a Fats Domino fan (real name, Ernest Evans) who made a career out of one dance, the twist
- Mary Martin, one of the most gifted and sweet-voiced Broadway stars of all time; she was in the original cast of the *Sound of Music*
- Frank Sinatra, the most famous and respected of the post-swing pop singers
- The Drifters, one of the classic vocal groups of the fifties and early sixties
- The Kingston Trio, three pleasant-voiced singers who started the folk revival in the late fifties and early sixties.

Most of these performers, especially the major stars, have a distinctive, easily recognizable performing style. The cultivation of a personal sound is the ultimate extension of the timbral variety of popular music. It is variety at the most local level. As this list suggests, popular music embraces a wide range of styles, even within a narrow time span: Broadway, pop, rock, country, blues, rhythm and blues, jazz, and folk.

However, the variety goes well beyond the differences from style to style. Almost as pronounced are the personal differences within each general style. Most of these artists sound like themselves even though they may be part of the same general style. For example, although both were jazz-influenced popular singers and career contemporaries, Nat "King" Cole and Frank Sinatra sound quite different from one another. Anyone familiar with forties and fifties popular song would know their styles and would be able to distinguish between them immediately. This microdiversity is the product of popular music's flexible and pragmatic approach to musical standards—if it communicates, use it—and its almost limitless stylistic variety. Performers can listen to an astounding range of sounds and draw into their style anything that catches their ear.

Indeed, what seems to distinguish many of the most critically admired performers is the way that they filter disparate influences through their own musical conception to create their distinct personality. Their sound is seldom a "pure" example of the general style to which it's linked. It usually has elements of other styles as well: steel instead of pure iron. Frank Sinatra's career is instructive in this regard. His early recordings with Harry James and Tommy Dorsey reveal a crooner with a voice much like the other male band singers of the forties. As he grew older, Sinatra's voice traded sweetness for grit. It was that exchange that gave Sinatra such a recognizable sound.

Popular music's enormous range in performing styles grows out of a philosophical difference between popular music and the classical and folk music from which it came. In classical music (and popular styles heavily influenced by classical music—such as operetta and pre-1970 film music)—there is a "correct" way to sing or play an instrument. Performers spend years learning how to produce the most desirable sound from their voice or instrument. Although there are subtle but telling differences in tone quality among the finest artists, overall there is little variation in sound production.

Likewise in folk music, there is a traditional way to sing or play an instrument, which is passed down orally from generation to generation. Although there are certainly individual performers who stand out from the rest, in general there seems to be relatively little variation in singing style from artist to artist, and region to region. As in classical music, the differences are subtle but significant, but the overall impression is of a homogeneous style. Even in as folk-oriented a popular style as country music, there was considerably more variety in the thirties than in the early twenties, when most country music performers were folk musicians rather than professional entertainers.

In popular music, by contrast, the rule seems to be "Anything goes," as long as it works. Some of the most revered performers in popular music sing or play in a way that would not be acceptable in classical music, folk music, or even previous generations of popular music. The singing of Louis Armstrong and Paul McCartney or the trumpet playing of Miles Davis fall well short of classical standards. But their music has an individuality and a personality that draws us to them, that makes their "failure" to meet classical standards of performance totally immaterial. In fact, their performances would not be as effective if their style were more classical. In this context, it's worth noting that one measure of excellence in popular music is individuality, the extent to which performers or bands cultivate a distinct sound identity.

DYNAMICS

The most common musical term for intensity is *dynamics*. In this age of almost unlimited amplification, an enormous dynamic range is possible: from just barely audible to an earsplitting volume level. Popular music takes full advantage of all possibilities. More than in classical or folk music, dynamics may be central to the message of a particular style. A number of rock styles—punk and various metal substyles—convey their rebelliousness most immediately through their "in your face" loudness. At the other end of the volume spectrum, cool jazz in the fifties, the folk music of the early sixties, and the "Windham Hill" music of the eighties included a low dynamic level as part of their esthetic. Interestingly, all three found loyal constituencies among white college students.

A more subtle use of dynamics is *inflection*, the note-to-note dynamic shading of a singer or instrumentalist. A performer may choose to stress a syllable or note to highlight its verbal or musical importance. Inflection is an expressive device of many different kinds of music, but it is especially pronounced and spontaneous in much popular music. It is one of the most important expressive devices available to a popular-music performer. A com-

II-21
III-1
IIB-10
IIIA-1

parison of two performances of "All of Me," one by Billie Holiday and the other by Russ Columbo, illustrates the expressive role of inflection (see Examples 10.2 and 10.3).

RHYTHM

Duke Ellington said it best: "It don't mean a thing if it ain't got that swing." Rhythm is the heart of popular music. So often, and in so many different kinds of music, the infectious beat of a song pulls us in, asking—demanding—that we respond. We tap our feet, clap our hands, sway our hips, bob our head. From the Brazilian samba and Benny Goodman's swing to hip-hop and Afro-pop, we move to the rhythms of popular music because we must: they're irresistible.

When we think of rhythm in popular music, we may think of its beats: the relentless throb of a disco hit; the groove of a great rock 'n' roll song; the toe-tapping pulse of swing and jazz; the supercharged tempos of thrash or speed metal; or the sequenced syncopations of rap and hip-hop.

However, rhythm includes more than the beat. In its fullest meaning, rhythm is the time dimension of musical sound: It encompasses any musical event heard as a function of time. This view of rhythm certainly includes the beat—often a complex interaction in itself—but it goes well beyond the simple marking of time. Still, the beat is central to an understanding of rhythm. It is the rhythmic point of entry into a performance and its main point of reference. As such, it serves as a useful point of departure for our discussion.

In popular music, there are at least three connotations for "beat." It can be qualitative, expressing a listener's impression of the rhythmic feel of a performance: "that song has a good beat." It can be quantitative, measuring the division of time into regular intervals. And it can be stylistic, identifying the rhythmic foundation of a style. In this chapter, we are most directly interested in the quantitative and stylistic connotations.

The beat is (usually) that regular division of time to which we can most easily respond physically. In popular music—as well as many other kinds of music—regular division of time may occur at several different speeds. At one extreme, there are very fast repeated sounds—drums, cymbals, other percussion, synthesizers—that sound eight to ten times a second. At the other extreme, there are slow rhythms: chords that change only three or four times a minute. The beat falls in between these extremes, at the speed we tap our foot.

tempo

We use the term *tempo* to define the speed of the beat. The "comfort range" for beat speed in most popular music lies between eighty and 140 beats per minute, roughly equivalent to the range of speeds to which we can walk. For example, most marches and disco songs have a tempo of about 120 beats per minute. If the clearest regular rhythm of a song moves at a speed considerably less than eighty beats per minute (as does Pink Floyd's "Breathe" from their album, *Dark Side of the Moon*), then we tend to look for a less obvious, but faster rhythm to move to. Likewise, we may seek slower-moving values if the most obvious regular rhythm seems too fast. New-wave music—such as almost any Ramones's song—is an exception to this rule: part of its impact stems from its quick tempos, which are too fast for walking but just right for bouncing!

Almost invariably, there are other regular rhythms besides the beat. In most contemporary popular music, division of the beat into two, three, or four equal parts is common. And beats are usually grouped into longer rhythmic units called *measures*. Most measures have two or four beats in them.

measure

Although the beat of a song may often be a prominent feature, rhythm in popular music is much more than the beat. Some patterns and accents confirm the beat and other regular rhythms; others may conflict with it or float over the regular marking of time. The interactions of beat-confirming and beat-defying rhythms produce the rich rhythmic textures so characteristic of popular music. These textures have their roots in African music.

accents

AFRICAN-AMERICAN RHYTHMS IN POPULAR MUSIC

The rhythms of almost all twentieth-century popular music grow out of an African-American reinterpretation of African rhythm. To understand African-American rhythm, we must first identify the main characteristics of African rhythm. There are three qualities that characterize the rhythms of traditional west African music. First, beats and/or other regular rhythms typically receive the same amount of emphasis. (This is unlike European music, in which beats typically have different amounts of emphasis. The OOM-pah-pah rhythm of a waltz is a good example.) Second, there is typically a lot of rhythmic activity, with five or more parts, several of them percussion, creating layers of repetitive rhythmic patterns. Third, some of the rhythmic layers mark the beat and other regular rhythms, while other layers do not coincide with the steady, evenly emphasized rhythms. These conflicting layers can be regular or irregular; they can be consistent or intermittent. The rhythmic conflict that occurs when accents do not coincide with the beat is often called *syncopation*.

syncopation

African rhythms were considerably diluted in the United States. Unlike most other African slaves brought to the New World, African-Americans were denied access to percussion instruments during slavery, for fear that they would be used for communication as well as recreation. As a result, their music was not as rhythmically dense as that of other Afrocentric musical styles in the New World, such as Afro-Cuban or Afro-Brazilian music. Still, essential qualities of African rhythm were present.

They first surfaced in popular music as African-American interpretations of European march and polka rhythms: ragtime and the ragtime-based dances of the early part of the century, including the fox-trot. By the twenties, they had become part of the fabric of popular music. After 1925, most dance music and Tin Pan Alley songs were fox-trots, and were performed with a clear fox-trot rhythm. Those that weren't were considered out of date.

Present in this music were the two features that have defined the sound of African-American rhythm in American popular music: the *rhythm section* and the *backbeat*. The rhythm section introduced percussion instruments and percussively played instruments into the accompaniment of popular song, thereby increasing the rhythmic density. The backbeat was the most direct and consistent evidence of African-American rhythm.

rhythm section

backbeat

In this century, the backbeat has been the *fundamental* expression of African-American music. It is a simple but syncopated rhythmic layer that African-Americans created with their bodies. It is virtually unique to African-American music; it is not a consistent feature in African music or African-based New World musics (only the Brazilian samba has something like it).

The *backbeat* is a percussive sound that occurs on the second and fourth beat of a four-beat measure. The simplest way to produce a backbeat is by clapping your hands. You can experience the feel of a backbeat by counting to four in a steady rhythm while clapping on two and four:

Count:	1	2	3	4
Clap:		X		X

Chuck Berry's first hit, "Maybelline" (Example 2.3), is a classic example of the backbeat and its pervasive use in popular music. In this two-beat pattern, Berry alternates a strong bass note (on 1 and 3) with a crisply played chord (2 and 4). The backbeat is the heavy accent that falls on the chord. A reverse accent two-beat is characteristic of the hard-country, honky-tonk style that evolved in the thirties and forties (see Hank Williams's "Your Cheatin' Heart" [Example 12.1] and Ray Price's "Much Too Young to Die" [Example 12.7], for example). In discussing the genesis of "Maybelline," Berry mentioned that he had originally conceived the song as a country song, based on the traditional dance-song, "Ida Red." His use of a two-beat rhythm with a heavy beackbeat confirms the song's connection with country music.

Since its incorporation into the mainstream, African-American rhythm has strengthened its hold on American popular music. African-American performers are more prominent, and their music has increasingly influenced the styles of white musicians. In this century, the center of gravity in popular music has shifted from melody to rhythm. Moreover, the rhythms of popular music have gravitated toward a more African conception. Examples 2.4 through 2.7 illustrate the close affinity between African rhythm and the rhythms of contemporary popular music.

"Tutsi Drums" (Example 2.4), performed by Watutsi ceremonial drummers, and "Isn't She Lovely" (Example 2.5), written and performed by Stevie Wonder, have virtually identical rhythms, although Stevie Wonder's song adds additional layers of rhythmic conflict. "Yoruba Chorus" (Example 2.6) and "Ladies' Night" (Example 2.7), performed by Kool and the Gang, both begin with a steady rhythm that moves twice as fast as the beat. Voices and instruments overlay this quick rhythm with riff-like figures. The instruments are different, the language is different, but the underlying rhythmic approach is uncannily similar.

Although the rhythms of popular music share a common conception and its most persistent expression, the backbeat, they have taken on quite different forms. The march-based rhythmic foundation of the syncopated dance music of the teens and twenties is a far cry from the active textures of today's dance music. To explore the similarities and differences among the various rhythms of popular music, we will consider the third connotation of "beat": the rhythmic foundation of a style.

THE BEATS OF POPULAR MUSIC

The term "beat" commonly describes the characteristic rhythm of a family of musical styles. When we refer to a "rock beat," we are identifying the characteristic rhythm of a rock song. Here, beat identifies the fastest layer of equally emphasized rhythm. We measure this layer by the number of equally emphasized notes in a measure that lasts four beats. A rock beat is typically identified as an eight-beat rhythm, because the fastest rhythmic layer moves twice as fast as the foot-tapping beat. So, in a measure of four beats, there will be eight equally emphasized notes.

A distinctive rhythmic foundation has defined each major new style in popular music. During the twenties, people danced to music with a fox-trot beat, a two-beat pattern. By 1940, the four-beat rhythm of swing had entered the mainstream. The eight-beat rhythm of rock, a novelty in the fifties, was a current and pervasive popular rhythm by 1965. By 1980, the sixteen-beat rhythm of Latin and African-influenced music had become a widely used alternative to rock rhythm.

Each new beat adds a layer of regular rhythm that moves twice as fast as the previous layer, heard in relation to the backbeat. In the two-beat, fox-trot rhythm, bass instruments establish a regular rhythm in alternation with the backbeat: there is a bass note, then a backbeat. Swing, the four-beat rhythm, adds a regular rhythm at beat speed; bass and guitar mark each beat with unvarying emphasis. In rock, the new layer, played by guitar and drums, moves twice as fast as the beat. This is commonly identified as an eight-beat rhythm. In sixteen-beat rhythm, instruments like drums, choked guitar, and/or their electronic equivalents play four attacks per beat. (Keep in mind that beat, when referring to a style-defining rhythm, no longer refers to toe-tapping speed, but the number of attacks in the fastest layer of regular rhythm in a four-beat measure.)

"Whispering" (Example 2.8), recorded by the Paul Whiteman Orchestra in 1920, is an early example of the fox trot. In this performance, the fox-trot rhythmic foundation is clearly in place once the song gets under way. Bass notes alternate with a crisp backbeat emphasized by the strummed banjo:

I-7
IA-7

two beat

Beat	Rhythm Section Roles	1	2	3	4
Backbeat	Played by banjo or guitar, cymbal, piano chord		X		X
Regular rhythm	Played by bass, piano bass	x		x	

"Jumpin' at the Woodside" (Example 2.9), performed by Count Basie's orchestra, is a classic big-band swing performance. Its introduction is a primer on swing rhythm. The piano begins by laying down a walking-bass figure. Bass and guitar join in on the first repetition. Jo Jones, the great swing drummer, enters playing the characteristic swing "ride" pattern on an alternately opened and closed hi-hat: long, short, short/long, short, short/long, short, short . . . , etc. The backbeat is audible in the choking of the cymbal sound as the hi-hat closes:

I-8
IA-8

four beat

Beat	Rhythm Section Roles	1	2	3	4
Backbeat	Played by closing hi-hat (swing and jazz) or on snare drum (R&B)		X		X
Regular rhythm	Played by string bass, guitar, (bass drum)	x	x	x	x

During the opening statements of the melody (called the *head* in jazz), the rhythm section provides steady support for the interaction of short riffs in saxes, brass, and—in the restatement of the melody—piano. Textures like this, with four distinct rhythmic layers and considerable rhythmic tension between riff figures and the steady reinforcement of the beat, move popular music much closer to African rhythmic concepts.

eight beat   Rock (or eight-beat) rhythm features two key ingredients: (1) a heavy backbeat; and (2) the division of each beat into (usually) two equally emphasized parts:

Beat	Rhythmic Section Roles	1	2	3	4
Backbeat	Played at least by snare drum; handclap, rhythm guitar, tambourine accent also used		X		X
Twice beat speed	Usually played by electric guitar, drums, perhaps bass guitar	/ /	/ /	/ /	/ /
Regular rhythm	Drums	x	x	x	x

As in the transition from fox-trot to swing, the fastest layer of regular rhythm of rock moves at twice the speed of swing in relation to the backbeat; there are two equally emphasized notes per beat instead of one. The rhythmic layer moving at twice beat speed is the essential rhythmic feature of a rock-based style; it brings soft and hard rock under the same umbrella.

    Chuck Berry's "Nadine" (Example 2.10) lays down a clear and basic rock beat. Bass and rhythm guitar play repeated notes that move twice as fast as the foot-tapping beat, and four times as fast as the backbeat; the eight-beat rhythm is unmistakable.

 I-9

 IA-9

sixteen beat   A new beat appeared around 1970, based on sixteen-beat patterns. As disco, it exploded brilliantly (if briefly) on the popular-music scene in the midseventies. But it also served as the rhythmic foundation for much Latin, Caribbean, African-American, and African-American- and Latin-influenced music in the seventies and eighties. As with swing and rock, this new beat adds a layer of rhythmic activity that moves twice as rapidly as that of the preceding style. The fastest rhythm now divides the beat into four equal parts. However, most "new beat" songs also make use of the slower regular rhythms; a heavy backbeat is typical:

Beat	Rhythm Section Roles	1	2	3	4
Backbeat	Played at least by snare drum; handclap, rhythm guitar, tambourine accent also used		X		X
Four times beat speed	Choked guitar, drums (usually on a closed hi-hat), other percussion	* * * *	* * * *	* * * *	* * * *
Twice beat speed	No one instrument typically assigned to this layer	/ /	/ /	/ /	/ /
Regular rhythm	Bass, drums	x	x	x	x

Disco stars Chic. L to r: Alfa Anderson, Bernard Edwards, Luci Martin, Niles Rodgers, Tony Thompson.

In "Good Times" (Example 2.11), Chic's quintessential disco song, the sixteen-beat rhythmic layer is heard on a closed hi-hat and choked guitar. This rhythmic layer combines with a distinct backbeat and an assortment of rapid riff-like figures occurring at rock and sixteen-beat speeds.

I-10

IA-10

MELODY

There are two melodic trademarks that give popular song a distinctively American sound, regardless of style. Both of them are rhythmic in origin. One is the construction of the melody from a short, clearly delineated melodic idea. The other is the use of a natural, speech-like rhythm in the melody. Both entered popular music in the teens—Irving Berlin's 1911 hit "Alexander's Ragtime Band," which begins "come on and hear," is arguably the first modern popular song—and have remained a consistent feature of mainstream popular music since.

The most commonly used term for these short melodic ideas is *riffs* riff Most riffs contain between two and seven notes. Often they contain syncopations. They stand out because they are isolated from the melody around them by silence. "It Had to Be You," the opening riff from a 1924 Isham Jones song, is a good example. It has six pitches/syllables, is separated from its restatement by a long pause, and has a syncopation on the syllable "you." The opening phrases of two earlier examples, "Maybelline" and "Good Times," are also good examples of riffs.

The best popular songs have absorbed not only the idiom and vocabulary, but also the cadence and inflection of vernacular (or everyday) American speech. Their lyrics often have a conversational flow, and they sound almost as good spoken as sung. The rhythms and melodic peaks and valleys should highlight, rather than fight, the natural delivery and inflection of the lyrics.

I-11

IA-11

Popular song's incorporation of vernacular language was influenced by the blues songs of the teens and twenties. This influence is clearly evident in popular singer Ruth Etting's recording of the classic twenties fox-trot song, "Deed I Do" (Example 2.12) written by Walter Hirsch and Fred Rose.

This song has unpretentious, conversational lyrics, set to a melody developed from a short opening phrase. The melody begins with a two-note riff, sung to the words "Do I." A rhythmically similar but melodically different continuation ("want you") completes the first phrase of lyric and melody; the entire phrase is two measures long. The second phrase ("Oh my, do I"), although identical in length and rhythm, differs melodically from the first. The final phrase ("Honey, 'deed I do") begins with the same riff used in the previous phrases. The breakaway from the riff rhythm on the last three words helps bring the section to a close. This final phrase is four measures, twice the length of the previous two. Even in this brief section of melody, we can clearly hear both the use of riffs as a melodic building block and the speech-like rhythm and inflection of the melodic line.

We can further highlight these trademark melodic features by contrasting them with the familiar "Take Me Out to the Ball Game," (a hit in 1906). This song is, of course, as American as apple pie in its subject matter, but shows the considerable influence of European music in its melodic style. It has a long, flowing melody and a melodic rhythm bound to the OOM-pah-pah waltz rhythm of the accompaniment. In a waltz song, the first beat generally receives more stress than the other two beats. Here the bass notes emphasize the first beat; so do the long syllables: "take"; "out"; "ball"; "game"; etc. As a result, the rhythm of the words as sung is quite different from the same words as spoken, because of the unnaturally heavy accents on syllables like "out" and the slow pace of the words themselves.

To sense the difference in melodic style between early and modern popular song, perform this simple test. Speak the words to the chorus of "Take Me Out to the Ball Game," then say them to the rhythm of the song. You should discover a significant difference between the way you would say the words without music and the way you have to speak them to follow the rhythm of the melody: "take" is too long, as are "ball" and "game." Then try the same procedure with the words to "Deed I Do" (or just about any current popular hit). Chances are that the sung version conforms pretty closely to the rhythm and inflection of the words as spoken.

hook

The use of riffs and speech-like rhythm has been common practice in popular music for the last eighty years, despite considerable variation in melodic style. Yesterday's riff is today's "hook"—the short, memorable, frequently repeated phrase in the chorus that tags the song. Riff-based melodies and speech-like rhythms helped mark the beginning of the modern era in popular music. Like the rhythm section and the backbeat, they signaled the emergence of a distinctively American popular style and have been enduring features since.

HARMONY AND TEXTURE

Instrumentation, rhythm, and melody all have accessible points of entry: the buzz of guitar distortion, a finger-popping beat, and a catchy riff. Harmony and texture, the next two elements we will discuss, do not; it's harder to sing along with a power chord than a riff. Although their use in popular music may often be less apparent, they still play a significant role in most performances. Harmony and texture have a complementary but usually subordinate relationship to melody. Harmony completes the organization of pitches; texture completes the organization of instrumental and vocal parts.

HARMONY

In music, harmony is the study of chords: what they are; how they are formed; how long they last; and how they succeed one another. If you have ever sung or heard a four-part hymn, you are already familiar with all four of these concepts. When all four parts sing at the same time, they produce groups of pitches, or chords.

The complementary relationship of harmony and melody is perhaps most apparent in a hymn, because all the parts generally move in the same rhythm. The top, or soprano, part is the melody. The series of chords formed by the four parts is the harmony. Harmony and melody are like coordinates on a graph: melody the horizontal axis; and harmony the vertical axis.

The other qualities of harmony are just as clearly evident in a hymn. Typically, chords change in a steady rhythm, once every syllable. Because chord change is usually clear and regular, the sequence of chords is easily heard. Chord sequences often become predictable, especially at the ends of phrases. For example, the sense of finality suggested by the closing "A-men" comes largely from the sequence of chords sung to those syllables.

Chords are most easily recognized when all pitches sound at the same time. But there are other ways of presenting harmony; most are more subtle. For example, OOM-pah accompaniments present the lowest note of the chord (the bass), followed by the rest of the chord notes. Or, chord pitches may occur one at a time. We use the word *arpeggio* to describe a chord in which the pitches are presented in succession.

Over its history, popular music has had a rich harmonic vocabulary. At its core are three chords, commonly identified as I, IV, and V. (Note: the value of Roman numeral indicates the note of the scale on which the chord is built; its case indicates the quality of the chord. The I chord is a major chord built on the first note of the scale: this is the chord outlined in the opening notes of the "Star Spangled Banner.") These chords entered popular music as the primary chords of European classical music. They have served as the main chords in popular song since its beginning. Many nineteenth-century songs are harmonized only with these basic chords. In this century, I, IV, and V have been the main chords in popular song, virtually the entire harmonic vocabulary of blues and early country music, and the focal chords of rock. We can hear these chords presented in sequence in Ritchie Valen's 1959 hit, "La Bamba" (Example 2.14).

I-13

IA-13

In European-derived styles, chords typically appear in a consistently used sequence, called a *progression*. In a chord progression, there is a sense of connection between the chords. The chords are not simply following one another, but forming a larger unit that leads toward a goal chord. Certain chord progressions appear so regularly that they create a sense of expectation. When we have heard part of the progression, we have a sense of what will come next.

I-12

IA-12

When a progression reaches a goal chord, it helps punctuate the musical flow; the arrival point is usually called a *cadence*. For example, the opening two phrases of Stephen Foster's "Oh! Susanna" (Example 2.13) both end with a cadence. Both phrases begin on a I chord. The first cadence uses the V chord as a goal, while the second uses the I chord. Both have the same rhythm and almost the same melody. The first cadence (on the word "knee") says "go on," because it pauses on the V chord. The second cadence (on the word "see") comes to a stop, because it returns to the opening chord, the logical resolution of the phrase. Because the first progression ends on the V chord, it suggests only a partial punctuation of the musical flow, like a comma or semicolon between clauses. The return to the opening chord at the end of the second phrase completes a harmonic sentence, suggesting a strong punctuation, like a period.

European harmony is a meaningful system of pitch organization comparable in many respects to a language. The harmony of most African music is the diametric opposite. Much African folk music has no harmony: it is simply voice(s) singing one line accompanied by percussion. "Chords," when they happen, are simply two or more pitches sounding simultaneously. There is no common vocabulary. As a result, there are no chord progressions in the European sense of a connected series. Chords may succeed one another, but they do not imply movement toward a goal in the specific way that European harmony does. In addition, African harmonies, when they do occur, tend to change very slowly. A chord or chord-like occurrence may last for several measures.

Not surprisingly, an African harmonic conception surfaced in African-American music. In African-American popular styles, it has often taken the form of reinterpreting European harmony from an African point of view. The earliest illustration of this reinterpretation process was the blues. The chord rhythm of country or early urban blues is much slower than the popular songs of the same era. Although the chord vocabulary of the blues comes from the familiar harmonies of European music, the chords are used in a radically different way. In blues styles minimally influenced by European music, there is little sense of a chord progression, even though the same chords may form standard progressions in other contexts. The most popular blues chord (an intensified form of the V chord) is a highly directional chord in European harmony. It demands resolution to the "I" chord. In a blues, however, it is used as a stable, nondirectional chord on all three scale tones. It is an isolated event, with no sense of leading to another chord.

Much contemporary popular music, especially by African-American performers, has shifted even further toward an African approach to harmony. The one-chord jams of rock guitarists and two chord grooves of pop-jazz saxophonists are ample evidence of this shift. The most influential artist in this regard has been James Brown, whose music substituted textural interest for harmonic variety.

TEXTURE

As we have noted, melody and rhythm offer easy points of access: the tune; the beat. In popular music, texture has two dimensions: melodic and rhythmic. When examining *melodic texture*, we are concerned primarily with the distribution of melodic interest. In this respect, the melody offers a convenient yardstick. By definition, it has the most drawing power, so we can use it as a gauge for the other parts. Which parts, if any, are of almost comparable melodic interest, and which parts are of lesser interest?

The *rhythmic texture* of popular music is likely to be fuller than the melodic texture. Each voice or instrument has a rhythmic as well as a melodic role. In addition, drums and other nonmelodic percussion instruments usually enrich the rhythmic texture in popular music. As with melody, the beat offers an easy point of entry into texture. Unlike the melody, however, the parts that confirm the beat are likely to be the least interesting parts of the texture. Strict timekeeping, as in a waltz-song accompaniment or a generic disco song, may produce a clear beat but little interest. A good beat, in the qualitative sense, depends on the interplay between those rhythmic layers marking or implying a regular rhythm and those that conflict with it or soar over it.

The rhythmic texture of much popular music can be heard as a number of layers superimposed on a regular rhythm. Since the consolidation of the rhythm section in the teens, most popular music presents a *stratified* texture. Each part may have a distinct role. It may have considerable rhythmic interest but negligible melodic interest or vice versa. The independent but interdependent division of labor among the rhythm section and melody instruments and voices is a trademark of popular music.

As is the case with harmony, the textures of pre-ragtime popular music and the African-influenced popular styles of today are polar opposites. European-influenced textures of nineteenth-century popular song are hierarchical. The melody is the primary—in many cases, the sole—source of melodic interest. Accompaniments are generic, interchangeable among dozens of songs. Contemporary popular music, like the African music that influenced it, is more democratic. Melodic and rhythmic interest is diffused throughout the group. Interest is a collective effort, a product of the interaction of several different parts, none of which may be interesting enough to stand alone. The main vocal line is first among equals, not the completely dominant part.

FORM

Form is, as we have noted, the organization of music in time. Popular music makes use of a number of different formal patterns. Some, like the multisectional form used in ragtime or the AABA form used in Tin Pan Alley song, were borrowed directly from European music. Others, like the standard AAB blues form, originated within the popular tradition. Often, such forms help define a style, so we will identify the characteristic forms of a style in the genre discussions that follow.

However, there are two aspects of form so widespread in their use that they deserve mention here. The first is the use of a *chorus*, the second is the ongoing tension between *hierarchical* and *sequential* approaches to form. A chorus is a phrase or section of music periodically repeated throughout a song performance that uses the same words and melody at every repetition. Precisely because both words and music are repeated without variation, the chorus is usually the most memorable part of a song. The chorus has been part of popular music since its inception in the 1840s. As we will see in

chorus

hierarchical form

sequential form

Chapter 4, a recurrent, well-defined chorus helps distinguish the minstrel and plantation songs of the new popular style from the more European parlor songs.

The tension between hierarchical and sequential approaches to form is one aspect of popular music's ongoing dialectic between European and African musical traditions. European forms tend to be hierarchical. Small formal units form larger formal units, that form still larger formal units . . . the process continues to the largest level: the performance, considered as a whole. This hierarchical approach is much like the hierarchical organization of language: letters group into syllables, that group into words, phrases, sentences, etc.

In the hierarchical forms used in popular music, sectional outlines tend to be clearly defined by a drop in energy in one or more elements. A harmonic cadence, the subtraction of an instrument—for instance, the piano interludes between vocal sections of a song—and the consequent thinning of the texture, a descending melodic line, a long note or pause in the rhythmic flow: any and all can help delineate sectional boundaries. Moreover, there tends to be a correlation between the energy drop and the size of the section it marks off. Bigger sections are more emphatically defined by coordinated decrease in energy in several elements. In this respect, energy drops in a hierarchical form function much like punctuation in language (as was suggested in the discussion of harmonic cadences).

A sequential approach to form differs in two fundamental respects. First, there may be little or no hierarchical organization: sections simply follow one another without forming larger units. Second, the boundaries between sections—if in fact they are sharply defined—are likely to be defined by an abrupt shift in one or more elements, not by a relaxation of the musical flow. Even the perimeter of a performance—its beginning and end—may not be clearly marked. The layered beginning and fadeout ending so common in contemporary popular music is evidence of a sequential approach. The African roots of a sequential approach to form are discussed in greater detail in Chapter 3.

PUTTING IT ALL TOGETHER

The Rolling Stones' "Honky Tonk Women" (Example 2.15) can be used as a case study in harmony, texture, and form. We can observe how harmony and texture help shape a performance and see both types of form in operation. The song takes the following form:

Introduction

Verse, consisting of four phrases. Each phrase begins much the same way. The first and third phrases are identical from beginning to end, while the second and fourth end differently from the other three. (We can indicate this plan as: AA'AA", where A is the first statement and its literal restatement, and A' and A" are variants of A.)

Chorus, consisting of two phrases. The second is a variant of the first (AA').

Verse: different text set to the same melody as the first verse.

Chorus: same in both words and melody.

Verse: performed now as an instrumental interlude.

The Rolling Stones, c. 1971. L to r: Mick Taylor, Charlie Watts, Mick Jagger, Keith Richard, Bill Wyman.

Chorus: same in both words and melody, but with an even richer instrumental and vocal accompaniment.

Chorus: as before, but with the addition of a short, concluding phrase.

This outline clearly shows how the form of this song emphasizes the chorus. With the verse, it forms a larger section: verse plus chorus. Unlike the verse, it is virtually the same in every statement. An extra statement is added for emphasis at the end (in case we missed the point the first three times). "Honky Tonk Women" is like many other popular songs in its emphasis on a recurring chorus. Where it differs is in the ways in which the form is outlined.

One of the harmonic options of rock in the sixties was to build a song out of the three basic chords. Of all the major bands of the rock era, none used these three chords with more imagination and variety than the Rolling Stones. In the verse, each of the three basic chords serves as a point of departure or arrival. We hear the I chord first. The IV chord harmonizes "Memphis," the V chord "ride," producing a "comma" cadence. The same basic progression harmonizes the second phrase. However, it returns to the I chord, which brings the verse to a harmonic close (a "period cadence"). The chorus is even more minimal harmonically: it uses only two chords.

What makes the use of these three chords especially interesting is the variety in their presentation. The first version of the I chord is incomplete, giving it a hollow sound. Both the IV and V chords are embellished with a smoothly connecting chord. At the time of this recording, this embellishment was on its way to becoming a rock cliché, but here it sounds fresh. And a different chord from the three precedes the V chord, giving the progression a richer sound.

The Rolling Stones introduce considerable harmonic variety to a simple progression through variation and embellishment. This gives the song a distinctive harmonic identity without the use of an elaborate vocabulary. Other Rolling Stones songs achieve a similar goal by a different route.

"Honky Tonk Women" is even more interesting texturally. Unlike many rock songs, there is considerable textural interest, in part because of its primary role in outlining the form. Instead of maintaining the same instrumentation and sound throughout the song, the Stones alternate between a relatively transparent texture during the sung statements of the verse and a dense sound on the chorus, when bass and steel guitar are added and the other instruments become more active.

The rhythmic texture is similarly rich. The song begins with a mildly syncopated pattern played on a cowbell. Both guitars and drums enter with repetitive rhythmic patterns, but none of them mark the beat. The drum pattern mixes several different drum sounds—bass drum, snare, and so forth—to provide even further rhythmic differentiation. This sense of rhythmic unrest is maintained until the chorus of the song. When the bass enters, the percussion instruments reinforce a rock rhythm so that an even denser, more varied rhythmic texture prevails. The instrumental version of the verse is the thickest section of all, with the addition of horns to an already full texture. The alternation of relatively thin texture in the verse with dense texture in the chorus casts the form of the song into clear relief.

Harmony, texture, and form show the influence of both European and African music. Formally, the song sends mixed signals: the form of the melody and harmony is hierarchical, while the rest of the texture suggests a more sequential approach. A hierarchical arrangement is particularly clear in the verse. There are four short phrases that group into two longer units: AA' and AA". Because the first phrase pair (AA') ends on the V chord (a comma cadence), and the second (AA") ends on the I chord (a period cadence), they in turn form one larger unit, the verse. Verse and chorus combine into a still larger unit, which is repeated three times. (Remember that the third verse/chorus statement features an instrumental version of the verse.) This hierarchical verse/chorus organization had been used in popular music for over a century by the time this song was recorded.

By contrast, the instrumental accompaniment suggests a more sequential approach. The song gets under way layer by layer: first cowbell, followed in turn by drums, guitar, and voice. The underlying rhythm remains constant throughout the song. Sectional divisions are most decisively defined by the addition and subtraction of instruments: added at the chorus, subtracted at the second verse, thickened even more for the final verse/chorus statement.

"Honky Tonk Women" is certainly a rock classic and arguably one of the best illustrations of a group conception in the popular music repertoire. It is a fitting song with which to end this chapter, because it is a virtual catalog of popular music's distinctive style features. In its instrumentation, it shows the central role of the rhythm section, the use of saxophone as the primary horn, and the pragmatic use of instruments from outside the style: the cowbell is a "found" instrument adopted by Afro-Cuban music, and the steel guitar is used as seasoning to give the song a slightly country flavor. Mick Jagger's performing style will never be confused with Luciano Pavarotti's, but who could sing this song better?

"Honky Tonk Women" shows several key rhythmic features as well. The stylistic connotation of beat is clear: Using the backbeat (played on the snare drum) as our point of reference, we can easily measure the eight-beat rhythm that characterizes the song as rock. We also hear the quantitative and qualitative connotations of beat. The beat (quantitative) is easy to find:

The song has the relentless groove for which the Rolling Stones were so justly famous. The layered beginning, which begins with rhythmic conflict in the cowbell and mixes in the eight-beat regular rhythm with several additional conflicting layers, shows, as well as any example can, that a *good* beat is more than beat marking. The melody, with its long phrases, is more reminiscent of country music than blues (which, given the theme of the song, shouldn't surprise us); in the accompaniment, however, are plenty of riffs. They're particularly evident in the instrumental version of the verse, where they are piled on top of one another.

With the features and parameters presented in this chapter firmly in mind, we can turn our attention to the sources of popular music.

Terms to Know

accent	arpeggio	backbeat
beat	chorus	duration
dynamics	form	harmony
hierarchical form	hook	inflection
instrumentation	intensity	measure
melody	melody line	part
pitch	rhythm section	riff
sequential form	syncopation	tempo
texture	timbre	verse

Study Questions

1. Name the instruments found in a standard rhythm section.

2. Explain the three connotations of the word "beat," as presented in the text.

3. Establish a backbeat by slapping one hand on your left leg. Then create, in succession, a two-beat, four-beat, eight-beat, and sixteen-beat rhythm by tapping the other hand on your other leg. (You may want to begin with a slow tempo, or slow down the tempo as you shift from beat to beat.)

4. Compare the attitude toward performing styles in folk, popular, and classical musics.

5. With the help of two or more classmates/friends, create a layered rhythmic texture using percussive sounds. Include at least a backbeat and an eight-beat or sixteen-beat rhythm layer. Use primarily found instruments: handclap; soda bottles; pencils; shakers of any kind; tin cans; table tops; and so on.

6. What are the two most distinctive features of an African rhythmic conception?

7. Choose three current pop songs. Analyze the form, texture, and rhythmic basis of each song.

CHAPTER THREE
The Sources of Popular Music

Popular music is a hybrid. Its distinctive sounds have their roots in two dissimilar musical cultures, that of western Europe and west Africa. European music brought to and nurtured in the United States was of two distinct kinds: art music and music composed in a similar but simpler style, and Anglo-American folk music. By contrast, Africans found it almost impossible to keep their musical traditions intact, because during slavery tribes and families were split up and much of their music making was suppressed. Despite this suppression, African musical values have gradually resurfaced in popular music. The following discussion highlights salient features of each tradition and their connections to popular music.

THE EUROPEAN HERITAGE

European music well known in nineteenth-century America ranged from Italian opera and German *lieder* (art songs) to folk songs from the British Isles. The wide range of styles reflected the diverse population that enjoyed them. The east coast, urban upper class formed the main audience for the grandest classical music, for example, operas by Rossini or Bellini. Adaptations of Italian opera arias with English texts and simplified music found a much wider audience that included members of a growing middle class. Many of the most popular songs published in the United States before the Civil War used virtually the same musical language as classical music. An opera aria differed from a household song mainly in its difficulty and sophistication, less in its style.

Excerpts from "Casta Diva" (Example 3.1), an aria from the opera, *Norma,* by Vincenzo Bellini, "Woodman, Spare That Tree" (Example 3.2) by Henry Russell, and Stephen Foster's "Beautiful Dreamer" (Example 3.3) show how grand opera style could be simplified into a song for home use. There are many similarities. Musical interest centers on a flowing melody. The simple arpeggiated accompaniment clearly fills a subordinate role, and divides each beat into three equal durations. All have a moderately slow tempo with a clear, if lightly marked beat, and all use the same harmonic language.

They differ mainly in their elaborateness. "Casta Diva" features an

lieder

aria

 I-14

 IA-14

 I-15

 IA-15

 I-16

 IA-16

orchestral accompaniment and a florid, wide-ranging, often melismatic (a melisma is a series of pitches sung on the same syllable) vocal line. "Woodman, Spare That Tree" is set for voice and piano. Although simpler vocally, it unfolds on much the same scale as "Casta Diva." Like the aria, it has a long instrumental introduction, and its phrases are of comparable length: in fact, both open with phrases based on a descending scale like the opening of "Three Blind Mice."

melisma

"Beautiful Dreamer" has the simplest setting of the three vocal works. The accompaniment is modest, in easy reach of an amateur pianist. In addition, the song unfolds more quickly than the other two, as its phrases are considerably shorter. Interestingly, it has the most active vocal line of the three, full of skips and leaps. It would challenge the amateur singer in a way that "Woodman, Spare That Tree" would not. Foster's song is a "popular song" because it is simpler and shorter than Bellini's operatic aria, but it is not a popular song in our contemporary sense of the term. It does not represent a distinct musical style. That would only emerge from the interaction of European and African styles.

ANGLO-AMERICAN FOLK SONG

Settlers from England, Ireland, and Scotland brought a rich folk tradition with them. Many of these fiddle tunes, songs, and ballads entered the native tradition here. Although folk music has existed separately from popular music, it has influenced its growth. Many important styles—beginning with nineteenth-century minstrelsy—have drawn on folk roots.

Appalachian string band. L to r: Jeeter Gentry (banjo), Elmer Thompson (guitar and harmonica), and Fiddlin' Bill Henseley. Asheville, NC, 1937. Photograph by Ben Shahn. Reproduction from the Collection of the Library of Congress.

I-17

IA-17

"Old Joe Clark" (Example 3.4), recorded in the early 1920s, is a typical example of a Southern folk song, and it illustrates graphically the differences between folk and cultivated traditions. The text is much more colloquial and humorous in tone than "Beautiful Dreamer." It certainly paints a less flattering picture of the female subject of the song. The vocal quality is nasal, without the sweetness of the cultured style. In many ways, it communicates much more directly (like good contemporary music) than the parlor song. The melody is repeated over and over, with little or no variation. The song has little harmonic movement, unlike classical or art song. Both accompaniment and melody are based on a modal scale; there is no sense of chord progression. The rhythm is very active, with a fast tempo and fast-flowing notes in the accompaniment. Each beat receives equal emphasis, but there is no rhythmic conflict (syncopation). In form, the song uses a rudimentary version of the verse-chorus form featured in early minstrel-show songs, as well as many popular songs of the post-Civil War period.

Although several of the qualities that distinguish "Old Joe Clark" from "Beautiful Dreamer"—notably the nasal singing style and the instrumentation—would remain the exclusive property of folk or country music, there are features of this song that found their way into nineteenth-century popular song. These include: a fast tempo suggesting a dance rhythm; more colloquial language; and frequent repetition of the main idea of a song, in alternation with a story or short vignettes.

THE AFRICAN HERITAGE

As European influence on American popular music has diminished, African influence has grown. The initial influence of African slaves on popular music was almost exclusively visual: blackface entertainers cruelly caricatured the slaves' appearance and speech. From that lowly beginning, African values have slowly but inexorably permeated popular music. Indeed, the steadily increasing influence of African musical values is one of the most remarkable features of the evolution of American popular music. That the dominant music of a society would be increasingly shaped by a minority culture is surprising enough. That it would be shaped by a minority that was brought forcibly to this country and stripped of its freedom, its language, and its culture is even more surprising. That this minority would exert such an enormous influence on a dominant majority in spite of the often institutionalized racism that it encountered has been extraordinary.

Much of the musical heritage of Africans was suppressed, although their musical talent was recognized and even encouraged at times. During slavery, drums were banned from the plantation because masters recognized that they were used not only as musical instruments, but also as communication tools. Without a common mother language or preserved musical tradition, African-Americans created their own distinctive musical traditions, often by reinterpreting the music of whites. Spirituals, ragtime, and jazz were among the earliest styles to emerge from this ongoing reinterpretive process.

African values have profoundly and pervasively influenced virtually all American popular styles, from early blues and religious music to the vast majority of contemporary popular music styles. Parallels between the folk music of west Africa and contemporary popular styles are uncanny in their closeness and their comprehensiveness. In most cases, the differences between the two are more a matter of resources and technology than musical conception. We can hear their close affinity in the following series of examples.

Many west African languages are tonal: that is, the same syllable may have different meanings depending on its pitch or inflection. As a result, speech in these languages already approaches song. Singing, especially singing of the narrow-ranging melodic motives common to much African music, is simply an intensification of the natural inflection of the language. (This is in sharp contrast to the clear division between speech and song that was customary in nineteenth-century classical music.)

Blues performer Blind Willie McTell, c. 1928.

 I-18

 IA-18

griot

"Folk Story" (Example 3.5) performed by a Wolof *griot* (a singer of tales), and "Travelin' Blues" (Example 3.6), sung by Blind Willie McTell (1901–1959), a bluesman from Georgia, show an underlying similarity in vocal style and vocal and instrumental approach, despite the obvious difference in language. In the first example, the griot is telling a story. He begins each of several sections by narrating the story in rapid, highly inflected speech. These narrations periodically blossom into song. Of special interest vocally is the smooth continuity in sound between mostly spoken passages and sung sections; the transition from speech to song is gentle rather than abrupt. The same is true in "Travelin' Blues." As in the griot song, the shifts between speech and song happen almost imperceptibly as McTell alternates between narrative passages and blues-like refrains.

 I-19

 IA-19

There are instrumental parallels as well. Both performers use a strummed instrument. Moreover, they use the instrument in two distinct ways: to accompany the voice and to provide interludes between vocal sections. McTell also makes train and bell sounds, and whistles, as well as producing two different guitar timbres, the steady plucking and the imitation of the voice. The exploration of new sounds is very much part of the African/African-American tradition.

Griot playing the Kora (harp); Bamana tribe, Mali, Africa. Photograph by Eliot Elisofon, Courtesy National Museum of African Art, Eliot Elisofon Archives, Smithsonian Institution.

 I-20

 IA-20

Example 3.7 alternates phrases from recordings by an African-American (Henry Ratcliff, performing a free-form blues song called "Louisiana") and an African (a field worker in Senegal) to show a remarkable similarity in vocal style between the folk music of the two cultures. The most important of these similarities include:

1. Vocal timbre: the basic sound and inflection of the voice
2. Melodic shape: most phrases begin high and finish low
3. Rhythmic freedom of the delivery
4. Pitch choice: the reliance on pentatonic (five-note) scales
5. The use of melismas.

pentatonic

African values have influenced the instrumentation of popular music in both instrument choice and instrumental style. The most obvious impact of African music on American popular styles has been the extensive use of percussion instruments. This shouldn't be particularly surprising, because the preeminent African instrument is the drum. Drums come in many shapes and sizes, and are capable of different pitches. Thus, drums are able to imitate the tonal inflections of many west African languages, and can be used for signals. Other percussion instruments, such as cowbells, rattles, and gourds, are also used frequently in African music, as are handclaps and other human-produced percussive noises.

We needn't look further than the drum set, a staple of virtually all popular styles since the twenties, to gauge the impact of African values on popular-music instrumentation, although their growing influence goes well beyond this one instrument. There has been a steady increase in the use of percussion instruments, and percussive playing techniques on nonpercussive instruments.

The African approach to instrumental style has had a profound impact on popular music in two ways:

1. Leading musicians have cultivated distinctive sounds on their instruments. Their sounds become their signatures. A jazz fan can recognize Miles Davis or Charlie Parker in a few seconds.

2. Musicians have also experimented with ways to get totally unprecedented sounds from existing instruments, or even noninstruments.

Unlike Western instruments, which are more or less uniform from maker to maker, African instruments do not conform to a standard specification. They are usually made from available materials: logs, animal skins, and so forth, and may vary considerably from region to region. African-American musicians have been similarly resourceful instrument makers, inventing instruments out of everyday materials intended for a different purpose. The washtub bass and washboard percussion heard in some juke bands are an early example; the rhythmic record scratching heard on rap songs, a more current one. **washtub bass**

washboard

More significantly, however, pioneering musicians have developed new ways to play existing instruments. Every instrument commonly used in popular music has acquired new sound possibilities through the inventiveness of African-American musicians. To cite only one example, guitarists, particularly blues and blues-influenced guitarists, have developed an entire repertoire of new guitar sounds, like the so-called "bottleneck" slide style, which **bottleneck** has given the instrument an entirely different character. "Sunnyland" (Example 3.8), performed by Elmore James, is a blues song that illustrates the use of the slide.

 I-21

 IA-21

African music has shaped the texture of popular music in two notable ways, a general approach and one specific procedure. A preference for African-like textures has been increasingly characteristic of popular music since the swing era, while call-and-response patterns have been used in popular music since the minstrel-spiritual songs of the 1870s.

The texture of African group music tends to be dense and heterogeneous: many people perform different patterns at the same time. Musical interest is distributed throughout the texture. No one part, even a vocal line, stands out as preeminently important. Indeed, a single strand of the texture could not stand alone. (This is not the case with European-derived popular song. The many successful unaccompanied performances of "The Star Spangled Banner" at sporting events offer ample evidence of the preeminence of melody in this style.) In much African music, then, the whole is greater than the sum of the parts.

I-22

IA-22

I-23

IA-23

"Yarum Praise Song" (Example 3.9), performed by Fra-fra Tribesmen, and "Nubian Nut" (Example 3.10) performed by George Clinton, demonstrate specifically an African approach to texture and the stylistic kinship of the two cultures. They display typically heterogeneous African texture in almost identical fashion. There are three distinct elements common to both songs: (1) a quick moving percussion part; (2) riffs played by a pitched instrument; and (3) a vocal line.

The praise song is a relatively simple example. It features a percussion instrument—some kind of shaker playing a steady rhythm at sixteen-beat speed—a bowed string instrument playing a riff-like figure, and a vocal line. Clinton, one of the creators of seventies funk, offers a more complex and denser version of the same pattern in this 1983 recording. The same three elements are present. A prominent percussion part plays intermittently, also at sixteen-beat speed. Here, several pitched electronic instruments play riff figures. The solo vocal line flows over the instrumental parts, as it does in the African recording. There are, of course, additional elements in the texture: bass, heavy backbeat, and backup vocals are the most prominent. But these should not obscure the underlying similarity in texture, both in approach and result.

Ray Charles, c. 1960.

I-24

IA-24

D

call and response

Call and response is the regular alternation of two contrasting sound colors or densities: solo voice/choir; voice/instrument; or instrument/instrument (e.g., guitar/sax). A common feature in much sung African music, it has been widely used in popular music since the thirties. In both the Bulu Chorus (Example 3.11) and "Tell the Truth" (Example 3.12), performed by Ray Charles and the Raelets, a group of singers—the African chorus and the

Raelets, respectively—repeat a simple three-note pattern ("tell the truth," in the case of Charles's recording) over and over. At the same time, the solo singer comments between, and sometimes through, statements of the three-note response.

The previous examples highlight the influence of African music on vocal style, instrumentation and instrumental style, and texture. This influence extends to every other element: dynamics, melody, harmony, and form. For example, melodies and accompanying parts of several of the previous examples grow out of melodic ideas: the Yarum Praise Song, Bulu Chorus, "Nubian Nut," "Sunnyland," and "Tell the Truth" illustrate this style.

African music has had a profound influence on the form of American popular music. The African approach to form is the exact opposite of the forms of nineteenth-century popular song. Forms are open, not closed, and sequential, not hierarchical. We can hear the open form of African music most clearly at the beginning and end of a performance. Group music begins with the master drummer or other musician establishing a beat; others join gradually. The music ends when the ceremonial event is over. There is no sense of frame, no sense of a clear beginning and end. Both the Yarum Praise Song and "Nubian Nut" begin this way, as do many of the examples found later in the text. Some particularly good illustrations include Count Basie's "Jumpin' at the Woodside" (Example 2.9) and Herbie Hancock's second version of "Watermelon Man" (Example 18.4).

 I-8

 IA-8

The impact of African music on form is typically even more obvious at the end of a song than its beginning. The fadeout ending, which had become commonplace by the late sixties, is the most pervasive adaptation of an African formal conception to popular music.

 V-6

 VA-6

African group music seldom presents a clear formal hierarchy. Typically, sections simply follow one another. Divisions between sections result from shifts in rhythmic texture, melodic motive, and/or beat speed. There are no internal resting points. The Yarum Praise Song illustrates this sequential approach to formal organization in African music. Any of the rock-era "endless loop" songs, like the Rolling Stones' "Satisfaction" (Example 15.1), illustrate its adaptation into contemporary popular music.

"endless loop" song

Ⓓ

CONCLUSION

The similarities between African and African-American (and African-American influenced) musical practices are extensive and remarkably close, despite obvious differences in language, technology, and culture. African-American music has in turn shaped virtually all twentieth-century popular music, at least to some degree. African influence is evident in ragtime, blues, Tin Pan Alley popular song, jazz, swing, country, Latin music, rock, disco, and funk: in other words, just about every important style to emerge in the last 100 years.

The miracle of American popular music is that such an important musical language has developed from such disparate musical sources. As we have seen, the "pre-pop" (early nineteenth-century) popular song derived from European classical music and Anglo-American folk music are different enough. But classically influenced song and African and African-American folk music are more than just different: They are the complete opposite of each other in virtually every respect.

The interaction between European and African musical traditions has been the crucial factor in the creation of a distinctively American popular music and the catalyst for its evolutionary change. However, Anglo-American folk music has played a significant, if intermittent, role in the development of popular music. Its impact has been most noticeable in the middle years of both the nineteenth and twentieth centuries. It introduced vernacular speech in the 1840s and brought plain-spoken, everyday speech into the mainstream during the 1960s. At the same time, it made the music more familiar and accessible by introducing the recurrent refrain into popular song.

It's safe to say that popular music wouldn't be as distinctive, varied, accessible, infectious, or popular without the contributions of all three sources. Each has played an important, continually changing role. A new kind of music came from their initial interaction. Its evolution has been the result of their ongoing cross-pollination. The remainder of the book charts this evolution, and the music that has resulted, over the last 150 years.

Terms to Know

aria	bottleneck	call and response
"endless loop" song	griot	lieder
melisma	pentatonic	washboard
washtub bass		

Study Questions

1. What are the three main sources of popular music? What did each contribute to the sound and style of popular music?

2. Which style had the most influence initially? Which has the most influence now?

3. In what ways might classical and folk performances of a nineteenth-century song differ?

4. Compare European and African approaches to speech and song.

5. Listen to any contemporary rap song. How does this song combine spoken and sung lyrics? What are the similarities between modern rap songs and traditional African songs?

6. Choose two examples of "endless-loop" songs from the pop charts. Describe why they fit into this category.

7. Choose any two examples of current pop songs. Identify the European and African elements in each. Be sure to explain what makes these elements "European" or "African," as these terms are described in this chapter.

PART II
REVOLUTION 1

CHAPTER FOUR

The Birth of American Popular Music

In 1852, Stephen Foster's "Old Folks at Home" was all the rage. Introduced by Christy's Minstrels, the song was known not only to shopkeepers, but to their upper-class patrons. It's true that the more respectable members of American society looked down their noses at "the Ethiopian business." They considered the early minstrel show and anything associated with it as low-class entertainment (although many of the middle and upper classes patronized the shows). For musical entertainment, they preferred sentimental parlor songs and watered-down versions of the European classics. John Sullivan Dwight, whose *Journal of Music* served as the semi-official arbiter of good taste among the cultivated, likened Foster's "Old Folks at Home" to a "morbid irritation of the skin." Still, Dwight had to admit that "Old Folks at Home" was popular. As it turned out, Foster's song was a birthmark, not a rash. His songs have remained part of our collective memory for almost a century and a half, while much of the more genteel music that Dwight championed is long forgotten.

minstrel show; minstrelsy

parlor song

Foster's minstrel-show songs (such as "Old Folks at Home" and "Oh! Susanna"), marked the birth of a distinct popular style. Although cut from the same musical cloth as the parlor songs of the period (Foster was just as adept at composing parlor songs, as "Jeannie with the Light Brown Hair" and "Beautiful Dreamer" testify), his minstrel songs have vitality, humor, and a lack of pretension. The minstrel show set in motion the first revolution in American popular music: the creation of a distinct popular style. Minstrelsy was an American entertainment, and was recognized here and abroad as such. The songs of the early minstrel show, accompanied with scratchy fiddles and clacking bones, brought an entirely new sound to popular song. The introduction of these folk elements in a crude, unwashed form was its most revolutionary aspect.

If the revolution had been confined just to the minstrel show, however, it wouldn't have been much of a revolution. What made it far-reaching was the way in which the most popular minstrel songs wove themselves into the fabric of American life. Contemporary accounts tell us how everyone seemed to know and sing Foster's songs. People couldn't seem to get enough of them. Dan Emmett's "Dixie," introduced in 1859 in a minstrel show, spread like wildfire through the South and quickly became the rallying cry of the Confederacy.

Two qualities distinguished such songs: they were surpassingly popular; and they sounded homegrown. This represented a real shift in taste. These were songs by Americans, known to many Americans in Foster's case, better known than almost any others, with a recognizably American accent. European music would continue to exert considerable influence on American popular music for the rest of the century, but with the minstrel songs of Foster, Emmett, and others, a distinctly American popular-song tradition took root. It would wait over half a century to flower.

AMERICA'S EMERGING IDENTITY

The minstrel show and the beginnings of American popular song in the 1840s and 1850s constituted one aspect of a three-decade-long cultural awakening. It began with Andrew Jackson's presidency. Jackson was the first people's president. The previous six presidents had come from America's "first families," and were wealthy, well-educated Easterners. Jackson, the orphan son of a poor North Carolina frontier family, was largely self-educated and self-made. He won the election primarily with support from the South and West, where many shared his distrust of the Eastern establishment.

Blackface entertainment reflected these new Jacksonian values. It was informal, high-spirited, vigorous, and full of humor, bringing a breath of fresh air into the stuffy parlors of the nineteenth century. But it was also crude, cruel, even vicious in its stereotyped portrayal of a defenseless minority. It represented the best and worst of this new American populism.

The decades before the Civil War also saw the beginning of the Industrial Revolution in the United States. Fed by cheap immigrant labor, industry grew rapidly. Many companies were established to manufacture the host of inventions and improvements that touched so many aspects of American life. Trains made travel easier, Samuel Morse's telegraph made rapid communication possible, and John Deere's plow and Cyrus McCormick's reaper helped settle the prairie. One industry in particular affected the music business: piano making.

During these years, American piano builders patented several important improvements in piano design. The most significant of these was a single-piece iron frame, which supplanted metal-reinforced wood frames, permitting greater string tension, and producing a richer, more projecting tone. Alpheus Babcock patented this all-metal design in 1825; in 1843, Jonas Chickering, a Boston maker, applied the cast-iron frame to a grand piano. Sixteen years later, Henry Steinway combined the iron frame with over-strung bass strings (the lowest strings are strung across the lower middle strings, increasing their length and thereby improving tone and volume), completing the most important development in the evolution of the modern piano.

Piano manufacturers served a rapidly growing middle class, which often cultivated some musical skills. The piano was the instrument most people learned to play. Until well into the twentieth century, it was an essential piece of domestic furniture and the center of home entertainment. Gathering together in the parlor, families would sing the popular songs of the day, (usually) accompanied at the piano by one of the family members.

The majority learned songs from sheet music, the primary means of dis-   sheet music
seminating popular songs until well into the twentieth century.

STEPHEN FOSTER AND
THE DEVELOPMENT OF
A NEW AMERICAN STYLE

In the stack of sheet music on a parlor piano might be a copy of Stephen
Foster's "Old Folks at Home." It was a safe bet that Foster's song would be
there, because it eventually sold over twenty million copies. No song has
sold more.

Stephen Foster.

Stephen Foster was the most important songwriter in nineteenth-century American popular music. He was versatile and skillful; his songs were
well written, and often inspiring and innovative. From the beginning of his
career in the mid-1840s, he was equally active composing for the parlor and
the minstrel stage. Success came early with minstrel tunes like "Oh!
Susanna" and "Camptown Races," which remain popular to this day.
Particularly in the 1850s, at the apex of his career, he was a composer of real
skill. His best songs far outshine the work of his contemporaries and successors. The relative simplicity of his style came about by choice, not default,

plantation
song

I-28

IB-2

as he sought to create a specifically popular style. His most significant innovation was the creation of a new popular genre, the "plantation song."
"Plantation songs" like "Old Folks at Home" (Example 4.4) drew on both parlor and minstrel song styles. It was the first important instance of a new
popular style being created by mixing two established popular styles. It
would not be the last.

Foster left an enduring musical legacy. His music, especially his minstrel
and plantation songs, was influential. Virtually all post–Civil War songs
would feature at least some of the elements added to popular song via minstrelsy. Much of it is memorable. Many songs remain familiar after 150
years; two are official state songs. The next four examples illustrate the
sources of the new popular song style, the parlor song and the minstrel
show, and show their synthesis in the plantation song. The three Foster
songs convey some sense of his versatility as a songwriter.

PARLOR SONGS

Parlor songs (or household songs) are songs intended primarily for
home use. They are close relatives of the art songs of European classical
music. They resemble art songs in their setting for voice and piano, but are
generally simpler in both melody and accompaniment.

Parlor songs composed in America followed English middle class taste.
In America, as in England, the primary influences were Italian opera and
folk songs from the British Isles. We have documented the influence of
Italian style on Foster's "Beautiful Dreamer." His "Jeannie with the Light
Brown Hair" (Example 4.1) shows the influence of the Irish folk songs
popularized in Moore's *Irish Melodies*. Thomas Moore (1779–1852), an Irish
poet and musician who lived in England most of his career, set his own
poems to traditional Irish folk melodies. A skilled singer and pianist, he
made these adaptations himself and published them in ten volumes
between 1808 and 1834. According to Charles Hamm, they were, along with
the songs of Stephen Foster, ". . . the most popular, widely sung, best-loved,
and durable songs in the English language of the entire nineteenth century."

Moore's settings, circulated in sheet music versions, were genteel and
"correct" according to the musical standards of the day. In this form, they
appealed to and circulated among musically literate members of the middle
and upper classes. (The same songs also came to the United States as folk
versions in oral tradition. Irish immigrants, most of them laborers, farmers,
or tradesmen, would have brought the folk versions to America, passing on
not only words and melody, but also style by performing the songs among
themselves. This style found its first commercial outlet in the minstrel show,
as we'll soon see.)

"Jeannie with the Light Brown Hair" is a typical, and especially pretty,
example of the parlor song genre. Together with "Beautiful Dreamer," it
shows Foster's familiarity with Italian opera and Irish song, two of the most
influential European styles during his lifetime. It shares many features with
"Beautiful Dreamer": a smoothly flowing vocal line over an unobtrusive
accompaniment; a clearly articulated, hierarchical form; a discreetly kept
beat; and a soft dynamic level. Its Irish roots are most apparent in Foster's
use of a pentatonic scale. Many folk songs from the British Isles make use

I-25
IA-25

strophic
form

of this scale. The song also illustrates *strophic* form, in which the same
melody serves several stanzas of text.

MINSTRELSY

The parlor song exemplified the genteel side of American musical taste. Minstrel-show music was another matter entirely. The first minstrel show took place in Boston in February 1843. Four veteran blackface entertainers, all of them northerners, banded together to form the Virginia Minstrels. Their evening of entertainment was an immediate success. Following their lead, other minstrel troupes formed almost overnight. Within a few years, many cities had their own resident troupe, while others crisscrossed the country.

blackface
minstrel

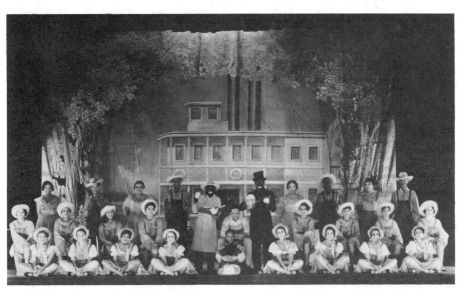

Minstrel show troupe, 1920.

Although stage impersonation of African–Americans predated the American Revolution, blackface entertainment really began with George Washington Dixon. Beginning in 1827 in Albany and a year later in New York, Dixon portrayed what would become the two most popular stereotypes of the minstrel show, the city slicker and the country bumpkin. In 1832, Thomas Dartmouth Rice observed (or claimed to have observed) an African-American street entertainer in Cincinnati doing a song and dance with a peculiar hop step, which he called "jumping Jim Crow." He copied the man's routine and introduced it on stage shortly thereafter. Rice and his impersonation of Jim Crow were a sensation here and abroad. The song he "wrote" for his act was, by one account, "the first great international song hit of American popular music." Two years later, Bob Farrell, another blackface entertainer, introduced the song "Zip Coon" on stage. With the success of Farrell's portrayal, the two stock characters of the minstrel show were in place: Zip Coon was the urban dandy, while Jim Crow was the naive, uneducated slave.

Although "Jim Crow," "Zip Coon," and other minstrel songs were supposed to depict African-American life, they were instead crude parodies of it. The song lyrics were written in pseudo-dialect. A short excerpt from "Zip Coon" shows the inconsistency in language: "I went the udder arter noon to take a dish ob tea." Some words are in alleged dialect; others remain unchanged. Similarly, the music of minstrelsy had little relation to authentic African-American music. As published, minstrel songs had much more in common with the folk music of settlers from the British Isles. Many passed into the oral tradition of country music: "Zip Coon," for example, became the fiddle tune, "Turkey in the Straw."

It is difficult to give a precise description of the minstrel show, because it lacked a consistent form and it evolved so quickly. By its very nature, the show was loosely structured. There were at least three minstrels: the *interlocutor* and the two *endmen*, Tambo and Bones, so named for the instruments that they played. The troupe sat in a semicircle, with the interlocutor in the center and the endmen at either end. The rest of the troupe filled the circle. There was no plot or story line, although there were stock routines and consistent roles. The subject matter, more than anything else, provided a sense of continuity. Comic exchanges between the interlocutor, who spoke with a resonant voice, proper diction, and a rich vocabulary, and the endmen, who spoke in a grotesque exaggeration of African-American speech, linked together a varied assortment of songs and dance numbers: a sentimental ballad here, a lively dance tune there. The interlocutor controlled the pacing of the show. According to the mood and response of an audience, he would allow routines to continue or cut them off.

The minstrel show evolved so rapidly in its half century or so of popularity that no single format became standardized. In the twenty years prior to the Civil War, it developed in several stages from the pre-minstrel solo and small group act to a full evening's entertainment, with a large troupe and orchestral accompaniment. One of the main motivations for this evolution was to refine the show, to make it more wholesome, family-oriented entertainment. Early minstrel shows were often crude, and their audiences were often forerunners of today's raucous rock-concert or soccer-match crowds. Because crowds were often so rowdy, "minstrel programs frequently listed 'Rules of Hall,' which pleaded with the audience not to whistle during the performances and not to beat time with their feet." Both show and audience became more well-mannered through the 1850s. As a result the show lost in vitality what it gained in polish.

The first minstrel shows, like the blackface entertainment that had preceded it, mixed singing, dancing, mock lectures, and comic sketches. Its stock characters gave the show its overall design. In these early shows, routines about the two most popular blackface characters were simply integrated into a full-length entertainment. The opening section portrayed "Zip Coon," the city slicker, and the closing section portrayed "Jim Crow," the country bumpkin.

Within a few years, however, the show had grown into three parts. The opening section alternated highly ritualized presentation of minstrel material with popular songs of the parlor-song variety, sung by a balladeer. The second section, called the "olio," was the variety part of the show. It usually featured a wide range of acts. Many of these were novelty routines, but there were also burlesques of current or classic "serious" material, for example, Shakespeare plays or Italian operas. The final section was an extended skit, originally of an idealized plantation life, but later topical comedy sketches. It concluded with a walkaround, which featured the entire minstrel troupe in a grand finale of song and dance.

interlocutor

endman

olio

The size of the minstrel troupe also grew. The Virginia Minstrels was a group of four entertainers who sang, danced, and played fiddle, banjo, tambourine, and bones. But other minstrel troupes quickly expanded beyond this nucleus. Christy's Minstrels, formed a year later, soon added other performers, then an orchestra. This growth would continue after the Civil War.

Professional black minstrel musician (known as Fiddling Jack) from Harper's Ferry, West Virginia, 1903. Photograph by John H. Tarbell. Reproduction from the Collection of the Library of Congress.

Dan Emmett's "De Boatman's Dance" (Example 4.2) heard here in a contemporary performance by Robert Winans illustrates the sound of early minstrel-show music. Emmett (1815–1904) was a blackface entertainer in the 1830s and one of the founding members of the Virginia Minstrels. He also composed (or adapted from folk repertory) a number of songs for the minstrel show, including "Dixie." Only Foster surpassed him as a minstrel show songwriter. "De Boatmen's Dance" predates the formation of the first minstrel troupe, and it was included on the first "Ethiopian Concert" of the Virginia Minstrels in 1843. Almost every aspect of the sound of this performance is startlingly different from the parlor song: its instrumentation; rhythm; tempo; accompaniment; and harmony. Many of the style features of early minstrelsy are shown in Table 4.1.

I-26

IA-26

Table 4.1	**Style Profile: The Minstrel Show Song**
Instrumentation	Four male singers, plus fiddle, banjo, tambourine, and bones.
Performing Style	The vocal style was modeled on classical harmony singing (something like today's barbershop quartets). The banjo is frailed (the right or strumming hand is held in a claw shape, with the nail of the index finger striking the

strings). The fiddle is played in a vibratoless, nasal style rather than the round, warm tone of a concert violinist.

Dynamics   Loud (considering the instrumentation).

Texture   An active texture featuring simultaneous statements of the melody by instruments and voices, accompanied by percussion. The melody parts carried by voice, fiddle, and banjo are all the same, with slight variations. The voice sings the simplest form of the melody, the fiddle often adds sustained tones (called drones), and the banjo interpolates extra notes to keep the rhythm moving at a fast speed. There is no clearly subordinate accompaniment, as in the parlor song.

Melodic Shape   The melody consists of a series of short phrases, usually descending, each of which is repeated. The melody of the song is pentatonic.

Rhythm   This song uses a quick, danceable tempo, with considerable activity in all parts. The tambourine often plays on the backbeat, while the bones add a percussive part that almost sounds like tap dancing. There is lots of animation but little syncopation in the several versions of the melody.

Form   The form of this song is one of its most interesting features. The performance consists of several statements of the melody, sometimes by instruments, sometimes by voices with instrumental accompaniment. The melody has three sections, each with two phrases, with the second repeating the first. The first and last sections act as a refrain, sung by the entire troupe. They frame a central solo section, which tells the "story." It is easy to visualize the song supporting action on stage. There was undoubtedly a great deal of movement by the troupe as they acted out the scenes described in the song, or simply danced.

To what extent did African-American music influence the sound of early minstrel performers? We can only infer the extent of its influence from secondhand evidence and contemporary parallels. Without question, there was some African influence. Bones and tambourine formed the first "rhythm section," and the banjo is an instrument developed from African models. And it is clear from drawings and accounts of the period that some white minstrels, at least, keenly observed the appearance, speech, and dancing of the African-Americans with whom they had contact.

But there is compelling, if indirect, evidence to suggest that white minstrels captured little of the quality of African-American music making. After the Civil War, African-American minstrels were enormously successful in portraying themselves as authentic "delineators" (as blackface entertainers were known) of African-Americans. Audiences saw it this way, too, to the extent that white minstrels all but conceded to African-Americans the right to perform the traditional minstrel show.

In the years before the Civil War, minstrel performers had only incidental contact with the African-Americans they supposedly portrayed. Most minstrel troupes resided permanently in northeastern cities: New York (especially), Boston, Philadelphia, and so forth. Given the contemptuous attitude toward African-Americans embodied in the minstrel show, it seems unlikely that white performers would have tried to copy African-Americans with anything approaching the same diligence with which today's white musicians emulate African-American artists, whom they respect. Even more important, early minstrels did not have the continuous access to African-American music that recordings provide.

The positive contributions of the minstrel show include four important firsts, all of which would figure prominently in subsequent generations of popular music. First, it was entertainment for the masses. Its primary purpose was to entertain, not uplift or educate, although these virtues sometimes slipped in the back door. Second, it made use of vernacular speech and music. Both words and music were low-brow, not high-brow, almost defiantly so. Members of the upper class (lawyers, doctors, politicians, and the like) were among minstrels' favorite targets for parody. And one of the recurring comic strategies of the minstrel show was to mock the Northern African-American for his upper-class pretensions by riddling his speech with malapropisms and bad grammar.

Third, the music of the minstrel show developed out of the synthesis of European classical and folk music. The process of forging a new style from several often dissimilar sources would become a trademark of popular music. Fourth, the minstrel show was the first instance of a pattern in American popular music that has continued to the present day: the periodic invigoration of the popular mainstream through energetic, often danceable music.

The performance of "De Boatman's Dance" recreates the song as it might have been performed in a minstrel show. The performance of Stephen Foster's "Oh! Susanna" (Example 4.3) illustrates how a minstrel-show song might be performed at home. There are several features that distinguish this song from "Jeannie with the Light Brown Hair" (Example 4.1). Among them are: the reinforcement of the chorus with a vocal quartet; the quick, dance-speed tempo, underscored by the use of a polka-like accompaniment in the piano interludes; and the use of a semistrophic form, in which the verse sets different text to the same melody, while the chorus repeats both words and music exactly. All three would become common features of post–Civil War popular song.

I-27

IB-1

Foster's early minstrel songs, like most others of the time, depicted African-Americans as mindless illiterates. ("Oh! Susanna" is no exception in this regard.) Lyrics described their features in grotesque caricature, and the songs themselves were simple, if artful. But in Foster's plantation melodies, lyrics portrayed African-Americans as real people with feelings, not subhuman stereotypes. In "Old Folks at Home" (Example 4.4), Foster finds a musical middle ground between the prevailing parlor-song style and the minstrel song. In its original sheet-music version, it has a tempo halfway between the languid pace of a sentimental melody and the brisk trot of a minstrel song. The setting is simply solo voice and piano, as in the parlor song. However, it borrows from the minstrel song a verse-chorus format. The periodic repetition of the chorus ensured that it would stick in the listener's ear. And, as

I-28

IB-2

in his more animated minstrel songs, Foster constructs a memorable melody from a pentatonic scale, a scale common to both Anglo- and African-American folk music.

CONCLUSION

The minstrel show was America's first indigenous popular music and its first musical export. It brought a welcome blast of fresh air to America's cultural life. Because of this, it's doubly unfortunate that its most indelible image is still the grotesque and cruel stereotypes of African-Americans. It cultivated prejudice and ignorance in some, and reinforced it in others. All else seems to pale beside the damage it did to race relations in this country.

Minstrel music was the catalyst for the development of an American popular-song tradition, but Stephen Foster was the one who, almost single-handedly, created it. Foster synthesized the two strains of European music, classical and folk, into a new, American song style. Because of his musical inspiration and his instinct for the middle ground between styles, his songs transcended class boundaries. His songs, and others in the same spirit, were the first genuinely popular American music.

Unfortunately, Foster's death in 1864 sapped the revolution of its energy. No one was musically ready to replace him. His most noteworthy successor as an all-around composer was the African-American songwriter James Bland, who began his professional career about a decade after Foster's death. Despite Bland's contributions, the three decades after the Civil War were the low point in the history of American popular song.

Terms to Know

blackface minstrel	endman	interlocutor
minstrel show; minstrelsy	olio	parlor song
plantation song	sheet music	strophic form
Tambo and Bones	vernacular speech	

Names to Know

George Washington Dixon   Daniel Emmett   Stephen Foster
Thomas Moore

Study Questions

1. Why was Stephen Foster one of the most important songwriters in nineteenth-century America? What were his innovations? What styles did he master?

2. Why was the music of the minstrel show different from other kinds of popular song? Why was it revolutionary? How did it help create a distinct popular style? What new elements did it introduce into popular music?

3. What were the positive and negative contributions of the minstrel show to popular song and American life?

4. How did the minstrel show change over the first twenty-five years of its existence? What features, if any, remained the same?

5. Choose a song by Stephen Foster that is <u>not</u> discussed in the text. What does it have in common with the songs discussed here? How is it different?

6. Why would it have been difficult for white actors in a minstrel show to portray African-American musicians? Should white musicians ever attempt to play African-American music? Why or why not?

7. How did the development of mass-produced, less expensive musical instruments encourage the development of popular song?

CHAPTER FIVE

Popular Music After the Civil War

The two decades before the Civil War saw the birth of popular music; the three decades after the Civil War saw the birth of the popular music *industry*. The minstrel show had shown that stage entertainment offered an excellent way to promote songs. Brisk sales of Stephen Foster's songs had revealed a large and lucrative market for sheet music. After the war, both stage entertainment and music publishing became more commercially oriented. Stage entertainment expanded and diversified, while an increasing number of music publishers began to publish only popular songs in order to maximize profits.

By 1895, the popular music industry was up and running. Musical comedy and vaudeville competed with the minstrel show for the stage entertainment dollar. Charles Harris's 1892 hit, "After the Ball," confirmed what music publishers already suspected: the existence of a large market for popular song. Musically, however, the thirty years after the Civil War were the least productive period in the history of popular music.

POST-WAR POPULAR SONG

VERSE-CHORUS SONGS

verse-chorus song

 I-29

 IB-3

Popular song in America hit bottom in the years immediately following the Civil War. There was little musical innovation and equally little music that has lived on. Textually, parlor songs and many of the minstrel songs were, if anything, even more sentimental than prewar songs like "Woodman, Spare that Tree." Musically, the biggest change was the adoption from the minstrel song of the verse-chorus format. In typical postwar verse-chorus songs, a verse section for solo voice alternates with a (usually four-part) choral refrain. The strophic verse sections narrate a story, while the chorus reiterates the central message of the song.

Henry Clay Work's "Grandfather's Clock" (1876; Example 5.1), one of the most popular songs of the day, is representative of the songs of the period both textually and musically. It begins with the verse, a narrative sung by a solo singer. The chorus enters with a refrain at the conclusion of the first segment of the narrative. The narrative resumes in the second statement of the verse. In a nice touch, the chorus periodically interrupts the narrative to highlight the fact that the clock stopped when the old man died.

The text of "Grandfather's Clock" has the sentimental bent that was so popular in the nineteenth century. It's hard to imagine anyone today getting excited about a clock that conked out when its owner did! Moreover, the music seems to have little to do with the text. The song moves along at a good clip and has a sprightly melody. Both melody and rhythm seem out of tune with the tear-jerking sentiment of the words. The text setting of the verse is awkward: The rhythm of the melody has almost nothing to do with the spoken rhythm of the text. Work's clumsiness in this regard is especially apparent when contrasted with the Foster songs studied in Chapter 4. The chorus is the most memorable and effective part of the song. The dramatic pauses after "stopp'd" and "short," and the nice rhythmic contrast between the quick pace of "never to go again" and the drawn-out rhythm of "old man died," are especially effective.

The design of "Grandfather's Clock" anticipates the emphasis on the chorus that would distinguish popular song after 1890 in two important respects: It is longer than the typical chorus of the minstrel song and it is the location of most of the musical interest. In Foster's minstrel songs, the chorus is the last part of a larger, essentially indivisible form. Verse and chorus blend into a larger whole, all of it easily remembered. (The choruses of "Old Folks at Home" and "Oh! Susanna" both end with the last phrase of the verse.) In Work's song, verse and chorus are distinct sections, complete unto themselves. Before long, the chorus would overshadow the verse to such an extent that it could stand alone as the entire song. George M. Cohan's "Yankee Doodle Boy" (Example 5.3) is an early example of this trend.

 I-33

 IB-7

The verse-chorus format served popular music well for almost fifty years following the Civil War. As stage entertainment became a more important outlet for popular song, alternation of solo and group became rarer. Instead, songwriters used the form to hammer the chorus into audiences' ears. By the 1920s, with the rise of the singable/danceable songs and the three-minute time limit imposed by early recording technology, the verse had become an optional, not obligatory, part of a song, except in songs performed in the theater. However, the verse-chorus idea would resurface in the 1950s and 1960s as the basis of a new kind of popular song.

The Birth of Tin Pan Alley

In the 1880s, a number of music publishers opened for business in New York. They differed from traditional publishers in that they sold only popular songs. Many publishing houses were owned by songwriters who wanted to reap the financial benefits of their creative labor. They would sputter along, often for years, until their first hit song gave them a financial foundation. At first, they were concentrated around Union Square, at that time the theater district in New York. Most soon moved uptown to 28th Street, still near enough to the theaters to have access to performers. This new breed of publishers marketed their songs much more aggressively than traditional publishers, who issued music of all kinds. They hired songpluggers, house pianists who could play a new song for a professional singer or prospective customer. Writer Monroe Rosenfeld dubbed 28th street "Tin Pan Alley" because the racket created when several songpluggers were trying out songs at the same time reminded him of crashing tin pans.

Tin Pan Alley

New York became home to both popular stage entertainment and popular music publishing. More significant events—opera productions and serious plays as well as mass entertainment like the minstrel show—opened in New York than in any other city in the country. The flood of immigrants, among them Irish, Germans, and then Jews, plus the migration of African-Americans into the city, swelled New York's population. Many immigrants found work in show business, either as performers or songwriters, or as theater owners, agents, publishers, and the like. Their activities further consolidated New York's control of popular entertainment. New York would be the center of popular music for decades, challenged only by Hollywood after the advent of talking movies.

Charles Harris's 1892 popular song "After the Ball" (Example 5.2) was the first big Tin Pan Alley hit, eventually selling over five million sheet music copies. The story of its road to success gives some insight into the growth of both stage entertainment and music publishing, the way they operated, and the extent to which they were intertwined.

Harris was a self-taught performer (on the banjo) and songwriter. (Harris never learned to read or write music and had to hire a trained musician to notate his songs.) However, what he lacked in musical skill or training he made up for in determination, chutzpah, and business savvy. Harris wrote "After the Ball" for a friend while living in Milwaukee. To promote the song, he approached several popular singers whose tours took them through Milwaukee. The first three, two vaudeville stars and a ballad singer in a minstrel show, unceremoniously turned him down. He finally convinced the fourth, who was starring in a touring production of *A Trip to Chinatown*, to interpolate the song into the show, one of the most popular musical comedies of the 1890s. Reportedly, Harris convinced the star to sing the song by promising him a glowing review—he represented himself as a correspondent for the New York *Dramatic News*—and giving him $500.

"After the Ball" was such a great success in the show that Julius Witmark, one of the new breed of Tin Pan Alley publishers, offered Harris $10,000 for the rights to the song. Harris figured, correctly, as it turned out, that he could make much more money by publishing it himself, so he set up his own publishing house. He understood public taste and had a knack for spotting potential hits. Although he never wrote another song as successful as "After the Ball," he made a fortune publishing both his own songs and those of other songwriters.

A half century had passed between the first minstrel show in 1843 and the success of "After the Ball" in 1892–1893. We can infer a great deal about the changes in the popular-music industry during that period from the story of Harris's song. Stage entertainment was considerably more diverse. A minstrel show that featured a ballad singer had moved some distance away from its folk roots. (One reason for this shift in content was the success of African-American minstrel performers after the Civil War in portraying the stereotypes that whites had created for them.) Vaudeville and musical comedy were new entertainment options.

Along the same line, popular-song publishing was a business unto itself. The publishers along Tin Pan Alley, like Witmark and Harris, no longer cluttered their catalogs with items that had little chance of brisk sales. "After the Ball" was the first song to demonstrate the full commercial potential of this

vaudeville

musical comedy

new branch of the music-publishing industry. In the wake of its success, even more publishers hopped on the bandwagon. By 1900, very few hit songs were published away from Tin Pan Alley. Harris's decision to go into business for himself suggests that the songwriter was the low man on the fame-and-fortune totem pole. It was the publisher who saw most of the profits and the singers who enjoyed celebrity.

Part of publishers' profits went toward recruiting singers to perform their songs. Then as now, the surest route to popularity was performances by the stars of the day, even when the song (like "After the Ball") was primarily intended for home use. It was standard practice to secure performances with gifts and bribes, just as record companies bribed disc jockeys 60 years later in the payola scandal of the late 1950s. The principle—or lack of principle—was the same. Only the players and the terms of the deals differed.

By the 1890s, popular stage entertainment and music publishing had become closely intertwined. Professional performers promoted new songs. Sheet music, which enabled people to learn the song at home, kept songs popular. Each fed off the other to a much greater extent than they did in Foster's day.

A footnote: An early recorded performance of "After the Ball," sung by George Gaskin, one of the Irish tenors who were so popular around the turn of the century, was a best seller in 1893. (Best seller is a relative term: commercial recording was only three years old at the time, distribution was difficult, and record players were expensive.)

DANCE RHYTHMS IN POPULAR SONG

The 1890s and 1900s also saw several dance rhythms invigorate popular song. Waltz songs were especially popular in the 1890s, George M. Cohan set many of his most memorable melodies to march rhythms, and the syncopated rhythms of ragtime and related styles found their way into popular song as well as dance music.

waltz song

march

Dance rhythms had been a part of American popular song since the rise of blackface entertainment. Minstrel songs were used for dancing, at least in the shows. Dance rhythms would also occasionally underpin songs for musicals and vaudeville. But the majority of popular songs were of the slow, sentimental sort.

In the 1890s, a fundamental change took place in popular song. Songs with sentimental texts were matched with accompaniments in a dance rhythm. Songs with dance rhythms were not intended for dancing—at least not social dancing. Rather, it was simply that dance rhythms were in the air. They found a home in popular song as well as the ballroom. The waltz was the first dance rhythm to enjoy widespread use in popular song. Many of the most memorable songs of the 1890s and 1900s had a waltz beat. In his chronicle of popular song, Charles Hamm lists sixteen commercially successful songs (sales of one million copies of sheet music) from these decades; thirteen of them have a waltz beat. Many of them are still familiar, most of all the 1908 hit, "Take Me Out to the Ball Game."

"After the Ball" (Example 5.2) was the first commercially significant example. It is typical of the waltz song popular in the decades around 1900. The waltz rhythm (a fast OOM-pah-pah, heard throughout in the accompaniment) pervades the song, often at the expense of fluent declamation of the

 I-30

 IB-4

text. (For instance, say the words "a little maiden" by themselves, then in the rhythm of the opening phrase and you'll notice that the musical accents don't always coincide with the accents of the text.) It's also worth noting that the relatively bouncy waltz rhythm does little to complement musically the pathetic story told in the song text.

The faster-paced waltz rhythm and the use of verse/chorus form most clearly differentiate this song from the Foster parlor songs. In most other ways, however, "After the Ball" grows out of the parlor song tradition. The affinities between "After the Ball" and "Jeannie" (Example 4.1) include:

1. The standard voice/piano instrumentation
2. (Presumably) an opera-influenced vocal style
3. A gently flowing melody
4. A texture with a dominant melody and relatively simple and unobtrusive accompaniment
5. Clear marking of the beat and measure in both melody and accompaniment
6. A clearly delineated, closed form.

"After the Ball" is even more closely related to "Grandfather's Clock." However, there is a noteworthy difference in their use of verse/chorus form. "Grandfather's Clock," like other verse/chorus songs of the period, alternated between solo voice in the verse and a four voice chorus in the (appropriately named) chorus. "After the Ball" retains the forms but does not outline it by adding and subtracting voices.

The waltz was by far the most popular dance rhythm in popular song around 1900, but other rhythms, notably the polka and march, also appeared with some frequency. March rhythm found its ideal vocal expression in the patriotic songs of George M. Cohan. Songs like "Yankee Doodle Boy" (Example 5.5) and "You're a Grand Old Flag" captured the spirit of a Sousa march in song. A march-like accompaniment also supported other songs of the period, especially those from the theater.

The use of dance rhythms was an important stage in the imminent merger of popular song and dance music. However, when the merger occurred in the late teens and early twenties, the dance rhythm came from African-Americans, not whites. The roots of this merger date back to the 1860s.

THE FIRST AFRICAN-AMERICAN ENTERTAINERS

After the Civil War, African-American musicians and entertainers found that doors previously closed to them had opened, although only a crack. They found two main outlets for their talents: jubilee choirs and the minstrel show. Jubilee choirs were a peripheral part of the popular-music world even during their heyday. Still, they were well enough known to serve as the source for the most important new song style of the 1870s and eighties, the minstrel-spiritual. Overall, however, the minstrel show provided much greater opportunities for African-American performers.

spiritual

Jubilee choirs were a success born of desperation. In 1871, a group of students from the newly formed Fisk University in Nashville, Tennessee, set out on a tour of the north to raise money for their school. Along the way, their director, George L. White, named them the Fisk Jubilee Singers to distin-

Fisk Jubilee Singers, c. 1880.

guish them from minstrel troupes. In their concerts, the Fisk Jubilee Singers performed spirituals—African-American religious songs—as well as popular songs of the day. A successful appearance at the 1872 World Peace Jubilee in Boston made the group's reputation. Singing groups from other African-American colleges and professional choirs soon followed in their wake. Among the professional groups was a reconstituted version of the Fisk Jubilee Singers, founded by a former member of the choir after the university withdrew its sponsorship.

Minstrel shows co-opted the spiritual almost immediately, integrating it into the scenes of plantation life. According to Charles Hamm, "from 1875, ensemble numbers featuring the entire cast singing pseudoreligious songs regularly opened and closed the performances of many minstrel troupes." A new kind of song, the minstrel-spiritual, grew out of the assimilation of the spiritual into the minstrel show. Its most distinguishing feature was the occasional use of call and response.

There had been isolated and short-lived African-American minstrel troupes before the Civil War. It wasn't until after the war, however, that African-American minstrels began to have a commercial and musical impact. African-American minstrel troupes, beginning with the Georgia Minstrels in 1865–1866, drew crowds as big as, or bigger than, the white troupes. During the 1870s, there were at least twenty-eight professional African-American minstrel troupes, none more successful than the one owned by Charles Callendar, a tavern owner turned entrepreneur. Callendar's Georgia Minstrels—in the minstrel show, at least, "Georgia" was synonymous with "colored"—was the best-known African-American minstrel troupe of the decade.

The "authenticity" of African-American troupes was a large part of their appeal. Even as the white minstrel show moved away from "the Ethiopian entertainments" of early minstrelsy, African-American minstrel shows, ironically enough, stayed closer to the original. Promoters billed African-American performers as "delineators," authentic portrayers of plantation life, so white performers chose to move away from the stereotypes instead of

delineator

competing. While African-Americans were certainly capable of portraying plantation life more accurately than whites, they had to perpetuate the stereotypes created by white blackface performers to satisfy white audiences.

These stereotypes even extended to their appearance. Bert Williams, the great African-American vaudeville performer of the early twentieth century, complained that he and other African-American performers had to appear in blackface so that they looked as white people thought they should. As the lingering stereotypes suggest, the minstrel show changed very little in sentiment following the Civil War. Postwar minstrel song lyrics suggest that the Civil War did little to create more realistic and enlightened racial perceptions among minstrels, songwriters, and their audience. Lyrics continued to portray the life of African-Americans during slavery as idyllic. The "happy darkie" myth had considerable staying power. Sheet-music covers of minstrel songs and, later, so-called "coon songs" pictured African-Americans in grotesque caricatures. One particularly interesting cover contains both a realistic portrait of the African-American songwriter James Bland and a typical scene of African-Americans singing, dancing, and praying. There was a huge gap between whites' perception of African-Americans and the reality of their persons and lives. Whites, at least those involved with the minstrel show, made no apparent effort to close it.

Despite continuing indignities on and off stage, the minstrel show gave African-American performers, according to Eileen Southern, "their first large-scale entrance into show business." W. C. Handy, himself a minstrel in the 1890s, noted that "All the best [African-American] talent of that generation came down the same drain. The composers, the singers, the musicians, the speakers, the stage performers—the minstrel show got them all."

Sheet music cover for James Bland's "Carry Me Back to Old Virginny" with stereotypical illustration.

Of all the black minstrels, James Bland (1854–1911) left the most endur-ing legacy. Although famous as a performer, singer, comedian, and banjoist during the 1870s and eighties, he is best remembered as a songwriter. Bland was the most successful composer of minstrel songs after Stephen Foster and the first African-American songwriter to achieve commercial success. Like Foster before him, Bland was fluent in all the popular styles of the day. His most famous song, "Carry Me Back to Old Virginny," became the Virginia state song in 1940.

Bland's song, "De Golden Wedding" (Example 5.3), is a good example of the postwar minstrel song. There is no prominent style feature (such as syncopation) that would identify Bland's song as the work of an African-American songwriter. Instead, the rhythmic inspiration for this song is the polka, a European popular dance in the latter part of the nineteenth centu-ry. Like "Grandfather's Clock," it uses a verse-chorus form, which identifies it as a post–Civil War song. Bland's use of dance rhythms presages the waltz-song enthusiasm that would develop in the 1890s. Unlike most of the African-American artists discussed in this book, Bland's African heritage had no evident impact on his musical style. James Bland was a fine songwriter, the most important nineteenth-century American songwriter after Foster; he just happened to be African-American.

POPULAR STAGE ENTERTAINMENT

Popular stage entertainment, already well established by the Civil War, underwent considerable growth in the postwar years. The growth spread in two directions: variety and size. By 1870, there were three entertainment genres: the minstrel show; vaudeville; and musical comedy. Within each genre, there were several varieties. The minstrel show diversified with the entry of African-Americans into professional entertainment. The first American musical comedy was staged in 1866, marking the beginning of the most enduring form of stage show. Beginning with Gilbert and Sullivan in the late 1870s, European operetta also found a home in the United States. Vaudeville also began directly after the Civil War, growing quickly from a small-scale variety show into the most popular form of stage entertainment.

Shows increased in size as well as variety. At least some of the produc-tions were gargantuan spectaculars, featuring huge casts and lasting for sev-eral hours. In this respect, they were in step with American attitudes of the time. Americans seemed to admire bigness, whether it was the personal for-tune of a Rockefeller or Carnegie, or one of Patrick Gilmore's colossal band spectaculars.

THE MINSTREL SHOW

Minstrel shows got bigger: they lasted longer and casts were larger. By the 1870s, each of the three sections of the minstrel show had grown into an entity complete unto itself. Moreover, the business was dominated by a few troupes big in name and number, like Leavitt's Gigantean Minstrels and Cleveland's Colossals. With the sudden popularity of African-American minstrels, the white minstrel show moved further away from its original format. The opening section remained much the same, although some performers chose not to black up. The olio grew into a full-fledged variety show, not much different from a vaudeville show. It included songs of all kinds, including parodies and spoofs of opera and other European music, as well as specialty acts.

Musical theater historian Gerald Mast describes the postwar third section as "a half-hour musical comedy sketch, often a burlesque of a major hit of the day, a little one-act musical in itself." Mast goes on to suggest that the three new forms of stage entertainment that became popular after the war grew out of the three independent sections of the minstrel show. In his view, the opening section became the "coon show" of the 1880s and nineties, the olio transformed into vaudeville, and the half-hour sketches grew into full-length musical comedies.

The late nineteenth-century minstrel show created a vogue for a song style, the "coon song," and a dance, the cakewalk, that would foreshadow the ragtime craze. There had been coon songs in the minstrel show prior to 1890, but the genre reached its peak in mid-decade with the popularity of such songs as May Irwin's "Bully Song" and "All Coons Look Alike to Me," written by African-American minstrel star Ernest Hogan. Coon songs of the 1890s gently introduced syncopation into popular song; the piano accompaniment of Hogan's "All Coons Look Alike to Me" anticipates the figuration of piano ragtime. Coon songs evolved smoothly into the ragtime songs of the 1900s.

The cakewalk also came out of the postwar minstrel show. By most accounts, it originated as a contest among slaves: Couples danced for a prize, generally a cake. The winners were the "pair that pranced around with the proudest, high-kicking steps." After the war, cakewalks served as the finale to the minstrel show. In the 1890s, it became a dance fad, moving from the stage to the dance floor. There, couples competed in cakewalking contests for prizes, not just a cake. As in the coon song, syncopation was gentle (listen to "At a Georgia Camp Meeting" [Example 6.2] to hear the characteristic syncopation of the cakewalk). But it was enough to prepare the way for ragtime.

I-36

IB-10

VAUDEVILLE

Vaudeville was a variety show, pure and simple, featuring a series of acts—singers, dancers, comics, acrobats, magicians, jugglers, and the like—without any pretense of dramatic unity. Acts would come onstage, do their routines, and leave, not to return for the rest of the show. The closest recent parallel would be Ed Sullivan's *Toast of the Town*, a Sunday night fixture of television's first decades. On it, rock groups—both Elvis and the Beatles made a big splash on the show—might follow trained animal acts.

Vaudeville had its roots in New York. Tony Pastor, a performer turned promoter, opened Tony Pastor's Opera House in New York's Bowery section in 1865. It flourished, and in 1881, he opened another theater, this one a little farther uptown on 14th Street. By that time, his was one of many vaudeville houses in New York. Vaudeville quickly became much more than a local phenomenon. There were chains of theaters across the country, managed by impresarios like Keith and Albee. Vaudeville was the most popular form of live entertainment in the United States in the decades around the turn of the century, replacing the minstrel show. Although vaudeville was not exclusively musical entertainment, it was a major performing outlet for popular song.

MUSICAL THEATER

By most accounts, the opening of *The Black Crook* in 1866 marked the beginning of American musical comedy. There had been popular musical-dramatic entertainments as early as the late eighteenth century, most notably European operas presented in their original or in watered-down versions. Burlesques and parodies were also popular, particularly in minstrel shows. The qualities that made *The Black Crook* more American than European were its irreverence, seemingly improvisatory style—in which unrelated acts are linked by the thinnest of dramatic threads—and its high spirits. All were qualities associated with, if not borrowed from, the minstrel show. The other factor that made the show a landmark was its popularity. *The Black Crook* ran for 475 performances in New York, which made it one of the longest-running shows of the century. Touring companies spread its popularity throughout the country, and periodic revivals kept it alive well past 1900.

Like the minstrel show, many of the musical comedies of the period had large casts and long running times. According to Gerald Mast, *The Black Crook* "had everything: melodrama, romance, comedy, dance, songs, specialty acts, spectacular scenic effects, elaborate costumes, and legs, legs, legs." To include all this, a typical performance lasted five and a half hours!

The Black Crook established a new branch of popular musical theater in America: musical comedy. Musical comedy offered an alternative to European operettas in subject, structure, and style. Both would prosper for over half a century. Only in the 1920s did European operetta lose its appeal. The distinction between European operetta and American musical comedy, relatively slight in 1866, became more sharply drawn over the years.

The most obvious difference between operetta and musical comedy was in the plot. Operettas typically told tales that took place long ago and/or far away. Some involved fairy tale-like settings, with handsome princes and beautiful princesses. Other similarly exotic settings also appeared with some frequency. By contrast, the stories of early musical comedies usually dealt with the here and now. Plots were often topical, made up of stories and incidents that, but for their exaggeration, could have come from the daily life of the audience. In the same spirit, many of the characters were stereotypes of the various ethnic groups that flooded New York in the latter part of the century. Both musical comedy and vaudeville featured stock portrayals of the Irish, Germans, Italians, Jews, and African-Americans who emigrated or migrated to New York.

Operetta and musical comedy also diverged in the extent to which they integrated music and plot. In operettas, the plot usually had some dramatic continuity, and the songs highlighted important moments in the story. In musical comedy, plots were at the mercy of song hits and star performers. It was common practice to *interpolate* songs into a show because they were hits or because star performers liked them, or because they were paid by the publishers or songwriters to include them.

Viewed from our current perspective, interpolation seems like a crude practice. For the last fifty years, we have expected songs in musicals to serve a dramatic purpose, even though the song may become popular outside the

interpolation

show. The idea of introducing a song into a show just because it is popular, or in the hope that it would become popular, rather than writing songs to fit the show, runs completely against contemporary practice. However, viewed in the context of the relationship between popular song and popular stage entertainment after the Civil War, interpolation is more understandable, a transitional step on the way to dramatically credible musical theater. Compared to the minstrel show, which had a deliberately loose story line—when it had one at all—and vaudeville, which was simply a variety show and had no plot, the surprise is not that the plot of a musical comedy was fair game for interpolation, but that it had a plot at all.

Interpolation was tricky. Because musicals had story lines, it would make sense that a song have some relation to the plot. In practice, plots were stretched like rubber bands to accommodate interpolated songs because the story of the song usually had nothing to do with the existing plot. Despite this hazard, interpolation was commonplace; audiences didn't seem to mind, because they came primarily to hear the songs and the singers.

For example, the three hit songs of *A Trip to Chinatown*, the longest running musical of the nineteenth century, were "The Bowery," "Reuben, Reuben," and "After the Ball." Although the show was set in San Francisco, "The Bowery" told the story of a naive young man who wandered into the wrong part of New York at night. The other two songs were interpolated well after the show opened, and had no dramatic connection with the original plot. Still, audiences came to hear those songs.

In the 1870s and 1880s, the most representative practitioners of the operetta and musical-comedy traditions were Gilbert and Sullivan and Harrigan and Hart, respectively. Gilbert and Sullivan's operettas, like *H.M.S. Pinafore* and *The Mikado*, were set in distant locations (aboard ship; Japan). Dramatically, they offered a "kind of musical theatre in which book, lyrics, and music combined to form an integral whole." Harrigan and Hart's shows, such as the series of Mulligan Guard shows (*The Mulligan Guards' Picnic, The Mulligan Guards' Ball, The Mulligan Guards' Christmas*, etc.), grew out of Harrigan's close observation of life around him in New York's lower East Side. Harrigan referred to his shows as a "continuity of incidents," plays with songs interspersed to catch the ear of the audience. While moving toward greater coordination of song and story, they lagged well behind the Gilbert and Sullivan operettas in this regard.

The Harrigan and Hart musicals, composed by a pair of an Irish immigrants, also give early evidence that the "Americanization" of musical comedy, the creation of musicals with a definably American sound and style, was largely the work of the disenfranchised, either immigrants or African-Americans. Their work also suggests that the lines between entertainment forms were lightly drawn. The team got their start in vaudeville, the other new entertainment genre of the post–Civil War period. Their first show, *The Mulligan Guards' Picnic*, also featured an olio, the variety part of a minstrel show.

Around 1900, operetta went through much the same process of development as musical comedy in the 1870s and 1880s: It acquired a native voice by way of immigrants. Victor Herbert, an Irish cellist/conductor/composer who emigrated to the United States to play in the Metropolitan Opera Orchestra, was the most important of several immigrant composers who wrote Broadway shows during this period. In words and music, Herbert found a midway point between the melodies of European operetta and the slang and syncopations of contemporary American popular song. Herbert and his two most important successors among immigrant theater composers—a Hungarian, Sigmund Romberg and a Czech, Rudolf Friml—kept the operetta tradition alive.

Although most operettas produced in the United States were composed by immigrants to America, European operettas—more specifically, the Viennese operetta *The Merry Widow*—captivated American audiences for almost a decade. Between 1907, the year that *The Merry Widow* opened in New York, and 1914, the beginning of World War I, Americans seemingly couldn't get enough of this Viennese music. After the onset of the war, however, Viennese operetta suffered guilt by association: Rising anti-German sentiment dampened enthusiasm to the point that no new productions succeeded after the war started.

George M. Cohan's musicals, the most noteworthy American musical comedy of the period, had no such problems. Many of them were unabashedly patriotic. No songwriter before or since has embodied patriotic sentiment so successfully in words and music. In addition to their memorable songs, Cohan's musicals were also noteworthy because their books and song lyrics used everyday speech, a practice that Cohan readily defended. As Gerald Bordman notes: "A number of traditional reviewers assailed [Cohan's] excessive dependence on slang. Cohan retorted that that was the way his characters would talk could they have come to life off stage. He was not writing 'literature,' he was creating an entertainment about people with whom his audience could identify." Cohan's musicals were a people's music, written for "the plumber and his lady friend in the last balcony."

Cohan also integrated music and drama more thoroughly in his shows. Cohan wrote his songs for the show and used them for dramatic purposes, to set a mood, advance the plot, or profile a character. This was in sharp contrast to the tenuous relationship between song and plot common in nineteenth-century musical comedy and still widely practiced in the early part of the century.

THE REVUE

As the minstrel show faded and musical theater became more dramatically credible, a void was created for a loose-jointed, breezy show with lots of song and dance and a skimpy plot to hold it together. The public craved shows that were topical, aimed at the masses, upbeat, and full of comedy, song, dance, and (in musical comedy) lots of girls. The revue filled that void for over twenty-five years.   *revue*

Florenz Ziegfeld's *Follies of 1907* put the American revue on the track that it would follow for over two decades. Ziegfeld, the greatest theater impresario of the era and the self-styled "glorifier of the American girl," combined promotional acumen, an eye for talent, and a sharp sense of public taste. His shows featured the top comics and singers of the day, along with lots of girls, dressed as revealingly as public taste would allow. Unlike earlier revues, Ziegfeld's *Follies* had a libretto (or script), however flimsy, but a believable story line was not the focal point of the show.

The "Follies" title had two connotations: it evoked the French *Folies Bergere* with its leggy female dancers; and it referred to the foolish actions of the famous people of the day. Ziegfeld's shows lampooned celebrities,

politicians, rich businessmen, and stars rather than the stock ethnic stereotypes. Perhaps unconsciously reflecting the reform spirit in the air, Ziegfeld's
shows moved away from comedy based on crude ethnic stereotyping to a
more sophisticated humor. Still, his *Follies of 1910* featured for the first time
two of the great comedians of the new century, both of whom excelled at
ethnic humor: Jewish comedienne Fanny Brice and the veteran African-
American vaudevillian Bert Williams.

Bert Williams in the Ziegfeld
Follies, *c. 1915.*

Williams's stardom in Ziegfeld's *Follies* gave evidence of the gradual, if
often grudging, acceptance of African-Americans into show business. It was a
good news/bad news scenario around 1900 for African-Americans in entertainment. The bad news was the decline of the minstrel show, which put many
African-American performers out of work. The good news was the greater
range of opportunities. Many of the leading African-American minstrel performers, like Williams and Ernest Hogan, found work in vaudeville, musical
comedy, and revues. An African-American vaudeville theater circuit, organized
in 1913, eventually became the famous, yet notorious Theater Owners Booking
Association (TOBA; nicknamed "Tough on Black Artists" because of the low
pay and generally poor playing conditions offered to African-American entertainers on the circuit) in 1920. Several of the African-American vaudevillians
moved on to the major white vaudeville circuits or to Broadway.

African-American songwriters also found wider acceptance for their work. In the 1890s, Gussie Davis became the first African-American song-writer to achieve success on Tin Pan Alley. The songwriting team of Bob Cole and the brothers J. Rosamund and James Weldon Johnson supplied music for their own shows and for interpolation into other shows. (One of their best known songs, "Under the Bamboo Tree," is discussed in Chapter 6; see Example 6.3.)

African-American musicals on Broadway were another point of entry. In 1898, two shows featuring all-African-American casts opened in white theaters. Cole and Johnson's *A Trip to Coontown* was first. *The Origin of the Cakewalk or, Clorindy* opened later that summer, and was a commercial and critical success. Their titles suggest a lingering identification with the minstrel show, a not unexpected circumstance. Five years later, *In Dahomey,* a full-length musical written by the poet Paul Lawrence Dumbar and composer Will Marion Cook, broke the Broadway color barrier. It was the first musical written and performed by African-Americans to play at a major Broadway theater. Its star performers, George Walker and Bert Williams, received rave reviews. African-American shows would continue to appear intermittently on Broadway and on the road until the early teens.

African-American musicians of the time usually wore many hats. For example, the most lasting contribution of the Johnson brothers was not in popular song, but their arrangements of Negro spirituals. They published two sets of them, in 1925 and 1926. Will Marion Cook, musical director for the Walker-Williams company in the 1900s, also composed songs in a style influenced by African-American folk song. Later he directed one of the leading syncopated dance orchestras of the time.

SONGS FOR STAGE ENTERTAINMENT

Around the turn of the century, popular songs for the stage reflected the variety of stage entertainment. Vaudeville could absorb any kind of song. With interpolation the rule rather than the exception, musical comedy was not far behind. Operetta, at least much of the operetta composed in the United States, drifted toward a more American popular style. The "coon song" was the sequel to the minstrel song; it was also its swan song.

The next pair of examples were two of the most popular songs of the era. They were written by Victor Herbert and George M. Cohan, the most celebrated composers of operetta and musical comedy, respectively, at the turn of the century. Taken together, they point up several of the differences between operetta and musical comedy. They also illustrate the transitional stage of both operetta and musical comedy at the time.

The Fortune Teller (1898), from which "Gypsy Love Song" (Example 5.4) is taken, was one of Herbert's first operettas. Like most operettas of the time, it tells a long-ago-and-far-away story. It involved a Hungarian heiress and her look-alike, a Gypsy fortune teller (a dramatic convenience, because they were to be played by the same person), who are attracted to a cavalryman and Gypsy musician, respectively. Not surprisingly, there are problems of mistaken identity, but everything works out in the end, per custom. "Gypsy Love Song" was the most popular song in the show. This recording, which dates from 1906, features Eugene Cowles, who created the role of Sandor, the gypsy musician, in the original production.

Like many songs from the operetta theater, this features a solo vocalist, singing in an operatic style, accompanied by full orchestra. There is little change in dynamics, although this may be due to the poor recording quality. In the verse, Cowles is accompanied with sustained chords. The chorus features a more active accompaniment with a strong bass line. The contour and rhythm of the melody also distinguish verse and chorus; in the verse, the melody lines are long and flowing, moving predominantly in a downward direction; the tempo is slow and fluctuating, to accommodate the delivery of the words. The melody of the chorus features short phrases, some of which move by step, others of which contain several big steps; its rhythm is steady and brisk. There is no rhythmic conflict in either melody or accompaniment.

The form of this song suggests a cross between the recitative and aria of opera and the verse-chorus form of popular song. Like the operatic accompanied recitative (a style in which the singer presents the text in almost a speech-like delivery), the verse does not keep a steady pulse. But the verse has a melody made up of regular phrases and a rich accompaniment, like a popular song, and the chorus is written in a modified AABA pattern.

Several features suggest that this song represents a style in transition. The out-of-tempo verse, its flowing melodic lines, and the total absence of rhythmic conflict throughout link the song to European operetta. But the chorus, with its short phrases and (modified) AABA form, anticipates the style of Tin Pan Alley and theater songs in the first half of the twentieth century.

George M. Cohan (1878–1942), born into a family of vaudeville performers, came into prominence around 1900 with a string of successful musicals that included many still-familiar songs. Cohan was a one-man entertainment industry, adept at all phases of the business: songwriting; performing; directing; and producing. He was among the most important and versatile entertainers of his age. His stage shows were more tightly knit dramatically than their predecessors.

I-33

IB-7

But it is as a "march" songwriter that Cohan's legacy endures. Songs like "Yankee Doodle Boy" (Example 5.5) have the energy of a great march, a vigorous, yet singable melody, and clever lyrics without a trace of nineteenth-century sentimentality. "Yankee Doodle Boy" is one of the best of Cohan's march songs. In the musical, it helps establish the character of Johnny Jones, a jockey who has come to England to ride in the Derby. Jones, played by Cohan in the original production, is, in the words of Gerald Bordman, "the cocky, slangy, identical twin of his creator." These qualities certainly come across in the song. "Yankee Doodle Boy" is an early example of the best kind of theater song: one that enhances the action onstage, but has a life apart from the show as well.

In its overall stylistic features, "Yankee Doodle Boy" is much like other songs from this period. It uses verse-chorus form, and it has a singable melody and simple accompaniment. (There are drums as well as piano in the accompaniment because this performance simulates a [modestly produced] theater production.) But it has several distinct, unique features:

1. *Emphasis on the chorus.* The most memorable part of this song is the chorus. For most people, it *is* the song. In this respect, "Yankee Doodle

George M. Cohan, c. 1905.

Boy" anticipates the greater emphasis on the chorus in twentieth-century Tin Pan Alley songs. (The same is true of "Gypsy Love Song.")

2. *Patriotic quotations.* The patriotic tone of the song is enhanced by direct quotation from several familiar songs. In addition to "Yankee Doodle," there are snippets from "Dixie" and "Star-Spangled Banner." (Cohan played both sides of the fence!)

3. *March rhythms.* In "Yankee Doodle Boy," the energy of the march finds its way onstage. This song moves at march tempo, faster than "Gypsy Love Song" or the waltz songs that were so popular during this period. Only the syncopated songs of the period—cakewalks and some ragtime songs—use the same beat and tempo.

4. *Syncopation.* When this song appeared in 1904, ragtime was already sweeping the country. This is not a ragtime song, because there is too little evidence of the rhythmic conflict characteristic of an African-American influenced style. But the cakewalk rhythm heard so frequently in ragtime songs (short/long/short) occasionally surfaces in lines like "Born on the Fourth of July."

5. *Use of slang.* Cohan used slang as a means of relating to his audience. The verse contains several slang expressions that give the song an easy familiarity: "all the candy"; "that ain't a josh"; and "phoney." Cohan wanted his characters to speak the same language as his audience. Slang helped achieve that goal.

THE CONCERT BAND AND THE MARCH

The most popular instrumental ensemble in late nineteenth-century America was the concert band. In an era without radio, TV, and other forms of mass communication, the touring concert bands, as well as municipal bands found in almost every town, were a primary source of musical entertainment. They supplied their audiences with a broad range of music: classical selections arranged for band; current hit songs; and, of course, marches, which they usually played sitting down.

The concert band was middle America's answer to the concentration of show business in New York. Bands had been a part of American life since the Revolution. Almost every city and town, large or small, had a municipal band. They performed on most public occasions, and gave concerts in season. After the Civil War, some of the bands that had formed in major cities became professional ensembles, playing concerts, dances, and enhancing public occasions. The most famous of these professional bands before 1890 was the band of the Twenty-second Regiment of New York, renamed the Gilmore Band when Patrick Gilmore became its director in 1873. Although

Patrick S. Gilmore (center) and members of his band and touring show, 1889.

he initially made his mark as a skilled performer on the cornet (a close relative of the trumpet), Gilmore, an Irish immigrant, was best known for organizing "monster concerts," particularly the National Peace Jubilee of 1869 and the World Peace Jubilee of 1872, which featured choruses of thousands, bands and orchestras of hundreds, plus world-famous soloists. He also raised the level of musicianship in bands, by arranging visits of the leading European bands to the United States, and by raising the standard of performance in the band that he directed. His band toured annually throughout the United States until his sudden death in 1892 (future operetta composer Victor Herbert took over the direction of the band on Gilmore's death). Gilmore's success set the stage for the great era of American bands.

In the 1890s (and well into the 1920s), the most popular concert band in the United States was a civilian professional band directed by John Philip Sousa. Sousa (1854–1932) was the most prominent bandleader and band composer of his era. He had established his reputation as a composer and conductor with the Marine Band, which he directed for twelve years. Sousa formed his own band in 1892, the year of Patrick Gilmore's death. For the remainder of his career, he led his band on annual tours throughout the United States, as well as several tours to Europe and one world tour, giving over 10,000 concerts. Sousa's band was known for its precision and musicianship and for the excellence of its soloists, several of whom subsequently led bands of their own.

A typical Sousa band concert included marches, original works for band, solos featuring the band's virtuoso instrumentalists, arrangements of well-known opera overtures, symphonic poems, program music, and the popu-

John Philip Sousa, c. 1880.

lar music of the day. The latter included the latest in syncopated music. (Example 6.2 is a Sousa band recording of the cakewalk "At a Georgia Camp Meeting.") In fact, many European audiences first gained exposure to ragtime's syncopated rhythms through Sousa's performances.

The role of professional bands in American musical life around 1900 was much like that of the contemporary pops orchestra. Both feature varied programming: a mixture of popular classical music and popular music, with star soloists. And they serve the same purpose, to entertain, rather than educate, their audience. Sousa made this distinction in an interview. Comparing himself to Theodore Thomas, the esteemed nineteenth-century orchestra conductor, he noted that Thomas "gave Wagner, Liszt, and Tchaikowsky, in the belief that he was educating his public; I gave Wagner, Liszt, and Tchaikowsky with the hope that I was entertaining my public."

The most popular and memorable music that the Sousa band performed was Sousa's marches. Although he composed other kinds of works—songs, operettas, and band suites—Sousa made his reputation as a composer of marches. Their popularity earned him the title "The March King" and made him America's best-known composer during his lifetime. Sousa wrote 136 marches between 1876 and 1931. However, most of the best known were written between 1888 and 1900: *Semper Fidelis* (1888), *Washington Post* (1889), and *Hands Across the Sea* (1899) are a few.

Around the turn of the century, marches by Sousa and others had an impact well beyond the parade and concert venues. Marches and march-like music were also used for social dancing. The rhythm and spirit of the march penetrated popular song (as we have seen). Most important, perhaps, the march also played a seminal role in the development of ragtime and jazz.

Sousa's most famous march, and probably the most famous march of all time, is *The Stars and Stripes Forever* (Example 5.6). Written in 1897 during Sousa's peak decade as a composer, it is the quintessential Sousa march. It has stirring and lyric melodies, subtle variation in accompaniment and rhythm, and a rich texture.

This march uses the standard concert-band instrumentation of brass, woodwind, and percussion instruments. Trumpets (or cornets), trombones, clarinets, piccolo (a high-pitched relative of the flute), and percussion are the featured instruments. Another important feature of the instrumentation is the periodic change of dominant instruments to help delineate sectional divisions within the march. For example, the use of the softer clarinets as the primary melody instrument at the beginning of the trio (the third of four main melodies) is customary in Sousa's marches.

Stars and Stripes employs a full dynamic range, from soft to loud. Also, there are many subtle gradations of dynamics within a phrase, and sudden dynamic changes help mark the beginnings of new sections. The basic texture here is melody plus accompaniment. But many phrases have countermelodies, melody-like parts that are not as prominent as the main melody. The piccolo part (called an *obbligato*) toward the end of the march is a good example of a countermelody. The final section, or strain, has three independent melodic lines.

Most of the dominant melody lines in *Stars and Stripes Forever* are not easily sung, because they move too rapidly at times (like the first main melody) or have wide skips (like the second). The third main melodic idea, which begins the trio, is composed in a lyric, or easily sung, style. Lyric trios

trio

are typical of Sousa marches. In contrast, the trombone break that follows features the most active melody in the entire march.

The standard march has two beats per measure (one for each leg!), and a tempo of about 120 beats per minute. Percussion and accompanying instruments clearly mark the beat. There are occasional exceptions, most notably in passages called *breaks*, which occur when steady rhythmic support stops. The trombone solo toward the end of this march is an excellent example of a break.

Like virtually all marches, *Stars and Stripes Forever* uses a multisectional form, containing several distinct sections linked together into a whole. Most marches have at least three different sections; four is the most common number (see Table 5.1).

multi-sectional form

Table 5.1   The Form of *Stars and Stripes Forever*

Section	Recognizable Features
Introduction	Short, played by entire band
First strain (A)	Trumpets are the dominant instrument
A	Repetition of previous strain
Second strain (B)	New melody played softly by clarinets
B	Same melody, played loudly by full band
Trio (C)	Midpoint of the march. New lyric melody played softly by clarinets. The sudden drop in dynamic level and the new, singable clarinet melody are the most recognizable features of the trio, and the clearest clue to the form of the march.
Break (D)	Fast moving trombone/tuba melody; no steady accompaniment
C	Original trio melody and instrumentation, except for added piccolo obbligato
D	As before
C	Trio melody, but played loudly this time by the entire band, with heavy percussion

---

Other Sousa marches exhibit the same general stylistic features heard in *Stars and Stripes*, although minor differences in form and rhythm are found from work to work.

Sousa's marches are the instrumental counterpart to Stephen Foster's songs. They share three important qualities. First, the most famous works by both composers were immediately popular and have remained among the best-known music from the nineteenth century. Second, they are musically significant: the best examples of their genres. Third, they are (almost indefinably) American, without obvious African-American influence. Together they comprise the most important legacy from nineteenth-century American popular music.

CONCLUSION

The period from the end of the Civil War to the close of the century was one of great change in American popular music. The boom in professional songwriting–centering in New York's famous Tin Pan Alley–showed that there was a strong desire for real, American songs. The favored form was the verse-chorus song, set to a lively waltz beat, such as the well-beloved "After the Ball." Meanwhile, African-American performers began to find more opportunities to work for urban white audiences, thanks to the popularity of jubilee choirs and "authentic" minstrel troupes. Although much of the material they performed was demeaning or perpetuated stereotypical images, still the music began to more accurately reflect African-American rhythms and melodies. Stage entertainment also reached a new level of sophistication, with everything from variety shows to light operetta drawing its own audiences.

As the nineteenth century drew to a close, American popular music had grown into an independent industry, headquartered in New York. The minstrel show, a stage entertainment specifically associated with America, had flourished for half a century and had only recently begun to decline in popularity. Vaudeville and an identifiably American musical theater had begun to take its place.

America had produced two composers, Stephen Foster and John Philip Sousa, whose music remains popular and identifiably American, if only by association. But no uniquely American style had yet emerged. The country awaited the impact of ragtime on popular music.

Terms to Know

delineator	interpolation	march
multisectional form	musical comedy	revue
spiritual	Tin Pan Alley	trio
vaudeville	verse-chorus song	waltz song

Names to Know

James Bland	George M. Cohan	Gilbert and Sullivan
Harrigan and Hart	Charles Harris	Victor Herbert
John Philip Sousa	Bert Williams	Florenz Ziegfeld

Study Questions

1. What was the major difference in form between pre–Civil War and post–Civil War popular song?
2. What were the two main components of the popular-music business before 1900? What city was the center of popular music in the late nineteenth century?
3. What kinds of stage entertainment became popular after the Civil War?
4. What are some of the differences between operetta and musical comedy?

5. In what ways did the minstrel show change after the Civil War?
6. What was the role of the concert band in American life in the decades around 1900?
7. In what ways did the introduction of dance rhythms influence the development of popular song?
8. Choose three popular songs that are examples of verse-chorus forms. Explain why they fit in this category.

CHAPTER SIX

Ragtime and Its Impact

ragtime

Ragtime began as an obscure folk-dance music played up and down the Mississippi valley in the last quarter of the nineteenth century. Before it faded away, it would significantly alter the sound of popular music; it was through ragtime that white Americans finally discovered the rhythmic vitality of a real African-American music. Some whites would have encountered African-American performers in minstrel shows or touring jubilee choirs. But because authentic ragtime performances could be realized from the sheet music, whites had a chance to study and savor the music. As a result, its influence was far more extensive than that of earlier African-American styles. Ragtime was the catalyst for the revolutionary changes in popular music that marked the beginning of its modern era.

THE MEANINGS OF RAGTIME

Throughout its history, the term "ragtime" has been used in three different ways: (1) to identify a body of music; (2) to describe a style of playing; and (3) to indicate its influence on another style. In its most limited meaning, the one most frequently used today, "ragtime" identifies a body of piano music, composed by Scott Joplin and others, that is clearly distinguished by certain stylistic features (see the following discussion of the "Maple Leaf Rag").

Ragtime has also referred to a way of modifying pre-existing material, "ragging" it so that it sounds like ragtime. In retrospect, we can see that the technique of ragging a song on the piano is relatively straightforward. Over a steady march-like (oom-pah) accompaniment, harmonize the existing melody, arpeggiating the chords (playing the notes of the chord in succession, rather than simultaneously) so that the original melody note occasionally produces accents between the bass notes of the accompaniment. This practice is the likely beginning of a common procedure in twentieth-century popular music: reworking an old song to produce an up-to-date sound.

Finally, ragtime (here used as an adjective) has also described other music influenced to a greater or lesser degree by the style, although not considered ragtime in the more limited and literal use of the term current today. In the first two decades of the twentieth century, almost any syncopated music, including songs and dances, was called ragtime. Relatively little of this music would be identified as ragtime today.

THE RAGTIME YEARS

The heyday of ragtime lasted about two decades, from just before the turn of the century to the end of World War I. Its history begins earlier, in the years after the Civil War. African-American musicians in the midwest had been playing ragtime–or at least syncopated music– well before the first rags were published in the 1890s, and even before the use of the term, "ragtime," became widespread. According to several accounts, at about the same time, African-American pianists up and down the East Coast played what would soon be called ragtime in bars and bordellos.

In the 1890s, syncopated sounds gradually infiltrated American popular music. There was the cakewalk of the minstrel show, and the coon songs popular in vaudeville and minstrel shows. National and international expositions, particularly Chicago's 1893 World Columbian Exposition, gave valuable exposure to African-American performers. African-American entertainers, especially ragtime pianists, also found employment in the restaurants, saloons, and brothels in the vicinity of the exposition. Most of the St. Louis ragtime pianists, Scott Joplin among them, migrated to Chicago in search of work.

cakewalk

Toward the end of the century, composers and songwriters began to use the terms "rag" and "ragtime" to identify this new style. Ernest Hogan's 1896 song, "All Coons Look Alike to Me," makes reference to a Negro "rag" accompaniment. The song is the first published example of rag-like piano style. The first published rags appeared a year later. With the publication of "Maple Leaf Rag" in 1899, ragtime became a household word.

John Philip Sousa, whose newly formed band performed at the Chicago fair, certainly heard some of this early ragtime. He quickly included it in his concert programs. Europeans first encountered American syncopated rhythms in Sousa's rag arrangements. His performance of Fred Stone's 1898 dance, "Ma Ragtime Baby," won a prize at the Paris World's Fair.

In this respect, Joplin's "Maple Leaf Rag" did not start a craze for syncopated music so much as give it a major push along two lines: It introduced more complex African rhythms to popular music, and made them available in sheet-music form. The rhythms of Joplin's early rags were more complex than the syncopated songs and dances of the 1890s. Rhythmically, they found a midway point between the improvised style of African-American ragtime pianists and the cakewalks and ragtime songs of the period. By doing so, his rags steered popular music in the direction of the more syncopated rhythms of the teens and twenties. Furthermore, ragtime was the first African-American music that looked on paper the way it sounded in performance. So, any competent pianist, African-American or white, able to read music could buy the sheet music to Joplin's "Maple Leaf Rag" and perform it in a reasonably authentic manner. In a time when recordings were limited, radio and television nonexistent, and live entertainment, especially by African-American performers, relatively rare outside of the big cities, sheet music was the best way to absorb new music.

ragtime
song

Although initially a piano music, "ragtime" quickly came to identify almost any syncopated music and even some that was not. (Irving Berlin's 1911 hit, "Alexander's Ragtime Band," is a thoroughly modern song for the time, but does not have even the modest syncopation of earlier ragtime songs.) Ragtime songs, sung by both African-American and white performers, were often interpolated into Broadway shows. Bob Cole's and the Johnsons's hit "Under the Bamboo Tree" (Example 6.3) first scored in a musical entitled *Sally in Our Alley,* which told the story of a Jewish merchant and his daughter. (It is difficult to imagine how they worked the lyrics—about a jungle maid—into the plot.)

syncopation

 I-37

 IB-11

There were ragtime versions of other repertoire. Ben Harney, a ragtime pianist who enjoyed great success on the vaudeville stage after moving from the Midwest to New York, illustrated in his *Ragtime Instructor* how to rag the familiar music of the day. Through his method, popular songs, classical compositions, and other well-known works were transformed into ragtime. His technique was probably similar to that used by ragtime pianist and songwriter Eubie Blake, who demonstrated in a television documentary how he used to rag a Wagner overture. The technique also applied to song. "That Mesmerizing Mendelssohn Tune," a big 1912 hit for the comedy team of Collins and Harlan, was a ragged version of Mendelssohn's "Spring Song."

piano rag

Ragtime soon became music for social dancing. Piano rags were scored for the dance orchestras of the period; Joplin's famous "Red Book" (so-called because it had red-colored covers), a collection of dance-orchestra arrangements of his popular rags, is the best-known example. Original dance music in a syncopated style also appeared throughout the late 1890s, 1900s, and into the 1910s. Some of it came from composer/bandleaders like James Reese Europe, who enjoyed a considerable following in white New York society in the teens.

ragtime
dance

turkey trot

In the 1900s, dancing to ragtime became increasingly popular despite disapproval from several quarters. As the cakewalk lost its popularity in the beginning of the decade, other simpler dances took its place. One of the first of these new ragtime dances was the turkey trot, the first of many animal dances to become popular in the late 1900s and early 1910s. The turkey trot was simple and awkward, but it permitted "lingering close contact," a novelty at the time. Body contact between couples (presumably) delighted the dancers, but scandalized the more conservative segments of American society. It was one reason for the hostile backlash to the music.

 I-38

 IB-12

In the teens, blues and jazz gradually superseded ragtime as primary African-American influences on popular music. Much of the music in mid-decade, especially by African-Americans, gives evidence of the transition between increasingly out-of-date ragtime and the fresher sounds of blues and jazz. James Reese Europe's "Castle House Rag" (Example 6.4) shows this transition well under way.

THE IMPACT OF RAGTIME

Ragtime had an impact on American music in three areas: It left a musical legacy of enduring value and appeal; it was responsible for a number of firsts in the history of both popular music and African-American music; and it influenced a wide range of music even as it reshaped popular music.

The classic piano rags of Scott Joplin and other distinguished composers

James Reese Europe's Clef Club Orchestra, 1914; Europe is at rear, holding baton.

comprise a repertoire of real artistic worth and individuality; there is no other music like it. As his later compositions showed, Joplin saw ragtime as a vehicle for serious artistic expression as well as entertainment. Accordingly, he thought of himself as a composer of art music in the tradition of the nineteenth-century nationalist composers. He believed that he had elevated a folk-dance music to concert status, in much the same way that Polish composer Frederic Chopin composed mazurkas (Polish folk dance), and Viennese composer Franz Schubert composed ländler (Austrian folk dances). Joplin's disciples approached ragtime composition with a similar seriousness of purpose, and his publisher, John Stark, identified him as a composer of "classic" rags. In keeping with its role as the preserver of a musical tradition, the classic ragtime style of Joplin and his disciples was the most conservative, or European, of the ragtime piano styles current around 1900. The East Coast ragtime of Eubie Blake and the New Orleans style of Jelly Roll Morton are considerably more African than Joplin's music.

Many found ragtime's mix of African-American and white influences unacceptable, musically and socially. Ragtime met with resistance from virtually every corner of the establishment, musical and otherwise. It was considered immoral, fit only for the saloons and brothels where it was played. It was musically inferior, the product of an inferior race incapable of the musical sophistication that Europeans had achieved. Ragtime was also seen as a cause of moral decay. The "Ragtime Evil" should not be found in Christian homes, according to one writer. There were, of course, overtones of racial prejudice in virtually all these arguments. Almost all prevailing views of African-Americans assumed their inferiority. They ranged from outright hatred to the kind of tolerance and affection one might have for a pet. During this low point in race relations, few whites accepted African-Americans as equals, so it's not surprising that few found African-American music to be of significant worth.

The demise of ragtime was reported regularly throughout its short history. Critics foretold it almost before it began, as this comment from 1900 suggests: "Thank the Lord [ragtime pieces] have passed the meridian and are now on the wane." Critics of ragtime were still singing the same song eighteen years later, when it was reported that: "It is gratifying to observe that this one-time doubtful feature [ragtime syncopation] is gradually losing favor and promises to be eventually overcome." Of course, it would not be overcome, but replaced with music that was even more syncopated.

Serious musicians stood divided on the question of ragtime's worth. Daniel Gregory Mason, one guardian of the cultivated tradition, sought to demean ragtime by drawing an unfavorable comparison of its syncopated rhythms to those found in Beethoven's and Schumann's music. Charles Ives, the most important American composer of that generation and an after-hours ragtime pianist, responded that the comparison showed "how much alike they [ragtime and Schumann] are." All in all, the reaction against ragtime and African-Americans for creating it was as virulent as the reaction would be against rock 'n' roll half a century later.

Ragtime flourished in spite of this hostility. Precisely because of its resilience, ragtime assisted in the process of reversing the stereotypes burned into the American consciousness by the minstrel show and minstrel-related sheet music. African-American syncopated dance bands played for white society in the 1900s and 1910s. Demand for their services was sufficiently great that African-American musicians' unions were formed in Chicago in 1902 and New York in 1910.

Ragtime, or at least the classic ragtime of Joplin and his peers, enabled African-Americans to become more aware of their own culture. Eileen Southern describes the process in this way:

> At last the black composer was involved in writing down the music he had been playing for his own people for many years. An improvisational music would be transformed into a notated music; a functional music, intended for dancing and entertainment, into a concert music intended for listening; a folk-style music, into the music of the individual composer, upon which he stamped his unique personality.

oral tradition   Prior to ragtime, African-American folk music had been passed on through oral tradition: Each new generation of African-Americans would learn the songs, dances, and religious music of their culture by hearing them and singing or playing along. It is frustrating to read pretwentieth-century descriptions of African-American music, because attempts by interested white musicians to capture African-American folk music in notation fall far short of the mark, no matter how sincere they may have been. Joplin's work marked the beginning of a movement among historically conscious African-American musicians to preserve their musical heritage. W. C. Handy, the "father of the blues," began collecting blues melodies and assembling them into songs, just as Joplin had done with rags. James Weldon and J.

Rosamond Johnson, brothers who were also active as Broadway composers, assembled and arranged spirituals, fitting them with piano accompaniment for performance at home, at church, and even in the concert hall.

Ragtime also represented the first *documented* instance of African Americans filtering through their own musical heritage the European music to which they had been exposed. By comparing pieces in rag style with their original versions and models, it is possible to filter out the specifically African elements in the rag.

Ragtime had a widespread impact on other musical styles. It loosened up popular music (both song and dance), helped shape jazz in its early years, and aroused the interest of several of the most important classical composers from the early years of the twentieth century.

In popular song, there was a new freedom in both words and music. Many of the songs of the 1890s and 1900s spoke more colloquially, with a vocabulary and delivery closer to everyday speech. Compare the first few lines of the chorus of "Hello! Ma Baby" to the lyric of "I Love You Truly," a song written four years later. "Hello! Ma Baby" begins:

Hello! ma baby, Hello!, ma honey, Hello! ma ragtime gal,
Send me a kiss by wire, Baby, my heart's on fire!

By contrast, "I Love You Truly" comes out of an almost bygone era:

I love you truly, truly, dear,
Life with its sorrow, life with its tear,
Fades into dreams when I feel you are near,
For I love you truly, truly, dear.

The minstrel show had introduced vernacular speech into popular music by way of the exaggerated dialect of the endmen's songs. The use of dialect declined in the minstrel song as the century progressed. In most turn-of-the-century "coon" songs, dialect is relatively mild (for example, the use of "dis" and "dat") or nonexistent. (The chorus of "Under the Bamboo Tree" [Example 6.3] is a significant exception. It was not acceptable for African-Americans to be portrayed romantically in a normal fashion, so Cole and the Johnsons had to resort to an imitation pidgin English. The contrast in vocabulary between verse and chorus is striking.) For the most part, coon song lyrics are colloquial, not dialect. "Hello! Ma Baby" uses only "I'se" and "coon."

Ragtime also made the music more lively. Its beat had more of a bounce, and its syncopated rhythms permitted a rapid, but relatively natural delivery of the words. The rhythm of "Hello! Ma Baby" as sung is almost identical to its spoken rhythm. (By contrast, melodies of waltz songs tend to move in a slower, more awkwardly patterned rhythm: "She's ooooon-ly a birrrrrd in a gilllld-ed caaaage.") Ragtime songs, particularly in the teens, often divided the beat into long-short patterns that conformed to the natural accentuation of the words. The opening phrase of Irving Berlin's "Alexander's Ragtime Band" (1911)–"come on and hear"–is a perfect example of this new rhythmic style.

There is such a smooth continuum between ragtime and early jazz that it is useful to think of early jazz as a dialect of ragtime. There is anecdotal evidence to support this view. Jelly Roll Morton, the self-proclaimed "inventor of jazz" and its first great composer, identified his jazz version of "Maple

Scott Joplin, c. 1913.

Leaf Rag" as New Orleans ragtime, as opposed to the St. Louis style used by Joplin. In any event, ragtime contributed repertoire and formal models to early jazz. Morton cast many of his greatest compositions in the multisectional form characteristically found in piano rags.

THE SOUND OF RAGTIME

I-35

IB-9

The most enduring music of the ragtime era has been the classic piano rags of Scott Joplin (1868–1917). These have remained familiar, especially since the ragtime revival of the 1970s. His "Maple Leaf Rag" (Example 6.1) was the first commercially successful piano rag, and his output of piano rags remains the core of the ragtime repertoire. A professional musician from his teenage years, Joplin played in saloons and clubs, at first along the Mississippi valley and eventually in Missouri. (The "Maple Leaf Rag" is named after the Maple Leaf Club in Sedalia, Missouri, his place of employment from 1894 until the turn of the century.) He also received formal musical training in the European tradition, principally through study at George R. Smith College in Sedalia, and was a fluent composer and arranger in the white popular styles of the day. After the turn of the century, Joplin devoted most of his effort as a composer and musician to legitimizing ragtime. In addition to a steady stream of piano compositions, mostly rags, he composed a ballet, *The Ragtime Dance,* and two operas, the now-lost *A Guest of Honor* and *Treemonisha.* (Joplin received a posthumous Pulitzer Prize for *Treemonisha* in 1976 on the occasion of its revival.)

From musical evidence in Joplin's works, we can also infer his dedication to bringing ragtime under the European art-music umbrella. The later rags are more melodious and less syncopated. The first half of the opening strain of "The Cascades" (1904) contains a flowing stream of fast notes and a big cascade (going up, not down), but no syncopation at all. And in both his tempo indications for rags and written commentary on the correct performance of ragtime, Joplin constantly admonishes pianists against playing ragtime too fast: Ragtime played at a slower tempo gains in dignity.

In Joplin's own performance of "Maple Leaf Rag," we can hear virtually all the significant features of traditional piano ragtime. This recording was made from a piano roll cut by Joplin in 1916. Like so many other African-American musical styles, the piano rag emerged from the reinterpretation of an established idiom, in this case, the march. (At this time, marches were almost as popular on the dance floor as in a parade.) Joplin and his peers simply transformed the march into ragtime by adding an African rhythmic conception and adapting the style to a single instrument, the piano. Table 6.1 details Joplin's heavy reliance on the march as a model.

Table 6.1	Style Profile: The Classic Piano Rag	
	African Elements	**March (European) Elements**
Instrumentation		Piano (later arranged for band or dance orchestra)
Performing style	Occasional "smear" group of notes run together) in the bass part	Played in the European manner, for the most part
Texture		Melody plus accompaniment
Harmony		Standard chord progressions
Melody		Either flowing, with some syncopation, or chords broken in "ragged" style. (That is: chords are arpeggiated in such a manner that the top notes come between beats as well as on them)
Rhythm	Bass notes equally emphasized; melody introduces rhythmic conflict	oom-pah accompaniment
Form		Multisectional, usually with four discrete sections: (here AA/BB/A/CC/DD). The march is the direct formal model.

As Table 6.1 indicates, there is little difference between a march arranged for piano and a rag, *except* for the ragged melody. Of course, that difference is crucial.

THE CAKEWALK, A PRE-RAGTIME STYLE

The cakewalk was a popular precursor of the piano rag. Although first popularized on stage, cakewalks soon appeared in sheet-music form for home use by amateur pianists. Kerry Mills's "At a Georgia Camp Meeting" (Example 6.2) was perhaps the best known cakewalk of the 1890s. It shows the close relation between march, dance, and ragtime at the turn of the century. Like the "Maple Leaf Rag," "At a Georgia Camp Meeting" uses the multisectional form characteristic of the march. The third strain in particular is virtually indistinguishable from the march style of the day. The cakewalk has only a fraction of the rhythmic conflict found in rags. Its rhythmic "signature" can be heard at the beginning of the first and second strains; it is easily recalled in the popular phrase, "here comes the judge."

This recording also highlights the role of the concert band in American music during this period. Band repertoire was not limited to marches, but included many of the popular hits of the day, as well as works in other styles. So it is not surprising to find "At a Georgia Camp Meeting," originally published as a piano piece, popularized by the Sousa band. Recordings of the band, although acoustically primitive, nevertheless reveal the precision and style with which it performed.

RAGTIME SONG

Ragtime songs were the successors to the coon songs of the 1890s. They remained popular for most of the first two decades of the century. Although a few piano rags acquired words (Joplin's "Pineapple Rag" is one example), they were the exception. Any song with even a touch of syncopation or even a snappy tempo was labeled a "ragtime song." "Under the Bamboo Tree" (Example 6.3), composed in 1902, illustrates the free use of the term ragtime during its peak period of popularity. It points up important differences between piano rags and ragtime songs. The dominant rhythmic pattern of the chorus is that of the cakewalk (compare the chorus with the Kerry Mills's work), and the verse has even less rhythmic conflict. So this typical ragtime song is considerably less syncopated than a piano rag.

Like most of the popular songs of the era, it employs the verse-chorus form, with the verse assuming a narrative function. It resembles popular waltz songs in its voice-and-piano instrumentation and melody-plus-accompaniment texture. It is the syncopated rhythm that distinguishes it from more conservative styles.

RAGTIME DANCES

James Reese Europe's "Castle House Rag" (Example 6.4) illustrates ragtime dance in the early teens, around the time of the animal-dance fads. Just as piano rags eventually developed into stride piano (a smoother, more jazz-influenced style of the twenties and thirties), ragtime dances gradually evolved into syncopated dance music, which was soon to become the dance music of a new generation. "Castle House Rag" documents the transition from ragtime to syncopated dance music. This music was recorded in 1913, at the beginning of the overlap between the ragtime and fox-trot eras. Although legitimately titled a rag, it also contains features commonly heard in the music of the late teens and twenties. These transitional features include:

A faster tempo. The tempo of ragtime music gradually accelerated during this period (despite Joplin's admonition to the contrary), and so the beat of this song moves considerably more quickly than "Maple Leaf Rag." A consequence of the quicker tempo is the use of the cakewalk rhythm at half speed (it is heard occasionally in the second and third strains). Fox-trots of the early twenties, like "Whispering" (Example 8.4), have an even faster tempo.

Instrumentation. This recording reflects the sound of the dance orchestra of the time, also in a state of transition. The violins hark back to the cotillion orchestras of the nineteenth century, while the drums anticipate the dance bands of the twenties and thirties.

Form. Like the Sousa march, Joplin rag, and Kerry Mills's cakewalk, "Castle House Rag" has a multisectional form. Unlike the earlier examples, however, the last sections are open-ended, offering the drummer a chance to "stretch out."

Syncopation. In general, there is less rhythmic conflict in this piece than in a classic rag. Grouping of beat divisions by three so that they periodically overlap the beat, one of the trademarks of later ragtime, occurs in the break before the third strain (the one with the bells) and the fourth strain, in which drums and strings are so prominent.

II-6

IIA-6

CONCLUSION

Ragtime was never the dominant popular style, even at the peak of its popularity; mainstream popular music was still largely unsyncopated. But no music from its era was more influential and no music of the period remains more popular. By the time ragtime died out as a style in the late teens, it had generated a substantial legacy, not only in the classic piano rags of Joplin and others, but also in its seminal influence on twentieth-century popular music. Even more important, it opened the doors of popular music to real African-American music. Blues, jazz, and gospel would all follow ragtime's path into the popular mainstream.

Terms to Know

cakewalk	oral tradition	piano rag
ragtime	ragtime dance	ragtime song
syncopation	turkey trot	

Names to Know

Eubie Blake	James Reese Europe	James Weldon Johnson
Scott Joplin	Kerry Mills	

Study Questions

1. What are the three meanings of ragtime discussed in the text?

2. In what ways was ragtime an important African-American style?

3. What elements of classic piano ragtime come from the European tradition? What elements are African in origin?

4. What is the characteristic rhythm of the cakewalk? Is a cakewalk likely to be more or less syncopated than a rag? A ragtime song?

5. Besides fuller instrumentation, how did ragtime dances differ from Joplin's piano rags?

6. Why was the white musical establishment so hostile toward the ragtime style?

CHAPTER SEVEN

The Blues

For much of the twentieth century, the blues have been the most direct and idiomatic musical expression of African-American culture. African-Americans have used the blues to convey their feelings in song, to describe their world and the most meaningful events and situations within it. Both text and music can communicate an extraordinary range of emotion—pain, sorrow, joy, humor—without the need for the flowery images or elaborate melodies of mainstream popular song. The blues are the quintessential expression of the African-American experience.

blues

BLUES STYLES

Around the turn of the century, blues was both a rural folk music and music for stage entertainment. As a folk music, it was often performed by an individual for his or her own amusement rather than for an audience—or at least a paying audience. This solitary aspect of folk blues differentiates it from most other African-American folk styles, including work songs and spirituals, which are based on collective music-making. Willie McTell's recording of "Travelin' Blues" (Example 3.6) and Robert Johnson's "Hellhound on My Trail" (Example 7.2) are good illustrations of country blues.

Shortly after 1900, blues also became a commercial music. Blues singers like Ma Rainey toured on the African-American vaudeville circuits, and W. C. Handy published a series of blues compositions, among them "St. Louis Blues" (1914), the most frequently recorded song in the first half of the twentieth century.

The advent of race records (recordings by African-Americans targeted mainly for the African-American market) in the early 1920s broadened the exposure of the blues, both within and outside the African-American community. Both rural and commercial blues singers, like Bessie Smith, were recorded. Jazz borrowed heavily from the blues; indeed jazzmen accompanied most of the commercial blues singers on recordings. Even popular songs (Jerome Kern's "Can't Help Lovin' Dat Man") and popular singers like Ethel Waters showed some blues influence.

Blues as entertainment declined precipitously in the thirties, but there

 I-19

 IA-19

 I-39

 IB-13

country blues

race records

were notable achievements by blues musicians. Although they were largely ignored at the time, the most influential recordings of that decade were made by Robert Johnson. Johnson performed in a country-blues style, singing and playing with great urgency and intensity. In another blues style, Jimmy Rushing sang jazz-influenced blues with Count Basie's big band. The influence of the blues in popular music grew steadily throughout the thirties, as a primary source of swing style and boogie woogie, a blues piano style that was an important precursor of rock 'n' roll.

The blues went electric after World War II, in the work of T-Bone Walker and Muddy Waters. The electric guitar injected a new vitality into this music and restored its commercial appeal. Like jazz, electric blues used a swing beat. So did the jump bands that were among the forerunners of fifties rhythm and blues. Jump bands and early electric blues provided a healthy antidote to the dreariness of post-World War II popular song. Rhythm and blues, although directed toward the African-American audience, began to attract a considerably larger white audience. Rock 'n' roll was an outgrowth of R&B, developed primarily by white artists. For example, Elvis's first recording, "That's Alright," was a cover of an R&B song by Arthur "Big Boy" Crudup. So a direct line of influence can be traced from the electric blues through rock.

The major figures of sixties rock drew even more heavily on the blues. Mick Jagger and Robert Plant owed more vocally to B. B. King than to Bing Crosby, and major guitarists like Eric Clapton and Jimi Hendrix used blues guitar styles as a point of departure for their own especially influential work. Meanwhile, the best soul performers—singers like Aretha Franklin, James Brown, Otis Redding, and Marvin Gaye—sang with an intensity usually heard only within the blues tradition. Performers like B. B. King, who remained well inside the blues tradition, also achieved some commercial success in the sixties and seventies. Pioneer heavy-metal bands like Led Zeppelin also used blues and blues-influenced rock as a stylistic springboard.

THE MEANINGS OF THE BLUES

In the popular-music tradition, the term "blues" has three specific connotations: It can describe a feeling; refer to blues style (a way of singing or playing); or indicate a form. One, two, or all three qualities may be present in a performance. All are salient features of the blues.

The statement, "I've got the blues," describes a state of mind that may have nothing to do with music. More often than not, blues songs are about problems: problems with a lover (or lovers), a job, the environment, or any other matter that the blues singer decides to sing about. Happy blues songs are the exception to the rule.

Blues feeling in music extends beyond blues songs. Many songs that are not blues in other ways, such as Harold Arlen's "I've Got a Right to Sing the Blues," may communicate something of the feeling of a blues song. Blues lyrics have also influenced nonblues styles. Blues lyrics generally state their message with a frankness that is in sharp contrast to the moon/June lyrics of pre-rock styles. Both the subjects and the language of contemporary popular song owe much to the blues.

Blues style is the way in which great blues singers have performed. Some of the recurring features of blues singers' styles include: a vocal part reminiscent of heightened speech, with a narrow range; a smooth continuum between speaking and singing; a delivery independent of the underlying beat; and a rough, highly inflected vocal timbre. Guitarists, saxophonists, pianists, and other musicians have sought to transfer the intense delivery of blues singing to their instrumental styles. Blues songs emphasize the instrumental role by often featuring call-and-response interchange between voice and instrument. Many of the major folk and electric blues singers, like Robert Johnson and B. B. King, have also been skilled guitarists. They can get their guitars to "talk" with the same impassioned eloquence heard in their singing.

In their commercial mode, the blues quickly assumed a stable poetic and musical form. In W. C. Handy's "St. Louis Blues," the first and last sections follow the regular twelve-bar blues form; in Handy's "Memphis Blues," an instrumental composition written in 1909, several sections follow the harmonic plan of the blues. With the advent of commercial recording of blues singers in the twenties, blues form took on a dependably regular design.

blues form

A blues song consists of an indefinite number of sections, or choruses, and has no standard length. Theoretically, at least, it can continue forever. Songs could be long or short, depending on subject and inspiration. Within a chorus, however, blues songs typically adhere to a strict form. Each chorus will follow a standard poetic, melodic, rhythmic, and harmonic outline; these are described in some detail in the discussion of B. B. King's "No Good" (Example 7.1).

B. B. King, c. 1970.

Because vocal statements within a chorus are usually short, with pauses in between, and because the first line of text is repeated, the blues is an ideal form for spontaneous creation. The quick and imaginative thinker can use the pauses to improvise new choruses. Bessie Smith's "Lost Your Head Blues" was reportedly improvised at the recording session.

THE SOUND OF THE BLUES

(D)

"No Good" (Example 7.1) features B. B. King, the acknowledged master of contemporary blues. B. B. King was born Riley B. King in 1925 near Indianola, Mississippi. His career began in the forties in his home state after service in the Army during World War II. A stint as a disc jockey in Memphis in the early fifties helped him gain a national reputation among blues fans. He was billed as "Blues Boy" King, which was soon shortened to B. B. His reputation spread to a wider audience during the sixties blues revival; a series of artistically successful albums, several recorded live, cemented his reputation as the most accomplished blues musician of recent generations.

King's recording of "No Good" is a textbook example of the blues. We can identify virtually all of the trademarks of a standard blues song in this performance. This song explores perhaps the most pervasive theme in blues lyrics: man/woman trouble. Typically, it tells its story in the direct, everyday, unsentimental language associated with the blues: "I read every word you had to say"; "my memory don't fail me"; "you know I remember the day you left."

King conveys the blues feeling musically through the traditional techniques of blues style. King doesn't have a highly individual repertoire of expressive devices; rather, he simply does those things that other blues musicians do, only better. They include:

Vocal style. This blues is song-as-intensified-speech. King's voice is always rough, and it cracks with emotion at particularly intense moments, on the word, "please," for example. Each phrase of the song stays for the most part within a narrow range, beginning high or reaching a peak early on, from which it gradually descends. Often, the final few words of a phrase are as much spoken as sung. And King's delivery of the words responds much more to their natural spoken cadence than to the underlying beat. In short, King sings the words to amplify the inflection that would typically be given them if simply spoken. He can slow down the delivery of the words without sounding mannered, he can give special emphasis to particular words and phrases, and by singing, he gives his voice extra resonance.

Instrumental style. King's guitar, which he named Lucille, talks when he doesn't. He has adapted key elements of his vocal style to the guitar; the bent notes, rapid vibrato (slight fluctuations in pitch on a single note), and variations in dynamics are the instrumental counterparts to his singing.

Other characteristic features of contemporary blues performance heard in this recording include:

1. Call and response between voice and guitar
2. A full rhythm section: drums, bass, keyboard, and rhythm guitar
3. An active, dense texture, with the keyboard player supplying melodically interesting background figures behind King

A typical blues song contains three phrases per chorus. Each verse follows a strict poetic, melodic, rhythmic, and harmonic form. The characteristics of each aspect of blues form are:

Poetic form. Each chorus in a blues song typically contains a rhymed couplet, two different lines of text with the first line repeated. So, the first line of text is sung to the first and second phrases of the verse, the second line of text to the third. **rhymed couplet**

Melodic form. Each line of text is sung to its own melodic idea. The second phrase of the melody (sung to the first line of text) is either a literal repetition of the first phrase or (more often) a slight variation of the first phrase.

Rhythmic form. Each phrase of a standard blues chorus lasts four bars; each bar (or measure) contains four beats. One chorus of a blues song contains twelve measures, so standard blues form is often identified as "twelve-bar blues."

Harmonic form. The harmonic framework of the blues is built on three chords. The first chord (I or tonic) begins and ends the first phrase of a section. The second phrase begins with the second chord (IV or subdominant) and returns to the first chord halfway through the phrase. The third phrase begins with the third chord (V or dominant); it also returns to the first chord halfway through (see Table 7.1).

Table 7.1   Basic Blues Harmony

	Beginning	Midpoint
Phrase 1	I	I
Phrase 2	IV	I
Phrase 3	V	I

Other harmonies can be—and almost always are—interposed between the main orientation points. But this outline is the standard harmonic plan for a vocal or instrumental blues performance. Even the most harmonically elaborate blues songs use this outline as a point of departure.

We can hear all four dimensions of blues form in "No Good." It contains six choruses: the first and fourth are instrumental; the other four are vocal. All follow the standard blues harmonic and rhythmic plan. The sung choruses add the poetic and melodic forms. The text of the first vocal chorus is shown below.

Line 1   Your letter reached me early this morning, baby,

                and I read every word you had to say.

Line 1   Your letter reached me early this morning, baby,

and I read every word you had to say.

Line 2   But if you love me like you say you do, baby,

I want to know why in the world did you go away?

THE SOUND OF EARLY BLUES STYLES

COUNTRY BLUES

Country blues, the earliest of blues styles, were sung throughout the rural south from the East Coast to the Southwest, certainly by the turn of the century and perhaps before. Country blues performers were recorded most frequently during the late twenties and thirties, some commercially and others by folklorists anxious to preserve an important expression of American culture. Despite occasional revivals, interest in country blues waned with the rise of electric and other forms of urban blues and as the increased availability of radio, TV, and records brought most African-Americans in contact with contemporary styles and trends. Country blues styles are distinguished from more mainstream styles by rougher vocal timbre, acoustic guitar accompaniment, irregular form, and occasional use of other acoustic instruments, many of them homemade.

Robert Johnson (1911–1938) was one of the great country blues performers. As a vocalist and instrumentalist, he captured the essence of all aspects of blues style. There is an astounding range of emotion in his voice, which often carried over into his guitar playing. Despite a brief career cut short by a violent death, and a limited number of recordings, Johnson was a major influence on many important blues and rock musicians, including the Rolling Stones, who covered his songs "Love in Vain" and "Stop Breakin' Down."

I-39

IB-13

The text of "Hellhound on My Trail" (Example 7.2) is exceptional in the power and vividness of its images; phrases like "Blues fallin' down like hail" and "there's a hellhound on my trail" give the narrative a frightening intensity. All the qualities associated with blues style and feeling are present to a great degree in this performance: blues singing as heightened speech; the vocal/melody line moving freely over the rhythmic base; multiple uses of the guitar (accompanying and answering the voice); the call-and-response pattern between voice and instrument; and a rough, untrained, but highly effective vocal timbre. Unlike B. B. King's "No Good," there is no regular pattern to the duration of the phrases; they constantly vary in length. A freer approach to form is one of the main differences between country and urban blues.

BLUES FOR ENTERTAINMENT

As African-Americans migrated to the urban areas in both North and South, they took the blues with them. What had been private or small-group entertainment in the rural South became, after the move to the city, music for public performance. In the first decades of the twentieth century, a group of blues singers, most of them women, performed the blues on stage, in clubs, and on records.

After the turn of the century, African-American vaudeville troupes often featured blues singers like Ma Rainey. They returned to the South to present urbanized versions of the blues. Throughout the twenties, with the opening of the recording industry to African-Americans through "race" records, the leading blues singers, like Bessie Smith, recorded extensively. However, African-Americans fell on hard times during the depression. Too few could afford to buy their records or attend the theaters and clubs where these blues singers performed. As a result, the market for this kind of commercial blues singing had all but dried up by the early thirties.

Blues songs that appeared commercially had lost some of their rough

Bessie Smith dancing the Charleston, 1924.

edges. Most of them employed the standard three-phrase/twelve-measure blues form, with call and response between singer and instrument. In performance, jazz bands with at least one rhythm/chord instrument and one horn accompanied the singer.

Bessie Smith (1894–1937) was the most important and influential of the women blues singers from the first third of the century. Her performances expressed the essence of the blues: each phrase is heightened speech, delivered with her unique vocal style and with great rhythmic freedom, which adds greatly to the expressive character of her performances. The melodic lines are typically narrow in range and usually descend.

Blues singers like Bessie Smith, who recorded only a handful of Tin Pan Alley songs, represented only one end of the stylistic spectrum among African-American women singers. Ethel Waters, one of the most popular African-American performers of the twenties and beyond, was also identified as a "blues singer" by herself and commentators of the period, even though she primarily performed popular material. The confusion between color and style—Bessie is unmistakably African-American in her musical style, Ethel much closer to the popular-music mainstream—recalls the similarly broad range of vocal styles among female African-American singers in the sixties, which ranged from the soul-defining style of Aretha Franklin to the recognizably African-American but more centrist sound of Diana Ross. The "blues" singers of the twenties had their counterparts among the "soul" singers of the sixties.

 II-1

 IIA-1

Smith's performance of the classic blues song, W. C. Handy's "St. Louis Blues" (Example 7.3), is one of her greatest recordings. W. C. Handy, known as the "father of the blues," gained this title because he was among the first to publish a blues song. Blues had been part of African-American folk music for decades, but it wasn't until 1912 that the first blues songs appeared in print. Among them was Handy's "Memphis Blues," discussed in Chapter 6.

"St. Louis Blues" (1914) is not one song but three. The first part lasts for two blues choruses. The second is not a blues, but a tango. Possible influences for this section include the "Spanish tinge" that Jelly Roll Morton suggested was an integral element of early New Orleans jazz, and the tangos that were popular in the dancing salons of New York. The final section returns to the blues, but with a new melody.

Spanish
tinge

There are several features that differentiate this song from "Hellhound on My Trail." Like most commercial blues, each chorus uses the standard blues form: three phrases setting a rhymed couplet, with each phrase lasting four measures. (Johnson's blues also contains three phrases per chorus, but their length strays from the usual four measures.) In its original form, "St. Louis Blues" was a fox-trot type song, with a bouncy two-beat rhythm.

The performance also distinguishes this commercial blues performance from Johnson's folk blues. The accompanying instrument is, unfortunately, a reed organ, played by Fred Longshaw. It is an inadequate substitute for the jazz rhythm section of the twenties. Louis Armstrong's trumpet responses redeem the instrumental side of this performance. In keeping with the mood of the song, the performance is slower than it would have been performed by bands of the teens. It has the four-beat feel of jazz and blues, at least in the rhythmic emphasis of both Smith and Armstrong.

As in Examples 7.1 and 7.2, we can hear key elements of blues style. Smith has a big, gravelly voice, and delivers the words with considerable

W. C. Handy holding a cornet, in bandsman's uniform, c. 1914–15.

rhythmic freedom and heightened inflection. For expressive purposes, she bends the pitch of certain emphasized notes. Her singing of the word "sun" in the first phrase of the song is an authentic example of the "blue note" so widely used by songwriters in the twenties and thirties. (Listen to Jerome Kern's "Can't Help Lovin' Dat Man," heard in Chapter 11.)

blue note

BLUES STYLE IN POPULAR MUSIC

"Alexander's Ragtime Band" (Example 7.4) was a big hit for Irving Berlin in 1911. This version, recorded in 1927, is one of the few non-blues recordings of Bessie Smith. It shows how blues style can easily apply to a popular song.

 II-2

 IIA-2

This recording, made well after the decline of ragtime, combines several different musical styles. It is: (1) a song about and presumably related to *ragtime;* (2) written in a style that shows little ragtime influence, but which predicts the style of the soon-to-be standard *fox-trot song;* (3) sung by the most important *blues* singer of the 1920s; (4) who is accompanied by a *jazz* band. In this performance, Bessie Smith inflects her version of the song with a blues-like feel. It's most audible in passages like the one set to "Alexander's Ragtime Band" at the end of the first phrase of the chorus. Here she narrows the pitch range, alters the rhythm slightly, and gives extra emphasis to the syllable "rag."

Smith's grafting of blues style onto popular-song performance was not immediately influential, perhaps because she recorded only two nonblues songs and because she was not widely known outside the African-American community. But it would influence important singers in subsequent generations. Billie Holiday, heard in Chapter 10, used the same kind of spontaneous rewriting of the melody in her version of "All of Me" (Ex. 10.3). She claimed Bessie Smith and Louis Armstrong as her two primary influences. The great song interpreters and jazz singers of the forties and fifties would also learn from Bessie Smith, either directly or indirectly.

III-1

IIIA-1

CONCLUSION

The blues has given more to popular music than it has taken in return. Despite standardization of blues form and steady assimilation of prevailing practices over the years (for example, the use of swing, then rock beats, and the gradual electrification of the blues band), the essential qualities of the blues have remained unchanged throughout its recorded history.

Blues gradually entered the mainstream of popular music not because the blues adapted to popular taste, but because leading popular musicians increasingly turned to the blues for inspiration. As a result, popular music gradually evolved to the point where the blues-based styles were accepted without sugarcoating, first by the musicians and then by their audience. For over half a century, the blues in their varied manifestations were the primary agent of stylistic change in popular music.

Terms to Know

blues	blues form	blue note
country blues	race record	rhymed couplet
Spanish tinge		

Names to Know

W. C. Handy	Robert Johnson	B. B. King
Bessie Smith	Ethel Waters	

Study Questions

1. What are the three meanings of the term "blues"? Can a song have a blues "feel" without having elements of blues style or form? If so, how? If not, why not?

2. Can a nonblues song acquire a blues "feel" if the performer sings it in a blues style?

3. Describe the poetic, melodic, harmonic, and rhythmic forms of the blues.

4. What qualities characterize blues singing? Which of these can be transferred to a musical instrument?

5. Describe some of the similarities and differences between country and commercial blues style.

6. Write three choruses of a blues song *as it would be sung*. (Then try to find a club that has an open mike night and sing your song!)

7. How was Elvis Presley influenced by the blues? Can you think of other rock singers or groups who have been influenced by this style? If so, how?

PART III

REVOLUTION 2

CHAPTER EIGHT

Syncopated Song and Dance

In 1925, a flapper (a young woman who ignored conventional social and moral restrictions) in Chicago might have visited a speakeasy (an illegal bar of the Prohibition era) with her escort to hear hot jazz by King Oliver, Bix Beiderbecke, or even a young Benny Goodman. Her counterpart in New York might be dancing the Charleston, freshly composed by jazz pianist James P. Johnson, at the Roseland Ballroom. She'd Charleston to the syncopated strains of Fletcher Henderson, whose dance band might still have included Louis Armstrong. She'd be wearing a short, loose-fitting chemise because the dance is so vigorous that the women's heavy dresses from early in the century were too restrictive.

flapper

A year later, our flappers' soulmate in Cleveland might be fox-trotting along with Paul Whiteman's band as they played Richard Rodgers and Lorenz Hart's first big hit "Manhattan." Whiteman's band would be broadcasting from another New York ballroom, but she could hear the band live via network radio, new that year. She'd be glad to "take Manhattan, the Bronx and Staten Island, too," because hearing the band over the radio put her in touch with a city she'd never seen.

All these experiences were consequences of the second revolution in popular music. Syncopated dance music, riff-based fox-trot songs with snappy lyrics, and jazz bands were barely on the horizon in 1910. In the teens, jazz and blues joined ragtime in reshaping popular music. Commercial radio stations, which began broadcasting in the early twenties, gave many Americans much readier access to these new musical forms. This massive infusion of African-American style into popular music gave it a new, uniquely American sound. For the first time in its history, the dominant popular music of the United States was not a pale imitation of European style but a distinctive amalgam of white and African-American music.

syncopated
dance
music

POPULAR MUSIC AND SOCIETY

The emergence of a distinctively American popular music expressed both the fact and the nature of America's coming of age. With its intercession in World War I, the United States had become a world power, reluctantly or not. Business, applying the assembly-line procedures used so successfully by

Henry Ford and the management techniques of Frederick Taylor, grew in size and efficiency. New products, particularly electrically operated home appliances, made domestic chores significantly easier. Skilled workers had more money to spend and more time to spend it. As a result, the entertainment industry flourished. Much of this entertainment, particularly popular music and films, reflected a distinct cultural identity. Politically, economically, and culturally, the United States relied much less on Europe for inspiration and guidance.

The teens and twenties were also a time of enormous social change. Immigration/migration and the sexual revolution particularly affected, and were affected by, popular music. Large ethnic and minority populations in cities like New York helped support their own musicians and entertainers. Most of the great songwriters of the period between the wars were Jewish or African-American: Irving Berlin; Jerome Kern; Harold Arlen; George Gershwin; Duke Ellington; and "Fats" Waller. So were many vaudeville stars: Eddie Cantor; Al Jolson; Bert Williams; and Fanny Brice. African-American musicians supplied dance music and entertainment for all levels of society in the teens and twenties, although bands remained segregated until the late thirties.

Prohibition gave many popular musicians jobs. Jazz spread from New Orleans throughout the country by way of Chicago's speakeasies, as King Oliver, Louis Armstrong, and other early jazz greats moved north in search of better-paying jobs. Benny Goodman, the "king of swing," also got his professional start in a Chicago speakeasy.

THE FIRST ELECTRIC REVOLUTION

Influx into urban centers brought musicians together and created audiences for their performances. However, the first stage of the electrical revolution of the twenties played a much larger part in swelling the popular-music audience. Through radio, popular music was available to anyone with access to a radio set.

In 1920, the first commercial radio station, KDKA in Pittsburgh, began broadcasting. Within two years, the number of commercial stations had grown from one to over 200. With few exceptions, each radio station generated its own programming, hiring local musicians and personalities to provide entertainment to its audience. By 1926, however, NBC (National Broadcasting Company) began broadcasting simultaneously on twenty-five affiliates throughout the Northeast and Midwest with a gala concert. Although AT&T had already experimented with broadcasts over several stations from one source, it was NBC's debut that celebrated the birth of a new industry, network radio. Soon, performances emanating from one location could be broadcast throughout the country, providing the nation with an unprecedented sense of unity.

acoustic broadcasting/recording

electric broadcasting/recording

microphone

amplifier

Important technological advances accompanied the rapid growth of commercial radio. None was more important than the conversion from acoustical to electrical broadcasting. Many of the earliest radio studios were equipped with long, conical horns similar to those used in acoustical recordings, into which performers spoke, sang, or played. These horns soon gave way to microphones that converted sound into electrical impulses, which were then converted into the broadcast signal or transmitted to network affiliates for local broadcast. Amplifiers and loudspeakers to restore the electrical impulses back into sound improved as quickly and as dramatically as microphones.

Microphones, amplifiers, and speakers found immediate application elsewhere, in recording, live performance, and instrument manufacture. In 1925, the recording industry converted from acoustic to electric recording almost overnight. As in broadcasting, microphones replaced the cumbersome and inefficient horns used for acoustic recording. The result was a dramatic improvement in recorded sound.

The most obvious benefit of amplification, developed in the early 1920s for commercial broadcasting, was greater volume in both live and recorded performances. However, amplification had an even more far-reaching effect on the sound of popular music, by enabling small-voiced singers to record and perform.

Before commercial radio, popular singers performed in theaters and auditoriums without any amplification. Many had classically trained, quasi-operatic voices suitable for the operettas fashionable in the early part of the century and for the more serious and conservative popular songs. Others, like Sophie Tucker, Bessie Smith, and Al Jolson, belted out their songs in a full voice that filled the theater.

The development of microphones, amplifiers, and loudspeakers created professional opportunities for singers whose voices would not otherwise project in a theater or record well using acoustic recording techniques. This new generation of singers broadened the spectrum of vocal styles heard in popular music almost overnight. By 1930, listeners could choose from the nasal twang of country's Carter Family, the intimate crooning of Bing Crosby or Russ Columbo, or the jazz-inflected, conversational style of Louis Armstrong. Amplification, as used in both recording and live performance, opened up commercial recording and performing careers to crooners like Frank Sinatra, hillbilly and country performers like Jimmie Rodgers and Roy Acuff, jazz and blues singers like Ethel Waters and Louis Armstrong, and performers like Fred Astaire and Ginger Rogers, whose major talent lay in other areas.

Except for Broadway performers and folk singers performing in small clubs, popular singers have not sung or recorded without amplification for over sixty years. In most cases, unamplified singing is inconceivable. Most singers do not have voices powerful enough to carry over the large and/or loud bands and orchestras that accompany them. Amplification is an essential technological component of popular music.

THE NEW SOUND OF SYNCOPATED SONG

The interaction of African-American music with white popular song comprehensively reshaped the mainstream popular style. Among the most significant and evident changes were:

1. *The merger of song and dance.* Popular songs before the teens had used dance rhythms but were not sung as music for social dancing. By 1920, syncopated dance music had integrated with popular song to make a music both singable and danceable.

2. *The formation of the syncopated dance orchestra.* Although dance

Paul Whiteman (with baton), leading his orchestra, c. 1928.

orchestras had existed in America since colonial times, none sounded like those of James Reese Europe in the teens and Paul Whiteman, Ben Selvin, and Fletcher Henderson in the twenties.

saxophone

There were two key differences in the instrumentation of these new dance orchestras: the full rhythm section and the use of the saxophone. The rhythm section came to the dance orchestra by way of the jazz band. An up-to-date sound in the early twenties had tuba and banjo laying down a fox-trot beat. The role of the drummer clarified in the mid-twenties with the refinement of two important pieces of equipment, the bass drum pedal and the hi-hat cymbal. By 1930, these were a standard part of the drum set.

The saxophone typified the sound of the twenties much as the electric guitar typified the sound of the sixties. In the twenties, the saxophone was an instrument new to popular music. It quickly became an alternative to—even replacement for—the clarinet as the reed counterpart to the brass section.

Violins, long the main melody voice of the dance orchestra, lost status during the twenties. In orchestras like Paul Whiteman's, they played a less-prominent role. In the jazz-influenced dance bands, like those of Henderson and Duke Ellington, they disappeared altogether.

3. *Crooning and other new singing styles.* With the electrical revolution of 1925, new kinds of singers entered the popular-music business. Light-voiced singers like Gene Austin, Cliff Edwards ("Ukelele Ike"), and even "Whispering" Jack Smith joined song belters like Al Jolson as popular recording and performing artists. The most commercially successful of the new group of singers were crooners like Bing Crosby and Russ Columbo. Their intimate singing, delivered in a soothing baritone, beautifully complemented the conversational tone of new song lyrics.

4. *A fox-trot beat.* Most songs in the twenties were fox-trot songs. In performance, a two-beat rhythm, played by tuba and banjo (or other bass and chord instruments) in alternation, anchored the melody of the song.

5. *New instrumental styles.* Popular instrumentalists, especially wind and brass players, cultivated ways of playing their instruments that distin-

guished them from band and orchestra performers. The two most obvious expressions of this different performing style were the use of a wide vibrato and, among brass players, the extensive use of mutes, plungers, and other timbre-altering devices. Both came from jazz and blues.

6. *Snappy, riff-based melodies.* Blues and ragtime influenced the melodies of popular song even more directly. As was discussed in Chapters 6 and 7, the influence is evident in three characteristics: (1) the use of riffs; (2) uneven division of the beat; and, (3) syncopation. All three in combination created melodic rhythms that closely corresponded to the natural inflection and rhythm of American vernacular speech.

7. *Conversational lyrics.* Lyrics matched the spirit and feel of the melodies. More often than not, words were one syllable long ("It Had to Be You"); phrases and sentences were short. Colloquial expressions replaced the more formal language of nineteenth-century song. Many contained surprising rhymes, e.g., "Manhattan" and "Staten (Island too)" in Rodgers and Hart's song by the same title.

8. *A chorus-oriented form.* Except in musicals, verses were all but scrapped. A performance of a song consisted primarily of several statements of the chorus. A fragment of the verse might be used as an interlude, particularly in dance-band arrangements. Typically, the band would play the first chorus, the vocalist would sing the second, and the band would take back the melody for the third and final statement of the melody.

chorus-oriented form

All these qualities are evident in "If I Had You" (Example 8.1), written in 1929 by Ted Shapiro, James Campbell, and Reg Connelly, and recorded in 1929 by Sam Lanin and his Famous Players, with Bing Crosby, vocalist. The arrangement of the song is typical of the period. Designed to fit on one side of a ten-inch, 78-rpm disc, it contains two-and-a-half choruses, plus an introduction, interlude, and short close. Instrumental statements—a full chorus at the beginning and two A sections at the end—frame Bing Crosby's fine vocal. The fox-trot beat is unmistakable: bass notes played by the tuba alternating with crisp backbeats from the banjo. They are the more prominent half of the full rhythm section that supports the rest of the band, including a typical lineup of trumpets (both muted and open), saxophones, clarinets, and trombones, in addition to the rhythm instruments. Both the muted trumpet sound and the wah-wah vibrato of the saxes help date this performance as a pre-swing era product.

II-3

IIA-3

The melody is a bit unusual, although still very much within the fox-trot style. Most phrases in popular songs develop from the opening riff; this one does just the opposite. It lops off the song's identifying riff ("If I Had You"—heard at the end of the phrase) from the fairly long (eight-syllable) opening statement. The four-note riff also serves as the material for the melody of the A section. The last syllable of the riff is syncopated, emphasizing the word "you," the verbal focal point of the melody. Lyrics are also in the spirit and style of the period. The opening A section consists only of one-syllable words. And, like so many songs of the twenties and thirties, the lyrics describe an idealized love relationship. Crosby's delivery is suitably low key: natural, not stiff. His style would prove to be very influential.

Bing Crosby, c. 1935.

FROM DANCE TO SONG

The ragtime-influenced dance music of the first decade of the twentieth century accompanied a number of notorious new dance steps. Most of them were adapted or borrowed from African-American folk dances. The most infamous of these new dances was a group of animal dances. The grizzly bear, the chicken glide, and the turkey trot all became popular in certain circles around 1910. "Respectable" citizens reacted violently to these dances, which were associated with sleazy establishments and disreputable people. As recounted in Dannett and Rachel's book, *Down Memory Lane*:

> A Paterson, New Jersey, court imposed a fifty-day prison sentence on a young woman for dancing the turkey trot. Fifteen young women were dismissed from a well-known magazine after the editor caught them enjoying the abandoned dance at lunchtime. Turkey trotters incurred the condemnation of churches and respectable people, and in 1914 an official disapproval was issued by the Vatican.

Irene and Vernon Castle, dancing to the syncopated strains of the African-American bandleader James Reese Europe, made dancing to syncopated dance music socially acceptable. The Castles, Europe, and W. C. Handy claimed to have invented the fox-trot, seemingly another of the animal dances of the period. Yet theirs differed from these other dances in an important way: the Castles purged it sufficiently of morally objectionable features to make it acceptable to mainstream Americans.

The process of its popularization began in 1912. The Castles had just returned from Paris, where they rode the crest of the tango fad. They began dancing at teas in a New York restaurant, and soon appeared in a Broadway stage show, *The Sunshine Girl.* In this show they danced the turkey trot, as ballroom and even tap dancing had begun to replace older dancing styles in musicals.

In 1914, so one story goes, Europe was touring with the Castles. One day, they overheard him noodling at the piano during intermission, playing strains of Handy's "Memphis Blues." The Castles immediately took to the number, and Europe suggested that they create a dance to perform to it. The result was the fox-trot; within a year, the dance was more popular than all the other dances in their repertoire. Their success led them to open Castle House, a dance-instruction studio. Almost immediately, the Castles and Europe's Society Orchestra became extremely popular among New York's high society.

Irene and Vernon Castle, c. 1914; note Irene's "bobbed" hair style and the couple's close physical contact, considered risqué at the time.

The Castles's success spawned an unprecedented enthusiasm for social dancing. More important, it also marked a fundamental shift in popular taste. For the first time, social dancing to a clearly African-American beat was acceptable to a significant percentage of the population. Fox-trotting caught on with all levels of society, from the Rockefellers on down. Although it may not have been condoned in all quarters, dancing to syncopated music was no longer a criminal offense. By the mid-thirties, dancing "Cheek to Cheek," as Fred and Ginger did so often on screen—even in a film biography of the Castles—was not only socially acceptable, it was the epitome of elegance.

The Castles's dance success even affected fashion. By the twenties, the

fox-trot

more emancipated women presented themselves less demurely without corsets, floor-length skirts, or other articles of clothing designed to obscure their charms, and with their hair bobbed. In this respect, they followed the lead of Irene Castle; she wore her hair short and dressed in looser-fitting garments the better to dance the more vigorous syncopated dances.

"Memphis Blues" (Example 8.2), composed by W. C. Handy and performed by James Reese Europe's "Hellfighters" Band, is generally credited as the first fox-trot. The recording has considerable interest for several reasons. First, it is a fine early example of syncopated dance music. Second, "Memphis Blues" brings together several different African-American styles in the air at the time. Handy had written the song in 1909, five years before he wrote his famous "St. Louis Blues." Although it's a blues, it has the multisection form of a rag, with three distinct melodies. The first and the last sections have the harmonic plan of a blues; the middle one doesn't. The tension between ragtime and blues style is also heard in the performance. There is contrast between the rather stiff syncopations in group playing and the blues-like slides into notes during the breaks in the last strain. Third, the recording provides us with one of the few examples of dance-band style in the teens. This performance, made in 1919, is stylistically similar in many ways to Europe's "Castle House Rag," recorded several years earlier. This recording features the instrumentation of a military band instead of a dance orchestra, but the playing styles are similar.

The next two examples, both from the early twenties, show the two most important aspects of the consolidation of the fox-trot style, clarification of the beat and its incorporation into popular song. "Copenhagen" (Example 8.3) clearly articulates the fox-trot beat in the rhythm section. Fletcher Henderson (1897–1952), the African-American arranger and bandleader who composed "Copenhagen," was one of the most important and influential musicians of the twenties and thirties. His dance orchestra was the first African-American band to broadcast regularly. Its alumni included jazz greats Louis Armstrong, Coleman Hawkins, and Benny Carter. During the early thirties, Henderson was instrumental in developing the sound of big-band swing, in conjunction with his saxophonist and coarranger, Don Redman. His contribution to swing style is discussed in Chapter 9.

"Copenhagen" dates from the early twenties, about ten years after "Memphis Blues" began to be used as a fox-trot. Unlike that song, which is clearly transitional, "Copenhagen" presents the sound of syncopated dance music in its mature form. First, it uses a complete rhythm section, including banjo, piano, tuba, and drums. Second, the rhythmic pattern of the fox-trot beat is clearly audible. The beat in this song has the OOM-pah pattern characteristic of the march, but with one important difference: the off-beat (pah) is a crisp, percussive backbeat played by the banjo. In this way, the march beat was transformed into an African-American rhythm by African-American musicians. Third, "Copenhagen" features the kind of syncopated riffs in conflict with a steady beat that would typify the swing sound of the thirties. Formally, "Copenhagen" is multisectional. Its form is its closest affinity to the ragtime dance-music tradition. The second section (or strain), played first by clarinets then Louis Armstrong, has the harmonic plan of the twelve-bar blues.

"Whispering" (Example 8.4), performed by the Paul Whiteman Orchestra, was a popular song in 1920, and Whiteman's first hit. It was also the first song to sell over one million copies of sheet music and one million records. Whiteman's recording clearly shows another major change in popular music during the early years of the fox-trot era, the use of a fox-trot song as dance music. By the twenties, popular song had acquired a steady dance beat.

"Whispering" is a conservative song for the time. It has a long, flowing melody that rises and falls gently. It is not syncopated, nor would its words (if we heard them) conform to speech rhythm. Nevertheless, the OOM-chuck of tuba and banjo can be heard clearly. For the first time in the history of popular music, popular song had to be equally suitable for singing and social dancing. As a glance at sheet music or record labels from the twenties shows, many of the songs were designated as "fox-trots," or in the case of at least one Paul Whiteman recording even more specifically: "fox-trot with vocal refrain." That tells it all.

THE HEYDAY OF POPULAR SONG

The twenty-five years between 1920 and 1945 saw songwriting ascend to a new plateau. Irving Berlin and Jerome Kern had been successful songwriters since early in the century, but they composed almost all their most memorable songs during these years. A new generation of songwriters—most important, George Gershwin, Richard Rodgers and lyricist Lorenz Hart, "Fats" Waller and lyricist Andy Razaf, Cole Porter, Harold Arlen, and Duke Ellington—began songwriting careers in the first few years after the end of World War I. They produced a seemingly endless stream of hit songs through the next three decades. Although they worked within the extraordinarily restrictive conventions of the Tin Pan Alley popular song, they displayed a level of craft and imagination in their best songs that far exceeded anything previously produced.

These years witnessed one of the rare marriages of creativity and popularity in popular music. Such marriages seem to come in the early maturity of a style, when its rhythms are vital and its bold new devices have not been reduced to cliché through endless imitation. The sudden expansion and diversification of the popular-music industry created an unprecedented demand for songs. They were needed for stage shows, radio, records, and, later, films. This demand, coupled with the superior quality of the songs, elevated the songwriter's status. They went from the virtually anonymous hacks of the late nineteenth century, pinned under the monopolizing thumb of their publishers, to acclaimed celebrities sought after by New York and Hollywood producers.

When a song became popular, through radio, stage, or even sheet-music sales, it appeared almost simultaneously in several different recorded versions and even more numerous radio performances (radio was live then). Standards, the enduring songs of this era, continued to receive performances over the years. Indeed, many were reprised in musicals and films.   standard

However, none of the myriad performances of a song were definitive. Unlike today's Top 40 hits, Tin Pan Alley songs had a life of their own independent of any particular performance. They existed as a melody, usually supported by a simple, if occasionally skillfully crafted, accompaniment. The "official" version of a song was its publication in sheet-music form, even though the song may have been written with a specific performer in mind. Only this form of the song accurately expressed the specific intent of the songwriter in such matters as melody, harmony, accompaniment, and tempo.

Relatively skimpy instructions for the performance of the song (for example, no clues to preferred instrumentation), coupled with the flexibility in the performing tradition, gave performers considerable interpretive license. Songwriters expected their songs to be interpreted in a variety of ways. For the most part, composers and performers formed two distinct groups linked symbiotically by the nature of their profession. Songwriters wrote songs; performers interpreted them, often modifying their melody, harmony, and rhythm.

Few songwriters were successful interpreters of their own songs. "Fats" Waller is a notable exception, and George Gershwin produced excellent piano versions of his songs. However, the vast majority never acquired the necessary performing skills. There was a clear division of labor between those who wrote the songs and those who performed them.

OLD AND NEW SONG STYLES

Throughout the history of popular music in this century, rhythm and melody have defined the polar extremes within a style. Songs with flowing melodic contours but relatively little rhythmic interest inhabit the conservative end of the stylistic spectrum, while songs based on syncopated riffs point to the future.

 II-7

 IIA-7

"April Showers" (Example 8.5), written by B. G. De Sylva and Louis Silvers and sung by Al Jolson, is a conservative fox-trot song. The melody of the chorus grows out of the musical idea accompanying the first three words, steadily rising in each variant of the opening four-note figure (the first two lines of text) and reluctantly descending in the second section. Both halves of the song form sustained melodic arches, giving the song a strong melodic profile. There is no syncopation or other energizing rhythmic feature.

The performance has several noteworthy features. Al Jolson was perhaps the most popular of the many Jewish entertainers in vaudeville during the twenties. He also starred in the first sound motion picture, *The Jazz Singer,* although he was not a jazz singer. His singing here illustrates the full-voiced, "song-selling" style that stage performers needed before microphones and amplification came into common use.

 II-8

 IIA-8

We have already noted that the saxophone joined dance and theater orchestras after World War I. It is during this period that the various saxophones (especially alto and tenor saxophones), with their heavier sound and collectively wider range, replaced the clarinet as the counterpart to the trumpets and trombones. Because of its novelty, the saxophone is identified with the twenties more than any other widely used instrument, especially when performed in the syrupy style used in this example.

rhythm song

"Fascinating Rhythm" (Example 8.6), words by Ira Gershwin, music by George Gershwin, sung by Fred and Adele Astaire, belongs to the most progressive subclass of Tin Pan Alley songs, the rhythm song. The rhythm song is exactly what it advertises: a song whose primary interest is rhythmic. It is

Al Jolson (right, at piano) in a scene from The Jazz Singer, *1927.*

Fred Astaire, George Gershwin, and Ira Gershwin at the piano, Hollywood, 1937.

usually performed at a fast tempo. Typically it begins with a melodically uninteresting but syncopated riff that undergoes little or no melodic variation or development.

Looking back, it's not surprising that George Gershwin composed "Fascinating Rhythm" and several other rhythm songs, because, more than any other songwriter, Gershwin incorporated the rhythmic language of ragtime and syncopated dance music into his songs. Typically, his songs, even his ballads, grow from a riff-like figure that's short and rhythmically interesting. "I Got Rhythm" applies to the song as well as to the person singing.

The fascination in the rhythm of the song "Fascinating Rhythm" occurs mostly in the A sections of the chorus. It's my suspicion that Gershwin indulges in some rhythmic one-upmanship in this song. One of the clichés of later ragtime and syncopated dance music was a repeated three-note pattern, with each pattern lasting one-and-a-half beats, so that its beginning went alternately in and out of phase with the underlying beat. (By way of example, "Memphis Blues" features several of these patterns in the instrumental breaks, as does the short interlude between the first chorus and verse in "After You've Gone.")

Gershwin goes these early jazzers one better. His version of this pattern in "Fascinating Rhythm" is considerably more complicated. The six syllables of each statement of the riff ("Fas-cin-a-ting rhy-thm") last three-and-one-half beats, with the result that the first beat of each new measure comes one syllable later each time the riff is restated:

Fas-ci-	na-ting	Rhy-thm,	(space) You've
1	2	3	4
got me	on the	go, (sp.)	Fas-ci-
1	2	3	4
na-ting	rhy-thm,	(sp.) I'm	all a
1	2	3	4
qui-ver.			
1	2	3	4

This is one of the trickiest of the rhythm songs of the era.

"After You've Gone" (Example 8.7) catalogs nearly all the new popular styles of the period. It also features several of the stars of the era: Paul Whiteman (this is a more representative example of his style than "Whispering" [Example 8.4]), a young Bing Crosby (again), and some of the best jazz musicians of the twenties.

Paul Whiteman (1890–1967) was the best-known and most respected bandleader of the era. He was instrumental in developing the "sweet" fox-trot sound kept alive by Guy Lombardo and Lawrence Welk, yet he hired some of the day's best white jazz musicians, and occasionally featured them. Bing Crosby got his professional start with Whiteman as a member of a vocal trio called the "Rhythm Boys." Whiteman recorded this song in 1929, eleven years after its composition.

The work of Henry Creamer and Turner Layton, an African-American songwriting team, "After You've Gone" was written in 1918, early in the fox-trot era (perhaps this accounts for its irregular form). However, its qualifications as an up-to-date fox-trot song in other respects—conversational lyrics, riff-based melodic style, use of syncopation—are unquestionable. The performance features voice plus full dance orchestra (strings, saxophones, trumpets, trombones, and a full rhythm section). The rhythm section contains brass bass, drums, piano, and banjo alternating with guitar (this is a rhythm section in transition, both instrumentally and rhythmically).

Crosby's singing is light-voiced and jazz-inflected. The texture is relatively dense, with several distinct, hierarchically arranged roles: voice or instrumental melody; obbligato parts in other sections; and steady harmonic and rhythmic support from the rhythm section. Melodic statements are short, and most words, including the occasional slang expression ("blue," "pal") are only one syllable. The melody grows out of the two short ideas that open the song: the first ends on a syncopation that—in true jazz-influenced style—gives extra emphasis to the word, "gone." A steady, danceable fox-trot rhythm, clearly played at the beginning by brass bass and banjo, underpins the melody throughout the initial statement of chorus and verse. Later in the performance, there is a shift to a four-beat rhythm.

Songs like "After You've Gone" that maintained their popularity past their introduction on stage, record, or radio became *standards* and entered the permanent repertoire of singers and musicians. So it's not surprising that Whiteman would decide to record a song over a decade old, because it had never really lost its appeal.

Like the popular songs of earlier eras, "After You've Gone" has both a verse and chorus; in this respect, its larger form is similar compositionally to waltz and ragtime songs. However, the sheet-music version of this song differs from its performance here. Arrangements of the song for a band like Whiteman's during this period, concentrated on the chorus. The verse was an optional interlude. If a singer was featured, she or he would be spotlighted in the middle of the performance, usually after the verse. Instrumental statements of the chorus would frame the vocal. In this recording, the verse appears only once. It is interpolated into the middle of the performance and played, not sung.

This version of "After You've Gone" illustrates, in its five choruses, several of the important performing styles of the late twenties. The sequence of events on this recording is shown in Table 8.1.

Table 8.1	**Form of "After You've Gone"**
Introduction	Full band
First chorus	Saxophones, then strings (fox-trot style)
(Short interlude)	
Verse	Mostly strings, but with background accompanying riffs by the saxes.
Second chorus	Voice, with guitar obbligato (jazz-influenced singing style)
(Short interlude,	
derived from the	
verse)	

Third chorus	Trumpet, then trombone, solos (early jazz style)
(Short interlude)	
Fourth chorus	Violin and guitar (jazz style)
Fifth chorus	Full orchestra, with trumpets playing melody return to fox-trot style, but with more syncopation)

The recording is a summary of changes in arranging and performing style that took place during the twenties. It begins in the conservative dance-orchestra style of the teens and early twenties and ends in a jazz-influenced style that anticipates thirties swing. The first chorus and the verse feature strings prominently. But by the end of the recording they're very much in the background, perhaps symbolizing their diminishing importance in dance orchestras as the decade wore on. The interlude between the first chorus and verse grows out of a repeated three-note pattern that recalls late ragtime and early syncopated dance music (like "Memphis Blues"). Through the opening sections, a clear, if stodgy, fox-trot beat, established by brass bass and banjo, provides a steady, danceable rhythmic accompaniment. The rest of the recording quickly brings matters up to date. All three solo choruses, Crosby's vocal (sung in the intimate style made possible by microphones and amplification), the trumpet/trombone solos, and especially the violin-guitar duet (played by Joe Venuti and Eddie Lang, respectively) have an unmistakable jazz feel.

At the beginning of the vocal chorus, the guitarist shifts from backbeats to a definite "chunk" on every beat, although the bass continues to play only on alternate beats. During the violin solo, the drummer plays an open cymbal on the backbeats, and the guitarist ends the solo with a very clear swing rhythm.

Both Crosby and the instrumentalists approach the swing feel and heightened inflection of jazz. Listen to the way Crosby sings "there's no denyin'" or "some day." Notice the "blue" notes emphasized with extra sound and a sliding approach at the end of both the trumpet and trombone solos, or the swoops and dips throughout Venuti's violin solo. This jazz feeling carries over into the final chorus. It's apparent in the more relaxed phrasing of the melody and in passages like the descending chords that accompany the second "After You've Gone." The orchestration also looks to the future: brass and saxes are prominent, as in the swing bands of a decade later, while strings are barely audible.

So, the performance of the Whiteman band runs the gamut of twenties styles: syncopated dance music at the beginning; crooning; and then small group and big-band jazz.

CONCLUSION

"If I Had You" and "After You've Gone" document almost all the revolutionary changes of the period. Everything about the songs and their performances is new: the dance orchestra/jazz band with its full rhythm section; the fox-trot beat underneath the melody; the melody itself; and, the style of the lyric. These changes mark the beginning of the modern era in popular music.

Terms to Know

acoustic broadcasting/recording   amplifier   chorus-oriented form
crooner   electric broadcasting/recording   flapper
fox-trot   microphone   rhythm song
saxophone   speaker   standard
syncopated dance music

Names to Know

Vernon and Irene Castle   Bing Crosby   George Gershwin
Fletcher Henderson   Al Jolson   Sophie Tucker
Paul Whiteman

Study Questions

1. What were the eight changes in popular song and its performance that came about because of the revolution in popular music in the twenties?

2. What was the role of jazz, blues, and ragtime in this revolution? In what specific ways did each style contribute to the new music?

3. What was the "electrical revolution" of the twenties? What innovations resulted? How did it affect the production and dissemination of popular music? In what ways did electrical technology change the sound of popular music?

4. How was social dancing different in the teens and twenties from earlier styles? Why did "respectable citizens" consider it immoral? How did it affect appearance and fashion? How was it connected with the sexual revolution of the same time?

5. What characteristics differentiate an "old" from a "new"-style song?

6. How did the dance orchestra change in the twenties? What instruments were added? What instruments became less-prominent or disappeared entirely?

CHAPTER NINE

Jazz, 1920–1960

Jazz has been called America's art music. Many regard it as the nation's most important and distinctive cultural achievement. The recordings of its greatest artists—Louis Armstrong, Duke Ellington, Lester Young, Charlie Parker, Miles Davis, and others—comprise an invaluable legacy. Despite this lofty status, jazz has been on the fringes of popular taste for almost all of its history. It's as if jazz has been the eccentric sibling in the popular-music family, the one who marches to a different drummer, often with highly creative consequences.

Jazz passed through three evolutionary phases in the years between 1900 and 1965; each lasted about 20 years. In the first, from about 1900 to 1925, jazz was mostly a regional music, despite the notoriety of the first recorded jazz performances in the late teens. It was performed mainly in New Orleans, or elsewhere by expatriate New Orleans musicians. Its repertoire consisted mainly of instrumental blues and jazzed-up rags, dances, marches, or other multisectional forms. The collective improvisation of its front-line players gave the music a distinctive sound that is still identified as New Orleans jazz.

Jazz intersected with the pop mainstream in the years between 1925 and 1945. During this period, the instrumentation of the rhythm section became standardized and the swing conception became widely understood and refined. Big bands found receptive audiences for dancing and listening, while small groups also flourished. The jazz repertoire shifted from rags to popular song, or—occasionally—jazz tunes or compositions based on popular-song forms. Blues remained an important source of repertoire and expressive devices. Jazz also became more of a soloists' music, especially in small group settings.

In the final stage of its evolution, jazz became an art music: music strictly for listening. This period saw the liberation of most of the rhythm section from swing-style timekeeping, the creation of a distinct song repertory (although blues and popular songs were still common vehicles for improvisation), and the development of a more complex harmonic and melodic language.

Jazz has made inroads into the pop market, especially in the twenties and thirties, and it has certainly influenced the performance of popular music since the teens. Several important jazz musicians, most notably Louis

collective improvisation

swing

big band

improvisation

Armstrong and Benny Goodman, have achieved fame comparable to many pop stars. On balance, though, jazz has had a different agenda. If one judges by musical results and anecdotal evidence, the primary motivation for jazz musicians is their own creative fulfillment. Faced with a choice between a relatively secure livelihood as a commercial musician and a more precarious life spent pursuing their art, they may opt for the latter, even if it jeopardizes their security. This may explain to some extent why jazz has seldom been a commercially important style.

melisma

This chapter has two primary objectives: (1) to identify both those qualities that jazz shares with other popular styles and those that differentiate it; and (2) to offer a panoramic view of the jazz styles that have evolved since the original New Orleans jazz musicians left for Chicago and points east and west in the late teens.

JAZZ IS

Jazz, as defined by the work of its most significant artists, is an art music built on the rhythmic foundation of swing. As documented on recordings, jazz was a continuously evolving style for four decades, from the early 1920s to the early 1960s, at which point the fundamental premises of a swing rhythmic conception were stretched to, and even beyond, the breaking point by some of the most adventurous jazz musicians of the time.

There have been several styles in addition to jazz that have used a swing, or four-beat, rhythmic conception. The classic blues of the twenties, urban blues of the thirties, more commercialized swing from the big-band era, swing-influenced popular singing styles of the post–World War II era, and the jump bands and electric blues musicians in the forties and fifties are the most noteworthy examples. However, two qualities distinguish jazz from all other swing-based styles: its greater rhythmic subtlety; and richer melodic and harmonic invention.

In jazz, there is greater complexity and subtlety in the interplay between the swing rhythm and the musical events of a performance. In general, jazz musicians play with greater rhythmic freedom and nuance than other popular musicians. Both the rhythm section and other band members are less likely to reinforce the beat consistently. As we will hear in several recordings, breaks from timekeeping are an important feature of jazz rhythm. There is more rhythmic conflict, either from strong syncopated accents or from melodic lines that soar over the underlying pulse, than is found in other musical styles.

Similarly, jazz musicians tend to use a much more extensive melodic and harmonic vocabulary than blues musicians. To cite just one example, one chorus of a basic blues song has four changes of harmony involving three chords (see B. B. King's "No Good," Example 7.1), and a fairly simple melody. "Bluesette," a jazz tune written by Belgian guitarist/harmonica player "Toots" Thielmanns, features perhaps the most extensive harmonic elaboration of a blues progression ever to gain widespread currency: each chorus is built on a progression of twenty different chords!

Ⓓ

A swing-influenced performance from the popular tradition may have melodic and harmonic interest but lack the rhythmic daring and heightened inflection of blues, while a blues recording may feature the declamatory rhythm of intensified speech but lack melodic or harmonic variety. Jazz combines both elements and adds a third, the improvisation of a new melody.

IMPROVISATION AND THE FORM OF A JAZZ PERFORMANCE

head

Most jazz performances, whether for large ensemble, small combo, or even solo performer, follow a theme-and-variation form. A performance generally gets under way with a statement of the theme used for the variations. The theme, usually called a *head*, may be a blues song, the chorus of a popular song, or an original composition by a jazz artist.

A series of variations follows. These variations may be improvised or composed, and may feature one performer or several.

The performance concludes with a restatement (either literal or varied) of the original theme. An introduction may precede the opening statement of the theme; the performance may conclude with a short extension of the final statement of the theme, sometimes called a *tag*. A typical jazz performance can be outlined:

Introduction (optional)
Head (theme or melody of the song)
Variation 1 (improvised solo/composed variant)
An indeterminate number of variations
Last variation
Restatement of head
Tag (optional)

Improvisation is the art of spontaneous creation. In jazz, it usually refers to the ability of a musician to invent on the spot a new melody based on the theme and/or the harmonic progression that supports it. An improvised solo may mix several kinds of melodic devices: (1) riffs; (2) paraphrase of melodic ideas from the head (theme); (3) running notes, based on arpeggiated chords, scales, or a mixture of the two; and (4) completely new melodic ideas that mesh with the underlying harmony.

Improvisation is customary in jazz performance, but not essential to it. Many memorable jazz recordings, like several of Duke Ellington's masterworks, contain little or no improvisation. Furthermore, most jazz performances include sections—for example, the statement and restatement of the head—where little or no improvisation may take place.

II-10

IIA-10

In "Freddie the Freeloader" (Example 9.1), recorded in 1959 by the Miles Davis Sextet (Miles Davis, trumpet; Julian "Cannonball" Adderley, alto saxophone; John Coltrane, tenor saxophone; Wynton Kelly, piano; Paul Chambers, bass; and Jimmy Cobb, drums), we can hear the form of a typical jazz performance and a mix of typical improvisational approaches.

This performance shows the affinity of jazz with blues and several of the differences between them. "Freddie" is a blues in form: a twelve-measure melody supported for the most part by standard blues chords. However, Davis nestles a harmonic surprise at the end of each chorus. There are other differences. The head is a simple call-and-response theme between horns and piano that recalls the sectional exchanges of big-band style, instead of the standard three-phrase blues melody. Time is kept lightly by bass and

Miles Davis, "Birth of the Cool" session photograph, 1949.

drummer using the ride cymbal; a blues band would tend to mark the beat   ride cymbal
more heavily. And of course, there are no lyrics.

After two statements of the head, everyone except the drummer takes an extended solo: Kelly (piano); Davis (trumpet); Coltrane (tenor sax); Adderley (alto sax); and Chambers (bass). Of particular interest is Miles's solo, masterful in its simplicity. He begins simply by stating a single note three times. From that, he spins out a long melody that sustains tension through silence by carefully placing the melodic peaks higher, almost step by step. Although invented on the spot, this solo is an architectural master-piece, an unbroken line from beginning to end. As such, it transcends even the most infectious blues riff or well-crafted popular song. Solos such as these raise jazz to the level of art.

JAZZ IN THE TWENTIES

The history of jazz properly begins in the early twenties, when African-American jazz bands began to record with some frequency. According to anecdotal evidence, jazz began around the turn of the century in New Orleans, but in the absence of recorded evidence we know little about how the music actually sounded. We can only extrapolate back to 1900 from the twenties recordings by older, more established New Orleans bands.

King Oliver's Creole Jazz Band, San Francisco, CA, 1921; note the stereotypical poses the band takes. L to r: Minor "Ram" Hall (drums), Honoré Dutrey (trombone), King Oliver (cornet), Lil Hardin (piano), David Jones (C melody sax), Johnny Dodds (clarinet), Jimmy Palzo (violin), Ed Garland (bass).

front line

Joe "King" Oliver (1885–1938) was one of the major figures of early jazz. His reputation rests on his achievements as a bandleader and cornet player. Like many New Orleans musicians, he emigrated to Chicago in search of better-paying jobs following the closing of Storyville, New Orleans's red-light district, in 1917. By 1920, he had assembled several of his New Orleans expatriates into King Oliver's Creole Jazz Band, the finest traditional New Orleans style jazz band preserved on record. It contains the standard rhythm section of the time: banjo; piano; brass bass; and drums. Its front line (a term jazz musicians use to identify instruments, usually horns, that play melodic lines instead of keeping time; the term derives from the placement of horn/melody players on the bandstand) also displays the characteristic instrumentation and texture of New Orleans style.

The three prominent front-line instruments usually play within a well-defined range, particularly when playing together. The role of each front line instrument is:

The clarinet takes the highest part, playing a fast-moving countermelody to the main part

The cornet (trumpet) is the midrange instrument that usually carries the melody

The trombone carries the lowest melodic part, usually in the form of "commentary" on the melody and clarinet part.

All three (or four, when there's an extra cornet or saxophone) melody instruments typically play at the same time, a procedure known as *collective improvisation*. Although there are occasional solos, most of the performance proceeds with all instruments playing simultaneously, and with no one instrument completely dominant.

As a cornet player, Oliver developed an influential style deeply rooted in the blues. His solo in "Dippermouth Blues" (Example 9.2) was one of the most frequently imitated jazz solos of that generation. "Dippermouth Blues"

 II-11

 IIA-11

King Oliver's Creole Jazz Band in Chicago, 1923, in a more formal pose. L to r: Honoré Dutrey (trombone), Warren "Baby" Dodds (drums), King Oliver (cornet), Louis Armstrong (slide trumpet), Lil Hardin (piano), Bill Johnson (banjo), Johnny Dodds (clarinet).

is a blues song in form. Each section is twelve measures long, with the characteristic harmonic pattern of the blues. It is also a blues song in style, which is nowhere more evident than in Oliver's famous cornet solo. His playing parallels the heightened inflection, narrow range, and unconstrained rhythmic delivery of a blues singer. The manner in which he slides in and out of important notes is an instrumental counterpart to blues vocal style.

"Dippermouth Blues" shows the deep blues roots of early jazz and its heavy reliance on improvisation. "Jelly Roll" Morton's "Grandpa's Spells" (Example 9.3) also in New Orleans style, shows the influence of ragtime and highlights the role of the composer in a largely improvised music. One of the most colorful figures in the history of jazz, Ferdinand "Jelly Roll" Morton (1890–1941) claimed to have "invented" jazz. He was certainly its first great composer and one of its great pianists. "Grandpa's Spells," performed by Morton and his Red Hot Peppers, is one of the best examples of his compositional style.

II-12

IIB-1

Morton's compositional control is especially evident in two areas: formal design and textural variety. The form of "Grandpa's Spells" is the march/rag form from the turn of the century. Subsequent jazz performances seldom used such a sophisticated formal plan. Morton's textural variety is even more striking, as a comparison between "Dippermouth Blues" and this recording reveals. Whereas Oliver maintains the same thick-textured sound of collective improvisation throughout much of the performance, with only the occasional solo chorus, Morton changes the instrumentation of the band with great frequency, while varying rhythmic support, dynamic level, and other elements at the same time. There is more textural variety in the first two strains of "Grandpa's Spells" than there is in the entire performance of

Jelly Roll Morton, Chicago, c. 1923.

"Dippermouth Blues." In the work of Morton and the other great jazz composers, composition does not necessarily eliminate improvisation; it simply controls the context in which it takes place. Table 9.1 outlines the formal plan and textural variation of "Grandpa's Spells."

Table 9.1	**Formal Outline of Jelly Roll Morton's "Grandpa's Spells"**
Section	Instrumentation and Other Features
Introduction	Full band
A	Guitar break/Full band answer
A′	Trumpet break/Full band answer (piano "comments")
B	Full Band with riff pattern in rhythm/piano break
B′	Clarinet solo with break at the end
A″	Trombone, bass solos, then full band (bass in walking 4 beat)

C	Muted trumpet with reduced rhythm section (bass in 2)
C'	Clarinet solo, with stop-time at beginning
C"	Piano solo-clarinet solo with banjo accompaniment
C'''	Full band (final rush to end)
Coda	Guitar break

With the influx of New Orleans jazz musicians like King Oliver and Jelly Roll Morton into Northern cities and the recording of both white and African-American musicians, jazz became a national music in the early twenties. Chicago was its crucible. The city was wide open—Al Capone and other gang leaders all but ran it—and musicians found ample employment opportunities in speakeasies and ballrooms. A generation of white musicians, among them Bix Beiderbecke and Benny Goodman, absorbed the sound of the New Orleans musicians firsthand, much as white rockers absorbed Chicago blues style in the sixties.

LOUIS ARMSTRONG, THE FIRST GREAT JAZZ SOLOIST

One musician whom Oliver brought to Chicago was a young cornet player named Louis Armstrong (1898?–1971). Soon Armstrong would outstrip his mentor, and establish himself as the first great soloist in the history of jazz, one of only two jazz musicians (Charlie Parker was the other) whose influence pervaded jazz for a generation. He set new standards for instrumental virtuosity, improvisational brilliance, and tone quality. Singlehandedly, he changed the direction of jazz performance from a balanced, collective conception to one in which soloists, each featured in turn, dominated the texture at any given time. By extending the range of the trumpet into that formerly occupied by the clarinet, he upset the balance within the front line, making his trumpet the dominant voice.

The dramatic change in the interaction of the front-line instruments can

Louis Armstrong, 1944.

II-13

IIB-2

be heard by comparing "West End Blues" (Example 9.4), in which Armstrong dominates whenever he's playing, to the more balanced interplay heard in "Dippermouth Blues."

In his book *Early Jazz*, Gunther Schuller identified four qualities of Armstrong's performing style that elevate him head and shoulders above his peers. They are:

1. His superior choice of notes and the resultant shape of his melodic lines
2. His incomparable basic quality of tone
3. His equally incomparable sense of swing, that is, the sureness with which notes are placed in the time continuum and the remarkably varied attack and release properties of his phrasing
4. The subtly varied repertory of vibratos and shakes with which Armstrong colors and embellishes individual notes, perhaps his most individual contribution

These criteria could also serve for evaluating the work of any major jazz soloist.

Schuller's four gauges of Armstrong's excellence are amply demonstrated in Armstrong's recording of "West End Blues." The introduction features a free-flowing cascade, spanning almost the entire usable range of the trumpet in two big swoops. This is the first of many examples in this recording of Armstrong's beautiful tone and melodic invention.

"West End Blues" is a blues in style and harmonic form. It appears as if it would also follow the melodic format of a blues song, until halfway through the first chorus, when Armstrong plays a series of flourishes, that while not very singable, have well-defined melodic and rhythmic profiles. The progress of this opening chorus, from the blues-like riffs with which Armstrong begins to the more elaborate instrumentally conceived ideas at the end, brings into focus one of the primary distinctions between blues and jazz. Throughout the solo, Armstrong informs his playing with the rhythmic nuance and heightened inflection of the blues. But while the opening phrase could be a blues song, the last half of the chorus exhibits the melodic and harmonic richness that separates even a heavily blues-influenced jazz style from its roots.

Armstrong closes out this chorus with a steadily rising arpeggio that ends on a sustained high note that gives an excellent illustration of his use of a shake to color the basic sound of an important note. Notice also that the chord instruments (banjo and piano) "chunk" out a steady four-beat rhythm, and the other front-line instruments are in a subordinate, not balanced, relationship with the trumpet.

The second chorus, performed by the trombone, offers a vivid contrast, showing the enormous difference in creativity and skill between Armstrong and the more typical musicians of his day.

Armstrong returns on the third chorus, but he performs as a vocalist rather than playing the trumpet. Armstrong reputedly invented scat singing during a record session when he forgot the words to a song, so instead sang a series of expressive nonsense syllables. The style became enormously popular, both for its expressiveness and humorous sound. Armstrong's musical conception remains the same, regardless of whether he plays or sings; when he sings, he offers the same kinds of ideas in a different package. As in the opening chorus, Armstrong breaks out of the limited melodic framework of the blues. The chorus begins with a call-and-response exchange between clarinet and voice. Armstrong's first few responses are relatively simple paraphrases of the clarinet riff, but after the fifth riff, he sings several wide-ranging phrases that quickly override the relatively simple and regular clarinet part.

The fourth chorus is performed by pianist Earl Hines. Hines was Armstrong's most important musical collaborator, and the only musician of the period whose virtuosity, swing, and invention matched Armstrong's. Especially interesting is the second phrase of the chorus, beginning a third of the way through, where Hines suddenly implies a tempo twice as fast as before. Hines adapted Armstrong's unique trumpet style to the piano (or perhaps vice versa; there was considerable give and take between the two), and it's heard most clearly from this point on.

Armstrong's final chorus is one of the great moments in the recorded history of jazz. He begins with a sustained tone at the top of his range that lasts for over ten seconds. He shows the subtlety of his sense of swing by playing five rhythmically varied statements of a simple four-note riff, none of which conforms exactly to the underlying beat. He breaks out of the riff with another of his patented top-to-bottom-to-top melodic flourishes, which he ends with a rip to the highest note in the last part of the phrase.

Armstrong's most significant contribution to jazz was establishing a standard of improvisational excellence. However, he also played a major role in another significant development in the late twenties and early thirties: jazz interpretations of the popular song repertoire. Much of the music recorded by early jazzmen, including many of Armstrong's small group recordings, were blues, multisectional rag-like works, or instrumentals. In the late twenties and early thirties, Armstrong crossed over into the popular market, singing and playing the Tin Pan Alley hits of the day. These recordings were extremely influential. Although he was not the first jazz musician to record popular songs, he, in effect, legitimized the practice—if Armstrong does it, then it's okay if we do it. He also showed how it could be done well. After 1930, most jazz performances were head/solos/head versions of popular songs or instrumentals (like "Wrappin' It Up" [Example 9.5] and "Harlem Air Shaft" [Example 9.6]) that used standard popular song forms. This shift in repertoire helped lay the groundwork for the commercial breakthrough of jazz.

BIG-BAND SWING: JAZZ AS COMMERCIAL MUSIC

In 1935, Benny Goodman and his orchestra exploded on the popular-music scene through a national tour and network radio broadcast series, "Let's Dance," bringing the sound of big-band swing to the American public. Their success opened the doors for several other big bands. During its relatively brief period of popularity, swing suddenly became an important dimension in popular music.

Swing was the jazz of the thirties and early forties. More than anything else, it was a dance music. It was jazz with a clear beat, lots of syncopation,

Benny Goodman, New York City, 1937.

and a rhythmic vitality to which a generation responded by dancing the jitterbug and lindy hop. It came into being with the standardization of big-band instrumentation and the clear marking of a four-beat rhythm by a full rhythm section (guitar, piano, string bass, and drums). As such, swing was a welcome antidote to the increasingly sentimental popular songs and crooning singing styles of the late twenties and early thirties.

Big-band swing had its roots not only in the jazz of Armstrong and others, but also in the syncopated dance orchestras of the twenties. Fletcher Henderson's dance orchestra (see Example 8.3) laid the groundwork for the swing style in the thirties, as did Paul Whiteman's band, which employed several leading jazz musicians of the twenties (see Examples 8.4 and 8.7) Duke Ellington led a dance/show band at Harlem's Cotton Club from 1927 to 1931, during which time it matured from a dance orchestra into a swing band.

Swing achieved its fullest artistic expression in the work of soloists like saxophonists Lester Young and Coleman Hawkins, clarinetist Benny Goodman, and trumpeter Roy Eldridge, and in the big bands of Ellington, Count Basie, Glenn Miller, Tommy Dorsey, and Goodman. It enjoyed its greatest commercial success in the music of the white swing bands. Only in the swing era was jazz truly a popular music, although some of the most popular swing bands did not really swing.

Fletcher Henderson (1898–1952), an African-American composer and arranger active from the early twenties, was a central figure in establishing the sound of big-band swing. In his arrangements, he organized the band into sections. He also established call-and-response patterns between sections, written-out sectional solos, and most of the other characteristic features of big-band style. Benny Goodman bought many of Henderson's arrangements for his band just before his rise to fame, so it was the

 II-5

 IIA-5

 II-6, 9

 IIA-6, 9

Henderson sound that Goodman popularized and other bandleaders and arrangers copied.

The characteristic features of big-band swing style are outlined in Table 9.2.

Table 9.2   Characteristic Styles Features of Big-Band Swing

Instrumentation	Rhythm section: guitar, piano, string bass, drums
	Sax section: five saxes (two alto, two tenor, one baritone)
	Trumpet section: three to four trumpets
	Trombone section: three to four trombones
Rhythm	Timekeeping: equal emphasis on every beat by guitar, bass, and bass drum
	Backbeat: drummer's hi-hat pattern: open/shut/open/shut
	Conflict: syncopated riff figures from brass and sax sections; piano "comping" patterns or riffs
Melody	Most big-band songs are simple riffs or riff exchanges between sections, developed into songs using blues or popular-song (e.g., AABA) forms.
Texture	Melodic statements almost always feature call-and-response exchanges between horn sections over a steady, timekeeping rhythm section. Other textural possibilities include solos with various kinds of accompanying figures: sustained chords and riffs are most common.
Form	Big-band performances generally follow the theme-and-variation procedure used in jazz: introduction; statement of the melody; a series of solos by different members of the band; perhaps a written-out variation featuring an entire section; and a restatement of the melody.

hi-hat

comping

The essential ingredients of Henderson's conception are present in "Wrappin' It Up" (Example 9.5). This early swing tune, performed by Henderson's band, is virtually a textbook presentation of swing style.

 II-14

 IIB-3

The introduction is a capsule summary of the rhythmic vitality of swing. It features the horn sections playing a riff figure that is syncopated against the rhythm section's steady four-beat foundation.

The first chorus, which contains the statement of the melody, shows the most important features of a swing arrangement. The rhythm section, essentially timekeeping in function, lays down a steady four-beat pattern. The sax section, treated as a unit, develops a melody out of a riff. The brass answer the saxes in the gaps between riff statements, an updated form of

Fletcher Henderson Band, New York, 1924. L to r: Howard Scott, Coleman Hawkins, Louis Armstrong, Charlie Dixon, Fletcher Henderson, Kaiser Marshall, Buster Bailey, Elmer Chambers, Charlie Green, Bob Escudero, Don Redman.

call and response. In the second phrase of the first chorus, the entire band plays the riff figure, which is highly syncopated.

After the opening melodic statement, the performance proceeds in a typical jazz theme-and-variations form. Perhaps the most interesting feature is the variety of accompanying patterns during the solos. For instance, the second chorus begins with an improvised sax solo, accompanied by sustained chords in the brass; this texture is sustained throughout the solo. The third chorus begins with a trumpet solo, supported this time with a more active riff figure in the saxes. Halfway through the first phrase of this chorus, the entire band joins together in a variation of the original melody.

The final chorus begins by featuring brass and clarinets (played by the saxophonists) in the characteristic call-and-response dialogue, and continues with a clarinet solo over sustained brass chords. The sax players then switch back to playing their main instruments for the second half of this chorus, which presents what amounts to a written-out solo for the entire sax section. The performance wraps up with the entire band.

This recording illustrates the most characteristic elements of big-band swing style. It has the four-beat rhythmic foundation with conflict between rhythm and horn sections, with the standard instrumentation of the swing big band, grouped by section. The head of the arrangement is a riff-based melody. And the various combinations of sections shows much of the range of possibilities in composing or arranging for big band.

II-15

IIB-4

Duke Ellington's "Harlem Air Shaft" (Example 9.6) illustrates the difference between good workmanship and real craft within the popular-music tradition. On the surface, it has much in common with the typical big-band swing compositions of the day. Its melodic form is borrowed from Tin Pan Alley, a four-phrase form in which the first, second, and last phrases are

Duke Ellington (at piano) with his Cotton Club Orchestra, 1931.

identical and the third phrase is different (AABA); each phrase develops from a riff. In addition, it basically follows the larger formal plan of a typical jazz performance of this era: a statement of the melody; a series of improvised variations on the melody; and a final somewhat varied restatement of the melody.

Ellington's artistry finds expression in two general ways: by including subtle variation or enrichment of the musical texture; and by superimposing a strong sense of beginning and end on the performance.

In the introduction, Ellington shows his fondness for varied instrumental color by spotlighting each section within the band (trumpets, saxes, and trombones in turn). Each section's statement not only highlights the instrument, but also anticipates the general character of that section's featured solo. After the introduction, Ellington upgrades the routine statement of the melody by contrasting the repetitious riff of the trumpets with a more interesting and sustained line in the saxophones. Textures enriched by several competing parts are an Ellington trademark.

Later, the source of additional interest is rhythmic: the B sections of both the second and third choruses feature supporting riffs that create excitement through rhythmic variation of a simple melodic idea, a short scale in the saxes, and a repeated note in the brass. None of these features represents a dramatic departure from standard practice in big-band swing. Rather, they represent ways in which Ellington does the same things that other composers do, but in a more interesting manner.

In the final chorus, we hear Ellington convincingly solve one of the most enduring problems of jazz performance: how to convey a sense of finality to the end of a performance in a style that is essentially open ended. Ellington's final chorus accumulates tremendous momentum as it moves toward the final notes. It begins softly, with an extended variant of the opening trumpet riff. At the B section, it builds in three ways: the drummer's heavy backbeat; a rise in volume; and the use of a shorter riff, combined with quick inter-jections from the clarinet. The final A section begins with an even quicker exchange of riffs (every four beats instead of every eight), a higher range, and louder dynamics; together they produce a climactic rise in intensity. The syncopated chords just before the end inject even more excitement into the proceedings. Ellington doesn't simply stop the performance after restating the melody. Instead, he creates irresistible momentum to the final chords, so that we feel that the performance is over because we have arrived at the end.

Ellington's stature as one of the great American composers is well-deserved. His craftsmanship finds expression in large-scale concerns as well as more subtle details. The extra measure of care and imagination help ele-vate his music to a level well above his many gifted contemporaries.

SMALL-GROUP JAZZ IN THE SWING ERA

Although big-band swing was more commercially successful and better known, small-group jazz remained a vital part of the jazz scene through the thirties and early forties. Many of the important bandleaders of the swing era, among them Benny Goodman, Duke Ellington, Count Basie, Artie Shaw, and Lionel Hampton, also performed and/or recorded with small groups, either from their own band or assembled specifically for a record-ing session. "I've Found a New Baby" (Example 9.7) brings together two of these bandleaders, Benny Goodman and Count Basie. They are joined by "Cootie" Williams, an Ellington alumnus, on trumpet, Charlie Christian on guitar, Georgie Auld on tenor sax, Arthur Bernstein on bass, and Jo Jones, Basie's drummer.

 II-16

 IIB-5

Benny Goodman (1909–1986), dubbed the King of Swing, left a sub-stantial musical legacy. He popularized jazz, helped integrate it racially, and performed it at the highest level. As we have noted, it was his band that launched the Swing Era, jazz's first and only flirtation with commercial suc-cess. He was the first white bandleader to tour with African-American mu-sicians, although he typically performed with them only in small group settings. Many stops on his tours did not permit performances by integrat-ed bands, so his big band was originally all white. His small group record-ings are among the finest jazz performances of the swing era.

Goodman's "I Found a New Baby" is particularly instructive in three ways. It gives us our first example of a jazz performance of a popular song; it presents, even more clearly than the two big-band recordings, the time-keeping in the rhythm section that was the foundation of swing style; and it illustrates three of the four jazz main improvisational strategies: melodic paraphrase, harmonically based running notes, and repeated riffs.

The performance begins with the most distinctive drum sound of the swing era: a ride pattern played on the hi-hat. This sound was Jo Jones's sem-inal contribution to jazz drumming. A highly syncopated riff then leads into the statement of the theme.

"I Found a New Baby" is a Tin Pan Alley popular song in AABA form. Perhaps because Goodman does not take a solo later in the performance, his statement of the head first elaborates, then diverges from, the melody rather than stating it literally. The first two phrases follow the original melody of the song fairly closely. But the bridge and final A section feature Goodman's own melodic ideas, not the tune. Throughout Goodman's presentation of the head, the rhythm section, with guitar and bass playing on every beat, lays down a rock-solid swing rhythm. They can be most clearly heard in the B section. Goodman's chorus is a good illustration of improvisation through melodic paraphrase.

The first solo belongs to electric guitarist Charlie Christian. His improvisation bears no resemblance to the melody; instead, he creates a new melody consisting mostly of streams of rapid notes, although it begins with a riff. These notes outline and embellish the chord progression that supports the song's melody. The streams do not fall into any regular pattern. They are varied in length and they begin on different beats within the measure. Toward the end of the solo (the beginning of the last A section), Christian plays a riff-like figure, then toys with it rhythmically by alternating two accented notes first on, then off the beat, before ending the idea with a final spurt. Christian's solo illustrates harmonically based improvisation. His style was an important influence on bebop—as well as electric blues guitarists like T-Bone Walker.

Count Basie's solo presents improvisation through riff repetition and variation, an option more customarily heard in big-band and jump-band performances. The riff used in the introduction returns in each of the A sections, setting up call-and-response exchanges between horns/guitar and piano. The rhythm section can again be clearly heard throughout this chorus, especially during the bridge (B section), when the riff gives way to an exchange of arpeggios between Basie and Goodman.

The next chorus features two half-chorus solos that contrast melodic and harmonic improvisational styles. Trumpeter Cootie Williams invents a new melody by combining riff-like figures, such as the series of repeated notes, occasional paraphrases of the melody, and melodic ideas borrowed from his personal inventory-ideas that he used frequently before and after this recording. George Auld's sax solo, particularly the opening phrase, consists almost exclusively of arpeggiated chords, arranged to provide the occasional syncopation.

This final segment of the performance lasts only half a chorus, probably because of the three-minute time constraint on recordings of this era. The first phrase features drummer Jo Jones, whose solo is punctuated periodically by riffs. The final phrase turns back the clock, recalling the collective improvisation characteristic of New Orleans jazz. The trumpet restates the melody, while clarinet and saxophone (replacing trombone) improvise complementary lines.

In this performance, all the connotations of "swing" are apparent. The performance swings because of the rhythmic interplay of the soloists with the rhythm section. This interplay takes several forms: the marked syncopations of the opening riff, Goodman's bent notes that glide over the beat, and, in Christian's solo, phrases that end abruptly off the beat and the on-again/off-again accents at the end. (Chuck Berry's "Johnny B. Goode" [Example 14.5] solo uses the same device, but superimposed on a different rhythmic conception.) The most recognizable elements of "swing" style are the instrumentation and beatkeeping style of the rhythm section and the call-and-response exchange of riffs in the second chorus. "I Found a New Baby" adheres to the typical formal organization of small group jazz perfor-

 IV-5

 IVA-5

mance: a series of improvised solos, framed by (in this case, paraphrased and incomplete) statements of the head. Each solo relates directly to the melody and/or harmony of the tune.

BOP AND POST-BOP JAZZ

bop

Bop was an art-jazz style that evolved directly out of swing. It was revolutionary in intent and execution. An outgrowth of the experimentation of a few musicians based in New York during World War II—most notably, saxophonist Charlie Parker, trumpeter Dizzy Gillespie, drummers Max Roach and Kenny Clarke, and pianists Thelonius Monk and Bud Powell—bop stunned the jazz world because it differed so radically from swing style. It stretched the rhythmic, melodic, and harmonic boundaries of swing past the comfort zone. In its rapid tempo, angular melodies, complex harmonies, and unpredictable rhythms, it was also clearly an art style, not music for dancing.

Bop was the original counterculture music. The musicians who developed it elected to cut themselves off not only from an unsophisticated public, but also from those musicians who weren't ready or willing to accept its innovations. In its mature form, bop represented:

Listening music. Bop was a jazz style unquestionably divorced from any association with dance. Its tempos were often too fast for dancing, and the rhythm section was less concerned with establishing an easily felt pulse and more concerned with creating a rich, rhythmically conflicting texture.

Music for an artistic elite. Bop was a style deliberately exclusionary in intent. It stretched the harmonic vocabulary of jazz, lifted the level of virtuosity demanded of its performers, and, with its rhythmically irregular phrasing, demanded a much more sophisticated rhythmic sense from them. Only a few jazz musicians in the forties possessed all these skills, and jam sessions became trials by fire for aspiring young musicians.

Musical expression of a counterculture philosophy. In their lifestyle, appearance, and music, bop musicians sought to isolate themselves not only from the white mainstream, but from more traditional African-American musicians. They envisioned their jazz as an art music comparable in value and interest to European art music. Their music expressed their sense of dignity and self-worth, despite the persistent racial discrimination institutionalized in so many aspects of American society.

 II-17
 IIB-6

Bop style revolutionized almost every aspect of jazz performance. "Koko" (Example 9.8), featuring Charlie Parker, along with Dizzy Gillespie, on trumpet and piano, bassist Curley Russell, and Max Roach, gives an excellent overview of these changes, including:

The emancipation of the rhythm section. Two changes identified the new sound of the bop and post-bop rhythm section. The guitar ceased to be a regular part of the rhythm section. It was used most frequently in bop and postbop either as a solo instrument or as an alternative chord instrument to the piano.

Charlie Parker, c. 1949.

Also, both piano and drums became almost completely liberated from timekeeping. Pianists "comped," or played occasional chord fragments to provide accents, often falling on the offbeats. Their role was to add to the overall rhythmic conflict even as they outlined the harmonies being used for improvisation. Drummers kept time only on the ride cymbal, using their right hand. They used the left foot to operate the hi-hat. The hi-hat was closed on backbeats, as in swing drumming. The right foot and left hand were used to provide intermittent, syncopated accents on bass and snare (or other) drum. Only the bass marked time in bop and postbop jazz.

Rapid tempos. Tempo took a quantum leap in bop. Up-tempo swing tunes, like the two big band examples included above, moved at about 200 beats a minute. "Koko" has a tempo of about 300 beats a minute, a 50 percent increase! One reason for this dramatic jump was simply the exhilaration the musicians felt improvising fluently at such daredevil speeds—it was the downhill skiing of music. However, there was, I believe, also a macho element. Cutting contests—extended jam sessions in which jazz musicians would compete like Old West gunslingers—had been part of the jazz world in the thirties and early forties, especially in Kansas City, where Charlie Parker grew up. Parker reportedly embarrassed himself at a couple of jam sessions while still a novice musician. Humiliated, he started practicing about ten hours a day. Within three years, he had acquired total mastery of his instrument, and could easily outplay those who had mocked him earlier. Bop was his revenge—a style that they couldn't understand, and couldn't play even if they had understood it.

asymmetrical melody line

Asymmetrical, irregular melodic lines. Bop lines came out in spurts: streams of fast notes (almost always ending on an offbeat) intermittently interrupted by silence or punctuated by irregular, riff-like figures. These lines typically elaborate the underlying harmony of the head, using an approach similar to that heard in the Charlie Christian solo (see Example 9.7). Because there was such a discrepancy between the statement of the head and the improvising style, bop musicians created new heads on standard blues and popular-song chord progressions. The staid "Whispering," (Example 8.4) became "Groovin' High" when fitted with a new, more bop-like melody. "Koko," the example presented below, is based on "Cherokee," the theme song of Charlie Barnet's popular swing band. Bop heads and improvisations represented a big jump in complexity, when compared to the regular riff figures and simple arpeggiations of swing style.

Complex harmony. Bop musicians enriched the harmonic vocabulary of jazz, adding an array of complex chords to the relatively simple harmony of blues and popular song. Like virtually every other feature of bop style, noninitiates found this difficult to master.

An aggressive sonority. Bop horn players, especially Parker and Gillespie, turned their back on the warm, mellow timbres of swing-era horn players. Parker, in particular, opted for a full but penetrating sound, usually produced with little or no vibrato.

JAZZ IN THE FIFTIES

Jazz in the fifties went through a period of consolidation. Musicians assimilated the advances of bop into a range of styles. East Coast musicians, mostly African-American, maintained the new freedom of the rhythm section while retreating somewhat from the rhythmic and melodic angularity of bop style. West Coast musicians, mostly white, developed "cool" jazz, a less emotionally charged style, but one that continued to extend the harmonic vocabulary of jazz. Some musicians and groups, like the Modern Jazz Quartet, Max Roach and Sonny Rollins, Charles Mingus, and Horace Silver, created highly personal idioms built on elements of bop style. "Django" (Example 9.9), written by John Lewis and performed by the Modern Jazz Quartet (Milt Jackson, vibes; John Lewis, piano; Percy Heath, bass; and Connie Kay, drums), illustrates one such style.

cool jazz

 II-18

 IIB-7

The work of the Modern Jazz Quartet gives evidence of a highly individual approach to jazz, one that has elicited comparisons with classical chamber music. One reason for this comparison is the sense of architecture conveyed by John Lewis's compositional approach. Much like Jelly Roll Morton in "Grandpa's Spells" (Example 9.3), Lewis shapes the overall structure of a performance without sacrificing improvisational freedom.

In "Django," Lewis superimposes an arch design onto the standard theme-and-variations form by carefully increasing, then decreasing, the amount of activity in the rhythm section. "Django" (dedicated to Belgian jazz guitarist Django Reinhardt) begins out of tempo: the first two phrases of the head have no underlying pulse. A steady beat is implied in the next few phrases by piano chords at the beginning of every measure. The final phrase of the head grows out of a syncopated two-note melodic idea.

In the vibes solo that follows, bass and drums begin by offering tentative support, the bass by playing only on alternate beats, drums by using brushes. As the solo progresses, all three rhythm instruments assume a more active role: the piano comps more busily; the bassist shifts to a walking pattern, then a riff; and the drummer trades brushes for drumsticks while increasing the amount of rhythmic conflict with offbeat accents on the snare drum.

At the structural midpoint of the performance, the last phrase of the head returns twice as fast as before: it is the keystone in the arch of activity Lewis has created. Bass and drums resume their prior level of activity as Lewis's solo begins. The bass riff introduced earlier returns; its gradual deceleration counterbalances the gradual increase in activity during the vibes solo. A final statement of the head, this time played with a steady, if mostly implied, pulse, concludes the performance.

The preeminent jazz musician in the fifties and sixties, especially after Charlie Parker's death in 1955, was Miles Davis (1926–1992). Davis had one of the most distinctive sounds in the history of jazz and was an improviser of great imagination. This alone would have secured his reputation. However, he was even more influential as the stylistic navigator of jazz. For over two decades, Davis created or oversaw almost all the important trends in jazz. Among them were the birth of "cool" jazz in the late forties, intersections with classical music (his unique "Sketches of Spain" album), and innovative jazz harmonies (see Example 9.10), through the jazz/rock fusions of the late sixties and early seventies. He also had a keen ear for talent and the prestige to attract it. Playing with Miles's band was a rite of passage for the top jazz musicians of the last several decades.

II-19

IIB-8

"So What" (Example 9.10), composed by Davis and performed by his 1959 sextet (Miles Davis, trumpet; Cannonball Adderley, alto sax; John Coltrane, tenor sax; Bill Evans, piano; Paul Chambers, bass; Jimmy Cobb, drums), revolutionized jazz harmony. Jazz harmony had become increasingly complex in many postbop styles. Chord progressions, the series of chords that served as the basis for improvisation, included more complex chords and changed from chord to chord more rapidly. These complicated chord progressions represented a challenge to even the most skillful musicians; they were an obstacle course instead of a vehicle of expression.

Jazz musicians had created these complex progressions in an effort to freshen the harmonic language of jazz. Davis took a different approach. He pointed jazz harmony in a completely different direction by simplifying it instead of making it more complicated. In "So What," he created a new chord by stacking the notes of the pentatonic scale, one on top of the other. At the same time, he slowed the chord rhythm down to a snail's pace. "So What," a thirty-two measure AABA form, uses only two basic chords per chorus: the original chord during the A sections, and the same chord at the next higher pitch during the B section. Davis's harmonic breakthrough influenced jazz in the sixties, especially the fusion styles that developed toward the end of the decade.

The harmony of "So What" is its most distinctive feature. The introduction is also unusual for a jazz performance of the period (or, for that matter, any period): the delicate, tentative bass/piano duet is a rare and beautiful beginning. By coupling the introduction with a fadeout ending, Davis breaks down the frame that a decisive beginning and end give to a performance.

In other respects, "So What" (like its companion example, "Freddie the Freeloader" [Example 9.1]) puts a new spin on conventional practice. The head is a good example. In its exchange of call-and-response riffs, first between bass and piano, then between bass and horns, "So What" harks back to the swing style of the late thirties. However, these exchanges showcase the bass, the least likely melody instrument in any jazz group.

The rest of the performance follows the typical head/solos/head format. All four solos are fine; two—Davis's and Coltrane's—are masterpieces. Davis's solo is a classic, another memorable example of his ability to create an expressive and logically structured musical statement on the spur of the moment.

It also illustrates what might be called Davis's "art swing." Jazz soloists typically create a sense of swing in two stages. They emphasize the beat by dividing it into a long/short pattern—DOO-bah-DOO-bah-DOO-bah-DOO-bah—then periodically replace one of the soft, short notes with a strong accent: DOO-bah-DOO-BOP. The opening phrase of the head of "Koko" is a clear illustration of this practice. In swing-based styles, beat and syncopation react to each other like magnets with the same electrical charge: the heavier the beat, the stronger the accent against it. The most exaggerated form of this kind of rhythmic conflict can be heard in the rhythm and blues of the forties and early fifties, like Joe Turner's "Shake, Rattle, and Roll" (Example 14.2).

IV-2

IVA-2

Davis's rhythmic approach goes in the opposite direction. His rhythm section lays down a much more delicate, flowing pulse. Davis floats over this pulse by deviating from it ever so slightly—a little before the beat here, a little after it there. The result is a swing that creates rhythmic tension without being overly obvious. This subtle rhythmic nuance is much more difficult to master, and Davis did it better than anyone else.

CONCLUSION

"So What," recorded for the same album as "Freddie the Freeloader," brings us full circle. Between 1920 and 1960, jazz progressed through a series of styles, from New Orleans to swing to bop and postbop. All were based on a four-beat rhythmic conception. Midway through this evolution, jazz changed from a dance-oriented music into a music strictly for listening.

In the work of its great artists, like Armstrong, Parker, and Davis, jazz combined the rhythmic freedom and intensity of expression of the blues with the harmonic, melodic, and—at times—formal sophistication of European art music. Some performances were largely improvised; others were composed, in part or almost completely. At their core, however, was always swing, the rhythmic high-wire act central to jazz of any style. Armstrong, Parker, Davis, Coltrane, and the other great jazz artists were able to defy the musical gravity of the beat by interspersing accents and patterns that reacted against it or floated over it without losing their awareness of the pulse. Jazz musicians swing; nonjazz musicians don't. It is as simple as that.

Terms to Know

asymmetrical melody line	big band	bop
collective improvisation	comping	cool jazz
front line	head	hi-hat
improvisation	ride cymbal	swing
walking bass		

Names to Know

Louis Armstrong	Count Basie	Charlie Christian
Miles Davis	Duke Ellington	Dizzy Gillespie
Benny Goodman	Joseph "King" Oliver	Modern Jazz Quartet
Jelly Roll Morton	Charlie Parker	

Study Questions

1. What is the organization of a typical jazz performance?
2. What is the role of improvisation in jazz? Is it essential to a jazz performance? Is it customary? What are some of the approaches to improvisation?
3. List some of the characteristics of the New Orleans style. What is its typical instrumentation? How do the instruments interact?
4. Explain "swing" as a verb, noun, and adjective (as in swing rhythm) in relation to jazz performance.
5. Jazz and blues are closely related. What qualities do they share? How do they differ?
6. What is the typical instrumentation of a big band? How many sections does it have? What are their roles?
7. How did the role of the rhythm section change from swing to bop style?
8. In what ways is bop different from swing-era jazz?
9. Choose either Louis Armstrong, Duke Ellington, Charlie Parker, or Miles Davis. Describe how his music fits into the history of jazz. What were his major innovations? How did he differ from other players?

CHAPTER TEN

Popular Song and Singing After 1930

The four decades between 1920 and 1960 were the golden age of Tin Pan Alley song. Almost a dozen superb songwriters turned out hundreds of memorable songs: standards that continue to please. In 1925, Irving Berlin and Jerome Kern had been active for over a decade. Gershwin's first hit came in 1919, and his first hit show in 1924. Joining them after 1925 would be Rodgers and Hart, Fats Waller, Cole Porter, Hoagy Carmichael, Harold Arlen, and Duke Ellington, among others. For the better part of two decades, they created hit after hit.

Tin Pan Alley song was simply "popular song" until the sixties. It was the mainstream style, so pervasive that it didn't require a qualifying term. Only when a song had an exceptional feature—a blues song (Harold Arlen's "Blues in the Night"), a rhythm song (Irving Berlin's "Puttin' on the Ritz"), a Latin song (Cole Porter's "Begin the Beguine")—did it acquire a more specific designation. It wasn't until rock became the mainstream style that it became necessary to distinguish between two types of popular song.

Songwriters brought everything together between 1925 and 1930. Lyrics were colloquial, yet often sophisticated, especially those of Lorenz Hart, Ira Gershwin, Cole Porter, and Andy Razaf. Both melody and accompaniment incorporated elements of jazz and blues. The new, chorus-oriented AABA form became standard at that time. It would remain the most widely used design for about three decades, and a point of departure for more imaginative forms, as we'll see below.

If there's one recording that epitomizes the new popular song style, it would be Irving Berlin's "Cheek to Cheek" (Example 10.1), performed by Fred Astaire. One of five hits to come out of the 1935 film musical *Top Hat,* "Cheek to Cheek" was unquestionably popular, arguably the biggest hit of the thirties. Several artists recorded it, and Astaire's version was the most popular recording of the decade. Even more significant than its popularity, however, was what the song represented: "Cheek to Cheek" symbolized the unquestioned acceptance by the establishment of the danceable, syncopated song. The elegant dancing of Astaire and Ginger Rogers—*Top Hat* was fourth of ten films they made together—was considered to be the epitome of style and grace. Even more specifically, the lyrics to "Cheek to Cheek" (. . . "I'm in heaven . . . when we're out together dancing cheek to cheek") glorify "lingering close contact." Only a generation earlier, such

Ginger Rogers and Fred Astaire in Swingtime, *1936.*

contact was considered so immoral that young couples were jailed for dancing so intimately.

Two aspects of the song and this performance are of particular interest. First, "Cheek to Cheek" illustrates, probably as well as any song he composed, Irving Berlin's craft as a songwriter. Second, both song and performance occupy the middleground between sweet and swing.

"Cheek to Cheek" is a long song. At seventy-two measures, it is over twice the length of a standard thirty-two measure AABA song. Its form is proportionally expanded. It contains three distinct phrases of melody, not two, in the following arrangement: A (sixteen measures), A (sixteen), B (eight), B (eight), C (eight), and A (sixteen). Each phrase has a distinct character. For example, the melodic contour of the B section, with its repeated hills and valleys, underscores the lyric. Similarly, the boldness of the lyric in the C section—"Dance with me; I want my arm about you"—is echoed by the distant harmonies and wide intervals in the melody. This degree of subtlety and complexity was rare in the popular songs of the era. At the same time, it is an extremely accessible song. It begins with the simplest of riffs: a two-note setting of the word "heaven." The first phrase develops directly from this two-note figure; almost every note belongs to a pair of notes derived from the opening riff. The subtly varied recurrence of the opening riff makes the phrase easily understood without being boring.

"Cheek to Cheek" illustrates two important dimensions of Berlin's genius as a songwriter. First, he was an extraordinarily versatile songwriter, so versatile that it's difficult to imagine the same man wrote both "White Christmas" and "Puttin' on the Ritz." Moreover, he put his versatility at the service of the situation: here he needed a buoyant fox-trot for Fred and Ginger's cheek to cheek dancing. Second, his best songs, no matter how

Irving Berlin, 1928.

sophisticated, had some immediately appealing feature, an easy point of entry: here it's one word—"heaven"—and two notes. We are into the song as soon as we hear them.

Stylistically, both song and performance are at the center of popular music during the thirties and forties, mixing old and new in balanced proportions. The melody of "Cheek to Cheek" develops from a riff (new), but has very little syncopation (old). This performance features a dance orchestra with full rhythm, saxes, brass (new), and strings (old). It also showcases the two most popular rhythmic conceptions of the era. A and C sections are sung or played to a two-beat rhythm, B sections to a (somewhat stiff) swing beat. Astaire sings with wonderful rhythmic subtlety. His light voice and impeccable style—never forced or overblown—seem ideally suited to the song. (Indeed, several of the great songwriters of the period, Berlin included, regarded Astaire as their ideal interpreter—quite a tribute for a man best known as a dancer.)

CROONING VERSUS JAZZ SINGING

Mixtures of old and new were not common in the thirties. By 1935, the year "Cheek to Cheek" hit the charts, Benny Goodman's success had established swing as a commercially viable alternative to the fox-trot song. At the same time, established popular song had retreated from the rhythmic advances of the twenties. Songs in this more conservative style, called "sweet" in the trade, were usually slower, set to a fox-trot beat, less syncopated, with more sophisticated and less colloquial language in the lyrics, and a more

sweet
songs

flowing melody. Swing and rhythm songs were just the opposite: faster, more syncopated, with a riff-based melody. Popular singing experienced a similar division at about the same time. Two new major singing styles had developed in the wake of electric amplification. One was crooning, a pleasant-voiced, conversational singing style, exemplified initially by Bing Crosby and Gene Austin. The other was jazz singing, best exemplified early on by Louis Armstrong.

 swing songs

Two versions of the still-popular 1931 hit, "All of Me," one by crooner Russ Columbo (Example 10.2) and the other by jazz vocalist Billie Holiday (Example 10.3), point out the clear division between crooning and jazz singing that developed in the thirties. Billie Holiday's version also anticipates an important trend in popular singing in the forties and fifties, song interpretation.

 II-21

 IIB-10

The interpretation of popular music is, if anything, an even more individual and distinctive art than its composition. Good performers bring a song to life by enhancing the qualities inherent in it. They can give extra emphasis to a key word or melody note, alter the written rhythm to impart an even more speech-like and personal quality, or perhaps add an expressive embellishment to the melody. They impose their personality, identity, and experience onto their audience, using the song to give us a glimpse into their souls. This personal element makes a great performance of a mediocre song possible.

 III-1

 IIIA-1

The two versions of "All of Me" illustrate the distinction between good and great song interpreters. Russ Columbo (1908–1934) was a popular crooner in the early thirties, similar in style to Bing Crosby; his version of the song is a good period performance. He sings expressively, with accurate

song interpreter

Russ Columbo, c. 1930.

pitch, and a warm, pleasing voice. He gives a mostly literal rendition of the song, but occasionally departs from the written version of the song to add musical and expressive interest. For example, he delays the start of the phrase that begins "Can't you see" to avoid a third statement of the same rhythm. His hesitation also helps tie the entire line of lyric together. Later in the same phrase, he alters the rhythm of the song to achieve more expressive emphasis by holding the melodic peak located on the word "good" longer than specified in the music.

The rhythm of the next two phrases also receives subtle alteration. As before, the first part of the phrase ("Take my lips") begins late. The second part moves more quickly than the indicated rhythm, so that the word "lose" comes slightly before the beat. Columbo's objective seems to be a delivery that floats over the underlying pulse, more closely approximating the natural cadence and the sense of the words. And Columbo prefaces the second "take" with an extra note, sung to the word "Oh," to give this second phrase greater urgency. The remainder of the song proceeds in a similar fashion.

Billie Holiday's recording brings into focus a crucial difference between a good and great interpreter: Columbo projects the song very nicely but Holiday projects *herself* through the song. As we listen to her recording, we are less concerned with what the words are saying, and more concerned with how she's saying them. Her performance transcends the sentimental lyrics to express the real and almost universal pain of lost love with an immediacy that the song by itself can't begin to attain. As written, words and music send one message; her voice sends a second, much deeper one. The contrast between the inimitable quality of Holiday's voice and Columbo's

Billie Holiday, New York, 1941.

smooth but almost generic baritone is immediately apparent. Hers is not a pretty sound, but it remains one of the most individual timbres ever to emerge within the popular tradition, unduplicated despite her profound influence on jazz and popular singers of every generation.

Holiday sings the first part of the opening chorus in a more or less literal fashion. But her voice is instantly recognizable, as is her characteristic expressive modulation of its basic quality. She gives the lyrics greater urgency through subtle alteration of pacing and emphasis. In her version of the second phrase, "Why not take all of me," each word with the exception of "of" is sung with greater breadth and intensity than in Columbo's version. Rhythmically, it's also more satisfying because it's freer: speech-like, but too intense for speech. She defies the musical gravity of the beat to give greater impact to the phrase.

As each major phrase in the first chorus progresses, Holiday paraphrases the original version of the melody more extensively to achieve greater expressiveness. Her reworking of the phrase, "Take my lips . . .," for example, begins much higher than it does in the original version. By using a higher range and freely altering the rhythm—especially to emphasize the words, "I," "want," and "lose"—she transforms the lyrics from poetic hyperbole to an emotionally credible statement.

But the real revelation in this performance is the second chorus. In it, Holiday transforms this straightforward popular song into a blues song. The melody's range narrows considerably, and most phrases begin high and end low. She sings this chorus in the top part of her range, giving her voice a particular urgency. The inflection of the melodic line becomes more intense, especially on the words "lips," "eyes," and "cry." The note values lengthen and the rhythm becomes freer, suggesting even more strongly than before that Holiday sings because simple speech cannot convey the emotion she wishes to express. She saves the very top note in the song for the climactic phrase "Why not take the rest"; as her voice descends, we can feel her despair. Her performance transcends the lyrics to express the *real* anguish of love lost.

Billie Holiday's art is not one of technical virtuosity. In one of the most fascinating paradoxes of jazz history, the greatest jazz singer of all time was never known as a scat, or instrumental-style, singer. Nor is it a style of conventional beauty. Instead, she communicates her feelings directly, unfiltered by inappropriate (for her) stylistic conventions, for example, a preferred vocal sound or literal adherence to the original melodic shape of the song. Like other great performers, she is a style unto herself, instantly recognizable, broadly influential, and widely, if unsuccessfully, imitated.

THE CRAFT OF SONGWRITING

Two qualities inform the best work of the great Tin Pan Alley songwriters. The first is their ability to respond to and transcend the limitations of popular song's restrictive musical conventions. The second is their ability to imprint their songwriting personality on their work, using highly personal musical traits that clearly identify a song as theirs, yet seem fresh in each new song. We can find both qualities in one of the great songs of the period, Richard Rodgers's and Lorenz Hart's "My Funny Valentine" (Example 10.4). It was introduced in their 1937 show, *Babes in Arms*. Although not

 III-2

 IIIA-2

Lyricist Lorenz Hart (at desk, holding pencil and cigar), librettist Herbert Fields (standing), and composer Richard Rodgers (at piano), in Hollywood, c. 1930.

immediately a hit during the run of the show, it was soon "rediscovered" by nightclub singers and jazz musicians, and it remains among the best-known Tin Pan Alley standards. Mary Martin's performance here is a beautifully sung rendition that is faithful to Rodgers and Hart's version of the song.

Richard Rodgers (1902–1979) has had perhaps the most unusual career of any of the great songwriters. In effect, he had two careers, the first with lyricist Lorenz Hart, the second with Oscar Hammerstein II. He wrote such markedly different music with each collaborator that his output seems to be the work of two different songwriters. Hart was his lyricist from their college days until Hart's death in 1943. Rodgers and Hart songs are very much in the spirit and style of the twenties and thirties. Many of them grow out of short riff-like ideas: "I'll Take Manhattan," the first line of their first big hit, is typical. Rodgers began his collaboration with Hammerstein shortly before Hart's death. Rodgers and Hammerstein songs, written for their enormously successful musicals, were more conservative in almost every way.

Hart was among the cleverest lyricists of the twenties and thirties, at once colloquial and sophisticated. Rodgers complements these qualities in Hart's lyrics with immediately accessible, yet subtly unified melodies full of sudden, quirky surprises. "My Funny Valentine" is one of Rodgers's most characteristic songs. In its chorus, we can hear two stylistic features that reveal both Rodgers's mastery of his craft and his personal style during his years of collaboration with Hart.

The first trademark is a melodic profile that resembles a seismograph during a short earthquake. Many later Rodgers and Hart songs begin by noodling around a group of closely spaced low notes. In "My Funny Valentine," Rodgers lulls his listener in the first two phrases, which set the words, "My funny Valentine, sweet comic Valentine." The third phrase begins similarly but then suddenly soars to a surprising high note (on the word, "smile"). This high note creates melodic tension that continues beyond the end of the opening section. Other phrases have the same bump, but in different ways. None are resolved until the final high note of the song ("stay").

The other outstanding trademark of Rodgers's Hart-era style is his effort to integrate all the sections within a chorus into a larger, unified, whole. To understand and appreciate Rodgers's craft we should review the usual way of writing an AABA song. Generally, Tin Pan Alley songwriters treat each A section as an independent unit; only the bridge connects to another section. Moreover, all three A sections are alike: the two repetitions of the opening section are melodically identical to the original statement. This is what we heard in "Deed I Do" (Example 2.12). There is little effort to link one section to the next, or to create musical tension within the opening section that is sustained through other sections and released only toward the end of the song.

In "My Funny Valentine," we hear an especially well-developed example of Rodgers's ingenious and inspired methods of unifying the chorus. Three features work together to achieve this goal: (1) creating melodic tension by highlighting a melodic peak, then building on it and finally resolving it later in the chorus; (2) linking sections together with melodic lines and harmonic progressions that flow easily from one section to the next instead of closing off periodically; and, most unusually (3) significantly varying and developing material from the opening section in the two restatements.

The musical tension appears in the first section. The high note on the word "smile" asks a musical question that remains unanswered, after which the melodic line descends but does not immediately resolve. The first two sections are joined together in two ways: (1) by a chord progression that begins at the end of the first section, on the word "heart," and concludes just before the beginning of the new phrase ("Your looks are laughable"); and, (2) by a melodic line that bottoms out and briefly reverses direction on the word "your."

The second section begins with the same melodic outline as the opening, but at a higher pitch. This produces a more intense version of the initial section. And the high note sung on the first syllable of the word, "favorite," escalates the melodic tension created in the opening section on the word "smile" because it's so much higher. Chord progressions and melodic contour also link the second and third sections. In the third section, three successive melodic peaks on the first syllable of "figure," "mouth," and "open," respectively return to and then fill in the melodic high points of the first two sections.

The final section compresses and climactically resolves the first half of the song. The first phrase of this section ("don't change a hair for me") repeats the opening phrase of the first section (A); the next phrase borrows the melody of the opening phrase of the second section (A1). This produces an abbreviated version of the melodic rise that had been spread previously over sixteen measures. The next phrase is the climax of the song, and its resolution. The high note sustained on the second "Stay!" justifies the sudden and surprising melodic peaks of the previous three sections. Only at this point of the song are these high notes understood as part of a logical, even inevitable, ascent to this climactic note.

Similarly, the final phrase in the extended last section of the chorus ("Each day is Valentine's day") resolves the endings of the first and second sections; their open-ended quality helped prepare the final resolution of the song in a key different from the one in which it began.

Rodgers's ingenuity gains in impact precisely because the formal, melodic, and harmonic conventions of Tin Pan Alley song were so well-entrenched. The calculated positioning of melodic high points, the subtle variation and expansion of the stock AABA plan, and smooth linking of each section to the next help "My Funny Valentine" transcend the formulaic efforts of less-inspired songwriters.

POPULAR SONG AFTER WORLD WAR II

III-6

IIIA-6

jump band

The spectrum of popular song and singing styles broadened even further after World War II. At one end of the spectrum were the songs of the Broadway musical and those who sang them in the shows. With the enormous commercial and critical success of Rodgers and Hammerstein's *Oklahoma!*, Broadway rediscovered its distant, unsyncopated past. As we'll see in Chapter 11, Rodgers and Hammerstein updated the operetta style from the early part of the century. "Oh, What a Beautiful Morning" (Example 11.3) is a waltz song with a flowing melody—more reminiscent of popular song in 1903 than in 1930. Many of the new generation of Broadway stars, like Mary Martin and Alfred Drake, who created the role of Curly in *Oklahoma!*, had trained, quasi-operatic voices. Mario Lanza, an operatic tenor turned pop star, epitomized this shift away from a distinct popular stage style previously represented by song belters like Ethel Merman and Al Jolson. At the other end of the spectrum, swing combined with blues to create the jump bands of the late forties. It marked the return of an authentic

Frank Sinatra in his young, crooning days, c. 1944–45.

blues style to commercial prominence. Ranging over much of the territory in between were the song interpreters. Following the path marked out by Billie Holiday, the great ones—Frank Sinatra, Nat Cole, Peggy Lee, Tony Bennett, and a very few others—have brought an emotional commitment to their best performances. All had an immediately identifiable sound, and moved easily between ballads and swing numbers.

Frank Sinatra is the song interpreter without peer. In his best performances, he wasn't just singing the song, he was living it. His sound became his alone; it remains one of the most identifiable, if widely imitated, vocal styles in popular music. At the same time, his range broadened: He could invest a ballad performance with tremendous intensity or swing irresistibly. His style was the perfect synthesis of his two main influences: Bing Crosby and Billie Holiday. "Here's That Rainy Day" (Example 10.5) and "I've Got You Under My Skin" (Example 10.6), both recorded by Sinatra in the fifties, show something of his musical and emotional range.

"Here's That Rainy Day," one of the best of the postwar popular songs, is an ideal vehicle for Sinatra the interpreter. The lyric paints an unsentimental if metaphorical portrait of lost love. Sinatra's singing sounds like he's lived the experience. There is an edge, a bite, to his voice; a rawness that is moving precisely because it's not sweet and smooth. He tells the story, altering the melody to give a more natural rhythm and emphasis to the lyric: Compare his opening line with the straightforward version of the melody played by the violins. The humanness of his voice and the directness of its emotion contrast with the lush accompaniment. It's like seeing Paul Newman dressed in a tuxedo: he may look elegant, but we know he hasn't spent much of his life in formal wear.

We hear just as much of Sinatra the interpreter in Cole Porter's "I've Got You Under My Skin." His interpretation begins with a rhythmic reconception of the song. Porter's original version, written for the 1936 film *Born to Dance*, was Latin-tinged, a sequel to his 1935 hit "Begin the Beguine." Sinatra sings it as a swing tune, allowing him to deliver the words more flexibly. He modulates his vocal quality just as flexibly, adopting a conversational tone in the early phrases, growing more resonant and charged with emotion at the climaxes. His vocal style—timbre, nuance, rhythm, diction—seems to amplify his personality rather than obscure it. It convinces us, even if just for the moment, that the song could be autobiographical.

Both performances give us some insight into the growing conservatism of mainstream popular song and its performance after 1935. Increasing European influence is evident in both songs. The melodies have longer phrases, which unfold slowly. Although each begins with a short melodic fragment ("Maybe"; "I've Got You"), the overall impression is of a long, unbroken line. (Compare them in this respect to "All of Me" or "Heaven.") Their harmony is richer and more complex, with surprising chords at strategic points (for example, the chord that supports the high notes on "Here's That Rainy Day"). The forms are longer, or at least take longer to unfold, and are less predictable in sequence. Syncopation is virtually nonexistent in the "official" versions of the songs, although Sinatra adds plenty in his performances.

The setting of the song in these performances shows the same trend. A lush orchestral string sound is a prominent part of the accompaniment, especially in "Here's That Rainy Day." The two-beat rhythm that supports "Here's That Rainy Day" has slowed from a trot to a crawl; it is now too slow for dancing. Following the same trend is the performance of "I've Got You Under My Skin." Its rhythm might be described as "swing-lite": the bass plays in two most of the time, even though the song has a clear four-beat feel. Both songs and performances indicate a spectral shift. To an even greater extent than the sweet songs of the 1930s, "Here's That Rainy Day," signals a retreat from the rhythmic advances of the 1920s (compare it to conservative songs from the period, like "Whispering" and "April Showers," or even Mary Martin's performance of "My Funny Valentine"). Sinatra's version of "I've Got You Under My Skin" finds a happy middleground between swing and sweet. Indeed, big-band style, which all but disappeared in live performance when most of the top bands disbanded after World War II, lived on in the recording studios during the fifties and into the sixties.

Swing-influenced popular song went in three directions after 1940. One was the synthesis of swing and pop, such as that heard in Example 10.6. Another was the continuation of jazz singing, most prominently in the work of Billie Holiday, Ella Fitzgerald, Sarah Vaughan, Carmen MacRae, Mel Tormé, Joe Williams, and Billy Eckstine. (Often the difference between jazz singing and jazz-influenced pop was a matter of context and material. Ella Fitzgerald was unquestionably a major jazz singer, but her songbook albums, such as her massive Gershwin songbook with arranger Nelson Riddle's lush settings, certainly straddle the line between jazz and pop.) The third was a reuniting of blues and jazz. This took two important forms. One was the formation of the electric blues band (see Chapter 14). The other was the creation of the jump band.

The jump bands of the late forties simplified and exaggerated the most accessible elements of swing style. The most significant differences between the jump band and the swing-era big band are the presence of a lead vocalist, reduced instrumentation, and a heavy backbeat. Jump bands maintained, even intensified, through the use of a shuffle rhythm, swing rhythm, while often giving the backbeat much more emphasis. ("Shake, Rattle, and Roll" [Example 14.2] is a swing-beat tune with a heavy backbeat.) And they relied heavily on riffs, both in the head and during solos. The jump bands were usually much smaller than their swing-era predecessors, a result of postwar economics. They often consisted only of a vocalist, rhythm section, and sax, although bands with three or four horns, usually trumpets and saxes, were also common. Jump bands linked swing with fifties rock 'n' roll.

"Choo-Choo-Ch-Boogie" (Example 10.7), performed by Louis Jordan, is a rhythm-and-blues hit from 1946, and one of the best jump tunes. Its style clearly mixes big-band swing with the blues. Here, the riffs repeat rather than develop and the lyrics are full of the street talk of the time. What the song may lack in melodic sophistication, it makes up for with an infectious beat. It features a "shuffle" beat, a beat-heavy version of swing rhythm. The consistent long/short pattern within each beat marks the beat even more strongly than the single-note emphasis typical of regular swing style (listen to the piano for the shuffle rhythm).

The vocal sections of the song alternate verse and refrain. All the verse sections follow the harmonic blues form. And the entire song, not only the vocal sections and piano and sax solos, is built out of riffs. This storytelling type of song, popular in both blues and country music, would decisively influence rock song. Formally, Chuck Berry's "Johnny B. Goode" (Example 14.5) is a direct descendant of this song.

shuffle
rhythm

 IV-2

 IVA-2

 III-3

 IIIA-3

 IV-5

IVA-5

Louis Jordan and His Tympany Five, 1946. L to r: Josh Jackson (tenor sax), Bill Davis (piano), Louis Jordan (alto sax), Jesse Simpkins (bass), Aaron Izenham (trumpet), Eddie Byrd (drums); unidentified showgirls in front.

CONCLUSION

The songs and singers presented above show the extent to which popular song and singing diversified after 1930. Songs ranged from a melodious ballad with a barely discernible pulse to a toe-tapping riff tune. The important singing styles are also represented: straightforward popular singing (in the case of Fred Astaire), Mary Martin's music theater singing, Russ Columbo's crooning, Billie Holiday's jazz singing, Sinatra's song interpretation, and Louis Jordan's friendly and lighthearted blues. We also heard several examples of the craft of songwriting: whether it was the imaginative adaptation of the formal conventions of the time ("My Funny Valentine" or "Here's That Rainy Day"), a departure from those conventions for expressive reasons ("Cheek to Cheek" or "I've Got You Under My Skin"), or the creation—or at least the early use—of a new formal convention ("Choo, Choo, Ch-Boogie"). It is an impressive legacy.

Terms to Know

jump band	shuffle rhythm	song interpreter
sweet songs	swing songs	

Names to Know

Fred Astaire	Irving Berlin	Nat "King" Cole
Russ Columbo	Lorenz Hart	Billie Holiday
Louis Jordan	Peggy Lee	Cole Porter
Richard Rodgers	Frank Sinatra	

Study Questions

1. What were the jazz-based singing styles that emerged in the forties?

2. What are some of the characteristics that identify the popular songs of the thirties and forties?

3. What are some of the important differences between crooners and song interpreters? How did Frank Sinatra change from a crooner in the forties to a song interpreter in the fifties?

4. In what ways do typical songs of the late thirties and forties differ from those of the twenties?

5. How does the song "Cheek to Cheek" mix elements of old and new song styles?

6. What is the conventional form of a Tin Pan Alley song? How do "Cheek to Cheek," "All of Me," "Here's That Rainy Day," "My Funny Valentine," and "Choo-Choo-Ch-Boogie" modify or depart from this conventional form?

CHAPTER ELEVEN
American Musical Theater, 1920–1960

The four decades from 1920 to 1960 were the heyday of Broadway and Hollywood musical productions. Musical stage entertainment was the primary outlet for popular songs in the twenties, and remained an important source of new hits through the early sixties. *Show Boat,* produced in 1927, anticipated the best musicals of the forties and fifties in its integration of music and drama and the relative seriousness of its plot. Twenty years later, its influence was evident in most of the important musicals produced on Broadway.

During the twenties, musical stage entertainment was at the center of the popular-music industry, more than at any time before or since. The decade

Jerome Kern, 1930s.

saw the heyday of vaudeville and the revue, and the beginning of a new era in musical comedy. Theatergoers could attend stage productions of unprecedented variety, lavishness, and quality. Stage entertainment served as the primary outlet for popular song, especially those by songwriters of high caliber. A majority of the hit songs in the twenties and thirties were originally written for revues or musical comedies, even though they would eventually achieve a popularity independent of their function within the show.

Musical comedy, an integral part of American entertainment since the end of the nineteenth century, began a shift toward greater dramatic credibility in the twenties. As a rule, musicals from the early part of the century followed some kind of plot, but most plots were lighthearted and rather flimsy. Songs used in the show were purportedly written to express the feeling of the characters in the story, but producers seldom hesitated to interpolate a song into a show if it was a current hit or if a star demanded it, even if it required rewriting the story line.

American musical comedy matured gradually in the years after World War I. Plots tightened, and the musical quality and dramatic usefulness of the songs improved. In the words of music theater historian Gerald Bordman, Jerome Kern's series of shows for the small Princess Theater, beginning in 1915, "brought American musical comedy into the twentieth century."

<u>SHOW BOAT</u> AND A
<u>NEW TYPE OF MUSICAL THEATER</u>

musical
theater

II-8

IIA-8

Two landmark musical theater productions were staged in the next decade. George Gershwin's *Lady Be Good,* which opened in 1924, brought the vital, syncopated rhythms of his early songs to a book musical; it featured some of his most memorable songs, including "Fascinating Rhythm" (Example 8.6). Oscar Hammerstein II and Jerome Kern's musical, *Show Boat,* which opened in 1927, instantly raised American musical theater to a higher level of quality. *Show Boat* was the first of the great modern musicals. It featured several wonderful songs that served a serious and dramatically credible plot. It treated a controversial subject, miscegenation, and eschewed the conventional happy ending.

In the credibility and cohesion of its plot and quality of its music, *Show Boat* was, in effect, the first American operetta. Like other operettas, it was set in an exotic (for New York) locale and time. On this occasion, however, the place was not some never-never land but the American Midwest; it's set on a riverboat on the Mississippi River and in Chicago in the late nineteenth century. It has less to do with fantasy and more to do with the reality of life in America at that time.

Show Boat was a musical without precedent. Its uniqueness was apparent from the moment the curtain rose. Most shows of the time began with a high-spirited number featuring a row of chorus girls performing an energetic dance routine. *Show Boat* begins with a single black stevedore singing "Ol' Man River." Both the song and the singer send the message that this show will be different.

III-4

IIIA-4

"Ol' Man River" (Example 11.1) is a sprawling song, with long phrases, a wide range, and a soaring melodic line that reaches a thrilling climax in the final phrase. It is a popular song written in the style of an operatic aria,

Show Boat, 1994 *revival, featuring Dorothy Stanley (top) and Joel Blum (bottom) on the deck of the "Cotton Blossom." Michael Cooper, photograph.*

not dance music (although it was inevitably used for that purpose). The song became a trademark for Paul Robeson, the singer/actor/lawyer/athlete who first sang the role of Joe (the stevedore) in 1928, and later sang it in revivals of the show.

Another memorable song from *Show Boat*, "Can't Help Lovin' Dat Man" (Example 11.2), shows—as few Kern songs do—the influence of blues style. Each of the A sections begins high and ends low. And the final phrase (on the words, "can't help lovin' dat man of mine") was a melodic cliché of song-writers in the twenties when they wanted to create a bluesy sound. The melody note on the word "man" is outside the normal scale for this song and was considered a "blue" note because it was borrowed from the blues scale. Its appearance here is related to the song's function within the show. The song was a featured number for Julie, a mulatto married to a white man. The blues tinge is Kern's way of characterizing her.

III-5

IIIA-5

Helen Morgan, the featured singer on this recording, starred as Julie in both the first and second Broadway production of *Show Boat*. She was one of the most prominent of the "torch" singers, so called because they sang as if "carrying a torch" for a man (twenties slang for unrequited love). They were white female vocalists whose singing style showed some blues influence.

In the sixteen years between *Show Boat* and *Oklahoma!*, few theater composers followed the lead of Kern and Hammerstein by creating dramatically coherent musicals. George Gershwin's three political satires in the early thirties were almost singular exceptions. The second of them, *Of Thee*

I Sing, won the 1931 Pulitzer prize for best play, one of only a few musicals to do so. Rodgers's and Hart's late thirties musicals also sought to bring more realism and greater integration of story and song to the Broadway stage. However, most shows, and filmed musicals as well, tended to be escapist entertainment, something to take the country's mind off the reality of the Depression. Cole Porter's hit show, *Anything Goes,* produced in 1934, is a successful example of this trend. Only with *Oklahoma!,* produced in 1943, and the postwar book shows of Rodgers and Hammerstein and others, did a true American operetta tradition sustain itself over a long period of time.

OKLAHOMA!

libretto

Rodgers and Hammerstein's *Oklahoma!* was a landmark musical in its integration of libretto, song, and dance, and the extent of its popularity. Theater critic Stanley Green identifies the uniqueness of *Oklahoma!* as the synthesis of its component parts into a complete theatrical entity of great beauty and imagination:

> Everything fit into place. . . . Not only were songs and story inseparable, but the dances devised by Agnes de Mille heightened the drama by revealing the subconscious fears and desires of the leading characters.

Its critical success was matched at the box office: *Oklahoma!* ran on Broadway for over five years; its 2,248 performances far exceeded any previous run.

Show Boat was the most direct precursor of *Oklahoma!.* Similarities between the two musicals went beyond their enormous popular appeal and emphasis on dramatic integrity. Both shows drew their plot from existing literature, uncommon in the twenties, but increasingly common by the early forties. Edna Ferber's novel, *Show Boat,* was the source of the musical, while *Oklahoma!* was adapted directly from Lynn Riggs's 1933 play, *Green Grow the Lilacs.* Additionally, both musicals featured stories set in America, but in a time and place far removed from contemporary New York. *Show Boat* takes place in the Midwest before the turn of the century; the Oklahoma of the musical was still Indian territory before 1910.

Most important, both incorporated significant innovations in: the depth of character portrayal; seriousness of plot; integration of song into the story line; disregard for convention (for example, both begin with a single male singer instead of a chorus line of dancers); and, in the case of *Oklahoma!,* the dramatically purposeful use of dance. The extraordinarily enthusiastic public support for a dramatically credible musical inspired a wholesale shift in values, by both creators and audience.

MUSICAL THEATER AS DRAMA

Of all these changes, none was more important than putting the song at the service of the story, rather than the other way around. Recall that around the turn of the century, the plot in a musical comedy was simply a scaffolding on which the songs were hung. Commercial appeal was the preeminent concern, and interpolation a common practice. As we discovered with "After the Ball" (Example 5.2), any song could secure a place in a show, so long as

I-30

IB-4

it was a hit. In shows like *Showboat* and *Oklahoma!*, commercial appeal was still a consideration: the songs, after all, were written in a popular style. But much more effort was given to write songs that responded to the dramatic necessity of the moment. Interpolation was a rare exception, not the rule.

In a musical comedy, operetta, or musical play, most of the dialogue is spoken, not sung. This observation leads directly to two series of questions:

1. What dramatic purpose(s) can a song serve? What are the advantages (and disadvantages) of replacing speech with song? What, if anything, can song accomplish dramatically that words cannot?

2. Why do the librettist and composer choose to incorporate a song at a particular location in the story? What dramatic purpose does it serve?

A dramatically effective song usually fulfills one (or more) of three functions: (1) it helps establish the mood of a situation; (2) it advances the plot; or (3) it gives the audience greater insight into the character singing the song. Spoken text can also achieve these ends, so the questions then become: how does the manner in which each achieves its purpose differ?; and, what are the advantages and disadvantages of song versus speech? The disadvantage of song—or at least the popular song of the musical—is obvious: song slows down the action. Words are delivered more slowly sung than spoken, and lines of text are often repeated; for example, we hear the chorus line "Oh, what a beautiful mornin'" over and over. But a dramatically effective song makes its text more immediate and meaningful; it projects the message of the text with a power and expressiveness that is difficult to achieve with speech alone.

Because it is based on a stage play, *Oklahoma!* gives us an excellent opportunity to study what makes a song dramatically effective and why a song appears at a particular point in the plot. This is made even more apparent because the original play also featured songs. However, the opening songs in *Green Grows the Lilacs* are decorative; they serve no significant dramatic purpose. In contrast, the first two songs of *Oklahoma!* are integral to the plot.

In *Oklahoma!*, we can sense the power of song right from the outset. "Oh, What a Beautiful Mornin'" (Example 11.3) serves two of the three purposes outlined above: it immediately establishes a mood and begins to sketch in Curly's character. The text of the song is a commentary on the weather and rural life. In everyday conversation, this is the most commonplace of topics: "Great day, isn't it?"; "Yep, sure is"; "Corn's sure growin'"; "Cattle have it easy, just stand around and eat all day, nothing bothers 'em." Rendered in speech instead of song, such a commentary would almost certainly have limited impact. It takes only a few seconds to evaluate the weather and life on the farm, and any speech rich in metaphor, as the song lyric is, would probably be inconsistent with the character speaking the lines. (Interestingly, both play and musical begin with song. Perhaps playwright Lynn Riggs also recognized the limitations of speech here.)

"Oh, What a Beautiful Mornin'" allows Curly to project the sentiments of the text with an exuberance that transcends speech. We share Curly's delight in the weather and rural life, learning why he thinks it's a wonderful day—"cattle are standing like statues" and "corn is as high as an elephant's eye"—details that help paint an idyllic picture of rural life. And the swing of

Oklahoma! *This posed publicity photo from the original production shows Curly (Alfred Drake) and Laurey (Joan Roberts) in the surrey with the fringe on top. Vandamm Studios, photographers; courtesy Performing Arts Research Center, New York Public Library at Lincoln Center.*

the melody of the chorus communicates Curly's sunny disposition; we are surprised to find a dark side to his personality that is revealed later on in the play.

What the song loses in pace, it gives back in expressive impact. We can stand to hear the chorus of "Oh, What a Beautiful Mornin'," over and over because the melody to which it's set draws us in and carries us along. The song establishes an upbeat mood right from the start and sustains it for several minutes; the intensity of this mood and the insight into Curly's personality more than compensates for the relatively slow rate at which the play unfolds.

The opening of *Oklahoma!* illustrates the principle behind the most dramatically effective use of song within a musical play. Song replaces speech when the emotion or situation at a certain point in the story requires the greater expressive power of music. "Oh, What a Beautiful Mornin'" is an appealing song, one that has enjoyed popularity apart from the musical. But it is also dramatically necessary, and its immediate appeal has a dramatic purpose within the play.

 III-7

 IIIA-7

"The Surrey with the Fringe on Top" (Example 11.4), Curly's second song in *Oklahoma!*, enables Curly to gain the upper hand at least momentarily in his repartee with Aunt Eller and Laurey. In the preceding dialogue and in the dialogue interspersed between choruses of the song, Curly is clearly losing his verbal duels with these two ladies. Only through song does the charm and persuasiveness of Curly's personality fully emerge. We also discover that he's got a bit of the huckster in him, a quality that comes into play later in the musical in his dealings with Jud.

When he talks, Curly manages to put his foot in his mouth, as in the exchange beginning right after he finishes singing "Surrey with a Fringe on Top." He is only in control when he sings, weaving a spell that completely, if briefly, entrances both Laurey and Aunt Eller, and he *needs* to sing to regain control of the situation.

THE LEGACY OF OKLAHOMA!

Oklahoma! marks the beginning of an American operetta tradition: most of the long-running shows of the forties and fifties were conceived as and understood to be musical theater dramas in which the music served the plot.

Many of these musicals drew on classics of one kind or another, for example, classical music (*Kismet* with music of the nineteenth-century Russian composer, Alexander Borodin), or famous literary works (*My Fair Lady,* an adaptation of George Bernard Shaw's play, *Pygmalion*).

West Side Story, staged in 1957 and filmed in 1961, was the landmark musical of the fifties: commercially successful in both stage and film versions, and creative and innovative in many important ways. Its inventiveness begins with its book, which puts a new twist on an old practice. As we have seen in *Showboat* and *Oklahoma!,* even American operetta told a story set long ago and far away. Composer Leonard Bernstein, lyricist Stephen Sondheim, choreographer Jerome Robbins, and librettist Arthur Laurents, the team that created *West Side Story,* started with such a story– Shakespeare's *Romeo and Juliet*–but reset it in contemporary New York. They turned the Capulets and Montagues into two street gangs, the white Jets and the Puerto Rican Sharks. Moreover, they chose not to sugarcoat Shakespeare's drama–even its tragic ending; the musical portrayed a contemporary issue with a realism unprecedented in a Broadway show.

choreo-
grapher

Two other distinctive features of the show stand out: Bernstein's music, both the songs and the dance music; and the total integration of dance into the show. Leonard Bernstein had been active on Broadway almost from the beginning of his musical career in the forties, but he was even more active as a composer, conductor, pianist, and commentator on classical music. Still, he had a strong interest in and affinity for jazz and theater music. In *West Side Story,* Bernstein brings his compositional range to bear in ways that songwriters, even those as skilled as Jerome Kern and Richard Rodgers, couldn't. Especially for such a conservative genre as postwar musical theater, his musical language is generally up to date. He wrote contemporary jazz for the Jets's dance numbers. For the Sharks, he wrote Latin, or at least Latinate, numbers. There is a mambo (a Latin dance popular during the early fifties) for the dance in the gym, but other music for Puerto Rican characters, like "America" and "I Feel Pretty," seems derived more from classical music by Latin composers than Newyorican popular music.

The love songs ("Maria," "Tonight," "One Hand, One Heart," "Somewhere,") use the Tin Pan Alley popular-song conventions as a point of departure but abandon them as necessary. "Maria" (Example 11.5) is the boldest of these songs, and it shows several of the distinctive characteristics of Bernstein's style. Perhaps the most apparent is his eagerness to break down the clear sectional outline of the standard popular song. In a typical popular song ("Can't Help Lovin' Dat Man" [Example 11.2]) verse and chorus are clearly differentiated, and each phrase of the chorus is clearly separated from its neighbors. Richard Rodgers, as we have seen in "My Funny Valentine" (Example 10.4), often tries to get around this problem by varying the A phrases, but he still preserves the distinction between verse and chorus and the sectional outline of the chorus.

 III-8

 IIIA-8

 III-5

 IIIA-5

Bernstein's song is much more integrated; the sectional outline is obscured by melodic momentum. Verse flows almost imperceptibly into chorus. The chorus itself has three long phrases, all irregular in phrase length (six, six, and seven measures, respectively) and all derived from the opening three note motive ("Maria"). The first phrase stays pretty much in place. Its restatement, however, climbs steadily, reaching a climax at the beginning of the third phrase. The melody recedes from this, suddenly, then gently. We are far more aware of the long arch formed by the second and third phrases than we are of its outline. "Maria" has its roots in Tin Pan Alley song—it develops from a riff-like melodic idea, after all—but it clearly transcends it. On the other hand, it is not a classical aria; it unfolds much too quickly for that. Almost uniquely within the popular tradition, "Maria" and its companions are poised somewhere between Tin Pan Alley and the opera house.

West Side Story, *rumble scene from the original production, with Ken LeRoy as Benardo and Micky Clain as Riff. Friedman-Abeles, photographers; courtesy Performing Arts Research Center, New York Public Library at Lincoln Center.*

III-9

IIIA-9

West Side Story was also exceptional for its use of dance. In the musical, dance is functional, not decorative; choreographer Jerome Robbins was a full partner in the collaboration. There are many extended dance numbers. None shows the integral role of dance better than "Cool" (Example 11.6). The dance features the Jets, who have reassembled in a garage after scattering to avoid the police. They have just finished a "rumble" with the Sharks that has left the rival gang leaders dead. Some of the Jets are almost boiling over in their urgency to gain revenge on the Sharks, but the new leader, Ice, cautions "Cool." We had noted in the discussion of *Oklahoma!* that songs appear when they're dramatically necessary. In this scene, however, action speaks louder than words, even when they're sung. The dance captures the repressed emotion of the gang, ready to explode at the slightest provocation, and kept under wraps only by the force of Ice's will. No song could do that.

The best of the post-*Oklahoma!* musicals were real musical theater. The revue, the heart and soul of Broadway in the twenties, was all but dead:

about three revues a season were produced in the fifties, down from an average of fourteen a season in the twenties. Broadway was a still an important source of popular song, but it was no longer the primary source.

This emphasis on musical theater grew out of the changing composition of its audience and the changing attitudes of its creators. At the turn of the century, musical comedy and its siblings were a primary form of mass entertainment. Audiences came from all strata of society. Over the next fifty years, other forms of entertainment, musical and otherwise, gradually drew off much of this mass audience. Films in the teens, followed by talking films in the late twenties; phonograph records and broadcast radio after World War I; nightclubs and ballrooms in the twenties and thirties; and television after World War II all provided cheaper and more accessible mass entertainment.

As a result, musical theater became an *alternative* to mass entertainment rather than simply another form of it. Likewise, its audience became increasingly elite, although not necessarily elitist. Ticket prices escalated: as early as 1927, scalpers' prices for *Show Boat* tickets reached $100 per seat. For most people, then, attending a Broadway show had become a special event, enjoyed only occasionally. Despite the regular appearance of Broadway show songs on the popular-music charts, musical theater had moved out of the popular-music mainstream. The Broadway stage was no longer the primary source of hit songs, as it had been in the twenties; it was simply one of several.

With *Oklahoma!*, the Broadway musical entered an artistically important period that lasted well into the fifties. Musically, this artistic sensibility is evidenced by a return to a more conservative style. The rhythmic vitality that had marked the music of the twenties and thirties disappeared. In many cases, there was virtually no influence from contemporary jazz or blues styles. Composers turned back the clock to turn-of-the-century waltzes or the straightforward fox-trot beat of songs like "Whispering."

Singers sang in a quasi-operatic style. Many of the most popular show songs featured long flowing melodies with little syncopation; any song from Rodgers and Hammerstein's *Sound of Music* is a good example. The musicals of Rodgers and Hammerstein and their emulators represent the transformation of the European operetta tradition—Franz Lehár, Arthur Sullivan, and their foreign-born imitators—into American terms. By looking back to Europe rather than ahead to Africa, musical theater grew increasingly isolated from the popular music mainstream. The 1964 show *Fiddler on the Roof*, which ran for over 3000 performances, would turn out to be the last hurrah for almost four decades of musical theater.

CONCLUSION

The Broadway stage reached its greatest heights from the late twenties through the mid-sixties. A new integration of music and plot was achieved by the greatest composers/lyricists/librettists, among them Jerome Kern, Rodgers and Hammerstein, and Leonard Bernstein and Stephen Sondheim. However, as the Broadway musical matured, it also moved away from its roots in popular song rhythms, recalling earlier styles such as the turn-of-the-century waltz song. The theater became just one of many places where songs were performed; because of the expense of attending a Broadway production, the audience became more discerning, and composers and lyricists became more ambitious in creating more "refined" music. The result was ultimately a conservative trend, one that resulted in a schism between Broadway and mainstream pop songs. By the late sixties, musical theater, like the rest of the popular-music world, had to come to grips with rock. How that happened is the subject of Chapter 16.

Terms to Know

choreographer	libretto	musical theater

Names to Know

Leonard Bernstein	Agnes de Mille	Oscar Hammerstein II
Jerome Kern	*Oklahoma!*	Jerome Robbins
Show Boat		

Study Questions

1. What are some of the major differences between musical comedy before and after *Show Boat*?

2. How did *Show Boat* create an American operetta tradition?

3. What were the most popular forms of stage entertainment in the twenties? Which remained popular in the thirties; which declined in popularity? Why?

4. How did the relationship between musical theater and its audience change after *Show Boat*?

5. What kinds of dancing were common in the revues and musical comedies of the twenties? How did *Oklahoma!* and *West Side Story* use dance differently than these earlier shows?

6. What dramatic purpose(s) can a song serve in musical theater? Which purposes do the songs from *Oklahoma!* discussed in this chapter serve?

7. What functions does a dramatically effective song serve in a musical? How can song be superior to dialogue to convey a feeling or emotion? What are the negative features of using songs to tell a story?

CHAPTER TWELVE

Country Music, 1922–1955

The term "country music" identifies commercially produced music associated with the rural white South and Southwest. Its history begins in the early
twenties with the introduction of two major aural media, broadcast radio
and the phonograph record, to a heretofore isolated population. The
increased accessibility provided by radio and records had an immediate
impact on both the performers of, and the audience for, the traditional
music of the South. It elevated the most accomplished and personable
musicians from being occasional performers at house parties, fiddle contests, medicine shows, and the like, to becoming at least part-time profes-
sionals with regional celebrity.

country
music

Appearances on radio and record often led to opportunities for live performances. Bands or solo acts with a weekly radio show would fill in the
days between broadcasts with engagements in cities and towns within the
listening area of their radio station. Moreover, radio and recordings aided in
the dissemination and cross-pollination of country music. By 1930, a guitar
player in Louisiana could learn Virginian Maybelle Carter's distinctive
accompanying style simply by buying a record and copying it.

Almost overnight, what had been a folk music—traditional material performed by nonprofessional or semiprofessional musicians for the enjoy-
ment of their neighbors—had become a business, with performers, songwriters, publishers, and promoters supplying a steady stream of music for a
relatively small, but growing and enthusiastic, audience.

THE BOUNDARIES OF COUNTRY MUSIC

Country music is a regional music with an international following.
Although it now attracts a worldwide audience, it remains rooted in
Southern culture and values. Nashville is the most obvious evidence of
country's strong Southern roots. As the home of the Grand Ole Opry,
Nashville became the most important city in country music. Now also the
home of the Country Music Foundation and major recording studios, it continues to be the spiritual, economic, and promotional center of country
music. Country music did not shift its operational base to New York or Los
Angeles when it entered the popular-music mainstream; the music industry

165

came to Nashville. Location is very much a part of the identity of country music.

Nevertheless, country music soon escaped its regional boundaries. Its geographical expansion reflected both the migration patterns of Southern whites and the interest in country music outside the region. Country music expanded westward, first into the Southwest, with the migration of Southerners to Texas and Oklahoma in search of greater opportunity, and then to Hollywood, with the production in the early 1930s of films featuring singing cowboys like Gene Autry and Tex Ritter.

The Depression years saw Oklahomans and other Southwesterners emigrate further west to escape the Dust Bowl. Many settled in the San Joaquin Valley, establishing Bakersfield as perhaps the major center of country music in the West. During and after World War II, many Southerners moved to other parts of the country, especially the industrial North and Midwest, in search of better jobs and living conditions. They brought their music with them. Listeners from outside the South could pick up country music on radio, especially at night. Signals from powerful clear channel radio stations (many broadcast from Mexico) could be received hundreds, even thousands of miles away. Hank Snow, a major country star in the 1940s and 1950s was first exposed to country music through radio broadcasts which he heard in his native Nova Scotia.

However, identification of country music with the South goes beyond mere geography. At its inception, country music expressed the values and traditions of the people who created and performed it: rural, mostly poor, Southern whites. Most of the early recordings featured repertoire that had been handed down aurally, often for several generations. As described by country music historian Bill Malone in his book *Country Music, USA*:

> The old 78 rpm records are treasure troves of virtually every performing style familiar to southern folk . . . British ballads and love songs, native ballads, religious and homiletic songs, instrumental pieces, blues and other Negro-derived material, and popular songs dating well back into the antebellum [pre–Civil War] era.

As country music became more commercially oriented, the repertoire of its performers expanded to include original songs, often written by the performers themselves. These new songs injected a personal element into country music, with the singers commenting on some aspect of their and their audience's common experience in direct, easily understood language. The most recurrent theme, not surprisingly, was the joy and pain of love won and lost. Many of the most enduring and popular songs of this period, like Hank Williams's "Your Cheatin' Heart," were autobiographical. Other popular subjects have included good and bad times, alcohol (both pro and con), nomadic life (on the railroad, out west, and, more recently, trucking), and the often difficult adjustment from country to city life.

MUSICAL BOUNDARIES

The development of country music has been a process of assimilation that began well before its "official" beginning in the twenties. It accelerated as the music entered the commercial mainstream. The two crucial musical elements of country music are a clear, honest vocal style, often nasal and without vibrato or fullness, and the fiddle style popular for generations throughout the South, and elsewhere, through the minstrel show. Both have been least susceptible to change, seem to predate any outside influence, and still define the country sound. Virtually every other element of country comes from another source. Country music historian Douglas Green details many of these influences:

> There were the sentimental parlor songs of the 1880's and 1890's, which have composed a large part of the country-music reper- toire from "Wildwood Flower" to "I'll Be All Smiles Tonight." There was the blues of the black man, and the guitar and the banjo, instruments that he introduced to the mountaineer. There was a score of other ethnic strains: polkas and their attendant accordion from central Europe: Norteno songs and the Mariachi brass from Mexico; Swiss yodeling; the striking fiddling and rich dialect of the Cajuns (Acadians) of southwest Louisiana; the dreamy tunes and the steel guitar from Hawaii; the pomp of small-town brass bands; the foursquare harmony and melody of Protestant hymns; and heavy borrowing from jazz and swing. Country musicians have always been quick to adapt other music to enrich their own.

The Carter Family, c. 1930. L to r: Maybelle Addington Carter (guitar), Sarah Carter (autoharp), and Alvin Pleasant (A. P.) Carter.

As they absorbed these various elements—popular songs, new instru- ments, blues riffs, etc.—into their music, many country musicians put a decidedly country stamp on them. The Carter family version of the nine- teenth-century sentimental song "Wildwood Flower" (Example 12.2) bears almost no resemblance to the way it would presumably have been per- formed in a middle-class parlor in the late 1890s. And although most of the instruments associated with country music—banjo, steel guitar, guitar, and mandolin—were brought into country music from outside, country musi- cians developed a distinctive way of playing them. In country music, rein- terpretation may often follow assimilation.

III-11

IIIA-11

The fluctuating balance between traditional and outside elements has defined the fundamental tension in country music. This tension can be expressed in several different ways: tradition versus change; conservative versus progressive; and pure country versus hybrid country (country pop or rockabilly). But the underlying questions remain: at what point in a performance do these external influences overwhelm the traditional elements, so that the performance loses its country identity?; and, what specific features of a song or style are most crucial to preserving the country identity?

This tension has been manifest from the beginning of commercial country music. The first country music hits were two songs recorded by Vernon Dalhart. Unlike most of the great country performers, Dalhart, although born in Texas, aspired to be an opera singer, and worked and recorded professionally in New York as a popular and light-opera singer under several pseudonyms. His first two hits, "The Prisoner's Song" and "Wreck of the Old 97," were country-type songs, in that they dealt with common themes in country music ("Wreck of the Old 97" may have been the first "railroad" song, but is very much in the tradition of "event" songs), and were similar melodically to other traditional songs. But Dalhart's singing, not surprisingly, has little affinity with vocal styles of folk performers recorded during the same period, and the viola obbligato on "The Prisoner's Song" has nothing to do with country fiddle playing.

"Tumbling Tumbleweeds," a 1934 recording by the Sons of the Pioneers, is clearly a "western" song textually. However, the song, with its rich harmony and sinuous, chromatic melody, has much more to do with Tin Pan Alley than Dallas, and its close-harmony vocal style recalls the sound of a barbershop quartet. Patti Page's 1950 recording of the "Tennessee Waltz" was extremely popular, much more so than a recording made two years earlier by the song's composers. But Patti Page does not sing in a country style, any more than the Sons of the Pioneers did. Both performances are identified with the country-music tradition, but it's questionable whether either can be considered a performance of country music.

More conservative musicians have resisted the incorporation of non-country elements. For example, drums were used in country music for the first time in 1935 in Bob Wills's western swing band. In his first and only appearance on the Grand Ole Opry in 1944, Wills and his drummer scandalized traditionalists among the staff, although the audience responded enthusiastically. Yet, no major style or important performer has been immune to change within the country-music tradition. Roy Acuff, widely recognized as a champion of traditional values in country music, recorded the "Wabash Cannon Ball" (see Example 12.4) with a band featuring amplified guitar and dobro (a steel guitar-like instrument) as the major solo instruments, instead of the traditional fiddle, and both the guitarist and dobro player had clearly been listening to blues guitarists. So, the gradually shifting core of country music is defined not only by the retention of the traditional vocal and instrumental styles, but also by the way in which newly assimilated elements are transformed by country musicians, who give them a distinctively country identity. Both banjo and steel guitar, for example, were "borrowed" instruments. (The banjo, of course, belongs to the prehistory of country music; the steel guitar was introduced into country music in the late twenties.) Earl Scruggs's three-finger banjo playing updates the banjo style of the early string band; it is unquestionably country despite its obvious debt to ragtime and blues guitar. Similarly, Leon McAuliffe, the

III-13

IIIB-2

dobro

musician who put the steel guitar in the country-music limelight, removed the Hawaiian associations from the instrument by creating a jazz-influenced style.

HANK WILLIAMS, SR. AND THE DEFINING VALUES OF COUNTRY MUSIC

The core of country music is clear; so is the ongoing tension within the music between tradition and assimilation. Both are embodied in the lives and music of its major performers. There is no better illustration of country music's essence and evolution than the life and music of Hank Williams, Sr. (1923–1953), the quintessential country singer.

Williams was born into a poor family in rural Alabama. While still in his teens, he performed in rough honky-tonks near his home and later in southern Alabama. His career received a boost from Fred Rose, a Nashville-based pianist, songwriter, and music publisher, and one of the most successful promoters in the history of country music. Williams gained widespread exposure throughout the South and Southwest through appearances on two radio shows, the Louisiana Hayride and the Grand Ole Opry.

honky-tonk

A Hank Williams performance typically featured all the qualities that distinguish country music. Any given song would express one of several recurrent themes or genres of country music—love problems being the most likely—in simple, direct language often rich in metaphor. His band included the fiddle and steel guitar, solo instruments closely associated with the country sound, as well as a full rhythm section. A simple melody and clear beat would provide the ideal setting for the most thoroughly country element of all, his highly individual, if often copied, conception of the traditional "mountain" vocal style: thin, nasal, flat, yet intensely expressive, plaintive or high-spirited as the song demanded.

steel guitar

Williams and his music are country in every way:

Geographical: Williams's roots are in the Deep South, and his career developed through agencies located in the South, e.g., WSM radio in Nashville, home of the Grand Ole Opry

Cultural: His songs spoke to his fellow Southerners about subjects that reflected their concerns and values—love, alcohol, God, good times, etc.—in their own language, even though these subjects also had great appeal outside the South

Musical: In rhythm, melodic style, instrumentation, and above all vocal style, Williams's songs express the tradition-rooted, yet continually evolving sound of country music.

All these qualities are evident in his classic "Your Cheatin' Heart" (Example 12.1), one of his most memorable performances. The recording shows the mixture of old and new that distinguishes country music from the folk music from which it emerged. As in traditional country music, the fiddle plays a prominent role. But the band behind Williams also includes a full rhythm section, including drums, plus the "newly traditional" country instrument, steel guitar. Williams's singing also blends old and new. It has a uniquely country timbre, but is drenched with blues. This was Williams's own synthesis, one that made him perhaps the most easily recognized singer in country music.

III-10

IIIA-10

Even more telling is the use to which Williams puts his voice. Like Billie

Hank Williams, 1949.

Holiday and Frank Sinatra, he is one of the great song interpreters. His songs when performed by a pop singer can seem banal. The intensity of Williams's rendition brings to life the pain behind the words. He's not just singing the song, he's reliving the experience that prompted the song in front of his audience. It's a gift few have had.

PARALLELS BETWEEN COUNTRY AND AFRICAN-AMERICAN MUSIC

Like many country songs of the late forties and early fifties, "Your Cheatin' Heart" was a hit in cover versions before Williams's version became nationally popular. In this respect, country music paralleled rhythm and blues: both offered songs that mainstream white audiences found appealing, but more palatable when sung by pop singers. Their history is similar in other respects.

From its beginnings to the emergence of rock, the commercial development of country music and much African-American music, especially blues and blues-influenced styles, ran along remarkably parallel paths. Each served a minority population assumed to be lower class by most of the mainstream majority. Both styles were identified within the popular-music industry by names with strong pejorative overtones. Recordings by African-Americans were called "race" records; early country music soon came to be known as "hillbilly" music. Both country music and blues were transmitted

hillbilly

aurally. As a result, radio and records were essential for widespread dissemination of both styles.

The term "hillbilly" had been in use since the turn of the century to identify rural white Southerners, but its musical association dates from a 1925 recording session with Al Hopkins, leader of a four-man string band. When asked by Ralph Peer, the talent scout who ran the session, to give the band a name, Hopkins replied "Call the band anything you want. We are nothing but a bunch of hillbillies from North Carolina and Virginia anyway." The term, even as it's used today, reflects both a strong, even defensive, sense of regional identity but also a self-deprecatory attitude. Other band names from the twenties, both African-American and white, suggest this same conflicting mix of pride and put-down: Gid Tanner's Skillet Lickers have their counterpart in the early jazz group the Chocolate Dandies.

string band

At mid-century, both blues and country stood apart from the popular-music mainstream, although they had moved closer to the center. Their move toward the mainstream, and vice versa, was evident both in the more complimentary and musically accurate name for each of these satellite styles. Hillbilly had become country and western, race had become rhythm and blues. In addition, "crossover" hits appeared on the pop charts with increasing frequency.

There are musical parallels as well. In both traditions, the most traditional and authentic vocal styles were instantly recognizable and far from the pop crooners. Their vocal sound was not "pretty," but powerfully communicative. Writing about Hank Williams, Bill Malone says:

> Williams sang with the quality that has characterized every great hillbilly singer: utter sincerity. He "lived" the songs he sang. He could communicate his feelings to the listener and make each person feel as if the song were being sung directly and only to him or her.

Change hillbilly to blues, and Malone's statement accurately describes a great blues singer, or blues-influenced pop singer, (as was suggested in the discussion of Billie Holiday in Chapter 10). Both blues and country music embraced the electric guitar almost as soon as it came on the market. Both also gradually filled out the instrumental accompaniment to include a complete rhythm section, blues in the 1940s, country in the 1950s.

But the role country music and blues have played in the development of popular music has been exactly the opposite. African-American music has been active in creating new styles; country music has been reactive, beginning with a traditional base and absorbing musical influences from a myriad of sources.

COUNTRY MUSIC: FROM ITS BEGINNING TO THE EMERGENCE OF ROCK 'N' ROLL

The first country music recordings spanned a broad spectrum of styles. At one end of the spectrum were traditional songs like "Old Joe Clark" (Example 3.4). There were also songs, like those of Vernon Dalhart, that drew heavily on the nineteenth-century, parlor-song tradition, ballads, cowboy songs, and gospel tunes.

 I-17

 IA-17

Most early country music recordings were made in the South by roving talent scouts representing major record companies. The most astute and successful of these scouts was undoubtedly Ralph Peer. Peer had negotiated a deal with Victor records wherein he retained publishing rights to the songs recorded by the musicians he discovered in return for his services as a field representative. This arrangement enabled him to form Southern Music Company, which in time became one of the largest music publishers of country music.

Peer would periodically tour the South with portable recording apparatus. A stop in Bristol, on the Tennessee-Virginia border, was one of the most fruitful in country-music history. As Bill Malone reports:

> In one of the great coincidences of country music history, two of its most influential acts made their first records for the same company in the first four days of August 1927. Jimmie Rodgers and the Carter Family took to Bristol, Tennessee, two of country music's most imitated styles and two of its most appealing impulses. Rodgers brought into clear focus the tradition of the rambling man which had been so attractive to country music's folk ancestors and which ever since fascinated much of the country music audience. This ex-railroad man conveyed the impression that he had been everywhere and had experienced life to the fullest. His music suggested a similar openness of spirit, a willingness to experiment, and a receptivity to alternative styles. The Carter Family, in contrast, represented the impulse toward home and stability, a theme as perennially attractive at that of the rambler. When the Carters sang, they evoked images of the country church, Mama and Daddy, the family fireside, and the "green fields of Virginia far away." Theirs was a music that might borrow from other forms, but would move away from its roots only reluctantly.

In their attitudes, and in the subjects and musical styles of their songs, the Carter Family and Jimmie Rodgers personified the conservative and progressive tendencies within country music. Table 12.1 outlines some of the differences between the two.

Table 12.1	**Comparison of the Carter Family and Jimmie Rodgers**	
	Carter Family	**Jimmie Rodgers**
Song Repertoire	Traditional songs or songs by A. P. Carter in the style of traditional songs	Almost all songs were originals, usually Rodgers's own
Vocal style	True "mountain" sound: clear, nasal, without vibrato and with little inflection	A highly individual amalgam of country, pop, and blues singing styles

Instrumental Accompaniment	Guitars and occasionally autoharp. Maybelle pioneered "thumb-brush" guitar style: melody on bass strings, harmony on upper strings.	Wide variety of accompanying instruments often added to basic voice/guitar combination; for example, early use of steel guitar and jazz-band horns

The Carter Family included A. P. Carter, his wife (after 1933, his ex-wife) Sara, and his sister-in-law, Maybelle. All three sang, Sara played guitar and autoharp, and Maybelle developed one of the most widely imitated guitar styles in the history of country music. A. P. Carter expanded their repertory by seeking out and arranging traditional songs. The Carters's professional career lasted from their discovery by Ralph Peer in 1927 until 1943. After World War II, Maybelle and her daughters continued to tour as the Carter Family, and subsequent incarnations of the group performed through the sixties.

Like many supposedly traditional country songs, "Wildwood Flower" (Example 12.2) was a nineteenth-century parlor song composed by two professional songwriters writing for a northern, middle-class clientele. The Carters's performing style does not represent the most traditional branch of early country music. In addition to Maybelle's innovative guitar style, these features suggest more recent influences:

III-11

IIIA-11

1. Absence of a fiddle
2. A clear distinction between melody and accompaniment, as opposed to the heterophony (each instrument playing the melody line more or less at the same time) of the traditional string band
3. Simple harmonic progressions in lieu of the ostinato patterns common in fiddle and string-band music

Jimmie Rodgers (1897–1933) had a brief but extraordinarily influential career. His musical legacy, preserved primarily through recordings, inspired an entire generation of performers to seek careers in country music. According to Bill Malone:

> Ernest Tubb estimated that perhaps 75 percent of modern country-music performers were directly or indirectly influenced to become entertainers either through hearing Rodgers in person or through his recordings.

Born in Mississippi, Rodgers spent much of his childhood and early adult life around the railroad, at first accompanying his father, a gang foreman, and then working off and on as a railroadman before contracting the tuberculosis that was to end his life prematurely.

Within a few months of his first recording for Ralph Peer, Rodgers's musical career was established. For the rest of his life, he enjoyed great popularity throughout the South through personal appearances, radio broadcasts, and his frequent recordings. Forced to move to Texas because of his illness, he gained an especially strong following in the Southwest. The greater receptiveness of Southwestern country music to outside influences is surely due in part to Rodgers's influence.

Rodgers's image of the rambling man roaming far and wide, one that he carefully cultivated in his songs, had great appeal for his fans. Musically, Rodgers borrowed liberally from all the styles with which he came into con-

Jimmie Rodgers in full rail-road regalia, c. 1928. This was a posed publicity shot taken when he was signed to Victor Records, to emphasize his working-class roots.

 III-12

 IIIB-1

tact; there are elements of Tin Pan Alley song, blues, and jazz in many of his recordings, as "Blue Yodel No. 11" (Example 12.3) demonstrates.

Rodgers was an extremely versatile singer. This song, his own composition, demonstrates his close affinity with African-American country blues. "Blue Yodel No. 11" is a typical blues song in textual content, melodic style, and form, although Rodgers's phrases are not consistently regular. More significantly, he sounds natural and very much at ease singing a blues. He has captured essential elements of the blues singing style: rhythmically free and unstilted delivery of the text; highly inflected phrasing (listen to the extra emphasis on the word "presents" in the third phrase of the first section); and a vocal style more expressive than pretty.

TRADITIONAL STYLES IN THE 1940s

The success of Roy Acuff (1903–1992) and the Grand Ole Opry are inextricably linked. After several tries, Acuff joined the show in 1938 and was an immediate success as a singer and personality. He became the host of the show a year later when NBC began its half-hour network broadcast. In the war years, Acuff was more closely identified with the Grand Ole Opry than any other performer.

 III-13

IIIB-2

"Wabash Cannon Ball" (Example 12.4) was a big radio hit for Acuff, but he only got around to recording it relatively late in his career, in 1947. The source and subject of this song attest to Acuff's conservative bent, but several features suggest contemporary influences, including:

1. The rich instrumentation: dobro and electric guitar are featured, and harmonica and accordion are also prominent

2. Dense, active texture, with countermelodies from several instruments often supporting the vocal line

3. Crisp honky-tonk style backbeat from the rhythm guitar

BLUEGRASS

Bill Monroe, a singer and mandolin player, is known as the father of bluegrass. Bluegrass emerged as a definite style in the years following World War II, perhaps in response to the increasing electrification and commercialization of country music. By the end of the 1940s, other musicians began copying features of Monroe's music of this period, which still remains the standard by which other bluegrass groups are measured. "It's Mighty Dark to Travel" (Example 12.5), sung and played by Bill Monroe and the Blue Grass Boys, is a classic early recording of this band.

bluegrass

 III-14

 IIIB-3

Bill Monroe (second from left) and an early version of his Blue Grass Boys, 1940.

The sound of bluegrass descends directly from the early string bands. The acoustic instrumentation and "mountain" vocal style preserve important country-music traditions. But there are some important differences as well:

1. *Expanded instrumentation.* Monroe and the Blue Grass Boys offered a complete array of acoustic string instruments: fiddle, guitar, banjo, mandolin, and string bass.

2. *Chop-chord mandolin style.* Bill Malone calls Bill Monroe's mandolin style "chop-chord." The "chop-chord," a percussive sound occurring in alternation with the bass, is bluegrass's answer to the honky-tonk backbeat.

chop-chord style

3. *Earl Scruggs's virtuoso banjo playing*. Scruggs developed a new style that combined the continuous stream of notes found in earlier banjo styles with the syncopated groupings of ragtime and the occasional blues lick, all at breakneck tempos.

4. *Collective improvisation*. The texture and form of a bluegrass recording has close parallels with New Orleans jazz. In both, there is a dense, active texture resulting from simultaneous improvisation on several melody instruments over a timekeeping rhythm section, with occasional interruptions for a featured soloist. This collective improvisation harks back to the heterogeneous texture of the string band, but there are more parts and their roles are more varied.

5. *Exceedingly fast tempos*. String band music was often dance music, but the tempos in many bluegrass songs are much too fast for all but the most agile dancers. This is listening music, although it invites a physical response. Part of the excitement of bluegrass is the skill with which its best performers reel off streams of notes at very fast speeds.

COUNTRY MUSIC IN THE SOUTHWEST

In the 1930s, the Southwest was the locus of stylistic innovation in country music. Cowboy and western music got its impetus in Texas and Oklahoma, even if it gained most of its notoriety further west, with the advent of the singing cowboy film. These films featured performers like Gene Autry and Tex Ritter, both of whom were authentic if derivative country singers before losing their rough edges in Hollywood.

Two other major country styles, *western swing* and *honky-tonk*, also developed in the Southwest during the thirties. Western swing blended the country string band with blues and jazz. The blues and jazz influence was most often evident in the heavier beat, fuller instrumentation, and solo styles.

No one did more to popularize the sound of western swing than Bob Wills, a fiddle player and bandleader from Texas, and few country musicians have played such a significant role in shaping the sound of country music. "Steel Guitar Rag" (Example 12.6) is a catalog of stylistic assimilations, most of which were eventually woven into the fabric of country music. Wills and the Playboys were not responsible for all of them, but, as the most popular band in the Southwest during the late thirties and early forties, did more than anyone else to popularize them. They include:

Western swing

 III-15

 IIIB-4

Bob Wills (far right, on horse) and the Texas Playboys in front of their tour bus, 1946.

1. *The use of an electrically amplified instrument.* Electrical amplification of guitars was still a very recent development in 1936, the year of this recording. Leon McAuliffe's amplified steel guitar, featured throughout "Steel Guitar Rag," did more than any other single performance to make the steel guitar an integral part of the country-music sound and also encouraged the more widespread use of amplification.

2. *The use of drums.* Wills was among the first country bandleaders to incorporate drums into a country band. In this recording, the drums are not particularly prominent, but they do reinforce the strong backbeat.

3. *Expanded instrumentation.* Wills merged a small jazz band (saxophones, trumpet, piano, bass, and drums) with a string band (fiddle, guitars, steel guitar, and banjo). Boots Randolph and the Nashville Brass to the contrary, horns have not been a consistent element of country music, but a full rhythm section became increasingly common after World War II.

4. *Honky-tonk beat.* The most characteristic rhythmic feature of honky-tonk music is a heavy backbeat superimposed onto a polka (OOM-pah) or waltz (OOM-pah-pah) rhythm. The result is similar to a fox-trot beat, but in western swing and country music, the backbeat is heavier and more closely related to swing and rhythm and blues. The fox-trot like rhythm with a heavy backbeat that would soon define the honky-tonk sound is heard clearly in this recording.

5. *Jazz and blues solo styles.* Steel guitarist Leon McAuliffe owes more to bottleneck blues guitar style than Hawaiian music, and both the sax and piano solos would transfer nicely to a jazz recording.

In his receptiveness to other styles, Wills certainly drew on Jimmie Rodgers's legacy. His stage demeanor, with his frequent words of encouragement to his musicians and yodeled expressions of pleasure, also recalls Rodgers's occasional spoken asides. In turn, he too left an enduring legacy of stylistic innovation.

HONKY-TONK MUSIC

A honky-tonk is a working class bar featuring country music, often performed by a live band. Honky-tonk also identifies the country-music style that emerged in the forties, in response to the conditions in those bars. The history of honky-tonk music begins in the Southwest in the early thirties. After the repeal of Prohibition, bars and dance halls catering to a working-class clientele sprang up all over the South, but particularly in Texas and Oklahoma. These bars were usually rough, noisy establishments, and musicians who performed in them needed to develop a new style that could be heard above the din. At the same time, their songs needed to articulate the problems and pleasures of the audience. Most of the traditional country repertoire, particularly sentimental or religious songs, would have been wildly inappropriate for a honky-tonk.

 III-16

 IIIB-5

Ray Price's 1954 recording of "Much Too Young to Die" (Example 12.7) is a good example of honky-tonk style as it developed in the two decades before rock 'n' roll. The style was defined principally by the following features, as we can hear on his recording:

1. Song texts that spoke plainly about problems encountered in a honky-tonk, or that would lead someone to frequent one: love, alcohol, hard times, loneliness, or life on the road.

2. A rough, nasal, vocal style far removed from the pop mainstream.

3. Instrumental backup that included fiddle, steel guitar, and complete or almost complete rhythm section of guitar, bass, piano, and drums.

4. Increasing use of electric instruments (for greater volume of sound).

5. A clear dance beat with a strong, crisp backbeat.

The greatest honky-tonk star was Hank Williams, Sr. He is also the most important performer in the history of country music, because he realized its expressive potential more than any other musician before or since. He was country music's great communicator; no one sang about life with as much immediacy or vividness. In a classic Hank Williams performance, the sympathetic listener hears his emotional message with a directness and impact that only a handful of singers within the popular tradition have equaled.

Along with music publisher Fred Rose, Hank Williams and Jimmie Rodgers were the first inductees into the Country Music Hall of Fame. Williams's and Rodgers's careers had other close parallels. Both died prematurely after only a brief period of commercial success (about five years in each case). Each was the most influential singer of his generation, spawning imitators too numerous to mention. Both men wrote many of the songs that they performed, although they also recorded material by others. For example, Williams's first commercially successful record was "Lovesick Blues," a popular song from the twenties. And both men blended a wide range of influences, including a heavy dose of blues, into a powerfully emotional style.

Hank Williams was the dominant country singer in the years immediately after World War II. His vocal style shows a variety of influences—country singers like Roy Acuff and Ernest Tubb, and blues and gospel music are the most prominent—yet Williams's singing voice, with its plaintive quality, naked emotion, and complete honesty, is probably the most distinctive and recognizable vocal sound in country music.

III-17

IIIB-6

"I'm So Lonesome I Could Cry" (Example 12.8) is one of Williams's classic songs and performances. Recorded in 1949, it is pure if slow honky-tonk, with its focus on the pain of separation, mournful vocal style, waltz rhythm with crisp backbeats, and definitively country instrumentation: prominent fiddle and steel guitar, piano and electric guitar fills, and a complete acoustic rhythm section (with the drummer playing brushes).

But it is far more than an ordinary country song. The text is much more elliptical and rich in metaphor than most country songs. The song is not a narrative, but a series of vivid images that makes Williams's heartbreak more meaningful than any story. We don't learn why Williams is lonesome until the next to last line, and that information is provided in an almost offhand manner.

Its melody is short and simple, yet well-crafted, with a nicely prepared climax at the beginning of the fourth line. The song is not a blues formally or melodically and the rhythm of the song has little to do with speech rhythm, but there seems to be a close affinity with the blues tradition nonetheless. This affinity is evident not only in the mood of the song, but also in the brevity of its melody, the use of strophic form (rather than verse-chorus), a blues-like chord progression, and heavy reliance on imagery in place of narrative. Poetically and emotionally, "I'm So Lonesome I Could Cry" has much more in common with Robert Johnson's "Hellhound on My Trail" (Example 7.2) than it does with Roy Acuff's "Wabash Cannon Ball" (Example 12.6) or the Tin Pan Alley hits of the day.

It is Williams's singing (which he called "moanin' the blues"), however, that elevates this performance to greatness. As we listen, we can hear his pain, perhaps because of the tension between the inherent fragility of his vocal sound it comes close to breaking several times and the intensity with which he emphasizes the long notes of the melody. Like Billie Holiday's, his is not a pretty voice, but that seems to be an advantage. Williams cuts through pop-vocal conventions to communicate directly with his audience. No country musician has done it more successfully.

CONCLUSION

The difference between the careers of Jimmie Rodgers and Hank Williams tells much about the commercial growth of country music in its first three decades. Although each was the most popular country star of his era, Jimmie Rodgers, for all his subsequent fame and influence, was strictly a regional celebrity during his lifetime. Outside the South and rural and small-town America, he was relatively unknown. He toured only in the South and Southwest, although he had made plans for tours of the North, West, and Canada prior to his death.

At the time of his death, Williams had a national, even international, reputation, although Southerners remained the core of his audience. His records sold widely, even outside the country and western market. Many of his songs were covered by pop singers like Tony Bennett and Rosemary Clooney. He signed a movie contract with MGM in 1951, although he died before appearing in any films. Williams's more widespread celebrity reflected the gradual acceptance of country music into mainstream culture.

Terms to Know

bluegrass	chop-chord style	dobro
hillbilly	honky-tonk	steel guitar
string band	Western swing	

Names to Know

Roy Acuff	The Carter Family	Vernon Dalhart
Grand Ole Opry	Bill Monroe	Ray Price
Jimmie Rodgers	Earl Scruggs	Hank Williams
Bob Wills		

Study Questions

1. What features distinguished early country music from Anglo-American folk music?

2. What role did radio and recordings play in the creation of country music?

3. What are some of the parallels between country and African-American folk music and folk-based styles (like the blues)?

4. Describe the ongoing battle between conservative and progressive forces within country music. What makes a country style "conservative" or "progressive"?

5. How do geography and culture help define country music? Why has Nashville been an important center for country-music making?

6. In what ways does Hank Williams's music embody country-music values? In what ways does it transcend them?

7. Compare Vernon Dalhart's singing style to Jimmie Rodgers's and Bill Monroe's. What are the similarities and differences?

CHAPTER THIRTEEN

Latin Music in the United States

Latin popular music has enriched musical life in America for over a century. Dances from Latin America, most notably the Argentine tango, the Cuban rumba and cha-cha-cha, and the Brazilian samba and bossa nova, have periodically invigorated popular music. Their sounds and rhythms have offered vibrant alternatives to mainstream pop. Just as significantly, Latin music, particularly from Cuba and Brazil, has increasingly influenced American popular music. In the first half of the century, each new Latin style first attained popularity as dance music, enjoying a brief vogue. It would then enter into the popular-music melting pot, where it would be used occasionally by songwriters, jazz musicians, and film composers.

tango

rumba

cha-cha-cha

samba

bossa nova

Since the early 1950s, however, Latin music has been much more than a source of variety. Its rhythms, instruments, and forms have helped shape rhythm and blues and jazz. In the 1970s, Latin music entered the mainstream. Afro-Cuban and Afro-Brazilian music were primary sources of the disco-related popular styles of that era.

Afro-Cuban

Afro-Brazilian

ROOTS OF LATIN STYLES

There are a wealth of Latin musical styles. Several of the countries and larger islands in the eastern part of the New World developed at least one distinctive idiom that eventually found its way to the United States. Like popular styles in the United States, these styles grew out of the interaction of African and European musical traditions, because the slave trade that brought Africans to the United States also brought them to other parts of the New World, particularly the Caribbean islands and Brazil.

Unlike their American counterparts, however, slaves in Latin America and the Caribbean kept much of their culture. They merged their tribal religions with the various forms of Christianity introduced by European colonialists. They created Creole dialects, hybrid languages that were part European, part African. Because drums, banned in the slave states of the United States, were permitted in most other parts of the New World, folk music from these regions has remained much closer to its African roots than almost all pre-1970 African-American music. Their music features more percussion instruments, and a denser, more complex rhythmic texture.

Despite their common origin in west African music, folk and popular styles vary considerably from country to country. This stylistic variety reflects most directly differences in the language and culture of the European nations that colonized them. The most dramatic instance of this variety would seem to be the contrast between Afro-Cuban and Afro-Brazilian music. Both have dense, rhythmically complex textures rich in percussion instruments. However, the rhythm of Cuban music is sharply articulated, while Brazilian rhythm flows smoothly from beat to beat. The contrast seems to parallel the difference between the harder consonants of the Spanish and the softer consonants of the Portuguese languages, representing the respective countries that colonized them.

LATIN MUSIC IN THE UNITED STATES

The most influential Latin dances and dance music in the United States have come primarily from two countries, Cuba and Brazil. Although these dances originated outside the United States, their sounds and rhythms have become part of the vocabulary of American popular music. Their assimilation parallels native "outsider" styles: a progress from exotic novelty to integral element. (Consider that in the first half of the century, old-time fiddle music or country blues would have been at least as alien to urban American ears as Latin popular music.)

The assimilation of Latin elements into the vocabulary of popular music has proceeded gradually over the last century. Three stages are discernible. In the first stage, Latin styles appeared as exotic novelties. They usually began as dance fads that provided occasional variety from mainstream fare. As popularized in America, they were only distantly related to their original realizations.

The second stage saw the emergence of hybrid or transformed styles. These grew out of the interpretations of Latin music by American musicians—and more significantly—the incorporation of American music into Latin styles. These Latin-influenced or Latin-derived styles were distinct from mainstream pop music until well into the rock era because of differences in rhythm and instrumentation between the two.

In the third stage, elements of Latin music have become part of the fabric of the dominant styles. Latin rhythms helped shape the rhythms of rock-era popular music, and Latin instruments appear routinely in a broad range of music. Latin music still stood apart from American popular styles, but the line demarcating them was not nearly so clear as it had been before rock.

These three stages have followed a roughly chronological progression. The first lasted until the early forties, the second peaked in mid-century, and the third spans the last third of the century. However, there has been considerable overlap, especially in the decade around 1960. Popular examples of all three stages coexisted easily during this time.

Both old and new Latin exotica found an audience. The tango, popular since the early teens, lived on in the musical. "Hernando's Hideaway," from the 1954 musical, *Pajama Game,* was probably the decade's best-known reincarnation of it. The cha-cha-cha surfaced as the last of the exotic Latin dance fads in the mid-fifties. One of the biggest hits of the genre was the 1958 remake of Vincent Youmans's 1925 standard, "Tea for Two," by the Tommy

Dorsey Orchestra. That a cha-cha-cha version of a Tin Pan Alley song played by a swing band would be representative of the style gives some indication of how modest the Latin influence was during the first stage.

Second-stage hybrids also flourished during the fifties and early sixties. Both the mambo—at least the "uptown" mambos of Tito Puente—and the bossa nova were styles created by Latin musicians who flavored authentic Latin music with jazz. Diluted versions of these styles were also abundant during their moment in the sun. Latin music also helped shape rock and rhythm and blues. Most of the R&B bands of the fifties included a few Latin numbers in their repertoire. Ray Charles's 1959 classic "What'd I Say" (Example 14.10) shows how Latin elements easily crept into rock and rhythm-and-blues songs.

mambo

D

The gradual acceptance of Latin music in the United States throughout the century has paralleled—indeed in many cases uncannily previewed—the assimilation of African-American elements into the popular mainstream. Through the first part of the century, a Latin dance fad foreshadowed each American dance craze: the tango was popular just prior to the fox trot; rumba predated swing; and mambo forecast rock. All these dances had rhythms different from the mainstream styles that they anticipated, but the overall pattern of rhythmic change was similar. In its Americanized form, each new Latin beat was rhythmically more complex than the one that preceded it. Disco, the most recent dance fad, broke the pattern. Here, Latin music became a primary source of a new beat, rather than a prelude to one.

STAGE 1: LATIN MUSIC AS MUSICAL EXOTICA

The story of Latin dance music in the United States begins over a century ago with the Cuban habanera. Its name is probably an abbreviated form of contradanza habanera—contredanse (a European ballroom dance) from Havana—and its characteristic rhythm is one of the first recorded instances of African influence on European music. The habanera developed during the early part of the nineteenth century with its popularity spreading beyond Cuba after 1850. In the decades that followed, it became known throughout the United States, Europe, and the rest of Latin America. The French composer Georges Bizet composed a habanera for his opera, *Carmen*, and Louis Moreau Gottschalk, the American composer/pianist/matinee idol, wrote several piano pieces that used the habanera rhythm. It also entered the United States by way of Mexico, where it had become popular in the 1870s. A Mexican military band performed the dance at an international exposition held in New Orleans in 1884–1885. They were the musical hit of the event, and their popularity led to the publication of several of the most popular pieces in their repertoire.

habanera

By the end of the century, the influence of the habanera was evident in more mainstream American popular music. The rhythmic signature of cakewalks like "At a Georgia Camp Meeting" (Example 6.2) and ragtime songs like "Under the Bamboo Tree" (Example 6.3) is identical to the habanera. Musical evidence suggests that the habanera also went south to Argentina, where it became the rhythmic basis of the tango.

 I-36

 IB-10

The tango was the first of the Latin dance crazes in the United States. It arrived in America in 1913 from Argentina by way of Paris. Irene and Vernon Castle had captivated Paris with their dancing of the tango. Upon their return to the United States, they introduced it in a Broadway show, *The*

 I-37

 IB-11

Don Azpiazu's Havana Casino Orchestra, c. 1931.

Sunshine Girl. Their dancing in the show was an immediate success. It helped to spark the enormous enthusiasm for social dancing that the Castles spearheaded. Although it never approached the popularity of the fox-trot, the tango became the first Latin dance to achieve a permanent place in American popular music. Tin Pan Alley songwriters featured occasional tangos in Broadway shows until well into the 1950s.

 III-18

 IIIB-7

The surprising success of Don Azpiazu's 1930 recording of "El Manisero," ("The Peanut Vendor" in English; Example 13.1) triggered the second of the Latin dance crazes in the United States: the rumba. Its success touched off a widespread enthusiasm for Latin music, sending publishers back to their catalogs for Latin numbers and inspiring a number of Latin songs by American songwriters. When performed by Latins, the rumba was a spectacular exhibition dance, but simplified rumbas were also widely used for social dancing. It remains the most popular of the Latin ballroom dances.

son

The rumba grew out of an Afro-Cuban dance called the *son*. The *son* apparently originated in eastern Cuba, developing from African and Hispanic elements. Brought to Havana around the turn of the century, it gained widespread popularity among all classes in Cuba in the twenties with the growth of commercial radio in that country. Much Cuban radio featured live performers, who were heard but not seen. In this way, Cubans of African descent gained access to audiences who would not normally hear them perform live.

There were important differences in the way in which the rumba and tango became popular in the United States. The tango was introduced by an Englishman and an American woman who had learned the dance in Paris. The first and most definitive recording of "The Peanut Vendor" was made by a Cuban bandleader named Don Azpiazu, whose Havana Casino Orchestra performed with a complete Cuban rhythm section. Even though rhythmically diluted versions of "The Peanut Vendor" and other Latin songs followed immediately (like the covers of 1950s rock 'n' roll hits), an authentic Latin performance was available. Interested listeners no longer had to settle for secondhand versions of Latin music.

Azpiazu's recording of "El Manisero" shows the necessary accommodation of Cuban music with American pop. The Cuban influence is most evident in the vocal, the prominent Latin percussion, and the (reverse) clave rhythm. (Clave rhythm is to Cuban popular music what the backbeat is to American popular styles: a consistent point of rhythmic reference.) In other respects, this is a period song: muted trumpet, and a piano style halfway between Cuban and cocktail piano. Still, it is a milestone: It marked the first incursion of authentically Latin-sounding music into popular music. The song and style were enormously influential for the better part of two decades, until an even more rhythmically complex Afro-Cuban style developed within the United States.

The rumba craze led to an increased presence for Latin music in the thirties. Songs by American songwriters, like Irving Berlin's "Heat Wave" (1933), showed greater sensitivity to Latin style, and songs by Latin composers—Cuban Nilo Melendez's "Green Eyes" and Ary Barroso's "Brasil"—became pop standards. Of the great Tin Pan Alley songwriters, Cole Porter was the songwriter most sensitive to Latin style. His "Begin the Beguine" (1935) remains the best-known of his many songs to use Latin rhythms. The Latin rhythms used by popular songwriters were not nearly so complex as those found in authentic Latin music, but they still captured something of the Latin rhythmic feel.

Both staged and filmed musicals featured Latin music more prominently. The 1933 film *Flying Down to Rio*, Fred Astaire's and Ginger Rogers's first film together, introduced an Americanized version of the samba. Latin performers like Desi Arnaz and Carmen Miranda began their American careers by starring in stage productions in the late thirties. Xavier Cugat, a Spanish-born violinist raised in Cuba, helped to establish a commercial Latin style as a bandleader at the Waldorf hotels in New York and Los Angeles and as the most filmed bandleader in Hollywood.

Xavier Cugat and Desi Arnaz represented the "downtown" form of Latin music: a rhythmically simplified, commercially oriented, hybrid style acceptable to white audiences. They gave the most visible evidence of a growing Latin musical presence in the United States, especially in New York. This increased presence resulted in large part from the emigration of Spanish-speaking Caribbean people. Most settled in east Harlem, in upper Manhattan.

The establishment of a Latin district, or *barrio*, in New York dates back to the turn of the century. One of the consequences of the 1898 Spanish-American war was the cession of Puerto Rico to the United States. Puerto Ricans were allowed to emigrate to the United States without restriction; many settled in New York. Latins from other parts of the Caribbean soon followed, and by the late twenties, there was a substantial community of Cuban musicians residing in the United States. Some appeared in vaudeville or worked in society dance orchestras, but many also played for the growing U.S. Latin community and recorded for companies catering to it.

Cuban immigrants passed on their style to Americans of Cuban and Puerto Rican descent living in New York. Among the Cuban musicians who moved to New York and, later, the Puerto Rican musicians who copied Cuban music, there was a clear division between downtown and uptown music, just as there was among African-American jazz musicians. The downtown Latin style was intended for the white American market. During the thirties, this commercial Latin music was usually performed by bands made up mostly of white Latin musicians. The music featured pop-song melodies and light percussion.

Uptown Latin music served the musical needs of the ever-growing Latin community in New York. This music was more African, with much heavier percussion and denser, more complex rhythmic textures. In the forties, cubop — uptown Manhattan would be home to the mambo and cubop, the first sustained experiment in Latin jazz. Both represented the second stage of development of Latin music in the United States.

STAGE 2: LATIN HYBRIDS AND TRANSFORMATIONS

In the second stage, U.S.-based Latin musicians and African-American musicians interacted and collaborated to create hybrid styles, or to transform an existing style by incorporating Latin rhythms. The first fruits of this interaction were the mambo and cubop. Mambo was Latin music with a jazz tinge. Cubop, as its name implies, merged bebop with Cuban rhythms. Two other styles appeared just prior to rock's British invasion. The cha-cha-cha, which became popular in the United States in the late fifties, was the last of the Latin dance fads. The bossa nova, very popular in the early sixties, was a Brazilian music heavily influenced by jazz.

The mambo was the third of the twentieth-century Latin dance fads, but the first to develop on American soil. It merged authentic Afro-Cuban *son*, as performed in New York by musicians like Arsenio Rodriguez, with big-band horns and riffs. The style was born in 1940, when Machito (Frank Grillo), New York's first important *sonero* (lead singer in a *son* band), formed his own band, Machito's Afro-Cubans, and hired fellow Cuban Mario Bauza as musical director. Bauza had worked in the African-American swing bands of Cab Calloway and Chick Webb and wanted to combine Cuban rhythms with the horn sound of swing. Their new style provided an uptown alternative to the commercial Cugat sound. By the end of the decade, Machito's style had been copied by other bandleaders.

By the late forties, the mambo had begun to attract notice outside of uptown New York. Downtown ballrooms like New York's Palladium Dance

Machito Orchestra, c. 1940s; Mario Bauza, trumpeter/music director, fourth from left.

Hall served as venues for this new dance fad. The mambo caught on with the non-Latin audience, first as a dance music, then as a popular song. Even the top singing stars occasionally dabbled in it. Both Perry Como and Nat "King" Cole recorded a song called "Papa Loves Mambo"; it was a million seller for Como in 1954. The mambo fad was not limited to pop music. Rhythm-and-blues bands of the fifties typically included a few mambo tunes in their repertoire. This would be the most important point of entry for Latin influence on rock-era music.

The dilution of the mambo as it entered the mainstream paralleled the watering down of the rumba in the early thirties or, for that matter, almost any "outsider" style in the first half of the century. What differentiated the fate of this Latin fad from the earlier one was the presence of a stable and supportive U.S. audience for Afro-Cuban inspired music. The expatriate Cuban musicians who popularized Latin music in the thirties had to accommodate popular taste to attain any commercial success. The audience for authentic Cuban music in this country was too small to support them. Twenty years later, that audience had grown large enough to support the Afro-Cuban based sounds of the mambo.

The presence of two "mambo kings" in the fifties brings to light the deep

Tito Puente, c. 1980s.

division between authentic and commercial Latin music. For white audiences, pianist/bandleader Perez Prado was king. His recordings, many of them called simply Mambo No. 1, 2, etc., were the sound of the mambo for the masses. The extent of his inroad into the mainstream market can be gauged by the success of his biggest hit, "Cherry Pink and Apple Blossom White," which topped the pop charts in early 1955 for ten weeks. But his style often had little to do with authentic Afro-Cuban music. In many of his recordings, Afro-Cuban rhythms and instrumentation are severely diluted or completely absent.

For Latins, the "King of the Mambo" was Tito Puente. Puente, born in New York of Puerto Rican parents, was an alumnus of Machito's band, in which he played timbales. By the early fifties, he had formed his own band, for which he also composed and arranged. His style, with its heavy brass and full Cuban rhythm section, appealed much more strongly to Latin audiences than Prado's music did.

timbales

The creation of the mambo reversed the normal pattern of assimilation in Latin music in the United States. In the past, Latin elements were absorbed into American music. Now, with a sufficient Latin audience in this country, musicians could perform authentic Latin styles, adding American elements to the mix.

 III-19

 IIIB-8

"Complication" (Example 13.2), recorded in 1958 by Tito Puente, shows how far Latin music in the United States had moved in assimilating both American and Afro-Cuban elements. The instrumental accompaniment mixes big-band style horns (brass and saxes playing riffs and sustained chords) with a full Latin percussion section.

tumbao

salsa

Particularly in the second section, it is possible to hear key elements of Afro-Cuban rhythm. The repeated riff conforms to the clave rhythm, and several layers of percussion produce a dense texture with considerable rhythmic conflict. The bass plays the offbeat *tumbao* pattern, while the piano plays figurations that recalls the syncopations of ragtime. There is little stylistic difference between this and the salsa of twenty years later.

Like country music, the Afro-Cuban mambo of Machito and Tito Puente was a regional music; however, the region was a slice of Manhattan and the Bronx, not the entire Southeastern and Southwestern quadrants of the country. Also like country music, the mambo was gaining a national presence in the years after World War II, most popularly in diluted forms, and it would play a significant, but not primary, role in shaping rock.

The other Cuban-inspired dance fad in the fifties was the cha-cha-cha. The cha-cha-cha became popular among white Cubans in the 1950s, and its popularity quickly spread to the United States. Both the rhythm and the dance step of the cha-cha-cha were simpler than the mambo and its tempo was slower. As a result, it replaced the mambo as the Latin dance of choice in this country.

The impact of Latin music on jazz dates from the time of its origins. Jelly Roll Morton, the self-styled inventor of jazz and one of its early greats, claimed that it was a "Spanish tinge" that differentiated jazz from ragtime. The presence of a "Spanish tinge" in early jazz is not surprising, because New Orleans had more contact with the Caribbean islands than did any other American city during the nineteenth and early twentieth centuries, as well as some Spanish settlers.

Latin music occasionally influenced jazz and popular music throughout the first part of the century. W. C. Handy's "St. Louis Blues," the most record-ed song of the first half century, sandwiches a tango/habanera middle sec-tion between two blues sections. Duke Ellington made extensive use of Latin rhythms and percussion in compositions like "Caravan." Dizzy Gillespie went a step further and hired Chano Pozo, a Latin percussionist, for the big band that he formed in the late forties. This sparked the development of Cu-bop, a true Latin-jazz style. At about the same time, Stan Kenton, who com-posed for and directed an innovative postwar big band, also incorporated Latin rhythms and instruments into extended jazz compositions.

Throughout the fifties, Latin-influenced jazz maintained a consistent if modest presence. Gillespie continued to experiment with Latin-jazz fusions, as did the popular British jazz pianist George Shearing. In the early fifties, Shearing formed a combo that included three Latin percussionists, as well as vibraphonist Cal Tjader. Cuban Mongo Santamaria, who played conga with Shearing, would play an important role in bringing jazz, rock, and Latin music together in the sixties. Other prominent jazz musicians, among them Sonny Rollins, Clifford Brown, and Horace Silver, also explored Latin-influ-enced rhythms.

The Latin-jazz fusions of the forties and fifties mixed jazz with Afro-Cuban elements. The sixties would usher in another major jazz-Latin fusion by way of Brazil. The fusion began with the bossa-nova fad of the early six-ties, but soon encompassed the rhythmically richer samba as well. This fusion would not simply provide an alternative to straight-ahead jazz. It would play a major role in creating the new jazz style of the seventies and eighties.

Bossa nova, a Brazilian music based on the samba, was the last of the Latin dance fads. Created in Brazil during the late fifties, the style first received international exposure in the 1959 film *Black Orpheus*. In 1962, bossa nova became popular in the United States almost overnight, first through the recordings of sympathetic jazzmen like Charlie Byrd and Stan Getz, then in performances by leading Brazilian songwriters like Joao Gilberto and Antonio Carlos Jobim. Its most enduring and covered hit was Gilberto's "Girl from Ipanema." Bossa nova enjoyed mass popularity for only a short time, but retained a loyal audience well into the seventies.

Although briefly popular as a dance, bossa nova had more sustained impact as music for listening. Bossa nova was a hybrid style developed by Brazilian musicians that combined samba rhythms with the harmonic rich-ness of American jazz. Its smoothly undulating melodies and subtly shifting harmonies drew on both the traditional flowing lines of Brazilian music, the forms and developmental style of American popular song, and the chord vocabulary of both. The lighter Brazilian rhythms offered a gentler alterna-tive to the rhythmic drive of rock. The rhythms of the Brazilian bossa nova were simpler than those of the samba. Its melodies and harmonies, on the other hand, were more complex.

"Desafinado" (Example 13.3), composed by Antonio Carlos Jobim and performed by Joao Gilberto and Stan Getz, was one of the most popular bossa novas of the early sixties. It brings together songwriter/vocalist/gui-tarist Joao Gilberto, one of the stars of Brazilian bossa nova, and Stan Getz, a leading jazz tenor saxophonist since the late forties.

"Desafinado," with its long, sinuous melodic line and rich, smoothly shifting harmonies may be the definitive bossa-nova song. Other features

III-20

IIIB-9

Stan Getz with Frank Isola (drums), 1957. Photograph by Paul Hoeffler.

also make this a classic performance: its slow tempo; the accompanying instrumentation of drums, bass, piano, and guitar; the gentle, yet syncopated, guitar chords behind the melody; and the quiet, but insistent regular rhythm, first on closed hi-hat, then on ride cymbal, that moves four times as fast as the bass.

Bossa nova was an early instance of a new pattern of mutual influence: the exportation of American popular music, its cross-fertilization with African-influenced music from other cultures, and the subsequent importation of the new hybrid style. The creators of the bossa nova blended American music with a native tradition, in this case American jazz and popular song with the Brazilian samba. The resulting new style then returned to the United States, where it helped shape new American styles, particularly the African-American music and new-jazz tradition of the seventies. Subsequently, styles like reggae and soca have followed a similar path. The world-music movement of the eighties is a global expansion of the same process. It is likely to continue into the next century.

Stage 3: Mainstream Influence

In the third stage, Latin music has woven smoothly into the fabric of contemporary popular music. Latin percussion and Latin rhythms, two of its most distinctive elements, have been an integral part of much of the music of the last thirty years.

The primary reason for the seamless integration of Latin elements into contemporary popular music is rhythmic. With rock, American popular music had become more African. Rock gave percussion a more prominent place in the musical texture. The additional percussion instruments, and percussive use of nonpercussion instruments, helped create denser, more complex rhythms. Both rock and Latin rhythms typically divide the beat into durations of equal length. By contrast, fox-trot and swing rhythms presume uneven (long/short) division of the beat. Since rock, then, Latin rhythms adapted into American popular music can be understood as variants of, rather than as alternatives to, the prevailing style.

The rhythmic compatibility of rock and Latin music disguised the influence of Latin music to some extent, at least among rock's audience. How many listeners would have identified Bo Diddley's famous beat as the clave rhythm, the rhythmic underpinning of Cuban music? The same question could be asked of James Brown's influential "Cold Sweat" (Example 15.11).

 IV-13

 IVB-1

Latin influence on sixteen-beat styles has been even more extensive. Much of the African-American music since the late sixties has incorporated Latin percussion instruments and denser rhythmic textures, especially the work of leading artists, including Marvin Gaye, Stevie Wonder, Aretha Franklin, Roberta Flack, and George Clinton. The most popular Latin-influenced music of the seventies was disco. Disco was a musical melting pot, combining popular song, rock, funk, salsa, and Brazilian music.

Disco, African-American music, and the new jazz were for Latin music what rock was for country music: the point of entry into the mainstream. Collectively, they represented a commercially significant family of styles of which Latin music was an integral, if subordinate, part. Like the use of country-inspired song forms in rock, Latin touches in this music are so much a part of its sound that they seldom seem exotic, as they would have in earlier styles. A perfect example is the use of the conga drum as the primary percussion instrument in Stevie Wonder's "You Are the Sunshine of My Life" (Example 20.4). Although Latin influence is certainly evident when it's present in heavy doses, more often it blends smoothly and almost imperceptibly into the overall texture.

conga drum

Since the fifties, Latin styles have introduced new colors and richer rhythms into popular music, rather than radically different beats. Other New World styles have also enriched the sound vocabulary of contemporary music. Three of them, calypso from Trinidad, mariachi music from Mexico, and reggae from Jamaica, enjoyed a brief vogue of about five years each in this country. During this time the most distinctive elements of the style—the steel drums and beat of calypso, the trumpets of mariachi music, and the unique backbeat of reggae—entered the sound world of popular music.

The seamless integration of Latin and New World elements into contemporary popular music was the most significant new development in Latin music in the latter half of the century. It came about in part because of the Cuban revolution. A flood of refugees from Cuba soon followed Fidel Castro's overthrow of the U.S.-friendly Batista regime in 1959, greatly increasing the demand for Latin music. But the flood was soon reduced to a trickle: following the severing of diplomatic relations between Cuba and the United States in 1960–1961, the emigration of Cubans ended.

Deprived of continuing contact with Cuban musicians, U.S.-based Latin musicians reacted in two quite opposite ways. Some created hybrid styles from Latin and American music, like the short-lived bugalu, Latinos' version of "soul music." The other, more significant, response was the development of salsa, the dominant Latin style since the early 1970s. Salsa (Spanish for "sauce") was fundamentally a "return to roots" movement, a successful effort to reestablish and popularize the Americanized Afro-Cuban *son* style performed in this country since the late thirties. It updated this traditional Afro-Cuban music with more varied instrumentation and other influences from non-Cuban styles like rock and Puerto Rican music. But these changes were mostly cosmetic; according to the accounts by both older and younger musicians, salsa retained its Cuban core. Significantly, the dominant figures in salsa were Latino, but not Cuban. New York-born Puerto Rican (Newyorican) musicians, like pianists Charlie and Eddie Palmieri, trombonist Willie Colón, and the Panamanian-born singer Ruben Blades, have been especially influential.

Newyorican

Willie Colón, c. 1980s.

III-21

IIIB-10

"Ojos" (Example 13.4), performed by Willie Colón with vocalist Ruben Blades, is an example of salsa. Willie Colón, trombonist and bandleader, remains one of the most respected and popular salsa bandleaders. His vocalist on this recording is Panamanian Ruben Blades, one of the most emotionally stirring of the younger *soneros*. Blades has also had a successful acting career.

This song exemplifies the salsa style that reaches back to the mambo and Cuban *son*. In it there are both Afro-Cuban and American elements. The Afro-Cuban features include:

1. *A dense rhythmic texture featuring several characteristic Cuban percussion instruments.* The most prominent are the conga, a long cigar-shaped drum with a drumhead on one end and a opening at the other end; timbales, two drums, just a little larger than the snare drum of the trap set; and bongos, two smaller drums that make a high-pitched sound. Other instruments—maracas, claves, and the like—also contribute to the extremely active and dense texture.
2. *Clave rhythm.* This five-note rhythmic pattern, best-known in American music from the several Bo Diddley songs that use it (something like: "shave [and a] hair cut, two bits"), is the basis of traditional Afro-Cuban rhythm. Everything else relates to it: melody; bass lines; piano *montuno* patterns; percussion rhythms; horn riffs.   *montuno*
3. *Tumbao bass.* Salsa bassists play a clave-derived pattern that falls off, rather than on, the main beats. This is one feature that usually distinguishes salsa from Americanized Latin music.
4. *Montuno piano patterns.* The pianist in a salsa band plays active, syncopated patterns over and over. Many of them are reminiscent of ragtime.
5. *The two-part form. Canto* (narrative) and *montuno* (rhythmic/instrumental)   *canto*

The major American feature is the brass writing, which has clear roots in the big-band style of the thirties and forties.

The form of this song expands on a typical two-part structure: canto and montuno. The montuno includes several sections. The formal highpoints in this song are:

Canto
Extended brass introduction
The Canto proper. This is the extended narrative section of a salsa song, much like the verse in a verse-chorus song. A major difference is the fact that the canto is only sung once. The canto ends with a decisive break.
Montuno. The montuno begins with a *coro.* Typically, the *coro* consists   *coro* of a short riff, followed by silence. In this recording, it is played first by instruments, then sung at least partially to the title words. Its brevity gives the *sonero* ample opportunity for solo flights. The next section alternates a brass figure with sections that bring the percussion instruments to prominence. Here the percussionists break out of their more restricted patterns to play in a rhythmically freer style.

The *coro* then returns; as before, an instrumental statement of the riff precedes a vocal version. The two are combined with an active piano montuno pattern before a reprise of the vocal part of the *coro* and the brass introduction to the song, which now serves as an ending.

Salsa and the related Latin styles remain the more-or-less exclusive province of Latin communities in New York, Miami, and elsewhere. But elements of salsa style have merged with other popular styles. The use of the conga drum is the most pervasive, as well as the clave rhythm, other percussion instruments, and *montuno* patterns by keyboard players.

Latin rock was one of the many rock-hybrid styles that emerged in the late sixties. Latin rock was simply rock plus salsa. It was basically a one-man movement: Carlos Santana created the style in the late sixties. Interestingly,

Sergio Mendes, c. 1970.

Santana, who was based on the west coast, is neither Cuban nor Newyorican. He is a Chicano (Mexican-American) who was attracted to the music of Tito Puente and other Latin musicians.

The bossa nova represented the deepest penetration of Brazilian music into the American market. Of all the Brazilian musicians, Sergio Mendes remained popular enough to update the name of his group from Brazil '66 to Brazil '77. However, Brazilian music found its most comfortable niche in the world of jazz. The jazz-samba fusion that produced the bossa nova was the beginning of a Brazilian-American exchange that is still going on. Evidence from the early seventies included the presence of Brazilian musicians in leading fusion bands and the samba-jazz synthesis heard in Chick Corea's especially influential album, *Light as a Feather.* There is an unmistakable Brazilian flavor in much of the new jazz since 1970. This new jazz echoes with the buoyant rhythms and colorful percussion instruments of Brazilian sambas. We hear both these qualities in a more traditional context in Example 13.5.

III-22

IIIB-11

"Quilombo" (Example 13.5) is an authentic samba written and performed by Gilberto Gil, one of Brazil's leading popular artists. Like many younger Brazilian musicians, he has incorporated elements from non-Brazilian popular styles into much of his music. Here, however, he shows his comfort with the more traditional music of his country.

"Quilombo" is very much in the spirit of the sambas performed during carnival time. Its melody spins out in long phrases. Rich harmony, although not as intricate as "Desafinado" (Example 13.3), supports the melody. "Quilombo" features a well-stocked percussion section, with many instruments playing regular sixteen-beat rhythms or patterns based on this fastest layer. Pitched instruments, especially guitar, also contribute to this dense rhythmic texture.

CONCLUSION

The presence and influence of Latin music in the United States has grown steadily over the last 100 years. A century ago, its influence was present but almost imperceptible. A touch of Latin rhythm crept into popular music via the habanera-cakewalk connection. A "Spanish tinge" distinguished jazz from ragtime, according to early jazz great Jelly Roll Morton. However, no distinctively Latin style enjoyed widespread popularity.

In the first half of this century, a series of Latin dance fads–tango, rumba, and mambo–introduced American audiences to progressively more authentic Latin sounds. From the dance floor they filtered into popular song and jazz. The Latin-inspired music that appeared between 1910 and 1945 was created by Americans who incorporated Latin elements into their work. Toward mid-century, New York-based Latin musicians Americanized Afro-Cuban music with the sounds and riffs of big-band jazz. The result was the first important Latin music created in the United States.

With the ascendancy of rock, both Cuban and Brazilian music became part of the fabric of mainstream popular music. Because of the similarity between Latin and rock rhythms, and the increased emphasis on rhythm in rock, the sounds and instruments of Latin music became part of a wide variety of rock-era styles. Music in which Latin elements predominated, like salsa or bossa nova, easily revealed their Latin roots. However, the gap between Latin and non-Latin styles, so evident before rock, had all but disappeared.

Latin music, once an exotic and largely misunderstood alternative to American popular styles, is now part of the fabric of popular music. It has helped shape the most rhythmically progressive music of the last quarter century, as we'll discover in Chapter 20, and authentic styles have a gained small but stable and enthusiastic audience in this country, Europe, and the Far East.

Terms to Know

Afro-Brazilian	Afro-Cuban	bossa nova
canto	cha-cha-cha	clave
conga drum	*coro*	cubop
habanera	mambo	*montuno*
Newyorican	rumba	salsa
samba	*son*	tango
timbales	*tumbao*	

Names to Know

Don Azpiazu	Ruben Blades	Gilberto Gil
Joao Gilberto	Machito	Perez Prado
Tito Puente		

Study Questions

1. What Latin dances became popular just before the: (a) fox trot; (b) swing era; (c) rock 'n' roll era? How did each dance fad differ from the one before it? Why was there no Latin dance fad in the seventies?

2. What is the clave rhythm? Can you clap it? Why is it important to Afro-Cuban music?

3. How did Latin music influence popular music in the thirties? Jazz in the fifties? Popular music in the seventies?

4. Where in the United States did a Latin music community develop around 1940? From what countries did the musicians and their audience emigrate?

5. Why are Latin rhythms different from fox-trot/swing rhythms and similar to rock-era rhythms?

6. Name two hybrid popular-music styles that include Latin influences. Identify the Latin elements in each style. Describe the other elements that go into making it a hybrid.

7. Identify two current hits on the popular music charts that show Latin influence. Identify the Latin elements in each song.

PART IV
REVOLUTION 3

CHAPTER FOURTEEN

The Roots and Early Years of Rock

Rock is by its nature an eclectic music. It is not so much a style as a family of styles. So it should not be surprising to discover that the sources and influences of rock are comparably varied. Mature rock did not come into being until the mid-sixties, when the British invasion groups reintroduced America to several seminal influences, many of them based on fifties popular styles. Country, jazz, rock 'n' roll, rhythm and blues, gospel, doo-wop, and rockabilly were all styles that went into the musical stew that would become known as rock. In this chapter, we'll look at several influences on the birth of rock, focusing primarily on fifties rock 'n' roll and rhythm and blues.

rock 'n' roll

rhythm and blues

gospel

rockabilly

THE ROOTS OF ROCK 'N' ROLL

Rock 'n' roll came together mainly from three rhythm and blues styles popular after World War II: electric blues; the swing-oriented rhythm and blues of the jump bands; and boogie woogie. Rhythm and blues was a term that came into use in the forties to identify most of the music performed by African-American musicians and supported by the African-American audience that was not pop or jazz. It was a big umbrella, including the three styles mentioned above; as well as popular songs sung in a bluesy style, such as those recorded by Dinah Washington and Fats Domino, and gospel-influenced singing groups (doo-wop).

electric blues

boogie woogie

Boogie woogie was a piano blues style that originated in the rural South during the early years of the century. Its creators were pianists who performed in noisy bars called juke joints. Needing to develop a way of playing that could be heard over the talking, shouting, and—often—fighting. They came up with a two-handed style that would cut through the crowd noise, even on an inferior instrument. Boogie-woogie is characterized by an active left hand pattern played in the lower part of the instrument. The left pattern often divides the beat into two equal parts, especially at fast tempos.

In the thirties, boogie woogie moved north to Kansas City and Chicago, and then became a brief national fad in the late thirties. Its influence can be heard in much rhythm and blues of the late forties and early fifties. Slower boogie woogie, in which the beat is divided into a long-short pattern, helped shape the shuffle rhythm heard in jump-band recordings like Louis Jordan's

III-3

IIIA-3

eight-beat
rhythm

IV-1

IVA-1

IV-2

IVA-2

"Choo-Choo-Ch-Boogie" (Example 10.7), as well as rhythm and blues songs from the fifties and sixties.

Fast boogie woogie, in which the beat is divided into two equal parts, gave rock 'n' roll its most distinctive musical feature, an eight-beat rhythm. Indeed, Chuck Berry's early recordings trace this aspect of rock's musical lineage. He had worked with Johnnie Johnson, the pianist on his major recordings, for years before signing with Chess. Johnson was an excellent boogie-woogie pianist. Berry simply transferred Johnson's left hand patterns to guitar. (Keith Richard discusses this point in the Chuck Berry documentary, *Hail, Hail, Rock and Roll*.)

We can hear this early, eight-beat conception in one of the most famous boogie-woogie recordings of all time, "Roll 'Em, Pete" (Example 14.1). The recording features singer Joe Turner (1911–1985), a former bartender who became a popular blues "shouter" for over half a century, and pianist Pete Johnson (1904–1967), one of the best of the boogie-woogie stylists.

From the jump bands, rock 'n' roll took its heavy backbeat. We can hear a pre-rock version of this backbeat in "Shake, Rattle, and Roll" (Example 14.2), a 1954 crossover hit for Joe Turner. This recording is also a good example of the postswing era jump-band sound. It has a walking bass, riff-like melodic figures, call-and-response exchanges between voice and horns, and a blues form adapted to include both narrative and refrain ("Shake, rattle, and roll"). The strong backbeat heard here has remained a characteristic feature of much rock music to the present.

Rock 'n' roll moved the rhythm section into the foreground and the electric guitar into the spotlight. Both were adapted from electric blues. For most of the twentieth century, blues had maintained a split personality. In

Joe Turner, c. late 1940s.

the deep South, it had remained a folk music–raw, often emotionally powerful, and simply accompanied. The country blues of Robert Johnson (Example 7.2) exemplify this style in the late thirties. At the same time, it had become a commercial music, in the blues songs of W. C. Handy and Bessie Smith, and the instrumental blues of Louis Armstrong and Count Basie. As blues intersected with other styles, its emotional impact was often diluted. Even the recordings of Bessie Smith, the most emotionally powerful of the commercial blues artists, occasionally lose something because of their sometimes tepid accompaniment. (Imagine her "St. Louis Blues" [Example 7.3] with an electric rhythm section instead of a reed organ!) That would change with the emergence of electric blues.

Some bluesmen who migrated north and settled in cities found employment in clubs. Like the country artists who created honky-tonk, and for the same reason (to be heard over the crowd noise), they started adding rhythm instruments to their sound, first piano, then bass and drums. In the forties, bluesmen transferred their guitar style from acoustic to electric guitar. By the late forties, the electric blues band was complete: vocalist/electric guitarist, piano, bass, perhaps another guitarist, and drums. This instrumentation became the nuclear rock 'n' roll band.

Although bluesmen incorporated the rhythm instruments and the rhythm of the swing band–most blues songs of this time used a swing or shuffle beat–this intersection with another kind of music did not dilute their style; their music gained in raw power. Nowhere is this more clear than in the music of singer/guitarist Muddy Waters (real name McKinley Morganfield [1915–1983]), the most important and influential of the postwar electric bluesmen. His vocal work retained the raw power of country blues, while his guitar licks–single string responses, and bottleneck-style slides– gained in power because they were amplified. We can hear both, as well as

Muddy Waters, 1964. Photo by Joe Alper.

IV-3

IVA-3

IV-4

IVA-4

the sound of the postwar blues band, in his eponymous recording, "They Call Me Muddy Waters" (Example 14.3). Waters had a profound influence on the development of rock. Chuck Berry sought him out when he came to Chicago in search of a recording contract. He was even more influential on British rockers in the sixties. The Rolling Stones took their name from one of his early hits.

The electric guitar has been the featured instrument of rock 'n' roll since Chuck Berry laid down his rock-defining licks in the late fifties. Although Berry had sought out Muddy Waters in Chicago, probably the major influence on his guitar playing and stage persona was T-Bone Walker. Walker was the most prominent and influential exponent of blues style on electric guitar. His playing was greatly influenced by his childhood friend Charlie Christian, the great jazz guitarist of the early forties. Walker was a showman, which contributed to his prominence. His blues style, as we can hear on "Stormy Monday Blues" (Example 14.4), straddles the boundary between jump-band rhythm and blues and electric blues.

Chuck Berry and other like-minded rock 'n' roll guitarists took their instrumental conception from the electric blues guitarists. Blues guitarists had always used their guitar as an instrumental counterpart to their voice as well as an accompanying instrument. Even the modest amplification of early electric guitars gave the instrument a presence comparable to the voice. For early electric bluesmen, the guitar could be used in at least three ways: to substitute for the voice; to respond to the voice with a different melodic idea; or to accompany the voice. All three are evident in Examples 14.3 and 14.4. They are evident in Berry's work as well.

As we have seen, the most immediate sources of rock 'n' roll are found in the array of blues styles from the forties and early fifties. Other styles–country, gospel, Latin music, jazz, even pop–had peripheral, sometimes indirect, but still meaningful influence. (To cite a nice example, Jelly Roll Morton's "Latin tinge" remained a part of the New Orleans sound for well over half a century. We can hear it in Professor Longhair's late 1940s recordings. From there it found its way into New Orleans-based rock 'n' roll, from Fats Domino and Huey "Piano" Smith to Dr. John.) By 1955, all the ingredients of a new style were in the air; it only required a few innovators to mix them together. What would emerge from the mix was a style clearly indebted to these sources, but–just as clearly–more than simply a blend of them.

THE EMERGENCE OF ROCK 'N' ROLL, 1955–1960

The seeds of the rock revolution began to flower in 1955, when Bill Haley's "Rock around the Clock" skyrocketed to the top of the charts. Only a year earlier, rock 'n' roll was waiting to be created. By 1956, it was a household word and Elvis was a household name.

1956 was the year when the music and the audience came together. The year before, Chuck Berry and Fats Domino had songs on the pop charts. Domino's song, "Ain't That a Shame," reached number one in a cover version by Pat Boone. Real rock 'n' roll did not reach the pop charts until 1956, but it did so in spectacular fashion. Little Richard woke the nation up with "Tutti Frutti." Elvis had eleven Top 40 hits that year; four reached Number 1.

Bill Haley and the Comets, 1958. Photo by Popsie Randolph.

The next few years were the glory years of rock 'n' roll. New artists included a string of rockabilly performers who followed in Elvis's wake: most notably Jerry Lee Lewis, Roy Orbison, Carl Perkins, and Johnny Cash. Pop audiences began to take their rock 'n' roll straight. Major African-American artists like Berry, Domino, and Little Richard reached the charts more consistently, while cover versions of songs declined. Buddy Holly offered a different and more imaginative form of rockabilly with a series of hits, including the number one "That'll Be the Day."

Rock 'n' roll began as an outsiders' music. Its first stars were mostly African-Americans or Southern whites. Its audience consisted of teenagers looking to break away from the enervated, if respectable, music of their parents. The history of Bill Haley's "Rock around the Clock," one of the first big rock 'n' roll hits, points this out. When it was originally released in 1954, it sold modestly. A year later, it became a Number 1 hit when used as the theme to the 1955 movie *The Blackboard Jungle*. The movie told the story of juvenile delinquents in a slum high school. Rock even then was a music of rebellion, although the song's message was certainly harmless.

The two dominant figures in rock 'n' roll were Chuck Berry (1926 or 1931–) and Elvis Presley (1935–1977). Chuck Berry, more than any other musician, defined the sound of rock 'n' roll—or at least the rock 'n' roll that led to rock—in his classic early recordings. He also captured the spirit of his largely teen audiences, talking about them ("School Days" and "Sweet Little Sixteen"), to them ("Rock and Roll Music"), and for them ("Roll Over, Beethoven [and Tell Tchaikovsky the news]"). Elvis was rock 'n' roll's strongest and most distinctive voice. More important, he was its image, capturing in every aspect of his appearance and demeanor what it stood for.

In "Johnny B. Goode" (Example 14.5), we can hear how Berry forged a revolutionary new style. Berry's voice is lighter and more transparent than Muddy Waters's, Joe Turner's, or even Elvis's. It has a unique quality, neither bluesy African-American nor sweet, but well-suited to deliver the rapid-fire

IV-5

IVA-5

Chuck Berry duck walks, 1956.

lyrics that are among his most recognizable trademarks. "Johnny B. Goode" features the standard instrumentation of the fifties rock 'n' roll band: electric guitar (perhaps with some overdubbing? Berry is the only guitarist acknowledged on the record jacket, but there are often two guitar parts sounding simultaneously), string bass, drums, and piano. With the overdubbed guitar, it is the same basic instrumentation as Muddy Waters's electric blues band; it only lacks the harmonica. Berry's recording also features the same dense texture as the blues band: walking bass, drums (here adding a heavy backbeat), steady rhythm guitar, lead guitar in solo choruses and in dialogue with voice, and an active piano obbligato.

The electric guitar plays two roles here. The background role simply transposes a standard boogie-woogie left-hand pattern to the guitar. By contrast, the lead guitar lines are something radically new. When Berry elevates the boogie lines to solo status, he transforms them, giving them much more melodic and rhythmic interest. We hear this from the first note of his famous opening solo. In the first complete measure (beginning with the fourth note), Berry plays the same chord *eight* times. In the next measure, he begins a descending pattern with the ninth consecutive statement of the chord, and again repeats a single chord throughout the third measure. Up to this point, Berry has divided each beat into two equal parts by spacing the attacks at twice beat speed. But even as he divides the beat equally, he creates rhythmic conflict with the beat through irregular accents. Instead of accenting every other note (**1** 2 **3** 4 **5** 6 **7** 8), which would emphasize the division of the beat into two equal parts, Berry accents the first, fourth, and seventh notes, which produces an irregular grouping of the repeated notes -3/3/2. Thus, a single strand in the rhythmic texture of "Johnny B. Goode" sends two different signals simultaneously: the opening series of notes divides time into regularly spaced segments; the pattern of loud and soft groups the attacks irregularly, producing rhythmic conflict with the beat.

Beginning in the fifth measure, Berry repeats the same note twenty-one times: two groups of ten, plus the beginning of the next idea. But he arranges the repeated note in a consistent long/short/long pattern, so that the long note is alternately in and out of phase with the beat. This guitar pattern, superimposed over the other guitar line that divides the beat into two equal parts, sustains the irregular grouping of the beat division heard in the opening measure over a much longer span. Berry was the first guitarist to consistently divide the beat in two parts and create rhythmic conflict at the same time. This explains in part his stature as the father of rock.

In "Johnny B. Goode," we can hear the three main influences on rock 'n' roll come together in Berry's music. From electric blues, he takes the instrumentation and the prominent place of the guitar. From boogie woogie, he takes the eight-beat rhythm. From rhythm and blues, he takes the heavy backbeat and the "narrative" blues form ("Shake, Rattle, and Roll" equals "Go, Johnny, Go").

At the same time, it's clear that the song is more than just the blending of these three influences. The guitar work, Berry's voice, the content and style of the lyrics: all were new elements, and all would prove extraordinarily influential. Berry's guitar breaks and solos are on the must-learn list of every serious rock guitarist. His lyrics, among the first to discuss teen life, are humorous, irreverent, and skillful. Both the content and style of his songs were widely copied. The surf music of the late fifties and early sixties, which glorified all aspects of the teen beach scene, is an especially good example of Berry's influence on song lyrics and musical style. No rock 'n' roll artist was more covered by the creators of rock—the Beach Boys, the Rolling Stones, the Beatles—than Chuck Berry was.

ELVIS PRESLEY

In 1954, Elvis Presley (1935–1977) appeared at Sam Phillips's Sun record company in Memphis looking to record. Phillips had been producing African-American blues singers but was looking for a "a white man with the Negro sound and the Negro feel." Presley, a Mississippi-born truck driver living in Memphis, answered his prayer. Presley recorded his first local hit in 1954. The record, a cover of bluesman Arthur Crudup's "That's All Right," sparked interest on country and western radio (although some stations wouldn't play it because Elvis sounded too African-American). Within a year he had reached number 1 nationally on the country and western charts with "Mystery Train" (Example 14.12).

Ⓓ

In late 1955, he signed a personal management contract with Colonel Tom Parker, who arranged a record contract with RCA. Elvis had become a national phenomenon before the end of 1956. Within two years, he had recorded several Number 1 hits, and made appearances on many network TV shows. He had become the symbol of rock 'n' roll for millions, both to those who idolized him and to those whom he disgusted.

Elvis Presley in a characteristic pose, 1957.

With his totally uninhibited stage manner, teen-tough dress, greased and pompadoured hair, and blues/gospel/country-influenced singing style, Elvis projected a rebellious attitude and sexual energy that many teens found overwhelmingly attractive. However, the musically significant part of Elvis's career lasted only three years; it ended in 1958, when he was inducted into the Army. Although still a major public figure in the sixties and seventies, he seldom recaptured the freshness of his earlier years.

(D) "Jailhouse Rock" (Example 14.6), the title song from Elvis's third movie, was written by Jerry Leiber and Mike Stoller, a songwriting team who supplied a string of hits for Elvis and others, mostly during the fifties and early sixties. "Jailhouse Rock" has all the ingredients of a fifties rock 'n' roll song, the kind that polarized generations and social classes. These include:

1. Straightforward lyrics that describe a less-than-respectable situation, instead of a sentimental love affair. The language is direct, not "sophisticated"; in this respect, "Jailhouse Rock" is akin to the blues and country music of the period.

2. Modified blues form. "Jailhouse Rock" follows blues form, except that the first phrase is considerably expanded to include a narrative.

3. The sound of a rock 'n' roll band. The backup band has four instruments: electric guitar; string bass; piano; and drums. The guitar plays a boogie-woogie style repetitive pattern in such a low register that it almost completely covers the bass.

Little Richard and his band c. 1957; note Richard's right leg, which is raised up above the keyboard.

4. A basic rock 'n' roll beat. Eight-beat patterning in the guitar and unaccompanied vocal sections, walking bass, and a heavy backbeat on the drums all contribute to the rock 'n' roll sound of the fifties.

Elvis epitomized rock 'n' roll. His enormous impact came from his unique singing style, his rebellious, sexually charged stage persona, and (because of these) his unparalleled commercial appeal. He was, by far, the most important commercial presence in rock 'n' roll; no one else came close.

It's worth pointing out that rock did not become the commercially dominant popular style until a few years after the British invasion of the early sixties. For all its subsequent notoriety, rock 'n' roll attracted only a modest percentage of the popular-music market share in the late fifties. The top selling albums of the late fifties were mostly soundtracks from Broadway shows and films. Even singles' sales, traditionally the province of teens, show that rock 'n' roll did not enjoy the unconditional support of America's youth. The top singles artists during the same period were mainly pre-rock stars (like Frank Sinatra and Perry Como) whose popularity continued through the fifties, younger stars in a pre-rock style like Andy Williams or Johnny Mathis, teen stars like Pat Boone (whose commitment to rock was lukewarm at best), or vocal groups like the Platters, whose repertoire included a large number of reworked Tin Pan Alley standards. Among the missing are such important and influential artists as Buddy Holly, Chuck Berry, Little Richard, and Ray Charles. Elvis was the exception that proved the rule, the only true rock 'n' roll artist whose commercial success compared favorably with pop stars. All that would change in the sixties. Rock 'n' roll, transformed into rock, would move to center stage.

Although rock 'n' roll was the primary source for rock and the rock-based music of the sixties, other styles helped shape the sound of popular music in the sixties. Chief among them were rhythm and blues and country music.

RHYTHM AND BLUES IN THE FIFTIES

The most important musical developments in rhythm and blues during the fifties were the secularization of African-American gospel style and its merger with pop and blues. Encounters of sacred and secular were nothing new in African-American religious music. Gospel music had developed around 1930 from just such an encounter. Thomas A. Dorsey (1899–1993), the father of African-American gospel music and composer of so many of its best-loved songs, was a commercial entertainer in the twenties, appearing most frequently as Georgia Tom. He brought this experience into the gospel style that he helped create, infusing African-American religious music with more than a touch of the blues.

Two distinct traditions, the male quartet and the female solo singer (with or without choir) dominated gospel music virtually from its inception. Most of the great solo performers in early gospel music—Mahalia Jackson, Rosetta Tharpe, Clara Ward, and Shirley Caesar—were women. By contrast, most of the small singing groups (quartets and quintets) were male: the Golden Gate Jubilee Quartet, the Swan Silvertones, and the Soul Stirrers were among the most prominent. Both traditions would have a significant impact on the rhythm and blues of the fifties.

a cappella

Male gospel quartets sang *a cappella*. With four (sometimes five) voices, they supplied both melody and accompaniment. At times, they supplied

Golden Gate Quartet, c. late 1930s.

much more, as "The Golden Gate Gospel Train" (Example 14.7) proves. This song, recorded by the Golden Gate Jubilee Quartet in 1937, shows how resourceful such groups could be in depicting images in sound. We hear the train whistle and bell, and the chug of the engine, which sounds much like the vocal equivalent of a rhythm section: guitar, bass, and drums. The performance also shows that some of the most pervasive tendencies in African-American music were not limited to secular music. These include the use of instruments (in this case, voices) in a percussive manner, the static harmony (the song never changes harmony), a melody of mostly descending phrases constructed from a pentatonic scale, blues-like inflection, and an active rhythmic texture. Despite obvious differences in instrumentation and inspiration, there are close parallels between this selection and Willie McTell's "Travelin' Blues" (Example 3.6).

Clara Ward's version of "How I Got Over" (Example 14.8) illustrates the other prominent pre-rock gospel style, the solo female singer. The song is one of several gospel classics written by W. Herbert Brewster (1899–). This performance, recorded in 1950 by Clara Ward and the Ward Singers, illustrates several other features of gospel style that would directly influence popular music: the urgency of Clara Ward's voice; her use of *melisma* (which has, unfortunately, increased in this half century to the extent that it frequently loses its expressive purpose; in a Patti Labelle or Mariah Carey song, it often degenerates into virtuostic display, which overshadows and detracts from an otherwise satisfying performance); her blues-like inflections of a basically hymn-like melody; the frequent call and response between lead

Clara Ward, c. 1950s.

and backup singers; and the use of the Hammond organ as an accompanying instrument.

In the early fifties, some of these gospel groups broke away from religious music. They began to sing popular and rhythm and blues songs in much the same style, but with the addition of full instrumental backup. The most influential of these early rhythm-gospel mergers was Billy Ward's Dominos. Ward's group featured Clyde McPhatter, who first worked professionally as a member of a touring gospel group, and later formed his own group (The Drifters) and then went on to a solo career. The Dominos were among the first groups to adapt the traditional gospel quartet sound to rhythm and blues. In "Have Mercy, Baby" (Example 14.9), a big R&B hit from 1952, their gospel sound enriches an otherwise typical jump-band song. The song is a blues whose melody, like so many other songs from the period, was constructed from a series of riffs.

 IV-8

 IVA-8

There are two new ingredients here. The first is McPhatter's gospel-like vocal lines. These are elaborations of a riff or phrases interjected between riffs. The second is the call and response between McPhatter and the Dominos. This feature was adapted from the exchanges between soloist and complementary section heard in African-American church music and big-band swing. (Notice, by the way, the close parallel between the accompanying figures in "Golden Gate Gospel Train" and the group response figures in "Have Mercy, Baby.") These two elements of gospel style continue to exert considerable influence on a wide range of popular-music styles. The backup singers of so many bands—African-American, white, rock, country—recall the secularized gospel quartets of the fifties.

Later in the decade, other gospel performers and many performers who had grown up singing gospel in church also began to sing nonreligious material. They preserved the vocal style of gospel but added backup instruments. Following in Clyde McPhatter's footsteps, Sam Cooke brought gospel into pop and became an even bigger star before his untimely death. He had been a featured singer with the Soul Stirrers, a gospel quartet, before starting a solo career performing secular (pop) material. Little Richard brought a less inhibited kind of gospel style into rock 'n' roll. It was one dimension of his seminal contribution to the new style.

The most important and influential of the gospel-inspired solo performers of the fifties was Ray Charles (1930–). More than any other artist, he was responsible for the synthesis of blues and gospel. His music merged the emotional intensity of both styles. His singing did not come out of the relatively smooth delivery of male quartets, as Sam Cooke's had, but the ecstatic, uninhibited shouting of holiness churches. Several of his songs, like "I Got a Woman," were thinly disguised adaptations of gospel songs fitted with new, nonreligious lyrics.

It shouldn't be surprising that Charles brought blues and gospel together. The major achievements of the early and influential part of his career were a series of syntheses. Charles has been a musician of eclectic tastes, and a strong enough musical personality to put his own stamp on everything he tried. He broke through as a rhythm and blues artist in the late fifties after an unsuccessful effort as a Nat Cole-style supper-club performer. During this time, Charles retained his interest in jazz, performing at jazz festivals ("A Fool for You" was recorded at the 1958 Newport Jazz Festival) as well as rhythm and blues events, and recording with major jazz artists like vibraphonist Milt Jackson (heard with the Modern Jazz Quartet in Chapter 9). In this respect, he was the main rhythm and blues connection in jazz's "return to roots" movement around 1960. Throughout this period, he also helped bring Latin music into rhythm and blues. Like many rhythm and blues artists of the period, he included a few Latin numbers in his act; this style had an obvious trickle-down effect on songs like "What'd I Say" (Example 14.10).

After establishing himself as the most important, innovative and influential rhythm and blues artist of the fifties, Charles reached out to two more styles: country and pop. Growing up, he had listened to country music along with various forms of pop music. After occasionally including country songs on earlier albums, he recorded two albums of country songs in 1962. Both were best-selling albums: the first topped all three charts (pop, R&B, and country) simultaneously. Charles's albums brought country songs to a wider audience, they inspired other noncountry performers to record country material, and they influenced a number of important country musicians, including Merle Haggard and Willie Nelson. His recordings of pop standards, like Hoagy Carmichael's "Georgia on My Mind," were similarly well-received and influential. His influence is evident in the vocal style of many rock-era stars.

"What'd I Say" (Example 14.10) and "A Fool for You" (Example 14.11) show several facets of Charles's blues/gospel synthesis. "What'd I Say" updates the pre-rock jump band style heard in "Shake, Rattle, and Roll." Charles retains its basic instrumental sound—vocal, rhythm section without guitar, and horns. He augments the sound with additional horns (his band includes two trumpets and two saxes) and female backup vocalists, the Raelets. In this song, Charles also augments the storytelling blues form (narrative alternating with refrain) heard in several earlier songs. He precedes the storytelling part with a long instrumental prelude and interpolates a rapid-fire call-and-response dialogue with the Raelets. With its layered beginning—bass and piano bass first, then drums and piano riff—the instrumental prelude recalls Count Basie's "Jumping at the Woodside" (Example 2.9) and anticipates much of the music we'll hear in subsequent chapters. The "storytelling" section is more cinematic than narrative, a series of images whose common thread we discover only in his dialogue with the Raelets. This section describes an earthly ecstasy, not a spiritual one, but its gospel roots are clear.

Charles's medium and uptempo rhythm and blues songs were the strongest link between pre-rock swing and rhythm and blues and much of rock era soul, jazz/rock, and other related styles. His influence can be heard on, among others, James Brown; Junior Walker; Blood, Sweat and Tears; Chicago; Aretha Franklin; the various incarnations of George Clinton's bands; and Earth, Wind and Fire.

"What'd I Say" shows Charles's ability to create a distinctive style out of several sources. "A Fool for You" (Example 14.11) shows how he expanded the emotional range of rhythm and blues by enriching a deep blues conception with the expressive vocabulary of gospel. Emotionally powerful blues singers like Bessie Smith and Robert Johnson concentrated their emotion into a narrow melodic framework. Charles begins "A Fool for You" in much the same spirit and style. As he warms to his subject, however, his melodic lines expand in range, his use of melisma becomes more frequent, and he periodically punctuates a phrase with the sung shouts so character-istic of the most unrestrained African-American religious music. The result is, I believe, one of the most emotionally powerful recorded performances in the history of popular music. It should be noted, too, that gospel influ-ence extends to the accompaniment and form; the song is a blues in spirit and basic vocal style, but Charles's piano playing is straight out of the church, and the song has the form of a gospel song, not a blues song.

THE INFLUENCE OF COUNTRY MUSIC IN THE EARLY YEARS OF ROCK

Two developments related to country music would have a powerful, if essentially subordinate, influence on rock in the sixties. One was the folk revival of the late fifties and early sixties. The other was rockabilly, a merg-er of country and western with rhythm and blues.

The folk revival had almost nothing to do with the country music of the fifties. Its stars–the Kingston Trio; Joan Baez; Peter, Paul and Mary; Bob Dylan, and others–came from outside the South: New York, California, even Hawaii. They performed in coffeehouses and nightclubs in big cities and col-lege towns. Their singing would never be confused with a traditional coun-try vocal sound. Baez, for example, mastered the guitar styles of traditional country acts, such as the Carter Family, but she cultivated a pure, unadorned singing style far removed from the nasal sound of Sara or Maybelle Carter. The folksingers' heroes were Woody Guthrie and Pete Seeger, not Hank Williams or Ray Price.

Nevertheless, the folk revival represented an important intersection of country and mainstream popular music. It brought the traditional country repertoire to an audience that had had little or no exposure to it. Joan Baez's covers of Carter Family songs like "Wildwood Flower" and "Gospel Ship" introduced a new audience to this music. These songs also served as mod-els for original songs by folk and folk-inspired musicians. For Bob Dylan and others who followed in his footsteps, it was a natural progression from tra-ditional repertoire to original material.

ROCKABILLY

Rockabilly was a different matter altogether. For the most part, it was an interpretation of rhythm and blues by white country musicians strongly influenced by blues and gospel music. Unlike traditional country music, which was headquartered in Nashville, the center of rockabilly was Memphis, also in Tennessee, but with a much richer blues tradition. Elvis, Carl Perkins, and Jerry Lee Lewis all began their careers as country musi-cians at Sam Phillips's Memphis-based Sun records. However, Elvis's early records and those of Perkins ("Blue Suede Shoes") and Lewis ("Whole Lotta Shakin' Goin' On") had a far greater affinity with rhythm and blues than they did with traditional country music or the then-new "Nashville sound" country pop. The distinction between rockabilly and rock 'n' roll was in many cases visual; there wasn't much difference between the sounds Little Richard and Jerry Lee Lewis made beating on a piano.

Many, including this writer, consider Elvis's Sun recordings to be his most musically successful work. "Mystery Train" (Example 14.12) is an excel-

(D)

Buddy Holly (left) and the Crickets in formal attire, c. 1958.

lent illustration. It is classic rockabilly, a blend of country, rock 'n' roll, and blues. The mixture is most clearly heard in the beat of the song and its form. The basic rhythmic premise established by the rhythm section is a honky-tonk beat, bass alternating with a heavy backbeat from the electric guitar. But the backbeat is modified with a quick rebound that begins alternately on, then off, the beat. Formally, the song is a modified blues: it has the poetic and melodic form of a blues song, but its harmony and phrase length are slightly irregular. Elvis's singing is the magical element in this performance. In both its basic timbre and its variety, his sound is utterly unique—the purest Elvis. It ranges from a plaintive wail on the opening high notes to the often-imitated guttural singing at the end of each chorus. Although imitated and parodied ad nauseum since the late fifties, Elvis's sound and style were absolutely fresh in 1955, the year of this recording.

Like so many other rock 'n' roll stars, Buddy Holly (1938–1959) crammed a successful and influential career into a short timespan: he was a national celebrity for less than two years, from late 1957 to his death in a plane crash in February 1959. Holly wrote or co-wrote many of his songs, and several were innovative in form, rhythm, and instrumentation. "That'll Be the Day" (Example 14.13), one of his better-known hits, showcases two especially influential style features. The instrumentation—lead singer, background vocals, two guitars, bass, drums, with no piano or keyboard—would become the most popular rock band instrumentation in the sixties; most of the Beatles's and Rolling Stones's early hits feature it. The form of this song was equally influential. Unlike most of the previous examples, this song is not a blues. Instead it offers a novel form in which a recurring refrain frames narrative sections that flesh out the story. This kind of form—several statements of a refrain separated by narrative sections that explain it—was used extensively by songwriters in the sixties; the Beatles's "Eleanor Rigby" (Example 15.4) uses the same formal organization.

IV-9

IVA-9

D

In the rock era, the interchange between country music and other styles became a two-way affair. Country helped shape other styles as well as borrowing from them. Its influence is most comprehensive in country-derived subgenres: folk-rock; country-rock; and the singer/songwriters styles of the seventies and beyond. It has been most pervasive in form: the refrain-oriented forms that distinguish rock-era song owe more to country music than to any other genre.

CONCLUSION

Rock 'n' roll ended as suddenly as it began. Elvis was drafted into the army in 1958. When he resumed his career two years later, he had lost the cutting edge that had defined his earlier work. Little Richard gave up his career to become a preacher. Jerry Lee Lewis married his thirteen-year-old cousin without divorcing his previous wife; the ensuing scandal seriously damaged his career. In 1959, Buddy Holly died in a plane crash. That same year, Chuck Berry was arrested on a Mann Act violation and eventually sentenced to a two-year jail term in 1962–1963. So, by the end of 1959, most of the major figures in rock 'n' roll were no longer active.

The payola scandal of 1959 also contributed to the sudden decline of rock 'n' roll. Because they controlled airplay of records, disc jockeys wielded enormous power. Some, like Alan Freed, used it to promote music that they liked. But many, including Freed, accepted some form of bribery in return for guaranteeing airplay. The practice became so pervasive that it provoked a governmental investigation. Also at issue was the question of licensing rights. ASCAP, the established licensing organization, reportedly urged the investigation to undermine its major competitor, BMI, which was licensing the music of African-American and country performers. Establishment figures viewed the investigation as proof of the inherent corruption of rock 'n' roll.

By the early sixties, it seemed as if rock 'n' roll was just a fad that had run its course. In retrospect, it was the calm before the storm. British bands would revitalize rock 'n' roll and help transform it into rock. Back in the USA, James Brown and producers like Motown's Berry Gordy and Atlantic's Jerry Wexler would turn rhythm and blues into soul. The story of their revolution is told in Chapter 15.

Terms to Know

a cappella	boogie woogie	eight-beat rhythm
electric blues	gospel	rhythm and blues
rock 'n' roll	rockabilly	

Names to Know

Chuck Berry	Ray Charles	Thomas Dorsey
Golden Gate Jubilee Quartet	Buddy Holly	Pete Johnson
Jerry Lee Lewis	Clyde McPhatter	Elvis Presley
Little Richard	Soul Stirrers	Joe Turner
T-Bone Walker	Clara Ward	Muddy Waters

Study Questions

1. What three styles came together to form rock 'n' roll? What did rock 'n' roll borrow from each style? In what ways was rock 'n' roll different from these styles.

2. Why was Elvis a dominant figure in rock 'n' roll?

3. Describe the sound of a rock 'n' roll band. What instruments are typically used? What is/are the role(s) of the electric guitar(s)? What is the bass instrument, and how is it used?

4. How did gospel transform rhythm and blues in the fifties? What was Ray Charles's role in the merge of blues and gospel?

5. Who were the major figures in rock 'n' roll in the fifties? What were they doing around 1960?

6. How did rockabilly combine country music with rock 'n' roll? What elements of country music are evident in the rockabilly recordings of Elvis and Buddy Holly?

7. Choose one recording by Elvis Presley and one by Ray Charles studied in this chapter. How are they similar? How are they different? What is it about each recording that makes it unique?

CHAPTER FIFTEEN

Rock, A New Musical Language

In 1966, you could have gone to San Francisco to hear the Beatles' final concert at Candlestick Park. With millions of others, you had seen them invade America in early 1964 via *The Ed Sullivan Show*. The same show had catapulted Elvis into the national spotlight almost a decade earlier. Now you and 50,000+ other people wanted to hear them live before it's too late.

You could have drifted over to Haight Ashbury to—in psychedelic drug guru Timothy Leary's slogan—"turn on, tune in, drop out." While cruising, you might have heard one of the first acid-rock bands: Jefferson Airplane, Quicksilver Messenger Service, or the Grateful Dead. Or perhaps you'd travel down the coast, find a not-too-crowded beach, and dream about "California Girls" while listening to (who else) the Beach Boys on your transistor radio.

After the new year, you'd sell your soul to be a fly on the wall of a recording studio in—of all places—Muscle Shoals, Alabama. You'd witness Aretha Franklin finding the groove that would make her the "Queen of Soul" by the end of the year. Backed by an integrated band, she would record a string of memorable hits, including "Respect," which would become an anthem for the women's movement. All these events were the consequence of the musical and cultural revolution that created rock.

rock

The rock revolution, fomenting for almost a decade, finally overthrew the popular-music establishment in the sixties. Almost overnight, the sound of popular music was completely transformed. Broadway, syrupy strings, and Sinatra were out, unless they hopped on the rock bandwagon; the British bands, Motown and Memphis, the California groups—surf music in

Motown

the South, hippies in the North—and the barely grown-up folkies were in.

Rock redefined popular music, how it was made, who it was for, and what it stood for. The music integrated African–American and white musical values into a new musical language, related to but separate from its roots in European and African culture. It was the first African-American-based style to become the commercially dominant popular music of a generation. The revolution that created syncopated song and dance in the teens and twenties produced an African–American-influenced popular style; this revolution produced a style in which African–American values predominated.

A ROCK ESTHETIC

Rock is a democratic music. Its fundamentally egalitarian attitude has found expression in every aspect: its songs; the identity of its artists; its relationship with its audience; the structure of its industry; and, most important, the music itself.

Rock began on the fringes of the popular-music industry. Its roots were in styles far removed from the popular-music mainstream: blues; rhythm and blues; Latin music; and country music. It attracted a minority constituency—teenagers. Its early hits appeared on small independent labels located in second-tier entertainment centers like Chicago, New Orleans, and Memphis. Even as it assumed an increasingly dominant role within the popular-music industry, rock maintained some sense of its identity as an outsiders' music, replacing the prevailing values of mainstream popular music with its own standards, rather than adopting them.

The democratic spirit of rock music is evident in three important ways: (1) an emphasis on group identity; (2) a broader geographic diffusion of the music industry during the rock era; and (3) rock's new attitude toward the popular-music landscape. Throughout the first half of the twentieth century, a star system usually prevailed. Popular-music performances generally featured a well-known singer or instrumentalist plus a supporting cast: Glenn Miller and His Orchestra; Bing Crosby and an anonymous group of studio musicians; even Elvis Presley and whatever backup musicians he chose to use.

In the fifties, the emergence of vocal groups—gospel-inspired African American harmony groups like the Platters and folk groups like the Kingston Trio—marked the beginning of a trend away from a hierarchical structure within a performing group. By the sixties, the transformation was complete. Most rock groups of the period were identified by a group title: the Beatles; the Rolling Stones; the Jefferson Airplane. The trend has continued to the present, with even more obscure names: Prong; Megadeath; Pearl Jam; and the Dead Milkmen.

Most early rock 'n' roll artists were recorded by independent labels, many of which were located in urban areas other than New York and Los Angeles. In the sixties, Detroit; San Francisco; Liverpool and London, England; and Nashville and Memphis, Tennessee, became major centers of activity. Even smaller cities like Muscle Shoals, Alabama; and Macon, Georgia; grew into important popular-music locations on the strength of a first-class recording studio and an outstanding roster of studio musicians. All that seemed necessary for a city to become a major center of popular-music activity, usually with an immediately identifiable sound, was a critical mass of like-minded musicians and a few individuals, like Motown Records chief Berry Gordy in Detroit or producers Kenny Gamble and Leon Huff in Philadelphia, who combined good artistic judgment with excellent entrepreneurial skills.

Moreover, rock music has taken on an international aspect since the British invasion of the midsixties. The exportation of American popular-music to Great Britain has come full circle with the continuing impact of British musicians on the American popular-music scene. The names of the most popular British acts—Beatles, Rolling Stones, The Who, Led Zeppelin, Elton John, David Bowie—are so much a part of our life that it's easy to forget that they're *not* American. The commercial and critical success of musicians like Van Morrison, born in Belfast, Ireland, or Dublin's U2, Jamaican Bob Marley, and Australian hard-rock band AC/DC show the continuing presence of foreign musicians in American popular music.

Rock formed a different bond with its audience than Tin Pan Alley popular song did. Tin Pan Alley songs offered listeners an *escape* from reality, whereas rock songs *intensified* the reality of life in the present. Songs could also be a form of social activism and commentary: Dylan's "The Times They Are A-Changin'" and Marvin Gaye's "What's Goin' On" are still powerful reminders of the social involvement of rock-era musicians.

Dylan pointed rock music in a new direction in 1964 when he told an interviewer that "I don't want to write for people anymore you know, be a spokesman. From now on I want to write from inside me." Dylan and the other singer/songwriters who followed his lead dealt with the present on a more intimate level. Songs about life, love, relationships, good and bad times, and other enduring themes of popular music became highly personal statements.

Most important, perhaps, because rock-era songwriters usually performed their own songs, the message of the song reached its audience in the most direct possible manner. Songs are not written *for* something—a musical or film—so much as to *say* something. For example, James Taylor's "Fire and Rain" (Example 19.6) captures in song a major event in Taylor's life. Taylor had been committed to a psychiatric hospital following problems with drug use; he befriended another patient, a young woman, at the institution, but was surprised when he discovered she'd been transferred out of the hospital. The story is told in stark, plainspoken language, not flighty metaphor. Compare the opening of the song—"Just yesterday morning, they let me know you were gone"—to the opening line of the pop standard "Misty"—"Look at me, I'm as helpless as a kitten up a tree." As with the majority of rock-era songs, the listener does not have to imagine the person behind the song; he or she is there for all to hear. "Fire and Rain" is song as heightened conversation, a special kind of public intimacy seldom achieved in a Tin Pan Alley song.

Rock's concern with the present, combined with its direct and often personal communication between song, singer, and audience, elevated the role of the music for many members of that audience from simple entertainment to (quoting noted rock critic Geoffrey Stokes) "a way of life."

In the sixties, the term "rock" came to encompass many different types of popular music. We can identify at least three different ways the word was used:

1. *"Pure" rock.* A new style in the sixties, rooted in but different from rhythm and blues, and undiluted by cross-pollination with other styles. The songs of the Rolling Stones are the clearest expression of the stylistic center of pure rock.
2. *Music by rock musicians.* Rock has also included any music played by musicians from within the rock tradition. The Beatles did more than any other group to stretch the stylistic boundaries of rock. For instance, a song like "Michelle" has no musical connection with rock style, other than that it was written and recorded by the Beatles. The eclectic approach of the Beatles, Bob Dylan, and others was widely imitated, and used as a point of departure by other creative musicians from the period.

Bob Dylan, 1963.

3. *Rock hybrids.* When it became clear in the sixties that rock had become the primary language of popular music, some musicians working within established nonrock styles—pop, jazz, musical theater, or country—merged their music with elements of rock, primarily its rhythm. These efforts added to the growing list of hyphenated styles—pop-rock, jazz-rock, folk-rock, and so on—camped under the rock umbrella.

The interaction of rock with the sound world of the sixties produced an extraordinarily varied musical landscape, one without precedent in the history of popular music. Rock music segmented into numerous substyles even as its stylistically definitive form took shape in the work of its major artists. The splintering of rock occurred from both within and without, by rock artists eager to expand the range of their music as well as by those who grafted elements of rock music onto existing styles to make them current. This trend has continued to the present.

THE IMPACT OF TECHNOLOGY

The themes of rock and its stylistic diversity are two expressions of the revolutionary changes rock brought to popular music. A technological revolution also played a major role in its transformation beginning in the sixties. Major changes include an enormous increase in amplification, invention of

multitrack recording

and improvements to electronic instruments, and multitrack recording.

The power of amplifying equipment took a quantum leap, enabling sound systems to produce many times more sound than in the past without distortion. This has had two major consequences: it has given musicians access to larger venues; and it has made the volume of sound that a band is capable of producing independent of its size. Seemingly limitless amplification meant that bands could create more sound simply by turning a dial. The power trios of the late sixties—guitar, bass, and drums—were aptly named. With amplification, they could play more loudly than big bands or symphony orchestras.

The sixties saw a wave of electronic instruments enter the mainstream

electric guitar

of popular music. Solid-body electric guitars became the preferred instrument of rock guitarists. The change to a solid body electric instrument affected the guitar's sound in two ways: first, the original guitar sound was converted immediately into an electrical current; and second, this electrical current could then be altered in a number of ways before finally reaching the amplifier. Of these sound-altering devices, the most important has been

looping

looping of the electrical signal so that the tone can sustain indefinitely, instead of decaying quickly as it does on a conventional guitar. The electric guitar can perform a singing melody with almost the same subtlety of inflection as any good singer. It is also an instrument for virtuosos, as major guitarists like Jimi Hendrix, Eric Clapton, and Eddie Van Halen have consistently demonstrated. In the right hands, it can produce high-velocity riffs and cascading runs and chords well beyond the capability and range of the most agile voice.

electric bass

The electric bass, also a solid-body instrument, developed in the late fifties and early sixties concurrently with the solid-body electric guitar. When it was appropriately amplified, it balanced the power of the electric guitar, giving rock bands the full bass sound they lacked in the fifties when the acoustic bass was used. Bass players like Larry Graham, originally of Sly and the Family Stone, soon discovered a new range of sound effects—mostly percussive—not obtainable on the conventional acoustic bass.

Hammond organ

Electric keyboard instruments developed along three lines. A new generation of smaller, more portable electric organs appeared in the sixties, and the venerable Hammond B-3 organ, long a fixture in African–American churches,

Jimi Hendrix, c. 1967.
Photograph by Bill Smith.

resurfaced in rhythm and blues and rock bands. Portable electric pianos also came into widespread use. Some, like the Fender Rhodes piano, merged a piano action with electronics to produce an instrument that retained the feel of a piano but added the power and tone color of electronics.

Both electric organs and electric pianos are relatively specialized instruments. It is the synthesizer that has most enriched the sound palette of popular music, providing close analogs to acoustic instruments, particularly with the advent of sound sampling, and adding a broad spectrum of sounds that could not be obtained with conventional instruments. The history of electronic synthesizers parallels that of the computer. Both began as large, unwieldly mechanisms that required a lot of work from the operator. In recent years, they have become more powerful, compact, and flexible through the application of microchip and digital technology.

Multitrack recording, the third technological breakthrough, involves recording parts of a song onto separate tracks instead of all at once, then mixing them together. It had been possible to record on more than one track since the late forties. Les Paul, a technological innovator as well as an outstanding guitarist, had experimented with *overdubbing* after World War II, and released several hit records using this procedure. However, multitracking did not come into widespread use until after spectacular results were achieved by the Beatles and their producer, George Martin, in the mid-sixties.

Multitrack recording has made it possible to record a project in stages instead of all at once. Strands of the musical fabric can be added one at a time, and kept or discarded at the discretion of the artist or producer. The ability to assemble a recording project one step at a time fostered a fundamental change in the creative process during the rock era.

From the outset, rock changed the relationship between composer and performer. Most of the early rock stars e.g., Chuck Berry, Buddy Holly, Little Richard, performed original material–Elvis was an interesting exception to this trend. In their music, the song existed as it was recorded and performed, not as it was written, if indeed they wrote it down. A song was no longer just the melody and harmony, but the total sound as presented on the record: not only the main vocal line, but also guitar riffs, bass lines, drum-beat patterns, and backup vocals. With the advent of multitrack recording and electronic sound generation in the midsixties, composer/performers could shape the final product even more carefully. Unlike earlier generations of songwriters, musicians in the rock era have had the capability of total artistic control of the entire creative process.

INTERDEPENDENCY OF THE ROCK BAND

The complete interdependency of the band is the stylistic innovation most expressive of rock's collective sense. In a pop performance, there is a hierarchical arrangement of musical interest. Melody instruments and solo voices are featured, while the rhythm section is subordinate. In a rock song, however, the meaning of the song is diffused throughout the group. With the exception of the rhythm guitar, which remains pretty much in the background, every part–vocal, lead guitar, bass, and drums–is essential to the song. A successful performance of a song without any one of the parts, or at least a different version of the same part, is inconceivable. Furthermore, the whole of the performance is greater than the sum of its parts. None of the lines has sufficient musical interest to stand alone.

Voice and guitar often share the melodic interest. In a song like the Rolling Stones' "Satisfaction" (Example 15.1), the most memorable melodic event of the song is not found in the vocal line; it is the guitar riff that opens the song. (This is easy enough to test: play any phrase from the vocal part on an instrument, then play the guitar riff; it should be clear that the riff identifies the song immediately and unmistakably, while the instrumental version of the melody is less quickly recognized.)

"Satisfaction" is an archetypical rock performance, providing a comprehensive inventory of those stylistic features that, taken together, distinguish rock from all earlier styles. It features standard rock-band instrumentation: voice, lead and rhythm guitars, electric bass, and drums. Although the drum set is not much different from that used by jazz or pop drummers, rock drummers invented a new way of playing. In earlier drum styles, the primary rhythmic focus was on the ride cymbal; in some early rock performances, like Chuck Berry's recordings as well as jazz and pop-rock styles, the ride cymbal is still used. In this recording, most of the timekeeping takes place on the drums and sock cymbal (this can be heard clearly on the drum break between "No, No, No" and "Hey, Hey, Hey"). Rock drum patterns tend to be complex, if repetitive, and rely on the interaction of bass drum with other drums and the sock cymbal. The drummer's role in this song is relatively straightforward: timekeeping at beat and twice beat speed.

Mick Jagger's vocal style adapts the speech-song continuum and rough-edged vocal quality of blues to a new context; some influence from Bob Dylan is also likely. Rock singers had no use for the smooth delivery of the crooners of the forties and fifties. There is also a marked difference in dynamics. Rock bands are loud, primarily because of rapid improvements in amplification. In a fifties rock band, only the guitar is amplified. In this recording, all instruments except the drum are amplified. Moreover, the amplifiers of the sixties produced more volume.

A rock song usually has three melodically interesting, if repetitive, lines (voice, lead guitar, and bass), plus an active drum part and chordal accompaniment from the rhythm guitar. Lead guitar and voice share most of the musical interest. In the transition from fifties rock 'n' roll to sixties rock, the role of the bass changed more than any other instrument. The bassist was liberated from his timekeeping role so that he could create distinctive lines with greater melodic and rhythmic independence.

Rock music features simpler harmony and a slower harmonic rhythm than the pop songs of the fox-trot and swing eras. There are two kinds of harmonic events in "Satisfaction." The first is conventional. The harmony throughout the first two sections ("I can't get" and "Yes I try") draws from the simple three-chord vocabulary of the blues, although the chord sequence is not that of a blues song. The other, which occurs at the beginning and at every recurrence of the guitar riff, seems, at least indirectly, influenced by African music, because the two harmonies that oscillate back and forth result from the coincidence of the guitar and bass riffs. Neither is a standard chord; both are incomplete. The rhythm guitar plays very faintly complete chords.

Like many earlier styles, rock melodies grow out of riffs. As this song exemplifies, however, there is considerably more repetition and less-complicated development of a riff ("and I try").

In this recording, the entire band shares a rock rhythmic conception, creating patterns whose fastest notes move at twice beat speed. More than any other quality, emphasis of this rhythmic layer by the entire band identifies the music as rock. Even forward-looking fifties rock 'n' roll recordings are transitional because the bass still played the walking bass line of the jump-band swing style. Rock reached musical maturity when the new rhythmic conception heard from Chuck Berry's guitar and Little Richard's piano extended to all instruments. The tempos of sixties rock songs tend to be slower than fifties rock songs, like those of Chuck Berry; their beat is also slower than the typical dance music of earlier styles.

"Pure" (nonhybrid) rock songs, like this one, often feature original forms influenced by blues and country music. "Satisfaction" has what might be called "endless loop" form, one of the most radical innovations of rock style. The song begins with the trademark guitar riff; bass joins quickly, followed by the other instruments. The vocal line consists of three different melodic ideas, an arpeggiated chord ("I can't get no"), a series of scale fragments ("Yes I try, and I try"), and a high riff ("I can't get no") that frames several words sung to a single note. Each idea leads smoothly into the next, as if it were a simple continuation of the previous musical phrase rather than new material. There are no harmonic-melodic cadences. The closest thing to an articulation between sections is the drum break, but even that seems to come in the middle of a section, rather than at the end, because the guitar riff is heard before and after it. The song ends with a fadeout.

endless
loop form

I-16

 IA-16

"Satisfaction" introduces a new formal conception into the popular-music mainstream. The closed form of nineteenth-century songs like Stephen Foster's "Beautiful Dreamer" (Example 3.3) presented a clear formal hierarchy. "Beautiful Dreamer" is strophic, with three stanzas of poetry set to the same music. Each stanza is separated by a piano interlude. Within each stanza, there are four sections, each of them clearly separated from the next by a cadence. "Satisfaction," by contrast, has an open form. It begins by simply getting under way and ends by fading out. More innovatively, it is sequential, but not truly hierarchical. Unlike closed-form songs, the musical momentum does not slacken at the end of sections. In fact, the opposite seems to be true. The guitar riff that begins the song supports the voice throughout the final part of each section. Because it serves both as the end of one section and the beginning of the next, it is impossible to pinpoint where the division between sections takes place.

hook

The climax of each section—the point at which the listener expects a catchy hook (a hook is a melodic idea that "hooks" the listener through frequent repetition)—has no melodic interest; Jagger sings the same pitch throughout. It would seem as though the Stones deliberately wrote a song without the kind of periodic ebb and flow heard in pre-rock popular song. Perhaps the lack of a climax is the Stones' way of musically underscoring the verbal message of the song (the singer, too, fails to be "satisfied"). Like an endless loop, the song goes round and round, without ever really starting, finishing, or pausing before beginning a new section.

THE DOMINANT
ARTISTS OF SIXTIES ROCK

Rock 'n' roll entered the 1960s tentatively, primarily because so many of its major figures were dead or out of circulation. Two breakthroughs, the British invasion and a surge in popularity of African–American music, soon changed that perception. The British invasion began late in 1963 when recordings by the Beatles began to appear in the United States; the group came in person early the following year. Other British groups soon followed: some memorable, others now all but forgotten. Just prior to their arrival, African–American acts were enjoying unprecedented popularity. By middecade, the Beatles were living at the top of the charts and African–American acts, especially Motown performers, were charting consistently. By the end of the decade, rock was securely in place as the mainstream style.

Although white and African–American performers shared Top 40 space, their music represented two distinct families of the new rock style. Both were remarkably diverse, as the discussion below suggests, and were quite distinct from each other. All camped under the rock umbrella.

The four artistically and commercially dominant rock acts of the sixties were the Rolling Stones, the Beatles, Bob Dylan, and Jimi Hendrix. Taken as a whole, their music not only presented rock as a newly established style, purged of all transitional elements, but also forecast the most important rock substyles of the next several years. The Rolling Stones updated fifties rock 'n' roll into rock. The Beatles, the premier melodists of rock, brought together rock and pop. Dylan connected rock with both country and folk music. Hendrix, who had listened seriously to Robert Johnson and B. B. King, formulated a style that brought together rock and electric blues.

The year 1965 was a watershed year for rock, the year that the music found its mature voice. Only a year earlier, the Rolling Stones were still primarily a "cover" band; Mick Jagger and Keith Richards had just begun to write original songs. Dylan was still a folk singer/songwriter, and the Beatles' songs fed teen fantasies and desires. The Rolling Stones' 1965 albums, *Out of My Head* and *December's Children*, included songs like "Satisfaction" and "Get Off of My Cloud" that, while strongly rooted in rock 'n' roll and electric blues, reshaped them into a completely new style. Meanwhile, Dylan enriched his accompaniment with a rock band, both in concert and on the albums *Bringing It All Back Home* and *Highway 61 Revisited*. The Beatles burst their bubblegum bubble with the landmark album, *Rubber Soul*, which included "Norwegian Wood" and "Michelle." These albums not only established rock as a serious, mature style, but prefigured, and in several cases shaped, the multiple forms rock would assume in the next several years. With the exception of a virtuoso guitar style, every major stylistic direction within the white rock tradition is, if not inaugurated by a song from one of these albums, at least represented there.

The Rolling Stones reaffirmed the essential connection between rock and blues, although it would soon find fuller expression in its solo-oriented form in the work of Jimi Hendrix, Eric Clapton, and, later, early heavy-metal bands like Led Zeppelin. While the Rolling Stones defined rock's center, Dylan and the Beatles stretched its periphery; the eclecticism that would mark the subsequent work of both was first heard in these recordings. Psychedelic (acid) rock, singer/songwriter rock, art rock, and folk-rock have their origins in songs from these albums. All three acts sustained a high level of creativity over the next few years. Hendrix and other significant talents soon joined them to make the last half of the 1960s the most musically productive period in the history of rock.

THE SOUND WORLD OF THE BEATLES

The most distinguishing feature of the Beatles' music is its range; there is extraordinary variety from song to song. John Lennon and Paul McCartney were a great songwriting team (or nonteam, after a while). But they did more than just write pretty melodies: They redefined what a popular song was: not just melody and chords—no matter how well-crafted—but a complete sound world, captured on record. Now, the recording, not the sheet music, documented the song.

The Beatles were the first great eclectics in popular-music history. They were not innovators so much as innovative users of the past and present. The Beatles drew on their sound world, which included not only rock 'n' roll, but English folk music, jazz, classical, East Indian music, Tin Pan Alley popular song, and many other styles. Elements drawn from these diverse sources imbued each of their songs with a unique character, although they still maintained their group identity. The result: each song is different, yet all are clearly by the Beatles. No artist or group has come close to matching the extraordinary variety of styles and sounds present in their mature music. They can evoke the sound image of a French cabaret in one song ("Michelle") and African–American gospel music in another ("Let It Be"), yet both songs have their distinctive personal stamp.

Their extraordinary range of expression has many sources. Four of the most important are:

Knowledge of styles. They had firsthand familiarity with a broad range of styles. In their dues-paying years, the band performed not only rock 'n' roll covers and original songs, but pop hits of all kinds. They clearly absorbed styles along with songs.

Melodic skill. The Beatles were the first important rock-era musicians to write melody-oriented songs that were in step with the changes in rhythm, form, and other elements that took place during this time. No one since has written so many memorable melodies.

Sound imagination. Aided by the development of multitrack recording, the Beatles enriched their songs by startling, often unprecedented, combinations of instruments and—occasionally—extraneous elements, such as the crowd noises and trumpet flourishes of "Sgt. Pepper." They also used audio effects to enhance the meaning of songs, for example, the eerie, backwards-tape effects featured in the background of "Tomorrow Never Knows."

Coordination of text and music. In their best songs, all elements of the song, not just the melody, but also such variables as the choice of instruments, rhythmic design, and form contribute to the meaning of the song.

The following four examples show these qualities in action.

"Yesterday" (Example 15.2) is a romantic ballad with strong roots in the Tin Pan Alley, popular-song tradition. The technique of melodic construction, the preeminence of the melody in the musical texture and clear formal outline recall the songs of the twenties and thirties. Like the typical Tin Pan Alley song, "Yesterday" begins with a phrase that develops from a short melodic idea. The opening (A) section consists of four melodic statements (1. "Yesterday"; 2. "all my troubles"; 3. "Now it looks"; 4. "Oh, I believe"). The first melodic statement is a simple three-note/syllable melodic idea. The next phrase varies the melodic shape of the opening idea ("far away") after attaching a prefix ("all my troubles seem so") to it. The third phrase maintains the rhythm of the second phrase while varying the melodic outline; the fourth phrase proceeds from the third without pause, highlighting the yearning for a less problematic "yesterday" expressed in the words. There are other nice surprises, particularly at the end of the second phrase. The end of the second phrase is cut short four beats to reinforce the word "suddenly."

The overall form of the song draws on the experience of their early years, when they paid their dues by playing all kinds of songs. Bands working in nightclubs usually played slow AABA popular songs one and a half times. They would begin with a complete statement of the melody AABA, then restate the B section and the last A. The pattern of "Yesterday," AABA-BA, takes precisely this form. "Yesterday"'s subtle use of rock rhythm (only in the acoustic guitar) brings it into the sixties, while its unusual instrumentation (guitar plus relatively low but sustained strings) gives it a unique sound seldom heard during the first half of the century. In this song, we hear quite clearly the four distinguishing features of the Beatles's music: reference to a popular style; strong emphasis on melody; imaginative instrumentation; and responsiveness to the text.

In "Lucy in the Sky with Diamonds" (Example 15.3) the kinds of contrast

The Beatles, c. 1965.

the Beatles made from song to song occur within the song itself. Each larger section (A+A1+B) begins delicately with a simple melody in a waltz-like rhythm, accompanied by a harpsichord-sounding instrument and bass playing once every three beats. A musical cloud created by electronic effects and continuous cymbal sound supply a foggy bridge to the beginning of the next phrase. This phrase is related to the opening both melodically and rhythmically, but has much fuller instrumentation and stronger emphasis on each beat. After the word, "gone," the song changes gears, shifting to straight-ahead rock 'n' roll for the refrain. The reprise of the opening phrase is an especially noteworthy feature of this song, because the final chord of the refrain simultaneously accompanies the return of the opening phrase.

Despite denials from the Beatles, several commentators have concluded that "Lucy" symbolizes an acid trip; the title/refrain purportedly suggests LSD. There is musical justification for this point of view. The sharp musical contrasts between sections suggest that the narrative sections describe a plausible acid trip, while the refrain explains a vision that includes "tangerine trees and marmalade skies." Seemingly, there is a musical purpose to the strong, disjunct contrasts from section to section: it parallels the discontinuity and disorientation of the drug experience.

Regardless of whether a connection exists between "Lucy" and the Beatles's drug experience, the song is a dramatic take on the updated verse-chorus form so common in rock-era music. In this song, all the elements, not just melody, combine to bring the storytelling sections to life. The musical imagery is so vivid that it almost seems cinematic. The song remains one of the most original inspirations of the era.

"Eleanor Rigby" (Example 15.4) is perhaps the most extraordinary of all the Beatles's songs, demonstrating the possibility of serious artistic expression within the rock tradition. Perhaps the most immediately startling feature of the song is its use of a string quartet (two violins, viola, cello), a sound closely identified with classical music, as the sole instrumental accompaniment. This, of course, was a radical switch from the standard rock-band instrumentation. If the only distinctive feature of the song were its unusual instrumentation, then the use of the string quartet would simply be a novelty, nothing more. But the string sound is an integral part of the song's conception; any other accompaniment is inconceivable, as innumerable failed "cover" versions have demonstrated.

The text of the song describes two lonely people, whose lives have been exercises in futility. The music expresses this sense of futility in several ways. The song begins without the customary orientation on its "home" chord and ends simply by grinding to a halt. Throughout the song, the harmony mostly oscillates between two chords without any sense of progression toward a goal. Similarly, parabolic melodic curves go up and come back down but don't lead anywhere; there is not the sense of melodic development within a phrase, such as that heard in "Yesterday." The strings abandon their usual role in popular music, to provide a cushion of sustained chords. Here, they serve as a rhythm section, with an active lower part (cello instead of bass) and strong beatkeeping in the other instruments.

The form of this song, an alternation of a persistent refrain with narrative sections that explain the refrain, is perfectly suited to the sense of the text that paints such a dreary picture of the two subjects of the song, because there is no musical tension or progression between the contrasting sections.

IV-9

IVA-9

This form has clear antecedents in the songs of Buddy Holly, whose music the Beatles knew well. For example, his song, "That'll Be the Day" (Example 14.13), also alternates an opening refrain with narrative sections that flesh out the story. But, typically of the Beatles, they adapt the material that they borrow. In their hands the form acquires a neutrality not present in the Buddy Holly song.

With 1965's "Norwegian Wood" (Example 15.5), the Beatles broke cleanly away from conventional rock style. Their songs from the previous year were barely removed from bubblegum status: catchy but simple songs about teen love set over a simple rock beat. "Norwegian Wood" breaks new ground in every way. The text talks about a boy-girl relationship, but not about love. We get a sketchy picture of their evening together: the events but not the emotions. And the title of the song is interspersed throughout, like a running gag. Musically, the song makes no reference to any previous rock style. It has a waltz rhythm, not a rock beat. It replaces the lead guitar with a sitar (an Indian instrument related to the guitar). Its melody consists of two long phrases. This song is identified with rock only because it's by the Beatles.

"Norwegian Wood" has several interesting musical features. Like "Satisfaction," it has an "endless loop" form, because the first phrase of the melody (A) is absolutely static harmonically and the second phrase (B) always leads back to the A section. The first phrase of the melody grows out of the rhythmic pattern set to the words "once had a girl." It has no rhythmic or melodic momentum; rather, it runs out of steam every eight measures. The B phrase also lacks momentum; it consists of a steady rhythm and minimal melodic movement. The absence of melodic or rhythmic energy suggests that the music echoes the noncommital attitude of the song's narrator. "Norwegian Wood" confirms the Beatles's departure from conventional rock, and signals their transition into a more musically mature and eclectic phase of their career.

BOB DYLAN

Bob Dylan, born Robert Zimmermann in 1941, began his musical career as a folksinger very much in the style of his early idol, Woody Guthrie. When he began to write his own songs in the early 1960s, he was soon recognized as the most articulate musical spokesman for the rapidly growing protest movement. His songs helped the folk movement rediscover its legacy of social activism. In 1965, Dylan "went electric," augmenting his acoustic guitar accompaniment with a rock 'n' roll band. He later teamed up with The Band, first in performance, then in the studio. The content of his songs changed as well, moving away from causes to social commentary and personal matters. Like the Beatles, Rolling Stones, and others, Dylan embraced nonrock styles, especially country music in the late 1960s.

"Subterranean Homesick Blues" (Example 15.6) is a particularly fine example of Dylan's eclectic electric style. As with most Dylan songs, the words are preeminent. The text presents a rapid-fire series of images, like a film that constantly cuts from one scene to the next; the words are all more spoken than sung. The quick "image" rhythm of the text is an important ingredient in the aggressive, hostile tone of the song.

Ⓓ

It can be argued that Dylan's embrace of rock was not a cop-out to commercial interests, as his earlier folk-purist fans maintained, but a musical necessity, brought about by the increasingly abstruse quality of his lyrics/poems. Dylan's song texts were not meant to be easily understood. Indeed, they were thoroughly analyzed apart from the music as significant poetry. Precisely because the texts in Dylan's electric-era songs had become more difficult, the musical message had to become more immediate. In these recordings, the function of the band is not so much to help express the text in music as to strike an attitude, which the text then explains and refines. The band finds a groove at the beginning of the song and maintains it all the way through. There is little interaction of the accompaniment with the melody of the song, because there is no melody to speak of.

A song like "Subterranean Homesick Blues" is the rock era's equivalent of a beat poet from the fifties, such as Kenneth Rexroth, reading his poetry over a jazz background. The instrumental accompaniment provides a constant reminder of the message of the song, but in general terms rather than specific details (as often happens on later Beatles's songs). The backup group sounds like a particularly nasty honky-tonk band by way of Chuck Berry's "Maybelline" playing a blues. They convey the rebellious attitude of the text in both the sound itself and the associations that the sound evokes.

Like several of the Beatles's songs, "Subterranean Homesick Blues" is not a rock song by any conventional standard; the instrumental accompaniment would serve many country singers well. Yet, when blended with Dylan's text and voice, it becomes part of the language of rock, pointing the way toward the expansion of its musical vocabulary.

"Satisfaction" showed what rock should be. The Beatles' and Dylan's songs showed what it could become.

JIMI HENDRIX: ROCK'S FIRST VIRTUOSO

Although rock is primarily a group music, it has had its share of virtuoso soloists. The best-known soloists of rock are the guitarists: preeminently Jimi Hendrix, but also Eric Clapton, Jeff Beck, Jimmy Page, and, on the fringes, John McLaughlin. All used electric blues as a point of departure, and greatly increased the range, volume, and variety of sound as they exploited the capabilities of the solid-body guitar, improved amplification, and new electronics.

Hendrix was the trailblazer both in his expanded vocabulary of riffs, scales, bent notes, and in his use of electronics. As described by *The Rolling Stone Encyclopedia of Rock 'n' roll*:

> Hendrix pioneered the use of the instrument as an electronic sound source. Rockers before him had experimented with feedback and distortion, but he turned those effects and others into a controlled, fluid vocabulary every bit as personal as the blues he began with.

Jimi Hendrix (1942–1970) and his various bands were among the original "power trios," three-man bands (guitar, bass, drums) with a strong solo orientation, in live performance if not so much in the studio. In "Purple Haze" (Example 15.7), one of his first hit songs, Hendrix adapts and expands the new language of rock. The following outline of the song highlights Hendrix's use of these new ideas:

Introduction. Oscillating two-note "chord"; strict beatkeeping

Section 1 (instrumental). Eight short phrases paired into larger groups (AABC). Opening phrases are rhythmically identical, melodically different four-note riffs drawn from pentatonic scales, final phrases slightly elaborated versions of these four-note patterns. Heavy beatkeeping in drums and bass enriched by subliminal marking of a rock beat in the drum part. No harmonic change.

Section 2 (vocal). Instruments shift to active accompaniment. Bass moves at rock-beat speed, drummer breaks away from marking the beat, and guitar plays riff-like (with a varied rhythmic pattern) chordal accompaniment. After two repetitions of the accompaniment pattern, the vocal line enters, building a phrase out of four slightly varied statements of a riff formed from just two different pitches. The section ends with an instrumental break under the last vocal phrase, followed by a short interlude featuring a short riff adapted from the opening instrumental section

Section 3 (vocal). Virtually identical to section 2, except that the opening two statements of the accompaniment pattern are omitted.

Section 4 (instrumental). This section begins as if it were the contrasting phrase of the vocal part, but soon turns into a guitar solo where Hendrix unleashes some of the devices in his electronic bag of tricks. The solo itself, during which Hendrix builds patterns by moving up and down a scale, is not one of his most inspired efforts. His second solo, which concludes the recording, has more shape and coherence.

Section 5. Identical to Section 1

Section 6. Identical to Section 3

Section 7. Open-ended version of Section 4

In "Satisfaction," the opening guitar riff and the vocal part shared more or less equal billing. In "Purple Haze," Hendrix shifts that balance toward the instruments. What had been an introductory guitar riff in "Satisfaction" has become a complete section with the riff fully developed instead of repeated a few times. Even when the voice enters, the accompaniment overpowers it, and the vocal line itself has minimal musical interest. The focus again shifts to the guitar in the solo section; the melodic material here is more elaborate than any vocal part.

SOUL: AFRICAN-AMERICAN MUSIC IN THE SIXTIES

In the sixties, African–American performers moved to the center stage of American popular music. They enjoyed unprecedented prominence: twelve of the top twenty-five singles artists or groups during the decade were African–American. A diverse group that included James Brown, Aretha Franklin, Ray Charles, Dionne Warwick, the Supremes, and Chubby Checker, they represented not one style but several.

Despite their commercial success, these performers did not share much common ground musically with their white counterparts. There are two main reasons for this. The first and more significant is the strong gospel tradition. Most of the major African–American performers of the sixties had grown up singing in church. There is no better example than Aretha Franklin, the "queen of soul"; Aretha's father was pastor of one of the largest churches in Detroit. Those that began their careers in the sixties had also been listening to the major rhythm and blues artists of the fifties. Their work continued the blues/gospel/pop syntheses of these fifties artists.

The other major reason for a distinct African–American tradition in the sixties was the artistic control of a few key producers. Chief among them was Berry Gordy, founder of Motown records and the man most responsible for the Motown sound of the sixties. Gordy exercised complete control over the performers under contract to him. He determined what songs they recorded, who performed on the recording (the Motown sound is due in large measure to Gordy's house musicians), what clothes they wore, their stage routines, and almost everything else related to their professional life. Eventually, some performers, like the Four Tops, left Motown or, like Marvin Gaye or Stevie Wonder, obtained artistic control over their records. By then, however, the Motown sound was well established.

Atlantic records, under producer Jerry Wexler's direction, and Stax records also helped develop a distinctive sound, which came to be known as "soul." The new name responded to a positive sense of racial identity that soul emerged during the decade: "black is beautiful" was the slogan of many politically active members of the community. Soul represented the blues and deep-gospel end of the African–American-music spectrum. This synthesis is heard most clearly in several recordings by Aretha Franklin; her hit, "Dr. Feelgood," is a blues performed in classic gospel style, in much the same spirit as Ray Charles's "A Fool for You." The "soul" movement seemed to end with the assassination of Martin Luther King in 1968. King's death touched off a series of inner-city race riots, which put a damper on the drive toward integration. Ironically, *Billboard* changed the name of its rhythm and blues chart to "soul" a year later.

At one end of the "soul" spectrum were the wildly successful African–American pop groups: the Supremes, the Shirelles, the Temptations, Smokey Robinson and the Miracles, and several others. These groups, mostly from Berry Gordy's Motown stable, mixed the lighter side of African–American music with the popular song of sixties rock. The musical result was usually prettier than soul, although seldom saccharine: generally more restrained emotionally, richer harmonically, more melodious, and with sumptuous orchestration. At the other end of the spectrum were James Brown, the "Godfather of Soul," and other like-minded artists, like Otis Redding and Percy Sledge. Their music typically featured rough, often unrestrained vocals, relentless rhythms, and active, open textures.

Smokey Robinson and the Miracles, 1963.

The following six examples show a wide range of African–American music in the sixties and early seventies. Smokey Robinson's "Tracks of My Tears" (Example 15.8), which mixes a flowing melody and conventional European harmony with a restrained African–American sound, shows the more restrained, pop-oriented end of the soul spectrum. Marvin Gaye's classic "I Heard It Through the Grapevine" (Example 15.9) mixes Gaye's intense vocal style with a varied accompaniment, rich strings but sinister keyboard and percussion. It retains some pop characteristics, but has more of the emotion associated with soul. The soul end of the spectrum is personified by James Brown (Examples 15.10 and 15.11). Viewed in retrospect, they were the real avant-garde music of the sixties. Examples 15.12 and 15.13 by Aretha Franklin show her ability to sing comfortably and communicatively in both a Motown-ish romantic pop style and the hard-core soul style linked so closely to James Brown.

Smokey Robinson and the Miracles were among the best of the pop-oriented groups to appear on Berry Gordy's Motown label. Robinson's gospel roots are clear in his use of falsetto (singing in the head rather than from the chest to extend a singer's range upward and produce a lighter sound) and occasional melismas. "Tracks of My Tears" (Example 15.8) helped create an African–American tradition of romantic song: a story of love lost, told in melodramatic language, set within a lush musical background. It has Motown's version of a rich pop texture, with full brass, strings, backup vocals, and rhythm supporting the solo vocal line. Its emphasis is on melody, rather than rhythm, and its form is as innovative melodically as James Brown's "Papa Has a Brand New Bag" is rhythmically. The African–American romantic song filled the void left by the decline of Tin Pan Alley song.

IV-10

IVA-10

Despite their common purpose, there are several differences between "Tracks of My Tears" and earlier Tin Pan Alley songs. The most obvious is the length of the song. A single statement of the melody requires all three minutes, whereas earlier songs typically included two or more statements of the chorus.

The melody contains three major sections, in an AAB pattern. The first two sections begin quietly, supplying the background information on the narrator. The song gains in intensity during the refrain as the words explain the title phrase. The last (B) section retains the intensity of the previous refrain statement through call-and-response exchanges, then a unison statement from voices and instruments that leads directly into the final statement of the refrain. Both within and between sections, the emotional weight of the song falls at the end: The first two sections grow from a quiet beginning to a climax just before the title line, and the AAB design gives a similar impression on a larger scale. The end-weighted AAB form was especially popular with songwriters, both African–American and white, in the late sixties and early seventies.

AAB form

Of all the Motown artists, none sang with more emotional intensity than Marvin Gaye (1939–1984). His turbulent life–stormy relationships with his wife and other women, drug and alcohol abuse, and his death by his father's hand–seems to find expression in his music. Whether singing about love, as in "Grapevine," or contemporary life, as in several songs from his groundbreaking 1971 album, *What's Going On,* he communicated an almost tangible range of feeling: pain, hope, joy, frustration.

"I Heard It Through the Grapevine" (Example 15.9) is one of the great recorded performances in the history of popular music. Like the Beatles's "Eleanor Rigby" (Example 15.4), it is a drama in miniature. It is beautifully integrated: every element blends seamlessly to convey the sense of the text, which gradually unfolds the story of love gone wrong. The introduction immediately establishes a dark mood with the opening keyboard riff, harmonized with open intervals. Other instruments enter in stages, leading to the entrance of the voice.

IV-11

IVA-11

Each statement of the melody of the song contains four sections. The first two are blues-like, in that they generally stay within a narrow range and go down more than up. The third builds to the final section for the hook of the song, "I heard it through the grapevine." It is the emotional center of each

Marvin Gaye at the Apollo Theater, c. 1964, with unidentified dancers.

statement. Like many songs of the sixties and seventies, including "Tracks of My Tears," this song uses a modified verse-chorus format. The first part of each statement describes the incident portrayed in the song; cumulatively they tell the story. The last part serves as the chorus, reminding us of the point of the song. The magic here is that the transition from verse to chorus is so seamless; it happens so effortlessly that we are hardly aware that the transition has taken place. The form of the song is outlined below:

Ominous introduction
First statement
a. "I bet you wonder how I knew . . ."
a. "With some other guy you knew before . . ."
b. "It took me by surprise . . ."
c. "I heard it through the grapevine . . ."
Interlude: strings and backup vocals
Second statement: AABC
Extended interlude: strings, brass, and backup vocals
Third statement: AABC
Fade-out

More than any other artist, James Brown has been responsible for the rhythmically progressive styles of the last two decades. In the late fifties, Brown followed much the same path as Ray Charles. Charles had overseen the merger of solo gospel singing with rhythm and blues. He had preserved the instrumentation of the jump band—a basic rhythm section (piano, bass, and drums) plus several horns (trumpets and saxes)—and had added from gospel not only his own florid vocal style but backup singers. Songs like

"What'd I Say" (Example 14.10) and "I Got a Woman," feature a call-and-response structure: Ray leading and either voices or instruments answering. Their exchanges updated the strong riff orientation of earlier rhythm and blues.

James Brown took this basic approach in a different direction. By the midsixties, he had achieved commercial success with a style that blended Ray Charles's gospel/rhythm and blues mixture with the rhythmic energy of rock and Latin music. Brown's 1965 breakthrough hit, "Papa's Got a Brand New Bag" (Example 15.10), is a dance song, although one with a difference. As such, its primary concern is laying down a good dance beat. It preserves many of the features of Ray Charles's R&B hits:

 IV-12

 IVA-12

1. Jump-band instrumentation: horns plus rhythm, but with guitar replacing piano
2. Alternation of blues form with sections featuring quick call-and-response patterns over a static harmony
3. A raw-edged vocal style of great intensity
4. Melodic ideas assembled from a series of riffs

But it also exhibits these differences:

1. Rapid call and response takes place between voice and instruments, not voice and backup group; the horns play short, crisp riffs in response to each vocal phrase.
2. The use of rock rhythm

The rock rhythm, as it is used here, has a much more "open" sound than that heard in more mainstream rock recordings. This results from lighter timekeeping and more rhythmic conflict. Rock rhythm (twice beat speed) is reinforced only on the drummer's ride cymbal and faintly by the guitar. The guitar is treated at times as a "percussion" instrument: the strings are not pressed down completely, so that, when strummed, the attack is heard clearly, but not the pitch.

Bass, drum, horns, and voice contribute to the considerable rhythmic conflict that is integral to the character of this song. The bass plays an intermittent, often syncopated line; the drummer similarly plays irregular, if periodic, patterns, either on the bass drum or between the bass drum and snare drum; horns typically time their responses to the backbeat; and the voice roams freely over all. The net result is a looser, less insistent, yet more active and complex rhythm.

"Papa's Got a Brand New Bag" was exactly what Brown said it was: a new bag, i.e., style. "Cold Sweat," (Example 15.11) released two years later, went even further. It substituted textural interest for harmonic interest: an even denser texture over absolutely static harmony. The opening section takes place on one chord; the contrasting section on an oscillation between two chords. The sense of harmonic progression evident in "Papa. . ." is completely absent. "Cold Sweat" was an extremely influential recording. Its echoes can be heard from Jimi Hendrix's music and Miles Davis's rock explorations to the rap and dance music of today.

 IV-13

IVB-1

Overall, Brown's style, with its denser texture, slow beat, more complex rhythmic interaction, and heavy dependence on riffs, was the most rhyth-

James Brown, 1964.

mically progressive African–American popular style of the sixties. Out of it grew the funk styles that in turn provided the rhythmic foundation for the progressive music of the seventies and eighties, as we'll see in Chapter 20.

The one performer who convincingly spanned the entire spectrum of African–American music in the 1960s and early 1970s was Aretha Franklin (1942–), one of the great talents in the history of popular music and perhaps the most outstanding solo performer of the last forty years. Although she was the daughter of one of the most sought-after preachers in the country, and had impeccable gospel credentials, she spent the early years of her professional career trying to become a pop singer. Jerry Wexler, a producer for Atlantic records, rescued her career by getting her to record rhythm and blues and cover current pop hits. Equally comfortable and effective with gospelish anthems like "Respect" and "Think," blues like "Dr. Feelgood," tender love songs like "Daydreaming," even pop and jazz songs, Aretha enjoys a range and versatility matched only by Ray Charles. When she covers a song, she transforms it so completely that it takes on a totally different character. And she is one of those rare performers who is able to communicate her experience through her songs.

Aretha was the first female singer to work successfully within the "hardcore" rhythm-and-blues style of Ray Charles and James Brown. "Think" (Example 15.12), one of a string of late-sixties hits, gives this genre a new direction, textually and musically. Like "Respect," "Think" is a lecture in song on how to conduct a relationship. Its subject and tone are more serious than a more dance-oriented song like "Papa's Got a Brand New Bag." Aretha's

 IV-14

 IVB-2

Aretha Franklin, c. 1967.

range of vocal effects, from the intensified speech of the opening phrase, the blues-tinged phrase that follows, the occasional Little Richard whoop, and powerful enunciation of "Freedom, Freedom . . ." gives ample evidence of her complete mastery of the style. The instrumental support provides a much richer backdrop for her artistry than that used in the James Brown song. The rhythm section is fuller: drums (with tambourine added); active bass, piano, organ, guitar (especially prominent in the second part of the song); vocal responses; and a "wall of sound" from the horns.

Recorded in 1972, "Until You Come Back to Me" (Example 15.13) is a love song very much in the mold of "Tracks of My Tears." As befits its later date, the setting is more sumptuous than that heard in "Think" or "Tracks of My Tears": strings, electronic sounds, extra percussion, and a jazz flute are some of the sounds that enrich this texture. The backup provides an ideal cushion for the more subdued side of Aretha's vocal personality. Using her repertoire of gospel devices expressively and with discrimination, she sings with an immediacy and personal involvement matched by few vocalists.

 IV-15

 IVB-3

"Until You Come Back to Me" is romantic without being saccharine. There is a successful juxtaposition of the underlying optimism of the music, expressed in its beat and gradual accumulation and release of melodic tension through each phrase (a musical confirmation of the title of the song, a way of saying "things will work out"), and the pessimism of the text and Aretha's bittersweet rendition of it. A song without the musical optimism would be too dreary, a version without Aretha's grit too sweet.

CONCLUSION

Rock music came to its full maturity in the sixties. Elevated by the work of artists like the Rolling Stones, the Beatles, Bob Dylan, Jimi Hendrix, Aretha Franklin, James Brown, and the Motown acts, the music reached new heights, setting the standard for the next two decades of popular-music making.

Terms to Know

AAB form	electric bass	electric guitar
endless-loop form	Hammond organ	hook
looping	Motown	multitrack recording
rock	soul	

Names to Know

Beatles	James Brown	Bob Dylan
Aretha Franklin	Marvin Gaye	Berry Gordy
Jimi Hendrix	George Martin	Smokey Robinson
Rolling Stones	Jerry Wexler	

Study Questions

1. In what ways was rock a revolutionary music? What external evidence is there that rock brought a new, more democratic attitude to popular music? What musical evidence is there?

2. What are the three connotations of the word "rock"?

3. How does rock differ from rock 'n' roll? What instruments are different? How are they used differently? How has the rhythm changed? In what ways are forms different?

4. What impact did technological innovation have on rock, its creative process, and its dissemination?

5. Describe the differences between pre-rock popular song and rock song. In what ways will the lyrics be different? How has the relationship between composer and performer changed? How is the interaction among performers different in the rock era?

6. Rock absorbed influences from many other styles. What styles did the following artists bring into rock: Bob Dylan; the Beatles; Jimi Hendrix?

7. In what ways was the African–American, rock-based music of the sixties different from white rock? What accounts for these differences?

8. How broad is the stylistic range of African–American music in the sixties? What are some of the key differences between James Brown and the Motown groups?

CHAPTER SIXTEEN

Song During the Rock Era

As the sixties began, rock was still very much the new kid on the block. Most of the best-selling *albums* before the British invasion were pop, stage and film musicals, and easy-listening music (largely instrumental versions of Tin Pan Alley-type songs). Frank Sinatra, having just formed his own record company (Reprise), charted seven albums in 1961 alone; the film soundtrack of Leonard Bernstein's *West Side Story*, released in 1962, spent over a year at the top of the album charts; Rodgers and Hammerstein's *The Sound of Music*, released in 1960, spent over three years on them. Rock may have made the most noise, but it was not the only player.

When rock 'n' roll broke through as the primary mode of popular music, other popular forms had to make a fundamental decision: to rock or not to rock. A genre could marry with rock to form a hybrid style or array of styles. Hybrids could be purely cosmetic, such as the addition of a rock beat to a Tin Pan Alley song. Or they could thoroughly integrate rock style with an established tradition to update a genre, as in *Hair*, the landmark rock musical.

rock musical

It was also possible to turn one's back on rock. In musical theater, those who ignored rock generally pursued one of three options: nostalgia; neo-traditionalism; or new directions. Much of post-1970 musical theater has been an exercise in nostalgia. Revivals are as common on Broadway as new productions. To cite just one example among many, *Guys and Dolls*, a hit show from the early fifties in both stage and film versions, has gone through several incarnations since 1970. There have also been new shows created from old material, such as the African-American revues *Ain't Misbehavin'* and *Bubbling Brown Sugar*. These shows were built around the pop song standards of the great African-American songwriters. Like the revues of the teens and twenties, these shows connected a handful of Tin Pan Alley-style tunes with a slender plot.

Neo-traditionalism—a new conception of an earlier style—is most successfully represented in the work of Stephen Sondheim, as we'll discover in the songs from *Follies* and *A Little Night Music* (Examples 16.3 to 16.5). Sondheim was equally creative in finding new directions, ones that neither incorporated rock nor recalled a specific pre-rock style. For *Pacific Overtures* (1976), a musical about Japan's contact with the West following Commodore Perry's 1853 visit, Sondheim integrated Japanese melodies and instruments into the score.

Nonrock options were not so clearly defined in the popular song of the seventies, for several reasons. One was certainly the difference in scope: the three-minute popular song versus the three-hour musical. Another was the absence of a songwriter, or group of songwriters, who were committed to a completely nonrock style and imaginative enough to chart a new course. In fact, the most imaginative continuation of Tin Pan Alley-type popular song involved some accommodation with rock, as we'll see.

POPULAR SONG

The Beatles, Bob Dylan, and other rock songwriters of the sixties sang the songs that they wrote. This departed from the standard popular-song practice of the previous generation, in which songwriters wrote songs for others to sing. Still, the older Tin Pan Alley approach to songwriting was still alive and well in the early sixties. By that time, however, Tin Pan Alley seemed to have shrunk to a single address: 1619 Broadway, otherwise known as the Brill Building. The building was home to several music publishers, most notably AlDon Music (named for partners Al Nevins and Don Kirshner), who set out to bridge the gap between rock 'n' roll and traditional popular song. Staff songwriters included future star singer/songwriters Carole King, Neil Sedaka, and Neil Diamond.

Throughout the sixties, the most inventive of the "Brill Building"-style songwriters was the team of lyricist Hal David and songwriter Burt Bacharach. Bacharach's songwriting was innovative: In the series of hit songs he wrote for Dionne Warwick throughout the sixties, Bacharach updated virtually every aspect of popular songwriting. Among his changes were:

1. The frequent use of wide melodic leaps, often in close proximity. These leaps typically produced jagged melodic contours, not the more smoothly flowing shapes of songs from the forties and fifties.

2. Unusual chords and chord progressions that decisively broke away from the "Heart and Soul" chord progression.

3. Rock-based, often irregular rhythms that highlighted the inflection and cadence of David's lyrics.

4. Unconventional forms that depart from the models of any era.

"Alfie" (Example 16.1) shows several of these changes in operation. It is innovative in its overall style, at least from a Tin Pan Alley perspective: the song finds a distinctive midpoint between Tin Pan Alley and rock. It shows its connection with pre-rock popular song in its emphasis on melody and sumptuous orchestration. The influence of rock is evident mainly in the rhythm, a trickle-down version of rock rhythm.

More individual and striking is Bacharach's fresh approach to melody. It is evident from the outset: the leap up on the word "Alfie" is a sung question. The next two phrases are classic Bacharach. "Is it just for the moment we live?" contains three big leaps back to back: "just-for," "for-the," and "moment." "What's it all about?" reiterates the opening question by beginning with two upward skips, the second larger than the first. The frequency, size, and irregular placement of the skips in this opening section are rare in pop-

*Dionne Warwick, c. mid-
1960s, when she was creating
hits with Bacharach and
David.*

ular song before Bacharach; they would become more common after 1970,
as they were perhaps the most widely imitated feature of Bacharach's style.
It should be noted that songs with such jagged, wide-ranging contours are
difficult to sing. Dionne Warwick sings "Alfie" effortlessly, which is certainly
one reason Bacharach recruited her to be his "hired voice."

Similarly, the form of the song updates the standard Tin Pan Alley
AABA form. Here it is used only as a point of departure. Each A phrase
begins the same way but ends differently. Moreover, the melody unfolds so
slowly that a single statement takes almost three minutes. In its length, it
resembles rock-era ballads, like Simon and Garfunkel's "Bridge Over
Troubled Water," or Elton John's "Your Song." By contrast, the chorus of a
typical AABA song from the twenties lasted less than a minute. "Alfie" has a
Tin Pan Alley-inspired form, but rock-era length.

"Do You Know the Way to San Jose?" (Example 16.2) contains sterling
examples of Bacharach's inventive harmonies, rhythms, and forms.
Although Bacharach's basic harmonic vocabulary is the same as any other
pop songwriter's, he often writes chords and chord sequences that depart

IV-17

IVB-5

from conventional practice. Underneath the phrase "In a week they'll make you a star" is a string of chords that is unusual both in the choice of notes that form the individual chords and in their sequence.

"Do You Know the Way to San Jose?"—like "Promises, Promises," and "I Say a Little Prayer"—also illustrates David's and Bacharach's patter-song style. In songs of this type—up-tempo, with rapid-fire lyrics—Bacharach periodically incorporates some kind of irregular rhythmic pattern, in response to the natural declamation of the lyric. In the opening section of this song ("Do you know . . . lose my way"), he adds a measure to what would conventionally be a four-measure phrase. The first phrase "Do you know the way to San Jose" is straightforward enough: two measures, with silence at the end to set it off from what comes next. Typically, the second phrase would use the same, or almost the same, rhythm for a variant of the opening phrase. (It's easy to create a conventional answering phrase by leaving out "I may go wrong.") However, Bacharach lengthens the phrase to accommodate the "extra" text instead of trying to cram it into four measures.

The opening five-measure phrase spins out into a highly unusual version of the standard pop-song form: A (five measures), A (five measures), B (fifteen measures), A, A, B, ending. The form is unusual in its proportions, not in the sequence of events. In particular, the B section—fifteen measures without a cadence to break the flow until the end—may be without parallel in the popular-song repertoire.

In melody, harmony, rhythm, and form, Bacharach and David offered novel alternatives to the old way of writing popular songs. The Bacharach/David style influenced the next generation of pop-song composers, most notably Barry Manilow, Paul Williams, and Marvin Hamlisch. In the early seventies, the merger of Tin Pan Alley-type song and rock had coalesced into soft rock. Soft rock blended the emphasis on melody and clear forms of Tin Pan Alley song with an understated rock rhythm. This style flourished throughout the seventies, particularly in the work of the Carpenters, Barbra Streisand, and Barry Manilow.

The rise of soft rock also marked the end of the fox-trot/swing-based popular song. There have been a few commercially successful older-style songs written in the last twenty-five years: Frank Sinatra's hit "New York, New York" is a familiar example, as is the soundtrack to Walt Disney's animated movie *Aladdin*. However, it has been far more common, and sensible, to perform new versions of fox-trot era standards instead of writing new songs in an old style. There are so many great songs from the pre-rock era that it seems almost superfluous to add to the repertoire.

Melodious popular song saw its market share diminish in the eighties. With the rise of rap, the resurgence of heavy metal, and the emergence of alternative rock, the center of popular music shifted away from melody. Even soft rock lost its commercial toehold. However, there are signals that the pendulum has begun to swing back toward melody. The strongest comes from country music, which has enjoyed unprecedented commercial success in the nineties. One reason for this success would seem to be its orientation to melody. In this respect, it is almost alone among the major contemporary genres.

Another signal has been the renewed interest in Tin Pan Alley-type songs and singing over the last few years by rock-generation audiences, for example the success of the soundtrack to *When Harry Met Sally* featuring

soft rock

Harry Connick, Jr.'s Sinatra-esque versions of fox-trot era standards (Isham Jones's 1924 "It Had to Be You"). The disc catapulted Connick to stardom. Natalie Cole's Grammy-winning album featuring remakes of her father's hits was also a commercial and artistic success.

The most symbolically significant effort may well be Frank Sinatra's multiplatinum 1993 *Duets* album. On it, Sinatra teams with singers from several generations, including U2's Bono, Aretha Franklin, and Luther Vandross, to re-record some of his most enduring hits. Because Sinatra epitomized the kind of music rock revolted against, the album seems to be not only a tribute to Sinatra but also a reconciliation between generations. A second volume with a similar group of partners was issued in 1994.

So the Tin Pan Alley popular song style that was so popular before 1960 lives on, both in reissues and new versions. In addition to Sinatra and Connick, his heir-apparent in the minds of many, cabaret singers like Bobby Short and Michael Feinstein have given old standards a fresh coat of paint. Classical singing stars, most notably Kiri te Kanawa, have given them an elegant new voice.

MUSICAL THEATER AND FILM

Broadway began the rock era on top of the popular-music world. The decade between 1955 and 1965 was a commercial and artistic highpoint. Four shows, beginning with Lerner and Loewe's *My Fair Lady* in 1956, exceeded the record for longest-running show set by *Oklahoma!* in 1943. *Fiddler on the Roof,* which featured Zero Mostel, began its record-breaking run of 3,242 performances in 1964. Original cast recordings dominated the album charts through the early sixties. However, by the decade's close, film and television had largely supplanted Broadway as a source of hits. Of the fifty original cast albums (recordings of Broadway shows) that made the Top 40 lists after 1955, only eight were released after 1965, and only two of these eight after 1975.

Soundtrack recordings (musical highlights from a film) showed a similar trend. During the late fifties and early sixties, most of the best-selling soundtrack albums were film versions of current Broadway shows like *West Side Story* and *The Sound of Music* as well as older shows like *Oklahoma!* and *South Pacific.* After 1963, however, far fewer soundtracks came from film versions of musicals. Many were music from popular films, like *Saturday Night Fever* and *Dirty Dancing.* Several featured hit songs by rock-era stars: Simon and Garfunkel's songs used in the 1968 movie *The Graduate;* the Bee Gees's hits for *Saturday Night Fever;* and Prince's songs for *Batman* are just a few.

The fame of composer/songwriters like Henry Mancini, John Williams, and Quincy Jones suggests the extent to which film and television supplanted Broadway as the primary visual media for popular music after 1960. In the pre-rock generation, Broadway-type composer/songwriters (for example, Gershwin, Berlin, Kern, or Rodgers and Hammerstein) were the marquee names, even when they wrote for films. Those who created background music were relatively unknown outside the industry. After 1960, composers with no Broadway affiliation became household names. Henry Mancini was the first. Mancini's breakthrough came in the late fifties with his jazz-based theme and background music for *Peter Gunn,* a television series about a detective. Mancini developed into one of the most versatile composers of the time, with scores for such films as *Breakfast at Tiffany's,* which included the lovely waltz ballad "Moon River," and *The Pink Panther.*

John Williams and Quincy Jones have enjoyed comparable fame since the seventies. Williams composed music for several blockbuster films, including *Jaws, Star Wars,* and *Superman.* From 1980 to 1994, he maintained a high profile as the conductor of the Boston Pops. Jones, who has worn many hats in his career, made his commercial mark with music for the television show *Sanford and Son,* the landmark miniseries *Roots,* and *The Wiz,* the 1978 film remake of *The Wizard of Oz;* he has also served as the producer of many of Michael Jackson's best-selling recordings, including the album *Thriller.*

ROCK ON BROADWAY

There were several popular and important shows in the sixties that reflected the spirit and style of rock. Most of the major pre-rock musicals had clung to the operetta plot conceit: stories about faraway places in long-ago times. (*West Side Story* was an important exception.) By contrast, many

Claude (James Rado) gets his hair cut in Hair. *Photograph (c) Martha Swope.*

rock-era shows were focused squarely on the present or recent past, which they viewed without the aid of rose-colored glasses. Just as rock songs had abandoned Tin Pan Alley "moon/June" love lyrics for singer/songwriter slices of contemporary life, rock-influenced musical theater traded in a largely sugar-coated "there and then" for a sometimes bittersweet "here and now."

Four shows from the late sixties and early seventies–*Hair; Promises, Promises; Company;* and *Jesus Christ, Superstar*–demonstrated the nature and range of rock's influence. The most revolutionary was *Hair*. Billed an "American tribal love-rock musical," *Hair* portrayed the counterculture lifestyle. Its sensational parts, like the nude and flag-burning scenes, got most of the press. However, *Hair*'s revolution went deeper than this surface sensationalism. It embodied counterculture attitudes in almost every aspect of its design: the ambiguity and relative insignificance of its plot; the absence of stars; and the racially integrated cast.

Promises, Promises (1968) and *Company* (1970) also showed the influence of rock. Both dealt with thorny issues in contemporary urban life rather than a fantasy land or historical event. Bacharach and David's *Promises, Promises,* a 1968 musical adapted from Neil Simon's film *The Apartment,* told the story of a young businessman who let his bosses use his apartment for extramarital affairs in return for job advancement. *Company* dealt with a bachelor in his mid-thirties who is reluctant to commit to a relationship.

Andrew Lloyd Webber's *Jesus Christ, Superstar* (recorded 1970, staged 1971) retold the passion of Jesus in contemporary terms. It portrayed the characters from a current psychological perspective and used rock-influ-

Ben Vereen as Judas and Jeff Fenholt as Jesus in the original production of Jesus Christ, Superstar. *Friedman-Abeles, photographers; courtesy Performing Arts Research Center, New York Public Library at Lincoln Center.*

enced music and everyday speech to make the story more up to date. Here, the relevance and immediacy associated with rock were evident not in the story, which is ageless, but in the way it was told. Lloyd Webber, the most commercially successful musical-theater composer of the rock era, has had a series of hit shows in the seventies and eighties. After *Jesus Christ, Superstar,* the most notable have been *Evita* (1976), *Cats* (1981), and *The Phantom of the Opera* (1985).

Lloyd Webber was musical theater's one-man counterpart to the British invasion of the sixties. There are striking parallels between the Beatles and Lloyd Webber that extend well beyond their British citizenship and their status as the commercially dominant artists within their genre. Both updated an established genre: the Beatles revitalized popular song; Lloyd Webber re-energized musical theater. And both brought their genre into the realm of art by drawing on classical models. The Beatles created beautifully crafted miniatures and concept albums that echoed the art songs and song cycles of nineteenth and twentieth century classical music. Lloyd Webber's compositions moved away from the dialogue-song alternation of musical comedy to completely sung stage works: operas with a rock beat.

Rock's influence on both content and style continued into the seventies and eighties. Two noteworthy instances came from director Michael Bennett. Bennett's *A Chorus Line* (1975) gave its audience an unsentimental glimpse into Broadway's life behind the curtain. His 1981 show *Dreamgirls* did the same for Motown-ish African-American pop groups of the sixties. Both offered a comparatively frank, unglamorous dramatization of the seemingly glamorous showbiz lifestyle.

STEPHEN SONDHEIM

Along with Lloyd-Webber, the major figure in musical theater after 1960 has been Stephen Sondheim, the most versatile American composer of this generation. Like few other theater composers, he has written both words and music to his shows. Moreover, he is musical theater's grand eclectic: the master of virtually every twentieth-century theater style.

Although thoroughly trained as a musician, Sondheim began his career as a lyricist. His first collaborations were three of the major musical theater events of the fifties: a revision of *Candide* in 1956, *West Side Story* in 1958 (both scored by Leonard Bernstein), and the 1959 musical *Gypsy,* with music by Jules Styne. The first Broadway show for which he wrote both lyrics and music was *A Funny Thing Happened on the Way to the Forum* (1962).

Sondheim flexed his compositional muscles in the early seventies in a trio of musicals: *Company* (1970), *Follies* (1971), and *A Little Night Music* (1973). *Company* portrayed a contemporary situation in mostly contemporary, for 1970, musical language. *Follies* looks back at Broadway during the heyday of the revue. Its music includes brilliant parodies of the music of the twenties and thirties. *A Little Night Music* looks back even further, to the turn of the century. To evoke the period, Sondheim set all the songs in waltz time, the most common rhythmic underpinning of popular songs during that period (recall "After the Ball" [Example 5.2]). The three shows are a musical tour back in time. In them, Sondheim visits/revisits stage entertainment in the three major time periods of twentieth-century popular music: after 1955; between 1915 and 1955; and before 1915. Sondheim writes in all

IB-4

I-30

styles with such apparent ease and authenticity that it's easy to imagine him at home musically at any time prior to 1970.

Within the popular tradition, Stephen Sondheim's music is unique in several respects. Most obvious is his stylistic range. Sondheim has mastered any style that he needed to express the dramatic intent of a work. More significantly, Sondheim puts his personal stamp on his work not by what he does, but by *how* he does it. Most major popular artists are most identifiable by musical trademarks, and these characteristics are typically style-specific. They are perfectly appropriate for the artist's work within the style, but less appropriate or even inappropriate for another style. Sondheim's approach is fundamentally different. His musical personality shows through not in specific style features, but in attitudes and predilections that surface in his music, no matter what the style, as well as in the lyrics and, for that matter, in the concept of a show.

Sondheim seems to revel in complexity, virtuosity, surprise, and a subtle, occasionally acerbic humor. The complexity in his work grows out of the multiple layers of meaning present in some aspect: a song; a turn of phrase; even the title of a show. Sometimes this complexity accumulates gradually. Both "Who's That Woman?" (Example 16.4) and "Soon" (Example 16.5) begin as simple solo songs, but end as spectacular ensemble numbers with several melodic strands sung simultaneously. On other occasions it may be implicit in a single event.

The titles of each of the three shows can be interpreted in different ways, revealing Sondheim's love of complex wit. *Company* refers both to the hero's inability to find "company," a mate, but it also has a theatrical connotation: a troupe with no real stars. *Follies* refers most obviously to Ziegfeld's *Follies*, the annual revue that was so popular in the early part of the century. A show about a group of chorus girls who return to see the old theater for one last time, it strips the Broadway life of its glamour and exposes another kind of follies: the folly of the human condition. The show ends with solo turns for the four principal characters; each song exposes a flaw in the character of the person singing it. *A Little Night Music* takes its theme from Ingmar Bergman's 1956 film, *Smiles for a Summer Night*, but it also refers to Mozart's famous string serenade, *Eine Kleine Nachtmusik*. Although there is no connection with Mozart in time, place, or style, the complicated plot—full of love gone awry and miscommunication—recalls some of Mozart's greatest operas; Sondheim's musical score emulates a Mozartian complexity.

Sondheim's virtuosity as a composer is evident on both a large and small scale. It shows on the broadest scale in his mastery of so many styles. In Examples 16.3 to 16.5, Sondheim demonstrates that he can write a rock-era patter song like Burt Bacharach, a jaunty fox-trot like Cole Porter, and a lilting waltz like Franz Lehar.

Sondheim's virtuosity is most obvious on a small scale in ensemble numbers. "Who's That Woman?" (Example 16.4) presents two songs, then combines them. "Soon" (Example 16.5), the last of a three-song number ("Now" and "Later" precede it), goes a step further. Sondheim assigns the first statement of the melody to one singer. However, when he reprises the melody, he interweaves the melodies of the two earlier songs so that all three are sung simultaneously. Sondheim's art renders this potential confusion not only comprehensible but delightful.

Surprise in Sondheim's music can take many forms. "Another Hundred

IV-18

IVB-6

People" (Example 16.3) beautifully illustrates two of the most common: harmonic sleight of hand and a sudden change in melodic direction or interval. The song begins with a patter phrase that climbs up a single chord, statement by statement, all over the same single static chord in the accompaniment. On the phrase "It's a city of strangers," Sondheim colors a sudden melodic leap up with a change of harmony. It's a wonderfully expressive gesture that underscores the poignancy of the text.

Sondheim's melodies tend to wander instead of staying in the same key throughout, and he often uses ingenious methods to leave or return to the home key. When he returns to a variant of the opening phrase ("They can find each other in the crowded streets"), it is in a different key and harmonized by a different kind of chord. This new chord makes it easier to change key again after the long note sung to "remark." Sondheim saves the best trick for last. Most of the phrases in the song reach a high point on the seventh note of a scale: "Another hundred people who got off of the plane"; "City of strangers"; "And they walk together." Most typically, the seventh note goes up to the key note. Sondheim does just the opposite: He brings the key note down a step so that it matches the melody. This bit of harmonic perversity has the additional benefit of returning the song to its original key.

Sondheim's humor can also be conceptual. In the song "Soon" (Example 16.4), Sondheim adds the two earlier songs, "Now" and "Later," in the reprise. In its second phrase, however, he twists the story line so each character sings about a different time: Anne, who had sung "Soon," enters first, singing "Now." Henrik, who sang "Later," enters immediately after, singing "Soon." Fredrik, who sang "Now," enters last, singing "Later." The humor is not only the rotation of the time roles but also that each singer enters in the sequence determined by his or her new role.

Musical expressions of Sondheim's humor are comparably subtle. Obvious humorous touches, like the saxophones that guffaw after the word "clown" in "Who's That Woman?," are rare—and added by Sondheim's superb orchestrator Jonathon Tunick. More often, it's the sheer delight that Sondheim's compositional craft inspires: the skill in combining two or three melodies so that all are intelligible, or the thick network of melodic and harmonic connections that give all the changes of direction in "Another Hundred People" (Example 16.3) an overriding logic.

There is also humor, or perhaps just the delight of discovery in allusion, even if it's only inferred by the listener and not implied by Sondheim. Marta, who sings "Another Hundred People," holds a number of specious theories. In one, she asserts that people who don't know a lot of Puerto Ricans are weird. So, in the rhythmic underpinning of her song, Sondheim adds the clave rhythm of Afro-Cuban/Newyorican music.

Sondheim has followed a tricky path between popular and art music. It has taken him through lonely territory; in musical theater, few have tried to blend the two, and only Gershwin and Leonard Bernstein have explored this middle ground with comparable artistic success. None have done it quite like Sondheim. Sondheim's dedication to this path has almost certainly cost him mass popularity. With the exception of "Send in the Clowns," Sondheim has not had a hit song.

There are two specific reasons a Sondheim song is unlikely to enjoy a life outside the musical for which it was written. First, it will almost certainly be more complex than a conventional popular song. Second, the meaning

Dean Jones and Elaine Stritch in Company. *Photograph (c) Martha Swope.*

of the song depends almost exclusively on its dramatic function within the musical. Remove the song from the context that the musical provides, and it is often difficult to understand.

Popular songs generally have an accessible melodic idea that is repeated again and again. Both the AABA form of Tin Pan Alley songs and modified verse-chorus forms of the rock era have a lot of repetition built into them. Sondheim, however, is reluctant to sit still through the extensive melodic repetition inherent in the most widely used forms. He uses the conventions of popular song as a point of departure rather than a model. So even though a song may begin simply, it typically develops into an extended statement rich in melodic ideas and interest.

"Soon" (Example 16.5) begins with a modest four-note idea, clearly set off from the variant that follows. Sondheim is undoubtedly leaving some elbow room for the other two parts that join in during the reprise. It is the kind of melodic idea—it's hard to call a motive in waltz rhythm a riff, but that is what it is, for all intents and purposes—that could serve as the basis for a standard AABA song. Sondheim develops the song much less conventionally. An expanded variant of the initial idea leads seamlessly into a restatement of the entire phrase in a different key. The end of this restatement links to a new melodic phrase, which is itself repeated. This second idea connects to still another new idea. When the dust finally settles, four melodic ideas have been stated and restated and a final climactic phrase has almost brought the song to an end; Henrik's cello rudely interrupts. With such an abundance of melodic material, it's not surprising that audiences don't walk out of the theater humming the tune: there's too much to remember.

IV-20

IVB-8

With Sondheim, it's not that the songs don't contain catchy melodic material. In these shows at least, most of them contain memorable, often striking, melodic ideas, very much in tune with the style that inspired them: "Who's that woman I know I know"; "It's a city of strangers." It's just that Sondheim builds them into grander, more intricately connected, less repetitive structures.

More than any other composer of musical theater, Sondheim has written his songs for the show. "Another Hundred People" (Example 16.5) is a superb example. It features Marta, one of the women Bobby the bachelor dates in his search for the perfect partner. The song, with its breathless, run-on melody and busy accompaniment, captures the frenetic pace of life in Manhattan, as described in the lyric. In the course of the song, the lyrics shift from an impersonal commentary on city life to a confused, tentative invitation for a date. As the focus of the lyrics turns inward and we discover Marta's inner turmoil, the music becomes more unstable: shifts in key; phrases begun but not ended; and ideas piling on top of each other.

The music of "Who's That Woman?" (Example 16.3) also works on general and specific levels, but in a different way. The song gives the chorus girl Stella a moment in the sun. Unlike "Another Hundred People," where the music illuminates the lyric, the music of "Who's That Woman?" belies the lyric. Its lighthearted mood, at least in the opening solo section, is very much at odds with the depressing commentary in the lyrics. The musical style of the song serves a double function. It nostalgically recalls the past–Stella's glory years–and at the same time underscores Stella's despair over the ravages of aging. Like the cracked face of a showgirl's statue that symbolizes the show, the conflict between words and music speaks cogently about its central issues: the gap between glitzy appearance and dreary reality; the pain of facing up to an unfulfilled life. Here, Sondheim's use of stylistic reference is ironic as well as evocative.

The total integration of song and story has been a trademark of Sondheim's musicals, more than that of any other Broadway composer. Sondheim takes this integration, begun in *Showboat* and widely followed from *Oklahoma!* on, to its logical conclusion.

It is difficult to discuss musical features of any serious musical theater apart from the dramatic context in which they appear. In Sondheim's case, it is doubly difficult, because the music responds so closely and so subtly to the events onstage and because Sondheim's musical "style" is the mastery of style. Still, we can find in these musicals certain recurrent themes, regardless of the circumstances of the plot. They include the portrayal of characters as real people, full of complex and often contradictory qualities and feelings. To do this, Sondheim uses his mastery of style in several ways: to evoke the time and place of the storyline, to heighten our awareness of the character's state of mind; or even to contradict or comment ironically on it. This helps us see the characters as vividly as possible.

Sondheim also clearly delights in creating challenges for himself and meeting them. After clarifying the range of his craft, he has roamed far afield: an excursion into Kabuki drama in *Pacific Overtures* (1976) and a musical about a painting–*Sunday in the Park with George* (1981)–are two examples. These self-imposed challenges occur not only in the subject of a show but also in its working out. The decision to write a show completely in waltz time is a clear instance of Sondheim putting himself in a compositional straitjacket and escaping with music so varied that we hardly notice the pervasive oom-pah-pah undercurrent.

These three musicals cemented Sondheim's reputation and the scope of his art. They also highlighted the three main directions that stage entertainment would take in the seventies and eighties: *Company* was in step with contemporary musical theater's accommodation with rock; *Follies* anticipated the revues and revivals; *A Little Night Music* pointed up the continued vitality of the operetta tradition. Indeed, Sondheim's later musicals *Sweeney Todd* (1979) and especially *Into the Woods* (1987) helped bring operetta into the late twentieth century.

CONCLUSION

Popular and theatrical song continued to flourish in the sixties, despite the great popularity of rock. Songwriters like Burt Bachrach and Hal David took some elements from rock and injected them into the popular-song tradition, thereby modernizing the older style while preserving its basic appeal. Theatrical composer Stephen Sondheim went the furthest in creating something entirely new; while not unaware of the rock revolution, he preferred to be a musical chameleon, molding the musical style to fit the style of the show.

Terms to Know

rock musical   soft rock

Names to Know

Burt Bacharach	Michael Bennett	Hal David
Quincy Jones	Andrew Lloyd Webber	Henry Mancini
Stephen Sondheim	Barbra Streisand	John Williams

Study Questions

1. Describe some of the similarities and differences between Tin Pan Alley popular song and soft rock.

2. Besides a rock beat, what innovations did Burt Bacharach introduce into traditional popular song?

3. How was musical theater affected by the rise of rock? How did it accommodate rock? How were attitudes and viewpoints associated with rock evident in the major rock-based musicals of the late sixties and early seventies?

4. Describe Stephen Sondheim's compositional range. Why is his style different from almost all other pop artists? Why haven't his songs become hits apart from the musicals for which they were written?

5. Compare *Show Boat* to *A Chorus Line*. What are the similarities and differences? How does *A Chorus Line* reflect the changes in the musical theater over the last few decades?

CHAPTER SEVENTEEN

Country Music in the Rock Era

Country music has followed rock along the road to popularity. It began the rock era as a mostly regional music far from the popular mainstream. Although country songs had begun to cross over, few country artists did. By the nineties, however, country acts routinely topped the charts, their videos were on several cable channels, and Nashville was a locus of power in the music industry. Its audience is no longer just white Southerners and Southern expatriates; it is now much more varied, although the South—and the rest of rural America—remain its core.

There were many reasons for country music's move into the main-stream. Among musical ones, two stand out. One was its many intersections with other styles. These took place on a two-way street: we have already seen nonrock artists reinterpreting country (the folk revival, Ray Charles's country albums) as well as country interpretations of noncountry styles (rocka-billy). More would follow in the decades ahead. Another musical reason for country's increasing popularity was the more open attitude toward nonpop styles that were a consequence of the rock revolution. As we have seen, rock accepted a far wider range of styles than pre-rock pop. Its artists explored non-pop styles—country blues and early country, for example—and its audi-ences accepted most of it. So it was a short step from the country-rock of the Byrds or the folk-rock of James Taylor to the hard country of Merle Haggard or the country singing/songwriting of Willie Nelson.

The assimilation of country into the popular-music mainstream has taken place in two stages. During the first, which lasted from 1955 to about 1970, the most popular country music crossovers were hybrid songs of some kind: rockabilly, country pop, and the like. The second stage began in the early seventies, when noncountry audiences began to take their country music straight. Artists like Merle Haggard, who made little stylistic accom-modation to rock or pop, found welcome ears outside traditional country markets. Country hybrids, like Kenny Rogers's "countrypolitan" style, were even more successful than they had been in the fifties and sixties, and more popular than hard country. But the big breakthrough for country was the fact that real country music now appealed to a noncountry audience. This stage has crested in the early nineties, with Garth Brooks, Billy Ray Cyrus, and other country artists selling as well as, or better than, top rock acts.

The commercial success of country music during the rock era has kept

country
rock

hard
country

country-
politan

alive country music's ongoing tug-of-war between its traditional and mainstream factions. It would seem that the mainstream faction is winning. The sharp distinction between country music and other popular styles in the years before rock has all but disappeared. Since the late sixties, there have been country acts that are country in name only. Glen Campbell, Kenny Rogers, and Charlie Rich were among the first; they have been followed by the majority of today's top country artists. At about the same time, the Eagles, Linda Ronstadt, and Emmylou Harris drew heavily on country music. Meanwhile, country traditionalists wrestled with two issues: preserving its essence and keeping older styles alive.

The essence of country music, then and now, is its themes, its plainspoken way of presenting them, its distinctive vocal styles, and its characteristic instruments—fiddle, steel guitar, and dobro. That has been retained to some extent. However, tradition in country music keeps shifting. Yesterday's progressive music is today's traditional sound. Traditionalism, even neo-traditionalism, means honky-tonk, maybe bluegrass, but not old-time fiddle music. Contemporary country musicians, preserving their role as popular music's proud rear guard, have transformed the Southern rock of the sixties and seventies into the latest "traditional" country style.

The landmark 1994 album *Rhythm, Country, and Blues*, that paired country artists with rhythm and blues artists, dramatically illustrates country's shift toward the mainstream. Younger country stars, like Vince Gill, Travis Tritt, and Clint Black, sound right at home with their R&B partners. It's clear that these country stars have spent some time listening to African-American music: there is relatively little discontinuity in vocal style in their exchanges. By contrast, the older country artists—Conway Twitty and George Jones—have preserved their country identity; their vocal style is clearly distinguished from their partners: Sam Moore (of Sam and Dave) and B. B. King. If a similar album had been made in 1950, the differences in vocal style between country and rhythm and blues artists would have been even more pronounced: imagine Hank Williams paired with Joe Turner, or Roy Acuff fiddling along with Clyde McPhatter. Despite this shift, country music hasn't lost its identity. It remains a distinct segment of the popular-music industry.

MAINSTREAM SUCCESS

The shift toward the mainstream began in earnest around the late fifties and early sixties with four country/rock intersections. Three of them—rockabilly; the folk revival and its aftermath (Dylan, folk-rock, country-rock); and Ray Charles's highly influential recordings of country songs—were discussed in Chapters 14 and 15. The fourth was the creation of the "Nashville sound." During the fifties, Nashville reinforced its position as the spiritual and commercial center of country music. The Country Music Association, formed there in 1957, served as the primary trade organization for the industry. Already the publishing center of country music, Nashville also became its recording center. Most of the major record companies rented, then built, studios there. The "Nashville sound" was a marriage of country and pop. inspired by the successful recordings of country songs by pop artists, some Nashville A&R (artists and repertoire) men, most notably guitarist Chet

Nashville sound

Atkins, sought to create a place in the mainstream market for country music. The result was a sound that supported smooth country vocalists like Jim Reeves with lush arrangements worthy of a Sinatra. A small number of musicians, including Atkins, pianist Floyd Cramer, and vocalist/choral director Anita Kerr, played or sang on many of these Nashville recording dates. Their continuing presence also contributed to the development of a consistent style.

Collectively, all four—the folk revival, rockabilly, Ray Charles's recordings, and the Nashville sound—set the tone for country music during the first two decades of the rock era: excursions into pop and rock from within, explorations of country repertoire from outside. They also created a crisis of conscience: Was country music losing its identity in its eagerness to assimilate into the popular mainstream? In the late sixties and seventies, that question would be answered outside of Nashville.

The seventies and eighties saw three important developments in country music. It achieved mainstream commercial success; recovered its identity; and continued to interact with rock to such an extent that it often became difficult to separate the two. For the first time in its history, country music attracted a large enough audience beyond its traditional constituency to make substantial inroads into the pop charts. Many of its stars gained national recognition: Merle Haggard, Johnny Cash, Tammy Wynette, George Jones, Loretta Lynn, and Willie Nelson all became household names. Dolly Parton went beyond that: she has become a pop icon, one of the handful of celebrities whose every move is grist for the tabloid mill.

There were many reasons for country music's increased popularity. In particular two political developments, the conservative backlash from the sixties and the election of Jimmy Carter, gave country music a boost. Country music continued to be identified with conservative points of view. Ironically, it also began to attract a young, non-Southern, posthippie audience—the very group that prompted the conservative backlash—at about the same time. Carter's election stirred Southern pride; he was the first president from the Deep South elected in the twentieth century. The White House became a major venue for country performers during his presidency.

Throughout the late sixties and seventies, country and its expanded audience met halfway. There was broad support for virtually the entire spectrum of country music from updated versions of traditional styles (Johnny Cash, Merle Haggard, and Willie Nelson), pop-oriented country (Glen Campbell, Kenny Rogers), to rock-country fusions (Gram Parsons, Linda Ronstadt). The clearest indicator of the strength of country's newly won popularity was the commercial success of hard-country acts. Haggard, Nelson, and other like-minded artists defied the conventional Nashville wisdom: Commercial success requires diluting country with pop. More than any other trend, their broad appeal signaled country's entry into the musical mainstream.

THE TRADITIONALISTS

Not surprisingly, the reaction against country's pop orientation took place outside of Nashville. In the mid-sixties, country music rediscovered its roots in Bakersfield, California. The San Joaquin Valley had become home for many Southwesterners after the Dust Bowl of the thirties. There, Buck Owens and his protégé, Merle Haggard, led a honky-tonk revival. In so

Willie Nelson, c. 1980.

doing, they redefined and updated the style. Because of songs like Haggard's "Okie from Muskogee," country music became identified with conservative American values and symbols: patriotism (my country, right or wrong); flags (made to be flown, not burned); only legal drugs (like alcohol); and short haircuts for men. This message had appeal far beyond the traditional country audience. As a result, radio stations devoted wholly or partly to country music increased nationally at an astonishing rate.

The redefinition of traditional country found another home in the seventies: Austin, Texas. Willie Nelson, who had tired of the Nashville treadmill, moved to Austin in 1971. He loosened up his image—wearing jeans and growing long hair—and started a Fourth of July festival that brought together, according to one commentator, "the hippie and the redneck." Nelson and Waylon Jennings started the "outlaw" movement, so called because of its defiance of Nashville's calculated commercialism—not because of any criminal wrongdoing on their part. As it turned out, Nelson and Jennings were more in tune with public taste than Nashville. Their 1976 album, *Wanted: The Outlaws,* was the first million-selling country album.

Their collaboration continued most noticeably on tour and in a series of "Waylon and Willie" albums. The first, recorded in 1977, included "Mamas, Don't Let Your Babies Grow Up to Be Cowboys" (Example 17.1), a Grammy-winning hit in 1978. The song shows the independent spirit of the two men in both words and music. It's most obvious in the words. The "cowboys" that

outlaw
country

 IV-21

 IVB-9

Nelson and Jennings sing about are, according to Bill Malone, "the free-living, good-timing good old boys that figure so prominently on southern back-roads and in southern folklore." The portrait they paint is far from flattering, but not unsympathetic: their cowboys like "clear mountain mornings" as well as "smoky old poolrooms," "little warm puppies and children" as well as "girls of the night." It's a mixed message: like them, but don't trust them.

 The music that supports this message is just as independent. It sidesteps the slickness of Nashville countrypolitan and the intrusion of rock (unless one considers the Beatles' "Norwegian Wood" [Example 15.5] an archetypical rock song–the two songs have the same beat and their melodies begin almost identically). Not surprisingly, given the traditional bent of both men, the roots of the song go back to the cowboy songs of the thirties and forties, like Eddy Arnold's theme song, "Cattle Call." This basic conception is flavored with the sounds of an up-to-date honky-tonk band: full, mostly electric rhythm section, steel guitar, and background vocals support Waylon and Willie's narrative.

Nelson has sung the music he likes. This has included not only traditional country material and his own music in a traditional style, but also Tin Pan Alley standards (his 1978 *Stardust* album) and blues-flavored rock songs in a collaboration with rock star/songwriter Leon Russell. This eclectic approach broadened his, and country's, audience considerably, making him the most successful country crossover artist of the seventies.

The music of Cash, Nelson, and Haggard showed the viability of "pure" country music outside its traditional audience. Pure country also flourished within its own world. Many who had begun their careers in the fifties enjoyed considerable success in the seventies. The most musically significant of these artists was George Jones. His career, which had begun in the late forties, reached a peak in the early seventies during his stormy marriage to Tammy Wynette. Despite their marital problems, which she cataloged in several of her hit songs, they made some of the best duet recordings in country music history. Like his idol Hank Williams, Jones can invest even the most sentimental song with the intensity of real emotion through the quality of his voice and the timing and nuance in his delivery. And like Williams, Jones wrestled with a serious drinking problem through much of his career; fortunately, for both Jones and popular music, he has overcome it. His recent work simply reaffirms his status as one of country's greatest living singers.

IV-22

IVB-10

No song shows Jones's interpretive abilities better than "The Grand Tour" (Example 17.2). Recorded in 1974, toward the end of his marriage to Wynette, "The Grand Tour" portrays the pain of divorce in a series of vivid images. Sung by a lesser singer, they could be merely sentimental. But Jones sings the song with such unmistakable anguish that the images come alive in our minds. He clearly feels the emotions behind the words; his voice lets us feel them just as urgently.

Jones's voice is so much the focus of the performance that it's easy to overlook the unobtrusive accompaniment. But it is well done, a honky-tonk foundation overlaid with subdued strings and choir. Unlike many of the Nashville-produced, pop-influenced accompaniments of the rock era, the rich setting never detracts from the performance. Jones's voice always comes through. All in all, it is one of the classic performances of country music, one matched in emotional power only by the best of Hank Williams, Sr.

It's worth reflecting for a moment on the art of song interpretation. We have listened to six performances by four great song interpreters, Billie Holiday and Frank Sinatra (Chapter 10), Hank Williams (Chapter 12), and Jones. Despite the differences in their "home" style, the four communicate their feelings in much the same way. They deliver the song simply and directly, without elaboration. When it occurs, paraphrase of the original melody makes the song less, not more, complex. Their art is in expressive nuance and timing, not in histrionics.

COUNTRY-POP

From the mid-sixties on, country-pop edged even closer to the mainstream market. There were two big differences between this generation's country-pop and country's earlier infatuations with pop. One was commercial; the most successful country-pop artists regularly rose to the top of the pop charts as well as country charts. The other was musical. Stars like Kenny Rogers had enormous crossover success in large part because their style found a midpoint between pop and country.

The first of the new generation of country-pop stars was Glen Campbell. After a decade of studio work as an excellent and versatile session guitarist, he broke through as a country-oriented singer in the late sixties. His pleasing, down-home but twangless singing became the voice of songwriter Jimmy Webb in songs like "By the Time I Get to Phoenix" and "Wichita Lineman," much as Dionne Warwick had been the chosen vocalist for Bacharach and David. During the late sixties and early seventies, other country singers made occasional trips to the top of the pop charts. Bobbie Gentry's "Ode to Billie Joe" was a number-one hit in 1967; Charlie Rich followed suit in the seventies with a string of hits.

Country-pop fusions, dubbed "countrypolitan" in the trade press, reached a commercial peak in the late seventies, particularly in the music of Kenny Rogers. "Countrypolitan," the rock-era sequel to the Nashville sound of the late fifties, placed country-sounding vocals in elaborately produced soft-rock settings. A typical country-pop song featured lush strings, a slow tempo, a subtle rock beat, and flowing melody. Only the vocal style and, often, its Nashville origins and marketing linked it with country music.

For Campbell, Rich, and Rogers, country-pop fusion was a natural outgrowth of their heritage and musical experience. Campbell's studio work included sessions for Frank Sinatra, Nat "King" Cole, and Elvis Presley, as well as Merle Haggard. Both Rich and Rogers played in jazz groups early in their careers and both had considerable professional experience outside of country. Before turning country, Rogers was lead singer in the pop group The First Edition, who had a big hit with "Just Dropped In (To See What Condition My Condition Was In)" in 1968. It was seemingly a natural step for them to integrate these varied experiences into a hybrid style.

FROM COUNTRY-ROCK TO FOLK-ROCK

Countrypolitan rubbed out the boundaries between country and pop. Like adjacent colors in a spectrum, it was relatively easy to identify "pure" country and "pure" pop but virtually impossible to discern where one left off and the other began in fusions between the two.

The boundaries between country and rock were even harder to draw, because travel between styles went in both directions. The road from coun-

Kenny Rogers, c. 1970s.

try to pop was a one-way street; pop musicians seldom borrowed from country. By contrast, exchange between country and rock musicians continued to go both ways. Not only were country musicians listening to and borrowing from rock, rock musicians listened to and borrowed from country. Indeed, several leading country musicians—Charlie Daniels, for example—began their careers as rock musicians, and gravitated over to country even as the country audience became more accepting of rock.

More than anything else, it was the deep interest of rock musicians in country that brought country music into the mainstream. In the songs of Bob Dylan and other folk-inspired artists, country music shaped the sound of the prevailing style for the first time in its history. The Byrds' *Sweetheart of the Rodeo* (1968) was the first country-rock album. Except for well-meaning but inauthentic vocals, it is hardly distinguishable from straight country. Dylan, a big influence on the Byrds, had anticipated this trend by recording several albums in Nashville, beginning with *Blonde on Blonde* (1966). He even altered his singing style to a countryesque croon on his 1969 *Nashville Skyline* album; the record also featured a duet with country star Johnny Cash, and many of young Nashville's better backup musicians.

By the early seventies, country-rock intersections had taken on several forms; Gram Parsons's efforts were the most innovative. During his brief life—he died in 1973 at age twenty-six—he worked harder and more effectively than anyone else to bring country and rock together. Parsons joined the Byrds for a few months in 1968, during the time that they recorded *Sweetheart*. After leaving the Byrds, he formed the Flying Burrito Brothers in 1969, which was the leading country-rock band until he left the group in 1972. Parsons influenced a wide range of musicians: the Rolling Stones,

Willie Nelson, Linda Ronstadt, Elvis Costello, and most decisively Emmylou Harris, particularly after Parsons went solo in 1971. Parsons recorded several duets with Harris just before his death. His work with her helped transform her into the pre-eminent country-rock singer of the seventies and eighties.

Southern rock and the singer/songwriters represented rock's more peripheral contact with country. Southern rock bands like the Allman Brothers and Lynyrd Skynyrd had their deepest roots in the blues, but also had a close affinity with country. The influence of Southern rock would become more evident in the country music of the eighties and nineties: e.g., much of the music of Garth Brooks.

Folk-based singer/songwriters began with a close affinity to country music. There was considerable overlap melodically and instrumentally; the basic folk-rock band used about the same instrumentation as a gentle country-rock band. In the early seventies, Kris Kristofferson epitomized the intertwining of the two styles. Kristofferson was a Southerner with an international perspective; born in Texas, he got his professional start in England while a Rhodes scholar. He made his mark as a songwriter with hits like "Me and Bobby McGee," successfully recorded by both Johnny Cash and Janis Joplin and "Help Me Make It Through the Night." To put an identifying label on him—country-rock/folk-rock/singer-songwriter, whatever—seems arbitrary, limiting, and ultimately pointless.

COUNTRY MUSIC TODAY

Country music has claimed even more squares of the patchwork quilt that is contemporary popular music in the eighties and nineties. Indeed, country has never enjoyed a broader audience than it does now. Its artists regularly chart on *Billboard*'s Top 200. TNN (The Nashville Network) is one reason for country's increased popularity. The enormous growth of cable television has aided the promotion of country music, because it makes specialized channels commercially profitable. TNN has given country music a face, and has made country music available nationally throughout most of the day to any household with cable.

Musically, country music has gone forward and backward at the same time. By the eighties, country had fully embraced rock. The rock beat had become the rhythmic currency of mainstream country music. Other elements of rock style—dense, percussion-enriched textures, lead guitar riffs— became commonplace as well. At about the same time, a neo-traditional movement revived the music of country's past, particularly honky-tonk and bluegrass. Both directions expressed the two enduring characteristics of country music, its inherent conservatism and the continuing tension between tradition and assimilation.

neo-traditional country

Much contemporary country music gives ample evidence of country's continuing gravitation toward pop. Top new country acts of the eighties and nineties—Alabama, the Judds, Hank Williams, Jr., Reba McEntire, Lyle Lovett, and more recently, Garth Brooks and Billy Ray Cyrus—typically expressed country-like themes in their songs: matters of the heart; testimonies to the working man; and nostalgic recollections of the past. Now, however, they often couched them in a musical language heavily indebted to rock. The popularity of several of these artists—not only in record sales and radio, but in national audience arenas like gossip magazines, major network TV shows, and major advertising campaigns—suggests the extent to which mainstream country is woven into the cultural fabric of all America, not just the South.

In the early eighties Ricky Skaggs spearheaded country's neo-traditional movement, breathing fresh life into hard country and bluegrass. Older acts like George Jones found their careers revitalized, while younger artists like Skaggs, Dwight Yoakum, and Randy Travis also found large and appreciative audiences. Many of the top acts move easily between old and new. The strength of the neotraditional movement highlights country's essential conservatism. For all its flirtations with other styles, country music—or at least a vocal minority within it—seems determined to preserve those qualities that define it.

IV-23

IVB-11

The song that launched the neo-traditional movement was Skagg's cover of Flatt and Scrugg's "Don't Get Above Your Raising" (Example 17.3). (Flatt and Scruggs were the team that did more than any other group to popularize bluegrass music.) Ostensibly a song about the conflict between a good-ol'-boy and his social-climbing girlfriend, "Don't Get Above Your Raising" was taken by many in country music as an allegory for country's loss of traditional values in its romance with pop and rock, and its need to rediscover its "roots": Skaggs's "gal" is country music.

Ricky Skaggs, c. 1982.

Musically, the song shows the eclectic mix of old and new that characterizes the best neo-traditional music. There is straight-ahead honky tonk in the rhythm section; bluegrass mandolin; some bottleneck guitar and its country cousin, the dobro; a little boogie woogie/rock 'n' roll piano; plus some rockish electric guitar. Interestingly, the song is a quirkily harmonized blues, which gives it a fresh sound. As this song illustrates, neo-traditionalism is not simply a nostalgic trip back to the past but a new interpretation of it.

No one country artist better exemplifies the significant trends in country music during the rock era—its growth in popularity, its continuing intersections with other styles, and its periodic reaffirmation of its heritage—than Dolly Parton. Parton, born poor in rural Tennessee, has become country music's biggest celebrity. Her fame transcends not only country music, but the music business as a whole. Her road to fame took her through Nashville, then to Los Angeles, where she ascended to superstar status. Despite her international celebrity, she retains a strong connection with her Tennessee roots. Dollywood, the amusement park that she built in Tennessee, symbolizes her attraction: Hollywood glitz placed in a down-home setting.

Parton's recordings suggest country's ongoing struggle between tradition and assimilation. Songs on her albums range from almost pure pop—although with her voice, a Parton album will never be pure pop—to traditional country. Two songs illustrate this struggle in her music and, by extension, country music since the sixties. Dolly Parton recorded "Coat of Many Colors" (Example 17.4) in 1971 at RCA's Nashville studio. Her theme song for the film *9 to 5* was recorded in Hollywood with Los Angeles studio musicians. A Number 1 hit in 1981, "9 to 5" (Example 17.5) was perhaps the most commercially successful country-based film song.

 V-1

 VA-1

In its most prominent features, "Coat of Many Colors" harks back to the early days of country music. Most obvious is Parton's crystal clear voice, unmistakably country. The guitar accompaniment owes much to Maybelle Carter. Storytelling songs are more common in country music than in any other American genre; this one is certainly part of that tradition. The simple style of the song—a mostly speech-like melody, limited harmonic vocabulary (just the three basic chords), and short, easily grasped phrases—does not divert attention from the words.

The form of the song looks back to the nineteenth century; it's identical to that of Stephen Foster's "De Camptown Races." Like Foster's famous melody, it is a strophic song. Each full statement of the melody contains six phrases, organized into pairs as follows: a, a'; a, a'; b, a'. Even more specifically, the signature of the song—the title phrase of the lyric, set to the song's melodic high point and reinforced by a chorus—is the contrasting phrase, the first of the third pair. Table 17.1 shows this correspndence.

Table 17.1   Comparison of "Coat of Many Colors" and "De Camptown Races"

"Coat of Many Colors"	"De Camptown Races"
Introduction: ("Back through the years . . . I recall a box of rags . . .")	**Introduction:** Instrumental statement of the melody

a ("There were rags . . .")	**a** ("De Camptown Ladies . . .")
a′ ("My mama . . ."	**a**′ ("De Camptown races . . .")
a ("As she sewed . . .")	**a** ("I come down dah . . .")
a′ ("Perhaps . . .")	**a**′ ("I go back home . . .")
b ("My coat of many colors . . .")	**b** ("Gwine to run all night . . .")
a′ ("Although we had no . . .")	**a**′ ("I'll bet my money . . .")

V-2

VA-2

Parton uses the introductory phrases of the song to set up the story, to bring us back to the time and circumstance of her childhood. The song proper begins with "There were rags . . ." It is from this point melodically that the form repeats in a different key. Although "Coat of Many Colors" clearly has a traditional orientation, it also has unobtrusive touches—a rhythm section featuring acoustic bass, drums, and electric organ—that bring it into the modern era. It reminds us that tradition in country music is a matter of emphasis and degree: the proportions in the mix of old and new.

Written nine years later, "9 to 5" is at the other end of the country-music

Dolly Parton, c. mid-1970s, in a characteristic, flamboyant pose.

spectrum, with only the most tenuous connection with traditional country. Its theme is a familiar one in country music: life on the job. Instead of a lonesome cowboy or trucker, however, its subject is a woman working an office job in the city. The only other clear connections to country music are Parton's voice and the form of the song. In keeping with the musical context, Parton's voice is grittier in "9 to 5" than in "Coat of Many Colors," and other aspects of her singing, for example, the inflected syncopations on "9 to 5," suggest that she'd been listening to and learning from rhythm and blues artists. Like many country songs, "9 to 5" has a verse-chorus form. By this time (1981), however, so did the majority of popular songs in other genres: rock, disco, and rhythm and blues. As a result, the form of the song does not immediately type it as country music.

The musical context for Parton's melody is more reminiscent of rhythm and blues than country. The instrumentation includes a full rhythm section, extra percussion, horns, and backup vocals. The song has a heavy rock beat, with multiple active rhythmic layers, many of them highly syncopated. Except for Parton's voice, this could have been an R&B hit.

Parton's excursions into the popular mainstream have dismayed country traditionalists who treasure the purity of her voice and prefer to hear it in more traditional settings. Her pop ventures also bring country music's never-ending identity crisis to the surface. Still, it is part of the country-music tradition and the tradition of American popular music to create new music by mixing styles. What's clear is that there is a place for both extremes within country music: traditional/neo-traditional and crossover.

CONCLUSION

In the period from the late fifties to today, country music has moved increasingly into the mainstream of popular music. It has done so through two sometimes conflicting trends. On the one hand, many country acts have attempted to mold their sound into a more middle-of-the-road pop style. Singers like Glen Campbell and Kenny Rogers performed a combination of crooning ballads and soft-rock tunes that had little country flavor. On the other hand, traditionalists like Merle Haggard, George Jones, and Ricky Skaggs did much to preserve both honky-tonk and bluegrass sounds. In the nineties, an avalanche of performers, including Garth Brooks, Billy Ray Cyrus, and Trisha Yearwood, have bridged the gap between pop and country, gaining great chart success.

Terms to Know

countrypolitan	country rock	hard country
Nashville sound	neo-traditional country	outlaw country

Names to Know

Glen Campbell	Merle Haggard	Waylon Jennings
George Jones	Kris Kistofferson	Gram Parsons
Dolly Parton	Kenny Rogers	Ricky Skaggs
Willie Nelson		

Study Questions

1. What cities besides Nashville were country-music centers in the sixties and seventies? Why did they emerge as alternatives to Nashville?

2. Why are the boundaries between country and pop and country and rock difficult to draw?

3. How has country music's audience grown? What musical reasons account for its inclusion in the mainstream?

4. How has the tug-of-war between conservative and progressive trends in country music been worked out in the rock era? How were the hard country of the sixties, the outlaw movement of the seventies, and the neo-traditional movement of the eighties representative of the conservative end of the country-music spectrum?

5. Compare Dolly Parton's "Coat of Many Colors" to her "9 to 5." What changes have occurred in Parton's style between these two songs? What do the songs share in common?

6. Choose a favorite country song from today's top ten by Garth Brooks, Reba McEntire, Alan Jackson, or Pam Tillis. What makes it "country"? What does it share in common with other popular styles?

7. Country music has become an increasingly popular style since the mid-seventies. Why? How does this reflect political and social trends in the United States?

CHAPTER EIGHTEEN
Jazz in the Rock Era

As the sixties began, jazz was at a crossroads. It faced the most radical style shift since it moved up river from New Orleans in the early twenties. Certain conventions of jazz performance had been in place from the late twenties through the late fifties: its rhythm, texture, form, harmony, and melodic style (see Chapter 9). Bop stretched the limits of these conventions, but did not alter them significantly. Pressure for radical change come from within and without. Jazz's evolutionary momentum had brought the music to a stylistic reckoning point, and rock demanded consideration. By 1970, it was clear that the crossroads was actually a fork in the road. One branch turned back on itself, preserving the swing-based jazz style of the past several decades in a precarious but often creative equilibrium. The other led to the formation of a new jazz style, one so different that it marked the beginning of a new jazz tradition.

REACTIONS TO BOP

The crisis from within was evident in several reactions to the harmonic and rhythmic complexity of bop. Some jazz musicians turned their back on its harmonic and melodic advances. Miles Davis introduced simplified harmonic alternatives in a series of recordings beginning with *Milestones* in 1958. His 1959 masterpiece, "So What" (Example 9.10), remains the classic example.

 II-19

 IIB-8

return to roots

Another reaction against the complexity of bop was the "return to roots" movement. This trend began in the late fifties but gained momentum in the sixties, most successfully in the music of Horace Silver and Cannonball Adderley. One motivation for this movement was the desire to create a style more accessible to both musicians and listeners. But there was also a social dimension: It was a powerful expression of the rising black consciousness during the civil-rights era.

The return to roots movement filled in the gap between rhythm and blues and jazz that had existed since the late forties. Rhythm and blues artists like Ray Charles and Hank Crawford recorded compatibly with jazz artists. Many R&B artists fronted bands whose instrumentation fell halfway between jazz combos and big bands: two or three saxes; two or three brass;

and rhythm. Each band, or studio group, had a top, jazz-influenced saxophonist: Maceo Parker worked with James Brown; David Newman and Hank Crawford accompanied Ray Charles; and King Curtis played on many Aretha Franklin dates.

jazz-rock fusion

The merging of jazz and rhythm and blues shaped a number of popular-music styles, like the jazz-rock fusion of bands Chicago and Blood, Sweat and Tears and the jazz/R&B fusion of the Crusaders (originally the Jazz Crusaders). It also established contemporary saxophone style, as heard in the music of Grover Washington, Jr., Tom Scott, David Sanborn, and others.

In a similar vein, the use of Latin elements in jazz increased. Dizzy Gillespie, a pioneer in the Cu-bop movement of the late forties, had made occasional use of Afro-Cuban instrumentalists. Horace Silver and other bandleaders included Latin-tinged numbers in their repertoire. Musicians like vibraphonist Cal Tjader and flutist Herbie Mann went further, building the style of their band around a Latin conception. The bossa-nova fad of the early sixties brought many jazz musicians to Brazilian music. The pop-jazz style of the seventies and early eighties created by Creed Taylor–produced artists like George Benson and Bob James used jazz-Brazilian hybrid rhythms extensively. Both rhythm and blues and Latin music helped jazz find the middle of the road by mixing in accessible, infectious rhythms and riffs.

By contrast, the jazz avant-garde tried to expand on bop's rhythmic and textural freedoms. Tenor saxophonist John Coltrane, a member of Miles's band throughout the late fifties, advanced the rhythmic language of jazz beyond bebop by creating such new devices as "sheets of sound" that divided the beat irregularly with streams of notes, and using a "stutter," the practice of repeating notes several times in patterns that flowed over the beat. Drummer Elvin Jones, a longtime collaborator of Coltrane's, often traded steady timekeeping of any kind for intricate rhythmic conflict and coloristic effects. Along the same line, bassist Scott LaFaro interpolated countermelodies into walking bass lines, effectively liberating the bass from its timekeeping role.

free jazz

Still others, most notably saxophonist Ornette Coleman, experimented with a style called "free jazz," a largely intuitive music that abandoned the standard preconditions–beat, chord progression, head melody–of conventional jazz performance. Free jazz replaced articulate discourse with unrestrained self-expression. The musical result was powerfully expressive at times but too often completely chaotic, jazz's answer to a primal scream.

 V-3

 VA-3

 V-4

 VA-4

The first two examples, John Coltrane's "Chasin' the Trane" (Example 18.1) and Miles Davis's "Fall" (Example 18.2), show complementary facets of these rhythmic and textural changes. "Chasin' the Trane," a 1963 live recording of Coltrane's quartet at the time (McCoy Tyner, piano; Jimmy Garrison, bass; and Elvin Jones, drums), is a terrific illustration of the tension between conventional practice and free expression that was such a dominant feature of the jazz scene in the early sixties. The head is a blues; the performance is one long solo. The opening of the performance is, for Coltrane and Jones, straightforward fifties jazz: a simple head, improvised lines that divide the beat into two and faithfully follow the chord progression, and standard timekeeping on the ride cymbal. As the performance develops, however, Coltrane strays from the underlying harmony, playing harmonically based lines far removed from the basic blues progression. At the same time, Jones's drumming begins to abandon timekeeping periodically to play patterns in serious

John Coltrane, tenor sax,
1955 (bassist Paul Chambers
is in the background). Photo
by Popsie Randolph.

rhythmic conflict with the pulse. By the midpoint of the performance (about three minutes), Coltrane has begun to add repeated notes and patterns completely independent of the beat to his solo, while Jones often ignores the beat to create complex polyrhythms. Throughout the rest of the performance, we can hear both musicians straining against the conventional boundaries of jazz performance, sometimes stepping through them, then retreating to, for them, more typical rhythmic and harmonic practice. Through it all, bassist Jimmy Garrison steadfastly plays a walking bass line, even though his part is often overwhelmed by the others. In other performances, Coltrane and Jones pushed the rhythmic and harmonic conventions of jazz past the breaking point. This performance captures them at the edge—the aural equivalent of the surface tension that keeps a liquid from spilling over the rim of a container. Within the jazz avant garde of the sixties, Coltrane and Jones influenced performing styles more than any other musicians did.

"Fall," a performance from Miles's 1967 album *Nefertiti,* is as introverted as "Chasin' the Trane" is extroverted. Its innovations are not nearly so obvious. (Indeed, John Ephland, the *Downbeat* editor who wrote the liner notes for the album, considers the performance a throwback, which it certainly is not, even when compared to the other performances on the album.) In retrospect, the approach of Miles and his collaborators (saxophonist Wayne Shorter, who also composed "Fall," pianist Herbie Hancock, bassist Ron Carter, and drummer Tony Williams) to all the elements—form, melodic and rhythmic texture, melody, and harmony—would influence the new jazz of the seventies more profoundly than Coltrane would.

The innovations of "Fall" touch every aspect of conventional jazz performance—right from the first note. To sense how comprehensive the innovations were, it will be helpful to recall the main features of a typical postbop small group jazz performance. Opening and closing statements of the head frame a series of solos. The head will usually be a blues, Tin Pan Alley-type popular song, or original composition using the harmonic language of popular song. The solos will consist of melodic lines based on the underlying harmony; during them, the soloist dominates the texture. Rhythm instruments adhere to well-defined roles: the bass walks; the drummer keeps time on the ride cymbal; and the pianist comps. All are subordinate to the lead or melody instruments.

"Fall" consists of eight choruses on a four-phrase, 16-measure melody. Each phrase has two parts. The first part is always a slowly rising three-note scale, the second some kind of answer. The first two phrases are identical; they share a response-like refrain. The third phrase has a higher scale and a different response; the fourth phrase ends with a one-note question.

This performance breaks down two important hierarchies within standard jazz performance: formal and textural. Instead of a clear distinction between head and solo, there is always head and always solo. The head can be heard in almost every phrase of every chorus, and the refrain always appears prominently. Solos occur over the first part of each phrase simultaneously. The solo line is simply a more elaborate version of the melody usually heard in another part. Head and solo are marbled together, as the recurrent refrain responses remind us. Surprisingly, the closest parallels to this kind of simultaneous melodic variation among the listening examples presented in this book are "Old Joe Clark," [Example 3.4] an old-time fiddle tune, and the bluegrass song "It's Mighty Dark to Travel" [Example 12.5]. They are unlikely antecedents.

 I-17

 IA-17

 III-14

 IIIB-3

There is comparable textural integration, primarily because all the parts—not only horns, but also piano and bass—have a strong melodic component. The bass line departs the most from its customary role. It seldom walks a steady four-beat rhythm. Instead, it alternates between harmonic reinforcement and melodic counterpoint, moving in a free rhythm. Tony Williams's drumming is especially sensitive, as much coloristic as timekeeping. When combined with the other parts, base and drums produce a wonderfully fluid rhythmic texture, with the pulse implied more than stated: indeed, at the beginning of the piano solo, there are at times three different tempos simultaneously.

Its formal and textural integration and fluid rhythmic texture suggest a collective conception that looked to the future, not the past. Its rich but not I-IV-V based harmonic vocabulary and progressions and slowly unfolding melody also foreshadow the future of jazz. For these reasons, "Fall" makes a decisive break with the jazz past. As it happened, Nefertiti was Miles's last pre-rock album.

The developments evidenced in "Chasin' the Trane," "Fall," and Ornette Coleman's work stretched the conventions of traditional jazz to and beyond the breaking point. As a result, the sixties saw the evolutionary end of the jazz tradition begun in the twenties. The road to the new jazz tradition went through rock.

JAZZ-ROCK

Jazz musicians turned to rock reluctantly. Early jazz-rock fusions were often awkward affairs. They lacked the density and energy of rock and the subtlety and harmonic richness of jazz. Despite occasional successes–e.g., many of Herbie Hancock's compositions–jazz-rock during the sixties is clearly a style in transition.

It was Miles Davis, since 1949 a leader of the jazz avant garde, who once again showed the way. After taking swing-based jazz to its limit (as we heard above), he reformed his band to become the "best damn rock band in the world." In two albums made in 1969, *In a Silent Way* and *Bitches Brew*, he created the most innovative and challenging synthesis of jazz and rock to that point.

Miles's breakthrough was the adaptation of the collective conception heard in rock and rhythm and blues to a jazz environment. He enlarged the rhythm section and replaced the solo-dominated format of swing and bop with open, active textures sustained by several instruments playing freely conceived riffs. Instruments might be highlighted but would seldom dominate. This texture paralleled the rock of the Rolling Stones or the rhythm and blues of James Brown, but replaced repetitive riffs with intermittent, often irregular melodic strands. The underlying rhythm of this new conception was usually the sixteen-beat rhythm of Latin music and what would become funk. But Miles treated it with a jazz-like freedom. Timekeeping was intermittent, not regular, and there was considerably more variation in rhythmic texture and conflict than in a standard rock or Latin song.

Miles's rock-based conception became the starting point of a new jazz tradition. His ideas were influential because they offered startling new possibilities for jazz musicians stuck in a jazz-rock rut. In addition, working with Miles became a rite of passage for a new generation of jazz-rock musicians. In the early seventies, alumni from his late-sixties bands took Davis's jazz-rock, now called fusion, in several different directions. Their fusions came in many forms: the Latin-tinged work of earlier editions of Chick Corea's Return to Forever; the electrically charged blasts of John McLaughlin and midseventies Return to Forever that rivaled any rock band; the art funk of Herbie Hancock; and the soundscapes of Weather Report.

We can hear jazz-rock mature into a new jazz tradition in Herbie Hancock's two recordings of "Watermelon Man." The first (Example 18.3) was recorded in 1963; the second (Example 18.4) a decade later. Hancock had spent most of the sixties as the pianist in Miles Davis's stellar quintet. After leaving Miles, he created a mostly electric "art-funk" style in the early seventies (heard below in the second "Watermelon Man"). This innovative direction brought him tremendous commercial success for a jazz musician–and cries of "sellout" from the traditional jazz community. The first "Watermelon Man" approaches jazz-rock from the "return to roots" route. Hancock uses the funky piano style popular around 1960, and the song is a blues form with an expanded final phrase. In this version, Hancock simply grafts rock rhythm onto a typical jazz tune. It results in a rhythmically restricted style; the rhythmic conflict and interplay that typifies so many great jazz performances is hard to come by because roles are so clearly defined and repetitive.

The second version of "Watermelon Man" completely overhauls the jazz-rock idea. The new version features a dense, layered texture in the opening, with the parts entering one by one, replacing the relatively thin and hierarchical front line/rhythm section arrangement of the earlier version. The conception is collective: there are no stars, and everyone contributes a little to

V-5

VA-5

V-6

VA-6

Herbie Hancock, c. 1970s.

the sound. In songs like this, Hancock's debt to James Brown and, even more, Sly and the Family Stone, is obvious. Harmony is slower, often static. And the sixteen-beat rhythm that would become the rhythmic trademark of the new jazz style is evident.

There is an interesting parallel here between the progression from jazz-rock to the new jazz style and the progression from syncopated dance music to swing. The jazz-related styles of the early twenties, in particular hot syncopated dance music, are caught in between a fox-trot and swing conception. It isn't until the late twenties and early thirties that the four-beat rhythm and more relaxed swing of mature jazz would become commonplace. (A comparison of Fletcher Henderson's recordings of "Copenhagen" [Example 8.3] and "Wrappin' It Up" [Example 9.5] illustrates this point.) In much the same way, the jazz-rock styles of the sixties are an awkward combination of two incongruous styles. New jazz doesn't find its groove until the early seventies,

 II-5

 IIA-5

 II-14

 IIB-3

when sixteen-beat rhythm, greater rhythmic freedom, and denser textures become commonplace. Both earlier and more recent jazz styles find a rhythmic home with a beat that moves twice as fast as the that of the prevailing popular style.

By the early seventies, a new jazz tradition was in place. The changes from straight-ahead jazz were comprehensive: many elements were significantly different, as Table 18.1 outlines.

Table 18.1   New Jazz Style

Instrumentation	Typical new jazz group includes full rhythm: piano, guitar, bass, drums, extra percussion. Horns are optional; most likely is saxophone. Considerable use of electronic instruments: keyboards, electric guitars and basses.
Rhythm	Eight or (most often) sixteen-beat rhythmic foundation, with dense rhythmic texture, much rhythmic conflict, and no single instrument responsible for marking the beat.
Texture	A more collective conception: as Joe Zawinul noted, "No one solos, we all solo." Dense, layered textures composed primarily of riffs are common. Bass completely liberated from timekeeping role. Even solo sections merge solo line with other melodic parts. Soloist may be preeminent but is rarely dominant.
Form	Long, sequential, multisectional forms are the norm. Most sections are fully worked out, with limited opportunity for improvisation.

We can see these features in one of the classic fusion recordings, Weather Report's 1977 hit, "Birdland" (Example 18.5). At that time, Weather Report included two Miles Davis alumni, keyboardist Joe Zawinul and saxophonist Wayne Shorter, the brilliant electric bass virtuoso Jaco Pastorius, drummer Alex Acuna, and percussionist Manolo Badrena.

 V-7
VA-7

"Birdland" is one of Joe Zawinul's many soundscapes, an evocation of his experience listening to the Basie or Ellington band at Birdland (a famous New York jazz club) after hours. The composition is a portrait, not a photograph: not the sound of a big band, but his impression of it, filtered through a modern sensibility. Accordingly, the musical language is up to date (for 1977): for example, "brass" and "sax" sections are electronic, not acoustic.

All the "new jazz" style features described in Table 18.1 are evident in "Birdland." The beat is on the bubble between rock and jam—a fast eight-beat rhythm with double-time tambourine. The texture ranges from transparent to thick—at its thickest it is comparable to any big band, despite the limited number of instruments. (Overdubbing helps!). More to the point, we can hear a more collaborative approach to music making: bass joins the other pitched instruments as a full melodic partner. A role inversion at the beginning of the performance highlights this point: Zawinul plays the opening bass riff on a keyboard, while Pastorius plays a midrange riff on bass. There is relatively little improvisation in "Birdland"; such solos as there are serve as obbligato parts that embellish the more prominent riff-based lines.

Weather Report, c. late 1970s.

The structure of "Birdland" also illustrates the more complex formal plans typical of the new jazz style. It consists of two statements of a form with four major sections, each tagged with a signature riff. Within each of these sections, we may hear just the riff, or it may be gradually overlaid with other riffs. Other sections may be interpolated between them. The first three sections build gradually toward the "hook" riff, which is repeated several times at the end of each statement. All the sections are open-ended; none close off with a cadence. The influence of rock form is clearly evident in the sequential relationship of the sections, the use of a "hook" and its placement at the end of the form—a new twist on the verse/chorus idea—and the overall length of the performance.

"Birdland" represented a relatively "pure" version of the new jazz style: it couldn't be any other style. There were, however, a number of jazz hybrids: depending on the artist, one could hear elements of rhythm and blues, rock, pop, Brazilian music, proto–new age, disco, or Afro-Cuban music. Nevertheless regardless of their ancillary influences, all these styles were distinctly different from post-bop jazz.

POST-BOP JAZZ AFTER 1970

Post-bop jazz, the established jazz tradition, received two severe setbacks in the late sixties. Coltrane died in 1967 and Davis defected to rock two years later. The loss of both men, one physically, the other creatively, dealt a devastating blow to a style already unsure of its creative direction. Around 1970, jazz-rock fusions were all the rage, both among jazz musicians and their audiences. There was comparatively little interest in or support for jazz musicians wishing to continue exploring the outer limits of bop-based jazz.

Post-bop began to make a comeback as its identity became more distinct from fusion. Herbie Hancock unofficially confirmed the division of jazz into old and new styles by forming V.S.O.P. in 1976. V.S.O.P., a quintet that reunited most of Davis's great sixties quintet (Freddie Hubbard replaced Davis), returned to and updated the "straight ahead" (swing-based) style of pre-fusion jazz. By forming the group and naming it V.S.O.P. (which identifies well-aged brandy of superior quality) Hancock labeled his two distinct musical personae. Since the midseventies, he has moved back and forth between the two jazz worlds. Memorable post–V.S.O.P. collaborations include sessions with Wynton Marsalis. The jazz media have also accepted this duality within the jazz world; Billboard now runs two jazz charts: jazz and contemporary jazz.

Trumpeter Wynton Marsalis is the main exponent of and spokesman for the strong neo-traditional movement that emerged in jazz during the eighties. Several of his early recorded efforts offered contemporary reinterpretations of jazz standards. Marsalis's 1986 performance of "Cherokee" (Example 18.6) shows his mastery of bop style and unparalleled technical fluency. "Cherokee" is the source of Charlie Parker's "Koko" (Example 9.8), so a comparison of his quartet's performance with Marsalis's measures the extent to which bop's innovations had become common currency in jazz performance, a point of departure rather than a goal. Parker's improvisations and Max Roach's drumming are timeless. However, Robert Hurst's bass line is more fluent and resonant, while Marcus Roberts's comping in the solo sections often goes beyond a few chords here and there to become melodic counterpoint. There's some nice rhythmic play in the middle of Marsalis's solo, of a kind that would not have occurred in 1948: the bass suggests a sudden drop in tempo by regrouping beats into threes in a long/short

neo-tradi-tional

 V-8

 VA-8

 II-17

 IIB-6

Wynton Marsalis, c. 1990.
Photo by Paul Hoefpler

pattern. For those who wonder how Parker would have sounded with an up-to-date rhythm section, an answer can be found in the soundtrack to the film *Bird*. Parker's part was extracted electronically from several recordings and re-accompanied by a contemporary rhythm section led by Herbie Hancock.

More recent Marsalis albums have turned the clock back even further. In some of the most significant jazz compositions in recent decades, he has revisited the early jazz of New Orleans, his birthplace.

The neo-traditional movement has helped both younger musicians and audiences appreciate many of those who helped create the jazz heritage in the years before rock. In the process, it revived the careers of many bop and post-bop jazz masters: saxophonists Sonny Rollins and Joe Henderson, for example, have found new and appreciative audiences. The veneration of jazz past found a particularly poignant expression in the critically acclaimed Bernard Tavernier film *Round Midnight* (1986). In the film, saxophonist Dexter Gordon, one of bop's founders, gave a moving, quasi-autobiographical portrayal of a troubled jazz musician. It has also spawned a younger generation of bop-fluent musicians. Pianists Kenny Kirkland and Marcus Roberts, and saxophonists Branford Marsalis, Joshua Redman, and Kenny Garrett are just a few of the rising stars.

In their "purest" form, swing- and rock/jam-based jazz styles are distinctly different, as a comparison of "Birdland" with "Cherokee" quickly reveals. However, the boundary between them remains fluid, because there is considerable bleeding of old into new and vice versa. One can find traditional chord sequences of old jazz over a sixteen-beat rhythm, or the expanded forms and richly layered textures of new jazz in a straight-ahead style. Given the fluency of many musicians in both styles, it shouldn't be surprising.

We can hear both the distinction between and the overlap of the two styles in the music of Chick Corea. Like Herbie Hancock, Corea is a pianist/keyboardist and Davis alumnus, and, like Hancock, has distinguished between old and new in the names of his groups: Electric Band (new) and Akoustic [sic] Band (old). The same core personnel have been in both bands since 1986: Corea, bassist John Patitucci, and drummer Dave Weckl. The Electric Band has also included saxophone and guitar; on the recording discussed below, they are Eric Marienthal and Frank Gambale.

 V-9

VA-9

 V-10

 VB-1

The final two examples come from two recent Corea discs: a 1989 recording of Cole Porter's "So in Love" (Example 18.7) by the Akoustic Band, and a 1988 recording of Corea's own "Eye of the Beholder" (Example 18.8) by the Electric Band. In most respects, "So In Love" is a straight-ahead jazz performance of a standard popular song, skillful—Corea is one of the great modern improvisers—but conventional in format: head/improvised solos/head form over a swing rhythm. However, three features clearly mark it as modern, Weckl's "sixteen-beat swing," Patitucci's virtuoso bass playing, and the accompanied drum solo.

"So in Love" oscillates between two tempos, a slow one in the head, and one twice as fast in Corea's solos. In the head, Weckl shifts in and out of the sixteen-beat rhythm, implying it in the A sections and stating it clearly in the bridge. When the tempo doubles during Corea's first solo, Weckl plays a contemporary version of the standard swing ride pattern. Periodically, however, he combines the ride pattern with active snare drum rhythms to reintroduce the sixteen-beat rhythm. Throughout the performance he oscillates

Chick Corea, c. 1980.

back and forth between the double time ride pattern and the sixteen-beat rhythm first heard in the slower tempo.

Patitucci's solo puts him in the select company of those bassists—Miroslav Vitous, Stanley Clarke, Pastorius, Eddie Gomez, and a few others—who have turned the bass into the new virtuoso instrument of contemporary jazz. The invention of a pickup allowed the acoustic bass to be amplified without a serious deterioration of tone quality. This in turn enabled bassists to lower the strings of the instrument and pluck with less force. Both adjustments greatly improved facility on the instrument. In the hands of a bassist like Patitucci, the bass is a solo voice as fluent as any horn or keyboard.

The accompaniment to Weckl's drum solo also shows the influence of contemporary practice. In bop-style jazz performance, the rest of the band typically shuts down during a drum solo; band members have been known to walk off the bandstand while the drummer enjoys his moment in the spotlight. In "So in Love," however, an outline of the melody is sustained through most of the solo. Here, the drum solo functions much like the improvised obbligatos in "Fall" or the saxophone and keyboard solos in "Birdland": it is primary, but not completely dominant.

"So in Love" is clearly a tradition-based jazz performance: standard tune, piano trio instrumentation, swing rhythm, conventional form, and the like. However, the three features mentioned above—sixteen-beat rhythm, virtuoso bass, and the collaborative drum solo—help give the performance a contemporary feel.

By contrast, "Eye of the Beholder" just as clearly exemplifies the new jazz tradition. It has a sixteen-beat rhythm, an extended, mostly composed, multisectional form, an interdependent, often dense texture—especially in the montuno section—and a full complement of electric instruments.

Of more specific interest is the pervasive influence of Afro-Cuban music on "Eye of the Beholder." It's evident in the form, rhythm, and specific features of the bass and keyboard parts. The sequence of sections recalls the form of Willie Colon's "Ojos" (Example 13.4): the opening melody functions much like a canto; a coro-like section follows after a drum break. This section is complete with an extended montuno section, which includes a complex piano montuno, timbale-like drum part, tumbao bass, horn riffs, plus an improvised synthesizer solo.

III-21

IIIB-10

It is to be expected that Corea should find inspiration in Afro-Cuban music. His musical apprenticeship included work with famed Afro-Cuban percussionists Mongo Santamaria and Willie Bobo and Latin jazz stars Herbie Mann and Cal Tjader. Corea has incorporated Latin influences into his music more thoroughly than any other major fusion artist.

CONCLUSION

Jazz split into two distinct style families around 1970. The established jazz tradition remained much as before, an art music based on a four-beat rhythmic foundation. The new jazz is, by analogy with the established jazz tradition, an art music based on a sixteen-beat rhythm. Discussions of the second "Watermelon Man," "Birdland," and "Eye of the Beholder" have identified other differences in conventional practice between established and new styles.

Two questions now stand out: (1) Is the new style really jazz?; and (2) What is its expressive essence? We can, I believe, address the first question most effectively by considering the relationship of new jazz to its style family and comparing it to the relationship enjoyed by swing-based jazz to the music of its time. New jazz aligned itself with the progressive end of rock's musical spectrum. When it finally coalesced in the midseventies after a decade or so of experimentation, new jazz belonged to the same rhythmic family as funk, Latin music, and black romantic song. However, its forms were generally more complex, its melodic lines more elaborate, and its rhythmic texture richer in implication and conflict than other popular music within the same style family. In these respects, new jazz is in much the same relationship to rock, funk, and disco as swing-based jazz was to popular song, blues, and country: It is a complex, nonfunctional music rooted in the style conventions of the period.

What of its expressive essence? Swing-based jazz was—and is—primarily an improvising soloist's music. As the discussion of Armstrong's "West End Blues" (Example 9.4) pointed out, the most expressive playing of its great artists has brought together swing, blues feeling, and melodic imagination. Many of its great moments were created on the spot; their nuance and timing were beyond musical notation.

II-13

IIB-2

New jazz would seem to have a different expressive esthetic. Its emphasis on composition over improvisation has limited the kind of spontaneous expression that is so much a part of swing-based jazz. As a result, expressiveness is more a group activity than an individual one; as in rock, it grows out of the interplay between several parts and the contrasts between sections. The new style can certainly accommodate the expressive solo voice. Many of them are rhythm and blues-influenced saxophonists: David

Sanborn and the Crusaders's Wilton Felder are two prominent and especially influential examples. In the most characteristic examples of the style, however, expression comes not from one voice but from many.

The birth and maturation of a new jazz tradition in the last twenty-five years and the resurgence of activity within the established jazz tradition have given convincing evidence that jazz of both kinds is still a vital music, that there is much yet to discover and create. It remains America's premier art music, a language of passion and subtlety.

Terms to Know

art jazz	free jazz	fusion
jazz-rock	neo-traditional	return to roots

Names to Know

Cannonball Adderley	John Coltrane	Chick Corea
Herbie Hancock	Elvin Jones	Wynton Marsalis
David Sanborn	Wayne Shorter	Horace Silver
V.S.O.P.	Weather Report	Joe Zawinul

Study Questions

1. Why did swing-based jazz stop evolving in the sixties? What has happened to the style since that time?

2. What musical changes give evidence of the maturation of jazz-rock of the sixties into the contemporary jazz style of the seventies and eighties? What role did Miles Davis play in the development of the new jazz style?

3. What evidence is there of two distinct jazz traditions? What are some of the important differences between them?

4. What is the rhythmic foundation of the new jazz style? What, besides its rhythm, has this new style borrowed from Latin music?

5. Trumpet player Wynton Marsalis has caused great controversy in the jazz world by dismissing much of the jazz of the sixties and seventies, and returning to earlier styles. In your opinion, does this represent a new direction for jazz? Why or why not?

6. John Coltrane's music had a large impact on the psychedelic-rock music of the sixties, especially the long guitar solos of players like Jimi Hendrix. What is the connection between Coltrane's music and this style of rock improvisation?

CHAPTER NINETEEN

Rock in the Seventies

In the sixties, rock music was like the Mississippi River, constantly swelling as tributaries fed into it. As the seventies began, it grew into a delta, fanning out into an ever-widening range of styles. The greater stylistic diversity of rock came from several sources. Rock hybrids of the sixties matured into generally well-defined substyles: folk-rock became singer/songwriter, acid rock sired heavy metal, and so forth. Rock drew on its past, recycling, reinterpreting, or recombining material from earlier styles and artists. Regional dialects emerged in New York, the South, London, and elsewhere. Improved technologies offered not only an expanded palette of sounds but new ways of processing them.

singer/song
writer
heavy metal

Even with rock's growing diversity, the seventies were a time of consolidation. The most important developments during the decade completed or expanded on changes begun in the late sixties. The reshaping of the popular mainstream, well under way by 1970, was a done deal by mid-decade. At the same time, the stylistic variety created by the interaction of the different genres of rock with established styles became more profuse during the seventies. It's as if popular music, starting with a box of eight crayons in 1965, had graduated to sixty-four by 1980.

CONSERVATIVE TRENDS IN SEVENTIES ROCK

Richard Nixon's election as president in 1968 marked a backlash by the "silent majority" against minority power, counterculture radicalism, and drugs. Still, other minority movements had learned from the civil-rights movement. Organizations representing women, Chicanos, Native Americans, and gays began their struggle for increased visibility and political and legal rights.

The rise of disco and the response to it expressed the increasing fragmentation and polarization of American society. Disco was an urban dance music, associated with blacks, Latinos, and gays. The virulent disco bashing of the late seventies was as much a reaction to its creators and supporters as it was to the music itself. The diversity of the sixties became increasingly polarized along racial and cultural lines during the seventies.

278

During the seventies, mainstream rock traded its hippie rags for a three-piece suit. Around 1970, the year that the Beatles disbanded, rock lost its revolutionary fervor and its evolutionary momentum. There were social and musical reasons for this growing conservatism. The mood of the country had changed, as it had in Great Britain. The social activism of the Kennedy and Johnson administrations and the counterculture that had flourished during that time dissipated under Nixon. Woodstock, the gigantic rock festival of 1969, capped off the peace-and-love era. Within a decade, rock music had officially become an industry. There was no longer any question that "rock 'n' roll was here to stay," and commercial considerations became paramount. Both the broadcast and recording industries were structured to ensure maximum profitability.

Nothing showed rock's corporate attitude more clearly than the profound changes in the recording and broadcast industries. Rock had originally been an outsiders' music available only on independent labels and on alternative radio programs. But by the end of the seventies many of the independent labels had merged or were sucked into a major label. As the eighties began, only six companies produced half of the popular-music recordings worldwide.

In pursuit of greater financial rewards, record companies used tours to help promote record sales. With improved amplification, the stadium or large arena concert became commonplace. Less musical event than spectacle, these concerts merely confirmed what the audience already knew about the music of a particular band. As a rule, there was little, if any, spontaneity in performance. Bands performed songs, usually from current or recent albums, to the accompaniment of light shows, fog, and other visual effects. At its most extreme, outrageous dress, make-up, and stage deportment replaced musical substance as a primary source of interest. Acts like Kiss and early David Bowie epitomized this theatrical aspect of seventies rock.

Corporate conformity was even worse in radio. The "underground" FM stations of the sixties had given new, musically original bands an outlet. But free-form FM programming of the sixties devolved into AOR (album-oriented radio). The restricted playlists (the rotation of songs played by a radio station) of AOR was a complete turnabout from the adventurous spirit of sixties FM. Disc jockeys relinquished most if not all of their independence to the program director, who selected a limited number of songs designed to attract a broad audience while offending as few as possible. Among reasons to air a song, artistic merit usually ran a poor second or third, behind commercial appeal and, too often, bribery from "independent" promoters hired by record companies. This commercialization of rock radio gradually reduced the play of African-American music on mainstream radio and put a damper on experimentation.

As African-American music developed a range of new styles—most built on the foundation of a new beat—African-American artists moved away from the rock mainstream. There were exceptions, particularly disco, an African-American/Latin/white dance music that found a massive white audience. Reggae, a different kind of African-American music, came to the United States from Jamaica by way of Britain. Here it found a steadily growing audience through the seventies.

Rock's facade still seemed to suggest a radical bent. The outlandish costumes of Elton John, Kiss's facial make-up, and the technicolor hair and

underground radio

AOR (album-oriented radio)

punk

new wave

art rock

body mutilation of the punk movement took sixties deviance in personal appearance to an extreme. But this was a cosmetic radicalism. Behind the scenes and in the music, rock had grown conservative.

This conservatism should not be surprising. The startling innovations of the late sixties could not be continued indefinitely; they required a period of absorption. Within rock, the seventies became a time of expansion, consolidation, and resynthesis in the mainstream, and a time of reaction against expansion and commercialization in the punk/new wave movement. Except for the punk groups and some heavy metal acts, bands got bigger and so did their sound.

Many of the new styles—heavy metal, southern rock, art rock, rock singer/songwriters—and major artists—David Bowie, Led Zeppelin, Bruce Springsteen—that emerged during this period continued the process of synthesis begun by Dylan, Hendrix, the Beatles, and others. Now, however, the syntheses were forged from rock substyles, rather than between rock and established styles. To cite just one example, Springsteen's early style (as we'll see) shows the influence of the Rolling Stones's group concept and the narrative emphasis and vocal conception of Bob Dylan.

Elton John, quantitatively the biggest star of the seventies, embodies the

Elton John in characteristic flamboyant stage outfit, c. mid-1970s.

contradictions, musical and otherwise, that characterized much of seventies rock. His early albums showed him to be a singer/songwriter of considerable gifts. Within a few years, however, John crossed over to the mainstream. He inundated himself in Top 40 while adopting a Liberace-like stage persona, donning elevator shoes, flamboyant costumes, and outlandish eyewear. His songs found the middle of the road and he found megastardom. Somewhere along the line he lost some of his musical individuality, trading it for familiarity and accessibility. And, like David Bowie, his visual identity at times deflected attention away from his real talent.

"Tiny Dancer," (Example 19.1) from his 1971 album, *Madman Across the Water*, gives evidence of the expansion of rock style in the seventies. It also shows John in transition musically from singer/songwriter to rock star. The expansion of rock style in this song is most evident in its form and resources. The song has an AAB form. As recorded, it takes over six minutes to perform, allowing for one and two-thirds statements of the form: AABAB. We can get some sense of the extent of John's expansion of popular song form by noting that each A section has its own internal AABA form. In other words, the opening formal section (the first A) of "Tiny Dancer" is equivalent to a complete chorus of a Tin Pan Alley-type song.

John uses a huge ensemble in service of his musical conception: his voice, piano, bass, drums, guitar, steel guitar, backup vocals, rich strings, and choir. The result is, when desired, a much denser and full-sounding texture. Moreover, John adds and subtracts instruments to outline the form and accumulate musical momentum through the A sections to the climax of the song in the B section. "Tiny Dancer" begins quietly enough, with just voice and piano, but instruments gradually join in—steel guitar at the end of the first A, drums and bass as the second A section begins, then choir at the end of the second section. The climax of the song is reached on the words: "Hold me closer." This is its melodic highpoint and "hook." The preceding material prepares this climax with a new, more agitated, beat pattern, shorter phrases, and more active harmony. Only the interlude set to the text, "softly, slowly," momentarily arrests the momentum.

"Tiny Dancer" sheds light on the fact and nature of rock's continuing expansion in the seventies. The expansion is not one-dimensional: just longer, louder, denser, or whatever. Instead, it is comprehensive: the supplementary instruments and voices—strings, choir, steel guitar—give shape to the expanded form of the song, articulating sections when they drop out, imparting a sense of movement toward a climax as they enter gradually. In this song at least, the expansion of rock style is artfully managed.

The song also shows John on the verge of his journey toward the middle of the road. He has always been a gifted melodist. However, in his early albums, he often accompanied his melodies with more modest instrumentation and more subtle rhythmic support. "Come Down in Time," from the early 1971 *Tumbleweed Connection*, is an especially fine example of a beautifully crafted melody supported by subtle accompaniment. In the four albums following *Madman Across the Water*, he substituted catchier riffs and a more obvious beat for the more restrained conception of his earlier songs. The result was, among other things, unqualified commercial success: all four were No. 1 albums; so was a subsequent "greatest hits" compilation.

Precisely because he was so successful after shifting to a more overtly commercial style, John seemed to epitomize the profit-driven corporate mentality that had taken over the rock rebellion. Perhaps John's musical legacy would be even more impressive if he had not gravitated to such a blatantly commercial style. The fact remains, however, that he was very good at it. His output in the seventies was far superior musically to that of many of his detractors, who had not yet discovered that attitude alone does not produce art—or even good music. Left unanswered was the question: Could it have been better if it had not been shaped so directly by popular taste? It was a question frequently asked throughout the decade regarding John and many other acts.

HARD ROCK

Within hard rock, mannerism replaced innovation in all aspects of the rock experience. Appearance and stage demeanor became progressively more outlandish, and special effects often replaced musical substance. Surface novelty substituted for fundamental change. This was evident in much art rock and glam rock, and some heavy metal.

glam rock

Art (or progressive) rock after 1970, as exemplified by groups such as Pink Floyd and Emerson, Lake and Palmer, had little of the subtlety of the Beatles's fusions of rock and classical music ("Eleanor Rigby" [Example 15.4]) or their beautifully crafted miniatures, like "Here Comes the Sun." Too often these groups opted for bombast and instant profundity. Overburdened with gimmick electronics (a new toy), art rock soon collapsed under the weight of its pomposity.

In a similar way, glam rock exaggerated the theatrics of sixties rock to the point of caricature. The personas of its stars became its defining feature. More ink was spilled on David Bowie's various incarnations (Ziggy Stardust) and his sexual preferences than on the nature or quality of his music.

Much post-Zeppelin heavy metal provided still another example of a style created through exaggeration. The roots of heavy metal reach back through power trios like Cream (with Eric Clapton) and the Jimi Hendrix Experience to the blues. Led Zeppelin, the best of the proto-metal bands, built directly on this base, combining the virtuosity of guitarist Jimmy Page with a tight group conception. But heavy metal soon developed into a style built on distortion in both a general and specific sense. Many metal bands exceeded the occasionally excessive guitar ramblings of a Hendrix, but with little of his skill or inspiration. Eddie Van Halen, who took guitar virtuosity to a new level, was a conspicuous exception to this trend. Intense sound distortion at hearing-damaging levels became the musical trademark of heavy metal, the feature that made it recognizable in an instant.

Heavy metal also acquired considerable extramusical baggage. Both bands and their audiences thrived on the obscure and the occult. In this respect, Led Zeppelin led the way with their untitled fourth record: runes (letters in a pre-Christian Anglo-Saxon alphabet associated with paganism) substituted for traditional album-cover information.

In the eighties, heavy metal has subdivided many times over, like a fast-growing bacteria. Left for dead at the end of the seventies, metal got new life in the new decade. Bands like Van Halen, Metallica, and Motorhead pointed the music in a variety of different directions.

The groundbreaking early metal of Led Zeppelin left an impressive legacy that subsequent bands have found difficult to match. In their work, the process of combination and recombination that typified rock after 1965 is clearly evident. "Black Dog" (Example 19.2), from Led Zeppelin's untitled fourth album, shows how quickly rock evolved in the late sixties and early seventies. Unlike a typical rock song, the song opens with some guitar mumblings. These are followed by an unaccompanied vocal by Robert Plant, whose high falsetto voice considerably extends the range of the white male rock singer upward, who is followed in turn by extended, complex guitar/bass lines that go well beyond the riffs and patterns heard in Hendrix's "Purple Haze" (Example 15.7). The opening guitar/bass line returns; it leads directly into an even more rhythmically daring line with irregular accents and contours. Still another texture follows, a rhythmically more secure passage featuring call-and-response exchanges between voices and guitar.

The unpredictability of the extended guitar/bass lines, tight organization, variety of texture, and rhythmic complexity of "Black Dog" provide an imaginative antidote to the sometimes self-indulgent excesses of power-trio jams. Page proves that a great rock guitarist can have his cake and eat it, too: Virtuoso guitar playing can be fully integrated into a group conception.

Art rock, glam rock, and heavy metal were defined by the expansion and extreme transformation of a sixties trend. The music got bigger, bolder, and flashier, but seldom better. All expressed rock's mannerist tendencies, in which a "can you top this?" approach to obvious features like appearance and volume moved the music further and further away from those qualities that had originally defined it.

For the center of rock, the seventies were a crash from the high of the sixties. The creative energy that had stamped the new music after 1965 all but disappeared. Death claimed several top stars. Jimi Hendrix, rock's most innovative guitarist, died in 1970, and no one stepped forward to point guitar playing in a new direction. Brian Jones of the Rolling Stones—the soul of the band in the opinion of many—had died the year before. They were two of many casualties of the drug culture. Jim Morrison of the Doors and Janis Joplin also died in 1970.

After releasing *Exile on Main Street* in 1972, the Rolling Stones went into a prolonged creative slump for the rest of the decade. They even ironically titled a retrospective collection of their music from this period *Sucking in the Seventies.* Each of the ex-Beatles tried to establish solo careers, but none achieved singly what they had achieved collectively; the most commercially successful was Paul McCartney. Bob Dylan's groundbreaking work was also behind him, although he continued to produce music of high quality. He spent most of the seventies seeking to recapture the cutting edge that he had enjoyed in the sixties. For the most creative rock musicians of the period, both established performers and recent arrivals, the seventies were a time of stylistic consolidation, not progress.

BACK TO BASICS

The glitz and commercialism of much early-seventies rock produced an inevitable "back to basics" reaction. Its two most important expressions came in the music of Bruce Springsteen, and the New-York based new-wave movement and punk, its London counterpart. Springsteen helped re estab-

Bruce Springsteen, c. 1970s.

lish rock's center through synthesis, much as the giants of the sixties had done in establishing it. His style, although heavily indebted to both Dylan and the Rolling Stones, offered a fresh sound by combining these influences with an original conception.

BRUCE SPRINGSTEEN

Critic/producer Jon Landau hailed an early club performance by Bruce Springsteen with the following statement, "I saw rock 'n' roll's future and his name is Bruce Springsteen." Landau's evaluation correctly identified Springsteen's prominent place in the rock of the next decade. His memorable songs and unqualified popular success have put him in the forefront of rock in the seventies and eighties. Although Landau's assessment certainly speaks accurately to Springsteen's subsequent commercial impact, it addresses rock's future only in the limited sense that rock was rapidly running out of evolutionary steam.

For all his commercial and critical success, Springsteen has not established a genuinely new style. Rather, his music has reworked and expanded on some of the best music of the sixties. Songs like "Born to Run" (Example 19.3) feature an emphatic rock beat, a much larger band, and sprawling forms. Table 19.1 gives a formal outline of the song.

Table 19.1   Formal Outline of "Born to Run"

Guitar, playing a memorable riff

A. In the day we sweat it out . . .
'Cause tramps like us, baby we were born to run

Guitar riff
A. Wendy let me in . . .

Girl I want to know if love is real

Sax solo

B. Beyond the Palace hemi-powered drones . . .
In an everlasting kiss

Extended interlude

A. The highway's jammed with broken heroes . . .
Tramps like us, baby we were born to run.

Tag/Guitar riff

In this song Springsteen brings together a number of important elements of earlier styles. Most obviously, it is a logical extension of Dylan's electric phase: The same concern for the primacy of the words in the midst of a dense, loud accompaniment pervades his music. This connection with Dylan is reinforced by Springsteen's singing; his quasi-spoken, rough-edged vocal style borrows directly from Dylan's delivery. But in "Born to Run" at least, the words are melodrama rather than social commentary; they do not have Dylan's detachment or poetic art.

The basic elements of rock rhythm form a strong undercurrent in this song: The eight-beat rhythm is reinforced by drums and repeated notes in both guitar and bass, while the backbeat is also clearly marked. Like the beat of punk and new-wave bands, this version of rock rhythm retreats from the increased rhythmic subtlety and richness of the best rock of the late sixties and early seventies. It is instead a rediscovery and update of the rhythmic language of the late fifties.

"Born to Run" also builds on and expands other, by now, traditional rock elements. It is a sprawling song: the entire performance consists of only one statement of the song, despite its brisk tempo. Every feature, with the possible exception of the sax solo, enlarges upon its direct or indirect model. Like its precedent in "Satisfaction" (Example 15.1), the opening guitar figure is the most memorable melodic event in the song. Unlike the riff from "Satisfaction," however, it is an extended, if incomplete, melodic statement.

The opening section, like so many rock songs, begins slowly and gradually builds to a climax. Both the approach and the climax are more sustained than typical songs from the sixties. And the extended interlude before the final statement of the original melody is also more elaborate harmonically, rhythmically, and texturally than the vast majority of its precedents.

The stylistic expansion of "Born to Run" is not simply a question of length. Like the opening guitar statement, every other significant feature takes on larger proportions. Perhaps the most direct example is the enrichment of the instrumental background. Springsteen extends Dylan's electric accompaniment to include several keyboards, extra percussion, and saxophone. The synthesizer-percussion "halo" that highlights the second part of the opening section ("Sprung from cages...") is a particularly nice example of the effective use of these expanded resources. This creative synthesis of contrasting elements—in this case, the rebellious tone of the lyrics versus musical sophistication of the accompaniment—marks Springsteen's best work. Rock critic/historian Ken Tucker has observed that "in (Springsteen), all things seemed to meet; naturalism and self-consciousness; recklessness and professionalism; a sense of rock history and a vision of rock future."

Punk Rock

Springsteen offered rock on a grander, more epic scale. In the mid-seventies and late seventies, a counterrevolution directed rock back to its past. Emerging in London and New York in the mid-seventies, punk sought to "purify" a rock industry that it considered decadent and bloated with its own success. It sought a return to the simpler kind of music and music-making of the early days of rock 'n' roll, the kind made by performers long on spirit but short on skill or imagination. In its simplest, most generic form, punk was a caricature of rock 'n' roll, an exaggeration of its most obvious features at the expense of subtlety.

Punk rock's most prominent musical feature was its beat: fast, loud, unvarying, with no rhythmic conflict. Despite its avant-garde pretensions—its stylistic sibling was dubbed "new wave"—punk was an essentially conservative trend, a reaction against the continuing evolution of rock rather than a step forward.

In the United States, the archetypal punk band was the Ramones. Perhaps the "purest" new-wave band, they turned out a string of interchangeable two-minute songs. All had a simple, unrelenting rock beat played at a breakneck tempo, Dadaist lyrics, and unrelieved, in-your-face loudness. The four alleged brothers—although they all took the last name "Ramone," the band members were not actually related—stripped down rock 'n' roll to its basics and then turned up the juice. Their songs are short, fast, loud, simple, repetitive, and very similar. One can go track hopping on their greatest hits CD and hardly miss a beat.

(D) "I Don't Wanna Go Down to the Basement" (Example 19.4) is typical of

The Ramones, c. 1970s.

many Ramones's songs. The lyrics simply repeat a meaningless statement, the title phrase. Such intentional meaninglessness may have been a response to the arty excesses of the day, an assertion that rock songs didn't have to have any meaning. The tempo is very fast, faster than walking speed or normal dancing speed. Guitar and drums pound out the rock rhythmic layer like a jackhammer. There is no subtlety here, no nuance, and little syncopation. True to its early rock-and-roll roots, the song is harmonized with only three chords. The melody is constructed from a series of short phrases that are repeated again and again. The texture is unchanging, and so are the dynamics. "I Don't Wanna Go Down to the Basement" is an intense two minutes. Like so many of their other songs, this is no-frills rock, a return to its early garage-band spirit.

However, the real keepers of the rock flame were, appropriately enough, the Southern rockers. Groups like Lynyrd Skynyrd and the Marshall Tucker Band continued the rock/blues fusion of the Allman Brothers. Unlike the music of Springsteen and the Ramones, Southern rock did not represent a back to basics trend, because Southern artists had never left the basics. Instead, they concentrated on refining rock's essence.

More than any other rock substyle, Southern rock—aka boogie—has consistently exemplified a process that might be called the "purification of the beat." Once a style reaches maturity, its conventions become widely known. Some artists are then able to distill those qualities that best express its rhythmic essence, purging it of any transitional features and excess baggage. The style becomes timeless at this point; the "purified" beat will remain fresh and unvarying, regardless of context. The sound of "old-time rock 'n' roll" remains virtually the same, whether it's performed by Lynyrd Skynyrd in the seventies, Huey Lewis in the eighties (his classic "Heart of Rock and Roll"), Garth Brooks in the nineties (in his country/rock synthesis, "Papa Loves Mama"), or by countless good bands that have found the rock 'n' roll groove since 1970.

boogie

Lynyrd Skynyrd's "What's Your Name" (Example 19.5) was a posthumous hit for the band. It was released in 1978, a year after lead singer Ronnie Van Zant and guitarist Steve Gaines died in a plane crash, and was one of their few songs to find its way onto the singles charts. It has the two crucial ingredients in any good rock 'n' roll song: a great beat, and a hook that won't let go. This song illustrates not only the distillation of the rock beat, but another dimension of the process of stylistic consolidation and synthesis that characterized so much rock in the seventies. At least in this song, Lynyrd Skynyrd brought together rock and soul: a Rolling Stones-type groove and excellent guitar work in combination with the horn sound of a soul band and boogie piano.

A note in passing: a closely parallel "beat purification" took place in the thirties. It is especially evident in the jaunty fox-trot songs of Cole Porter ("It's De-Lovely" or "You're the Top"); Irving Berlin's "Cheek to Cheek" is another good example. It's intriguing to think that "What's Your Name" and "Cheek to Cheek," which are so unlike each other in style and spirit, exemplify the same evolutionary stage in their respective styles.

Springsteen, the Ramones, Lynyrd Skynyrd, and Led Zeppelin represent the most important directions in hard rock during the seventies. Rock also had a softer side.

THE RENAISSANCE OF MELODY

The other main current in seventies rock was a return to melody. Much as hard rock took several forms, the revival of melody found expression in quite different ways. Three trends were particularly evident: a flowering of soft and pop rock; a continuation and refinement of African-American romantic music; and the emergence of the singer/songwriters. Each admitted considerable variety.

With only a few exceptions–e.g., some Beatles's songs, Frank Sinatra's late sixties hits, and the Bacharach/Hal David/Dionne Warwick collaborations–Tin Pan Alley type songs were eclipsed by rock in the sixties. In the seventies, popular song resurfaced with only a few differences. Most of these songs retained Tin Pan Alley's clear forms, more traditional harmony, and a dominant melody. The addition of a gentle rock beat to the mix seemed to guarantee commercial success, at least to the Carpenters, Barbra Streisand, and Barry Manilow. The more innovative music came from the singer/songwriters (discussed below) and African-American romantic music (discussed in Chapter 20).

SINGER/SONGWRITERS

Singer/songwriters were the most varied group of rock artists of the period. In addition to Dylan, they included folk-revival alumnae like Joni Mitchell, Brill Building veterans like Carole King, renegades like Randy Newman, and eclectics like Paul Simon, who drew on a broad background to produce a string of hits in a dazzling variety of styles.

Establishment songwriters derided rock 'n' roll songs for their crudeness–verbal, melodic, and harmonic–particularly when compared to the sophisticated songs of a Henry Mancini. However, in the early seventies, singer/songwriters created a new school of songwriting whose results rivaled the earlier Tin Pan Alley songwriters in sophistication, coherence, and expressive impact. The most innovative songwriters in the seventies updated the Tin Pan Alley song in several ways: they redefined its form, harmonic language, rhythmic background, lyric content, and melodic style.

Important changes include the use of an AAB form, typically with a climactic final section, as well as other forms that mix narrative and refrain. The songs also become longer and unfold more slowly. An entire record, three minutes or more, may contain only one statement of a song. Simon and Garfunkel's "Bridge Over Troubled Water" is a good example of this trend, as are the early hit songs of Jim Webb, like "Up, Up and Away." Most songs use at least a diluted form of eight-beat rock rhythm. The pulse may assume an irregular length to allow for a more speech-like rhythm, as in the songs of contemporary pop songwriter Burt Bacharach (see Chapter 16).

The most significant difference between rock-era and Tin Pan Alley songs is the length of melodic ideas. Tin Pan Alley songs tend to unfold quickly; the first idea may require only four or eight beats. By contrast, the opening idea of a rock song may often be twice that long. Two Beatles' songs underscore this difference. "Yesterday" is very much in the mold of a Tin Pan Alley song; it begins with a three-note melodic idea that, even with the silence that follows, still consumes only five beats. On the other hand,

"Norwegian Wood" (Example 15.5), a song written in a contemporary style, begins with an idea that continues for twenty-four (fast) beats before a pause. Most rock songs employ these longer melodic gestures.

These longer gestures are probably the most important *musical* contribution of the country-music tradition to popular music. The characteristically country preference for longer melodic gestures almost certainly came into rock-era songwriting primarily through folk music, rather than through the country music of the sixties. Original songs by the early sixties folksingers reflect the influence of the traditional songs that they sang at the beginning of their careers: Bob Dylan's "Blowin' in the Wind" and "Mr. Tambourine Man" are good examples of this folk/country influence. The harmonic language reflects the new approach to popular music, in which the standard "Heart and Soul" chord progressions are replaced by simpler, but more surprisingly ordered, patterns.

The most innovative songwriters of the rock era, including such songwriter/performers as the Beatles, Paul Simon, and Stevie Wonder, not only wrote the melodies of their songs but controlled the entire context in which they were presented. As a result, each song, because it is more than just a melody, has a more individual character.

One of the songs that helped establish the singer/songwriter genre is James Taylor's "Fire and Rain" (Example 19.6). Taylor (1948–), one of the most critically acclaimed and successful of the new generation of songwriters, followed a different, more gentle path down the folk-rock road than Dylan. His songs tell personal stories. "Fire and Rain" describes an experience during his stay in a mental hospital. In many of Taylor's songs—and those of others working in the same style, including Carole King—key ele-

James Taylor, 1971.

ments of rock style are present, but in a more muted form. Acoustic instruments substitute for the electric guitar and bass, and both components of rock rhythm (eight-beat rhythm and backbeat), while present, are much more in the background; the melody is the most important musical element of this song.

"Fire and Rain" is a further illustration of the dramatic and widespread change in popular-song form. The new formal plans depart not only from the typical Tin Pan Alley forms (AABA, etc.), but also from the blues and blues-related forms of earlier rock 'n' roll styles. The underlying principle is the alternation of narrative sections and refrain, with the narrative sections preparing and explaining the refrain.

Ⓓ "I Don't Know Where I Stand" (Example 19.7) written and performed by Joni Mitchell, is even more skillfully constructed and modestly set. Early in her career, Joni Mitchell (born Roberta Anderson in 1943) moved away from traditional folk songs to her own compositions while retaining the basic sound of the folk revivalists. Beginning in 1969, she created some of the most musically significant songs of the period. Her songs of this time featured lyrics rich in images and highly individual and expressive melodies responsive to the meaning of the text.

"I Don't Know Where I Stand" is a beautifully crafted song. The vocal line contains four phrases: the second expands on the first; the third—the climax of the entire phrase group—balances the second; and the fourth is a calmer variant of the third phrase: AA1BB1. The four phrases are thus integrated into a clear arch design, despite several minor changes of direction. Although Mitchell did compose traditional verse-chorus songs—"Both Sides Now" is the most famous example—her work tended to be freer in form, with meandering melodies that matched her thoughtful, often rambling lyrics.

Paul Simon (1942-) has had two distinct careers. The first, as one half of the folk-singing duo Simon and Garfunkel, brought commercial success. Simon and Garfunkel remained together until 1970, when they dissolved the partnership at the peak of its popularity. "Bridge Over Troubled Water" had just been released and both album and single had gone to the top of the charts. However, it was clear that they were headed in different directions professionally, and since the early seventies they have only performed together for special occasions. Since he became a solo artist, Simon has exploited the evocative possibilities of popular and folk styles more than any artist since the Beatles. Like the Beatles, he uses external reference to help convey the sense of his texts, which bear little resemblance to Tin Pan Alley-type "moon-June" songs.

Ⓓ Like many of the Beatles's songs, Simon's "Still Crazy After All These Years" (Example 19.8) is richly, yet unobtrusively orchestrated. The rhythmic foundation of this song derives from African-American gospel, and although it is considerably transformed, it retains the rhythmic energy of that music. A nice coordination of text and music occurs in the middle of the song, where the word "fade" introduces a brief interlude of dream music, like a cinemagraphic "dissolve" from one shot to the next, before the saxophone solo. Like the work of Joni Mitchell, this song takes on the quality of a long dramatic dialogue, with its melodic twists and turns following the singer's thought processes.

Examples 19.6 to 19.8 show the innovations in form, melodic style, and

Paul Simon, c. 1970s.

context that distinguished the songs of the singer/songwriters from those of earlier generations. Carole King's "You've Got a Friend," (Example 19.9), a hit song from her 1971 album, *Tapestry*, has been one of the most frequently covered songs of the entire rock era, and justifiably so. It shows how traditional songwriting procedures were updated as they were integrated into rock style. The song is as skillfully and subtly unified as any Tin Pan Alley standard. Here, however, these techniques serve a different purpose; to underscore the message of the lyrics.

    The song begins with a three-note ascending figure ("When you're down") and immediately stabilizes around the note sung to the word "down." There are a series of attempts to escape this central note: a slight

Ⓓ

inflection on "troubled"; a sudden leap to "need," and a more sustained upward push on the two "nothing"s. But all three lines return to rest on the central pitch. The note acts as a melodic millstone, pulling the melody back down to earth each time it tries to break away.

The next line ("Close your eyes") is a more urgent version of the opening line, with many more syllables sung on the same note. The final phrase finally ends (with the word "night") on a different note. It's lower than the other note—the night is darkest before dawn—but it marks the juncture between despair and hope, the point where the melody shifts direction.

The shift in melodic direction changes the tone of the song. As it rises, we can feel the weight of despair being lifted off our shoulders, just as we could feel it pulling us down earlier in the song.

At the beginning of the chorus ("You just call . . ."), the melody, building on the opening three-note scale, begins to move mostly in an upward direction. Each new phrase grows out of an earlier one. "Winter, spring, summer or fall" is a elaborated variant of the first line. Finally, the melodic climax ("And I'll be there") is reached, preparing the melodically understated punch line of the song ("You've got a friend").

The second major section is identical to the first, except for the noticeable omission of the phrase containing the punch line. This omission is significant because it does not give the musical resolution that we expect. Instead, the melody leads directly to the most intense part of the song. The music expresses this agitation right from the start. The phrase that reaffirms the punch line even as it replaces it ("Ain't it good...") is the most rhythmically active line in the song, the melody skips around on "hurt you and desert you," and the most daring harmonies are heard throughout this section.

Carole King, c. 1970s.

The final statement of the chorus resolves the preceding tension through its inherently reassuring qualities and its familiarity to us. The repetition of the chorus is not simply conventional; it is in direct response to the flow of the text.

It is not uncommon for a song, especially a good song, to create an overall mood, to convey the general idea of the lyrics in its melody, rhythm, and context. At the same time, the melody follows its own internal logic, so that it makes sense with or without words. What makes "You've Got a Friend" special is that the melody responds so specifically to the story told in the words. Few songs in the popular idiom have done this as well as it is done here.

CONCLUSION

Rock fanned out in several directions in the 1970s, almost all of them stylistically conservative. Early in the decade, hard rock divided and subdivided into several styles, most notably heavy metal, Southern rock, art rock, and glam rock. Style often triumphed over substance: the performer's image was more important than the music he or she created. As a reaction to the increased commercialization of mainstream rock, there were two concurrent movements, one a back-to-roots movement spearheaded by Bruce Springsteen and the other a primitive reaction to smooth and commercial music by punk and new-wave groups. Throughout the decade, a group of talented singer/songwriters created some of the decade's most memorable music. Their songs made melody a central element but married it to contemporary rhythms and textures.

Terms to Know

AOR (album-oriented radio)	art rock	boogie
glam rock	heavy metal	new wave
punk	singer/songwriter	underground radio

Names to Know

David Bowie	Elton John	Carole King
Led Zeppelin	Lynyrd Skynyrd	Joni Mitchell
Ramones	Paul Simon	Bruce Springsteen
James Taylor		

Study Questions

1. In what ways did rock become conservative in the seventies? How did the rock segment of the popular-music industry change? How did the music itself reflect a more conservative attitude?

2. How does the music of Bruce Springsteen, Led Zeppelin, Elton John, and other major acts illustrate the nature and extent of the stylistic diversity of rock of the seventies?

3. How diverse are singer/songwriters as represented in this chapter? What

common features distinguish their work from hard rock? How do they differ among themselves? What are the principal sources of the singer/songwriter styles? How are their songs different from pre-rock popular song?

4. What musical qualities distinguish punk and new-wave music from other rock of the seventies? In what ways was punk the "return to roots" movement within rock? In what ways is punk different from fifties and early sixties rock?

5. Can you think of another song in which the melody, structure, and accompaniment underscore the message, as they do in "You've Got a Friend"? Write a brief analysis supporting your point.

6. Compare Garth Brooks's song "The River" to either James Taylor's "Fire and Rain" or Carole King's "You've Got A Friend." How has Brooks carried forward the singer/songwriter tradition?

7. Select a recent song by the Rolling Stones such as "You've Got Me Rockin'" or "Out of Tears." How do these carry forward the traditions the band established in the sixties and seventies? How are they different?

CHAPTER TWENTY

"Jam": The New Beat

In the early seventies, rock split into two families of musical styles. One remained rock, at least for a decade. The other, having absorbed key elements of Latin music and hard-core rhythm and blues, took on a distinctly different musical personality. Among the latter group were the proto-funk of Sly and the Family Stone; Isaac Hayes's film score for *Shaft;* a new generation of African-American romantic music, evident in the work of Roberta Flack, Bill Withers, Aretha Franklin, and the Philadelphia-based Gamble/Huff stable of vocal groups; Stevie Wonder's breakthrough crossover albums; the funk of George Clinton's Parliament and Funkadelic bands; the jazz/Latin/rock fusion of Miles Davis's keyboardists-turned-leaders (Chick Corea, Herbie Hancock, and Joe Zawinul's Weather Report); the orgasmic sonic undulations of Barry White's Love Unlimited Orchestra; the infectious dance music of KC and the Sunshine Band; and the rich rhythms and textures of Earth, Wind, and Fire.

funk

African–American romantic music

CHARACTERISTICS

Much of the music of these artists shares several features that distinguish it from the rock of the period and all earlier styles. The most important difference is rhythmic. Groups are thinking in "sixteen," evidenced by regular rhythms and riffs that move four times faster than the beat, eight times faster than the backbeat. Instrumentation is enlarged, with the addition of Latin percussion instruments, synthesizers, horns, and backup vocals to the typical rock-band nucleus. Bands average ten players instead of the four or five of the typical rock band. These extra instruments help produce dense, varied textures, rich in supporting riffs, as well as sustained harmonies and active rhythms. Tempos are slower, due in large part to the faster durations within the beat. Roberta Flack's "Feel Like Making Love," Stevie Wonder's "Superstition," Parliament's "Give Up the Funk" (Example 20.3), and Herbie Hancock's 1973 version of "Watermelon Man" (Example 18.4) all fit under this same umbrella, despite their obvious differences.

We can infer that musicians "officially" recognize the existence of this beat. Rhythm machines on electronic keyboards routinely identify the style-defining rhythm as "sixteen beat." Sixteen beat refers to the fastest layer of

 V-13

 VB-4

 V-6

 VA-6

equally emphasized regular rhythm, by analogy with two-beat, four-beat, and eight-beat rhythms. However, unlike swing, rock, and even the two-beat fox trot, this contemporary rhythm does not have a widely used or accepted name.

jam

In this book, the sixteen-beat rhythm is called "jam." The decision to give this beat a name that does not have wide currency was motivated primarily by convenience and clarity. It's helpful to have a short, easily remembered term like rock or swing to identify a family of styles. Many of the jam-based styles have widely accepted names: disco; funk; rap; even the euphemistic urban contemporary. *Billboard* identifies the sixteen-beat–based jazz of the last two decades as "contemporary jazz." But all these names just designate styles within the jam family. This deficiency occasionally leads to awkward constructions, like Robert Christgau's well-intentioned, accurate, but somewhat clumsy phrase, "postpunk-postdisco fusion," which identifies various rock/jam intersections in the eighties. At least in the context of this book, the term "jam" should rectify the problem.

disco
rap

What are the jam-based styles? In the seventies, there were at least five distinct kinds of music and many more hybrids. There was the pre-funk of Sly and the Family Stone and the funk of the George Clinton empire: all riffs, rappish vocals, and open rhythms. There were uptempo dance numbers, like Stevie Wonder's "Superstition" and Earth, Wind and Fire's "Shining Star" (Example 20.1), both Number 1 hits, with even denser textures and more insistent rhythms. Disco offered an even more obvious rhythm, one thud per beat, usually overlaid with active riffs, busy, repetitive rhythms, and sustained strings. The most melodious of all the jam-based styles was what might be called African-American romantic music: songs about love, with nicely crafted phrases, delicate textures, soft dynamics, and slow to medium tempos. Jazz spanned all these styles, from sophisticated funk-based styles to romantic instrumental ones.

 V-11

 VB-2

Intersections, both within this style family and among these styles and Latin/Caribbean music, added even more variety. The pop-flavored jazz, or vice versa, of George Benson and Grover Washington is one example of an intrafamily blend. Latin influence was almost always indirectly evident because of the additional percussion instruments. At times, it became more overt. Stevie Wonder's Latin/Caribbean flavored songs, for example "Boogie On, Reggae Woman," or the samba-ish "Bird of Paradise," are examples, as is "Salsation," from the soundtrack of *Saturday Night Fever.*

The eighties and nineties have seen the continued evolution of jam-based styles. There have been several interesting developments. Rap, after a decade of bubbling under, hit it big in the late eighties, reaching out from African-American neighborhoods to MTV and the white suburbs. A new wave of dance music has reclaimed the territory forfeited by disco. Crossbreeding with rock added a bite to the new beat, evident in mainstream successes by Michael Jackson and the punk/funk syntheses of Prince. From the other end, jam raised the energy of metal bands to manic levels. In speed, death, and thrash metal, sixteen-beat rhythms shot out as if from a jammed Uzi. Alternative rock revisited jam's roots. Bands like the Red Hot Chili Peppers, Primus, and Living Colour have updated the hard rhythm and blues of the sixties.

punk/funk
fusion

Jam, definitely outside the mainstream in the seventies, has infiltrated most contemporary popular music in the last decade. Only country music has remained immune. By 1990, the majority of hit songs were using a jam beat, not a rock beat.

SOURCES

Jam's ancestral roots are in Latin America. Its dense, percussion-laden textures and active rhythms have been characteristic of the Cuban *son* and Brazilian samba for over half a century. The sounds and rhythms of these Latin styles define jam's essential qualities as surely as boogie-woogie and rhythm and blues defined rock's. In this respect, jam broke new ground. It was the first style family whose defining qualities did not come from the blues.

The Latin rhythms that coalesced into the jam styles flowed into popular music in two waves. The first wave had two streams. Both began in the late forties and lasted into the fifties. One was the mambo craze, the other Cu-bop, a marriage of bebop and Cuban rhythms (see Chapter 13).

Latin bands introduced the mambo to non-Hispanic audiences. They played ballrooms in the major cities, especially New York. Both white and African-American dance bands included Latin numbers in their repertoire, and most of the rhythm and blues group of the fifties also carried a few Latin songs. Bill Haley's "Mambo Rock," a 1955 hit for him, is a typical example. The influence of Latin rhythms surfaced in the music of Bo Diddley, Ray Charles, and particularly James Brown.

While dance bands mamboed their dancers to exhaustion, jazz musicians, especially Dizzy Gillespie, embraced Latin rhythms, and uptown Latin bandleaders, most notably Machito and Tito Puente, absorbed jazz influences into their music. Cu-bop began in the late forties. A decade later, Latin tunes were part of the sound fabric of post-bop jazz.

The second wave of Latin music came from Brazil. The bossa nova musicians—most notably Gilberto and Jobim—brought the lighter and more subtle rhythms of the samba to the United States in the early sixties, where they found a welcome audience. Some jazz musicians, most notably Stan Getz and Charlie Byrd, turned to the bossa nova as an alternative to the inevitable fusion with rock. Out of this initial blending of jazz and samba, a younger generation of musicians forged an array of Brazilian/Cuban/jazz fusions. Most influential and musically significant was Chick Corea's early Return to Forever group. Corea and his collaborators often integrated a samba beat, montuno-style accompaniments, and angular, almost bop-like melodies and solos into a unified conception.

A similar synthesis with even more far-reaching implications began in the mid-sixties. James Brown's brand of soul drew on not only blues and gospel, but also the open form, busy but airy textures, static montuno-ish harmonies, and prominent percussive sounds of Afro-Cuban music. Perhaps the most miraculous feature of Brown's conception was his emphasis on rhythm without the addition of extra rhythm instruments. Brown's band produced a percussive sonority by playing their instruments in a percussive way. The bassist played crisp attacks on syncopated notes. The guitarist choked the neck of the guitar to produce a sound more percussive than harmonic. Horns alternated between sustained and bitten-off notes. It wasn't necessary to add additional percussion instruments.

In the latter part of the sixties, Brown issued a stream of influential

IV-12

IVA-12

IV-13

IVB-1

recordings. Two in particular set popular music off in a new direction. The first was "Papa's Got a Brand New Bag" (Example 15.10). It established the mature James Brown sound: lots of riffs; an irresistible beat with relatively little timekeeping; plenty of syncopation; frequent call and response; and hardly any melody, at least in a conventional sense. "Cold Sweat" (Example 15.11) went even further. Half-sung, half-spoken over two alternating ostinatos, this song laid the groundwork for funk and rap. Both Sly Stone and George Clinton listened seriously to Brown's music.

The more tuneful group of jam styles borrowed heavily from Motown as well as James Brown. Philadelphia producers drew on the more European side of Motown–rich strings; flowing, singable melodies; clear forms–and frequently merged them with a more muted version of the jam beat. At the same time Motown artists like Marvin Gaye and Stevie Wonder explored this new rhythmic territory in albums like Gaye's *What's Going On* and Wonder's *Talking Book.*

Jam drew most heavily on Latin music, both Afro-Cuban and Afro-Brazilian, and hard-core rhythm and blues, with lots of rhythm, lots of blues, and very little pop. Particularly in the music of James Brown, they blended together to produce a rhythmic groove without precedent. It was not Latin, rock, blues, or gospel, yet it was indebted to each. Its unique sound would serve as the foundation for the most progressive trends of the seventies, eighties, and nineties.

THE SOUNDS OF JAM STYLES

"Shining Star" (Example 20.1), a Number 1 single from Earth, Wind, and Fire's top-selling 1975 album, *That's the Way of the World,* shows a middle-of-the-road jam style. It finds the medium groove that funk bands found so irresistible, but is more melodious than funk. Use of a sixteen-beat rhythm, here played by choked guitar, is the most obvious indication that the song belongs to the jam style family. Other jam-related style features include:

1. An expanded band, through the addition of several horns, backup vocals (from the band members), and additional percussion.
2. A dense texture, made up not only of the timekeeping instruments, but also riffs from singers and horns, plus bass lines that seldom mark the beat.
3. Sections of static harmony.
4. A tempo slower than the average rock song. The rhythm sounds busy because there's so much activity at faster-than-beat speed levels.

The most direct antecedent of jam style was the music of Sly Stone. His band, Sly and the Family Stone, took James Brown's conception a step closer to jam style. In his brief but influential tenure at the top of the pop charts, Sly Stone gave popular music a push in a new rhythmic/textural/harmonic direction. Many of his songs combined simple, repetitive riffs with complex textures. "Africa Talks to You" (Example 20.2) took the process even further. The intermittent vocal lines ride on a multilayered wave of sound. In the opening, a series of pitched rhythm instruments, first bass then keyboards and guitars, enter almost layer by layer. No one line, except

V-12

VB-3

Earth, Wind and Fire, c. 1980s.

perhaps for the high guitar line, stands out, but the blend is magical. The texture is like a densely woven fabric made up of contrasting strands of material. Everyone is busy, but no one seems to get in the way. The song harmonically one-ups (or one-downs?) James Brown's "Cold Sweat," in that it uses just one chord. The harmony is absolutely static; there is no sense of progression at all.

Sly and the Family Stone, c. 1968.

FUNK

George Clinton was the mastermind behind two important bands, Parliament and Funkadelic. Parliament, formed in the late sixties, was his first band. When forced to relinquish the Parliament name to Motown, Clinton formed Funkadelic. When Clinton regained control of the Parliament name in 1974, he used two names for the same band. He recorded the more outrageous material under the Funkadelic name and the tighter, more polished material as Parliament. Clinton's multinamed band was big for the time—twelve musicians. It shows in a denser sound.

 V-13

 VB-4

"Give Up the Funk" (Example 20.3), written by George Clinton and recorded by Parliament, shows Clinton's debt to the sources of funk and the special qualities that defined his style. The sound of the band is fuller than either James Brown's or Sly Stone's, because there are more instruments and all of them are busy. There are riffs and sustained chords from both horns and keyboards, high obbligato lines from a synthesizer, an active but open bass line, lots of percussion, and voices—both the choral effect of the backup singers and Clinton's proto rap. Clinton's debt to Brown goes beyond influence from his recordings and performances; Clinton recruited three key personnel from James Brown's backup band for his group: bassist "Bootsy" Collins; saxophonist Maceo Parker; and trombonist Fred Wesley.

AFRICAN-AMERICAN ROMANTIC MUSIC

African-American romantic music was at the opposite end of the jam style spectrum. Unlike rock, which had largely abandoned the romantic

George Clinton, 1979.

song in favor of a more direct and realistic view of love or its absence (the Beatles' "Norwegian Wood" [Example 15.5] or Lynyrd Skynyrd's "What's Your Name" [Example 19.5], which cynically describes a band member's one night stand with a groupie), African-American pop had retained the romantic view of love portrayed so frequently in Tin Pan Alley song. Motown was at the center of this romantic style. However, in the seventies, Motown's guiding producer Berry Gordy no longer dominated the African-American pop market. Both Marvin Gaye and Stevie Wonder demanded and got creative autonomy. At the same time, Gamble and Huff answered Motown with the Philadelphia sound, which carried Motown's slickness to the next level. Other new artists, such as Roberta Flack and Bill Withers, also contributed a series of hits, again mostly about love.

Of all the African-American pop artists in the seventies, no one enjoyed more commercial and critical success than Stevie Wonder (1950––). Stevie Wonder is one of the few artists to make the transition from child celebrity to adult megastar. In recent years, only Michael Jackson has made such a transition with similar success. After gaining his artistic independence from Gordy, Wonder produced a string of albums that sold well to both African-Americans and whites. They contained much of his most memorable music.

Stevie Wonder's success as a crossover artist can be explained at least in part by the fact that he has written real songs, not just riffs over a funky

Stevie Wonder as a child prodigy star, c. 1963.

beat–although he has done that as well. His melodies have continuity and
direction. They are usually accompanied by modified Tin Pan Alley harmony and supported by dense, usually electronically overdubbed orchestration.
Since the early seventies, Wonder has been deeply involved in all stages of
the creative process. In many cases, he has been the only performer on a
recording, adding each part through overdubbing. Although the melodies of
many of his songs are distinctive enough to cover easily, the songs are
always a total conception that extends well beyond the melody to include
instrumentation, rhythmic backdrop, and vocal parts. As a result, covers of
his songs never match the integrity of his original version and seldom
achieve comparable success, musically or commercially. Wonder has been a
tremendously versatile songwriter and performer. He is just as comfortable
in uptempo songs like "Superstition" as he is in his love songs.

The two Stevie Wonder songs discussed here show important features
of his style. They also show the entry of the African-American romantic
song into the jam style family. "You Are the Sunshine of My Life" (Example
20.4), released in 1973, is a rock song, although it has many of the features
of the newer style–in particular, the prominent use of Latin percussion and
a thick texture. By contrast, Wonder's 1979 hit "Send One Your Love"
(Example 20.5) has a clear sixteen-beat feel. In almost every other respect,
the two songs are very similar. Both have a deceptively subtle and contemporary form. Despite their clear formal outlines, the songs offer additional
examples of endless-loop form. In both songs, each statement of the melody
contains four phrases, in an AABB' (for "You Are the Sunshine of My Life")
or AABB (for "Send One Your Love") pattern. The last phrase is open-ended,
always leading back to the beginning instead of coming to a stop. The form,
texture, and beat of these songs were Wonder's contemporary spin on the
melodic and harmonic language of Tin Pan Alley song. Together, they illustrate the transition to jam's ballad style.

Disco

Although Stone, Hancock, Clinton, and Wonder all enjoyed popular success–Wonder was the dominant African-American artist of the seventies,
commercially and musically–it wasn't until disco was created that the new
beat rivaled rock in commercial importance.

Disco began to take hold in 1975 with its first hits: KC and the Sunshine
Band's "That's the Way I Like It" and Van McCoy's "The Hustle."
Discotheques had been venues for dancing as far back as the early 1960s, but
went underground during the first years of rock concerts. They re-emerged
as hot spots in the mid-seventies as some whites and several minorities–
African-Americans, Latins, and gays–flocked to them to rediscover the joys
of social dancing. In 1977, disco went mainstream with the release of the
film *Saturday Night Fever*. The film gave major career boosts to John
Travolta and the Bee Gees, and its soundtrack sold more than 11 million
units. Along with big-selling albums by Donna Summer, Kool and the Gang,
Chic, and more from the Bee Gees, it made disco the commercially dominant style in popular music for a short time.

Disco was not embraced universally. It was, among other things, a mul-
timinority music. In addition to African-Americans and Hispanics, its audience included gays, openly cultivated by groups like the Village People. It's
easy to infer sexual and racial prejudice in the virulent reaction against disco,

just as it's easy to infer racial prejudice in much of the condemnation of early rock 'n' roll. Homophobia was part of disco-bashing's hidden agenda. The 1979 anti-disco rally held in Chicago's Comiskey Park after a White Sox baseball game, where disc jockey Steve Dahl burned hundreds of boxes of disco records in a huge pyre in centerfield, was at least partially based on these feelings.

Still, disco was a commercial dance music designed for mass appeal. In line with this purpose, disco songs typically employed an obvious form of the jam beat. The beat is strongly marked by bass drum, and the sixteen-beat layer played on a closed hi-hat and/or a choked guitar. Like a compass zeroing in on true north, tempos vibrated around 120 beats per minute. Because there was so little variation in tempo and rhythmic feel, disc jockeys at discos became a kind of second-level performing artist. Their art was programming songs on two turntables so that the music would "peak" seamlessly. The unending flow of sound with periodic climaxes became a musical counterpart to the overtly sexual lyrics of many disco songs.

Disco's unrelenting beat was the biggest difference between it and other jam styles. There were other differences, however. Perhaps the most evident was disco's use of slow moving melody lines, usually played by strings or keyboards, contrasted with the activity of some of the rhythm instruments. This combination of lush sonority and rock-solid dance beat proved irresistible to many, if repulsive to hard-core rock 'n' rollers.

No act better expressed disco's message than Chic. Decked out in evening wear, they epitomized the elegance that style-conscious disco-goers aspired to. However, the band was more than just a pretty look. They made some of the best and most characteristic music to come out of disco. Their song "Good Times" (Example 20.6) typifies the best music of the style. There are several qualities that distinguish it from other jam styles. The beat, reinforced by the bass drum, is more clearly marked than in other jam styles. Despite this clear beat, the song has an open, airy texture—perhaps its most distinguishing feature. This texture occurs despite an impressive number of parts. In addition to the beat-marking bass drum, there are a sixteen-beat rhythm on a closed cymbal, hand clap, celeste-like sustained chords, occasional string figures, the riff-based vocal part, an active bass line, guitar chording (often choked and in a sixteen-beat rhythm), and slow-moving piano riffs and chords. Here, as in other jam styles, the sum is more than the individual parts; however, the effect is less dense and more open than funk because so many of the parts move so slowly (the keyboard and some string lines), or appear only intermittently (other string lines, voices). We can hear the details of this distinctive texture most clearly in the middle of the song, when it is taken apart and put back together, layer by layer.

 V-14

 VB-5

While its texture may be the most distinguishing quality, the harmony of the song is its most musically meaningful feature. Like the disco experience itself, the harmony keeps promising release from uninterrupted tension. In the disco, it is the skillful, seamless blending of songs that sustains the tension through climactic waves that never seem to get over the edge. Similarly, the two chords that serve as the harmonic underpinning of this song keep promising resolution to the tonic chord, but it never arrives. (If it did, there would be a letdown.) Harmonically, then, "Good Times" compresses the disco experience into a single song.

THE EIGHTIES

Like all dance fads, disco quickly ran its course. As a style, it disappeared soon after its initial mass success; it was dead by the early eighties. During its brief run, however, it brought the jam beat from the periphery to the center of popular music. It carried other jam-based styles along in its wake. Funk and contemporary jazz enjoyed unprecedented commercial success in the late seventies, while a new generation of African-American pop artists, most notably Lionel Richie and Michael Jackson (as solo artists) and Prince, incorporated it easily into their music. Earth, Wind and Fire, already established commercially before disco, maintained their popularity through the early eighties.

In the early eighties, Michael Jackson and Prince created the most commercially important jam-based style. Both found a middleground between jam and rock, moving easily between eight- and sixteen-beat rhythms and mixing the more open sound of the new beat with the harder edge of rock.

Both artists have been overwhelmingly successful. Indeed, the phenomenal sales of Michael Jackson's *Thriller* album (40,000,000 and counting) helped revive a relatively moribund recording industry. The commercial importance of this recording was not just in its big numbers. Over the years, the relationship between popular song and other media had been turned upside down. Before 1970, many hit songs were written for, or at least popularized through, shows or films. By the time of *Thriller*, the situation was reversed. Music videos, the short attention span mini-films of the current era, were created for hit songs, not the other way around.

Michael Jackson's enormous popularity also signaled a complete about-face from blackface. Most of the early African-American performers who played for white audiences had to cork their face so that they looked like the caricatures on the sheet music covers of the period. By the 1980s, however, some African-American performers were major celebrities, even role models. Michael Jackson, Prince, and Whitney Houston have found a huge, integrated audience. Michael Jackson's single, sequined, fingerless glove briefly became an essential fashion statement for youth of all races in mid-decade. Jackson suffered a setback in the early 1990s when he was embroiled in rumors about his sexual proclivities; his 1994 marriage to Lisa Marie Presley helped assuage some of this rumor mongering. As this is written, rap, the "blackest" and certainly the most racially hostile of the current popular styles, nevertheless enjoys a large following among whites.

It should be noted that integration of the popular music industry has not occurred quickly or easily. For example, MTV, which began broadcasting in 1981, stuck to a lily-white playlist during its first two years on the air; it all but refused to air videos by African-American artists. MTV executives justified their playlists by asserting that African-American music wasn't rock 'n' roll. Less than twenty-five of 750 videos featured African-American musicians, including those in integrated bands. Only when public demand for videos from Michael Jackson's *Thriller* album became overwhelming did MTV finally cave in and integrate its playlist. It quickly saw the financial reward for its decision, so its current playlist features a healthy racial mix.

Thriller also dramatized the increasingly crucial role of the producer in contemporary popular music. Producers like Quincy Jones, who oversaw

Thriller, continued to expand the musical responsibilities of the job. Even more than the archetypical producers of the sixties, like George Martin of Beatles's fame and Motown's Berry Gordy, they oversee recording projects from conception to completion. They assume several roles, some old, some new. Like the old sheet-music publishers, they keep their finger on the pulse of popular taste, so that they can advise the artists in selecting and arranging songs. Like the arrangers before rock, they may arrange the songs, or at least supervise the arrangements. There is a crucial difference between pre-rock era arrangements and those of contemporary arranger/producers, however. Traditional arrangements offer one way to present a song; contemporary arrangements become part of a song.

Taking advantage of the multitrack technology that came into its own in the sixties, producers may mix—or supervise the mixing of—the raw recorded material, often creating a song virtually impossible to replicate in live performance. In today's popular music, recording is seldom just a means of preserving a performance, but an art form unto itself—obtainable only, or at least most easily, in the studio. Producers are its new, multifaceted artists. If a record company were a football team, the producer might be the general

Michael Jackson, c. 1980s.

Ⓓ manager, coach, and at least one of the players. Michael Jackson's "Wanna Be Startin' Somethin'" (Example 20.7) is an ~~ideal example of the recording as a distinct performance medium, not a preservation of a live performance.~~

"Wanna Be Startin' Somethin'," one of the many hits from *Thriller* illustrates the fusion of rock and jam. Both Michael Jackson's vocal and the accompaniment have a hard edge more characteristic of rock than any of the jam styles. So do the lyrics. On the other hand, the song also has the dense, multilayered texture and sixteen-beat rhythm characteristic of jam styles, and an infectious dance beat. It deserved its popularity.

Michael Jackson was the star player on a musical team that produced the biggest-selling album of all time. Prince has been, through the miracle of multi-track recording, a team unto himself. He has been the primary—and often the sole—musical source in his recordings since his 1978 debut album *For You*. His blockbuster was the 1984 film, *Purple Rain*, described by Paul Evans as "essentially an ambitious long-form video, perfectly in sync with the new visual culture then being shaped by MTV."

Like Jackson, Prince has explored the middleground between rock and jam-based styles. In his case, the results have been even more wide-ranging. He is at home with an astonishing array of styles, which he can incorporate into his work without sacrificing its identity or personality. He uses this stylistic flexibility to help express the character of his songs. Indeed, it often seems that Prince's first language is music: his songs are organic expressions of his moods and preoccupations.

Perhaps no album better demonstrates the nature of his musical conception than the 1987 double album *Sign "O" the Times*. It shows off his stylistic range: included among the 16 tracks on the album are takeoffs on fifties doo-wop ("Slow Love"), a sixties soul ballad ("Adore"), and Led Zeppelin's "Stairway to Heaven" ("The Cross"); updated approaches to the classic Motown group sound ("Forever in My Life") and the early Beatles ("I Could Never Take the Place of Your Man"), as well as dance music ("Housequake"), an urban contemporary ballad ("If I Was Your Girlfriend"), new wave ("It"), an R&B/Latin/contemporary jazz synthesis ("Hot Thing"), and several punk/funk mergers.

Ⓓ No single song could adequately express this range; the two discussed below only hint at it. The first, "Sign 'O' the Times," (Example 20.8) offers a bleak vision of contemporary life, interlaced with anecdotal accounts of the fallout from drug use. The music is correspondingly bleak: a spare texture of synthesizer, bass, and guitar riffs and intermittent, mostly background, percussion support the vocal line. Only a rich, sustained synthesized chord underlines the refrain and hook of the song. There is no harmonic change outside the "hook" section, suggesting perhaps a despair that has no end.

Ⓓ "Sign 'O' the Times" reveals a brooding, thoughtful side of Prince's personality; "It's Gonna Be a Beautiful Night" (Example 20.9) finds him more upbeat, energized by an enthusiastic Parisian crowd. The song shows two characteristic features of his music: his ability to synthesize several styles into an integrated conception; and his irrepressible love of a rhythmic groove. It begins with a straightforward rock beat, played by the drummer. The horn line, with its double-time riffs, muddies the rhythmic waters somewhat: is it rock or jam? When bass, synthesizer, and extra percussion enter, there is no doubt: this is jam-based pop funk; the rock beat, in retrospect, was simply the scaffolding for a dense rhythmic texture.

In his mastery of a dazzling array of styles and ability to blend them to highlight the sense and mood of a song, Prince joins select company: the Beatles, Dylan, Paul Simon, and a few others. Where he differs most strikingly from them is in the styles he draws from. By the time he recorded *Sign "O" the Times*, rock was over thirty years old. So, he has been able to draw on the full range of rock-era styles, instead of reaching back into the past (pre-rock pop and gospel) or across styles (East Indian music, classical music). No one in the last two decades has done it more creatively.

The music of Michael Jackson and Prince represent the pop end of the jam-style spectrum. Rap lies at the opposite end: a music that makes almost no accommodation to prevailing popular taste. Still, rap has a large audience and considerable influence outside the African-American community, although conceived by and for African-Americans.

Because it's largely spoken, not sung, rap is the most immediately distinctive style to emerge since rock 'n' roll. It is easy to assume that it represents a completely new direction in popular music. However, there are clear antecedents for its most distinctive features, both textual and musical. The idea of reciting poetry over a popular-music background dates back at least to the fifties, when beat poets like Kenneth Rexroth read their work to the accompaniment of a jazz combo. Bob Dylan did much the same thing in his "Subterranean Homesick Blues" (Example 15.6), although the tone of the text is much more confrontational than the standard beat fare (and much closer to rap in style and intent).

Rappers blur the line between speech and song. Their delivery is more than just spoken text. It has pitch, although not the definite pitch associated with song. There are antecedents for this in both African culture (the *griot* heard in Example 3.5) and a wide variety of African-American musics: the preacher, the bluesman, and the cries of street vendors. Rap's more recent and direct lineage goes back to James Brown by way of George Clinton and Sly Stone. I-18 IA-18

Rap can also be seen as a logical consequence of the "percussionization" of popular music. We have noted both the introduction of percussion instruments into popular music—first the drum set, then the percussion instruments of Afro-Cuban and Afro-Brazilian music—and the adaptation of nonpercussion instruments to produce a percussive sound (plucked acoustic bass, choked guitar, slapped electric bass). In rap, the *voice* becomes a percussion instrument: rhythm is prominent, while pitch is indefinite. With the addition of sequenced drum tracks, scratching, and hand claps, rap is—or can be—almost pure rhythm. It's a total musical turnaround from the melodically oriented waltz songs from the beginning of the century.

Rap is the most recent instance of a popular style speaking to and for its audience. In a 1992 *Newsweek* article, Public Enemy's Chuck D called rap "Black America's CNN." In his view, it serves as the news service of the inner city, providing information and viewpoints not available through conventional media. Despite this specific orientation, rap attracts a much larger audience than the group to whom it is primarily directed. Chuck D feels that rap and rap videos give whites exposure to a side of African-American life that they could not get short of visiting a ghetto. V-15 VB-6

Public Enemy's song "1 Million Bottlebags" (Example 20.10), from the 1991 album, *Apocalypse 91. . . The Enemy Strikes Black*, illustrates all of rap's key features. The song is a commentary on alcoholism among African-Americans and an indictment of advertisers who exacerbate the problem by promoting alcoholic beverages heavily in the African-American community. The anger and frustration implicit in the text clearly comes across in the delivery of the rappers. The insistent (sixteen-beat) drum part reinforces the message conveyed in the vocal parts, which feature quick rhythms and rapid-fire rhymes. So do the siren-like stereophonic synthesizer riffs that mark the refrain, and the sound collages at the beginning and end of the song.

Rap songs like "1 Million Bottlebags" are popular music as social commentary. The impact of such songs comes not only from the text but from its musical and, in this case, aural setting. The words paint the picture, but the music sets the tone. Although these songs may appear simple—and many artists from both within and outside the musical community have attempted to record "rap" songs—the best rap is as musically sophisticated as other pop music styles.

CONCLUSION

Jam-based music continued to diversify in the eighties. Its embrace widened to include rap and dance music, some alternative rock and heavy metal substyles. Already international in its roots, jam became truly international in its scope with the world beat movement of the eighties. These intersections of pop and Afrocentric international styles included not only Brazilian music, but calypso, soca, and zouk from the Caribbean and Afro-pop. Much of this music shared jam's sixteen-beat rhythm; American popular music had finally caught up with the rest of the world. Intersections of Afrocentric folk and popular music with the popular music mainstream have gone both ways. Several leading popular musicians, among them Peter Gabriel, David Byrne of the Talking Heads, and Paul Simon, have actively promoted both the regional musics and their cross-pollinations.

The continuing multiplication of rock and jam styles and their ongoing intersections have created a stylistic panorama in the eighties and nineties comparable in many ways to that of the forties and early fifties. Certainly they are comparable in range and diversity. At one current extreme are rap, dance music, and world beat. Their parallels in the forties were electric blues, rhythm and blues, and the mambo. At the other extreme are the entire spectrum of country music and musical theater, retro-rock, and the neo-traditional movements in jazz and Tin Pan Alley popular song—Harry Connick's emergence and Tony Bennett's "rediscovery." This matches up pretty nicely with the conservative end of style spectrum in the forties and fifties, which also reached back not only to the early years of a style period, but before it, especially in the Rodgers and Hammerstein musicals.

Terms to Know

African-American romantic music	disco	funk
jam	punk/funk fusion	rap

Names to Know

Chic	George Clinton	Earth, Wind and Fire
Michael Jackson	Parliament	Prince
Public Enemy	Sly and the Family Stone	Stevie Wonder

Study Questions

1. Is it consistent with the history of popular music to link a group of musical styles because of a common rhythmic foundation? When has it happened previously? What is the rhythmic foundation that connects disco, funk, rap, and contemporary jazz?

2. In what ways has Latin music influenced the sound of jam styles? What has been its influence on instrumentation, rhythm, and texture?

3. Trace the line of development from James Brown through Sly and the Family Stone and funk and rap. What musical characteristics have remained the same or similar? What changes have taken place?

4. Why did disco provoke such a range of reaction from the popular-music audience and critics? What musical characteristics distinguish it from other jam styles?

5. Who were the commercially successful jam-based artists? Why did their music represent a synthesis of rock and jam styles?

6. What other musical features besides the beat typically distinguish rock and jam styles?

7. What are the distinguishing features of rap? How does it represent, as a style, the ultimate development of a rhythmically based music?

Postlude

As this is written, American popular music is just over 150 years old. Ragtime, the first syncopated popular style, is about 100 years old. Since ragtime, popular music has undergone a wholesale transformation, while the industry that supports it has experienced tremendous development.

We can get some sense of the extent and rapidity of this transformation by creating two hypothetical listeners, one from 1800, the other from 1900, and imagining that each could go about a century into the future and hear a popular song from the period. Suppose that our listener from 1800 could hear "After the Ball" in 1900 (recall that it was the first big Tin Pan Alley hit and was still very popular at the turn of the century), and that our listener from 1900 could hear "Wanna Be Startin' Somethin'" (if only because the album is still popular and the songs still familiar).

Our listener from 1800 would have found much to remind him of the music of his own time: its setting for voice and piano, although a piano with a much richer tone, a dominant melody supported by an unobtrusive accompaniment, traditional harmony, and simple rhythm confirmed by both melody and accompaniment. The waltz rhythm might come as a surprise, not because the rhythm was unfamiliar, but because it accompanied a tearjerker of a story. And, if he saw the song performed on stage, he might wonder what the story had to do with a trip to Chinatown.

By contrast, our listener from 1900 would have a severe case of future shock. Just listening to "Wanna Be Startin' Somethin'," perhaps on a personal cassette/stereo, would have taxed his credulity. The first record players had just been manufactured; although a real novelty, they were expensive, cumbersome, and primitive sounding. So, the sophisticated, yet accessible, technology of today might seem like a miracle. And if he could see the recording in progress, he would probably be equally amazed by the array of electronic equipment used to produce and record the music. The electronic keyboards would seem like a space-age version of the player pianos of his own time. The song itself would also seem foreign: virtually every feature–prominent percussion, syncopated rhythms, layers of riffs, Michael's distinctive vocal style, rapid-fire delivery of the lyrics–would be radically different from the popular music of his time. Other than its reiterated chorus and underlying dance beat, he would be hard pressed to find anything about Michael Jackson's song that would recall the popular songs of his own time. The differences between "After the Ball" and "Wanna Be Startin' Somethin'" are so great that the songs seem to have come from two different cultures that happen to share a common tongue–which is not far from the truth.

POPULAR MUSIC: THE ENGLISH OF MUSICAL LANGUAGE?

What is the future of popular music? There will, of course, be popular music in the foreseeable future. The more intriguing issue is whether there will be a Bach, Mozart, or Beethoven as well. Will popular music nurture the geniuses who can create music that transcends time, place, and culture to speak to us with the power and immediacy of the great European composers?

Will future generations respond to 200-year-old melodies the way our generation responds to the Beatles and the Rolling Stones?

We can speculate on this aspect of the future of popular music by considering the past. One consideration is the link between popular music and art music in the eighteenth and nineteenth centuries. Before the emergence of a distinct popular tradition, the difference between art music and the most popular music of the day was more a matter of the sophistication in the use of musical language than a different musical language. (This is what we learned from the three examples presented at the beginning of Chapter 3—a Bellini aria and songs by Russell and Foster are cut from the same musical cloth.) Even the greatest composers of the time were very much in the musical mainstream. J. S. Bach's most prodigious achievement was the composition of five years' worth of cantatas, music for Sunday and holiday worship in the Lutheran service. Granted that Bach was considered by some of his peers as the liturgical music equivalent of "too hip for the room," the fact still remains that these cantatas grew out of the hymns that the congregation sang. Mozart was delighted to hear people singing and humming arias to his operas when he visited Prague. Haydn used folk tunes in his symphonies and string quartets. So did Beethoven, who added a memorable folk-like melody to our collective consciousness, the famous "Ode to Joy," in his monumental Ninth Symphony. The list could easily go on, but the main point is clear: Audiences could understand the art music of their time more easily because it was expressed in the same musical language as everyday music.

This is no longer the case. In this century, we have seen the gap between art music and everyday music widen into a gulf. There has been much important "classical" music composed since 1900. At its best, it can be powerfully expressive and aesthetically and spiritually illuminating. However, it often demands more commitment from its audience—if only to become acquainted with its language—than many are willing to give. This does not mean that the music is less valuable artistically; it means only that it is likely to be less popular.

At the same time, we have seen the creation of a new musical language in the last third of the century. Much of the important rock and post-rock music that we have studied in the last several chapters is created in this new musical language. Part of the importance of the Rolling Stones' "Satisfaction" and James Brown's "Cold Sweat" comes precisely from the fact that they are speaking in a new musical language. As we near the end of the century, the musical language of pre-rock popular music seems farther removed from our everyday musical experiences. It is certainly not obsolete, but it is just as certainly not the only option.

We can project an answer to our original question—Is there a Beethoven in the future of popular music?—by drawing an analogy with the English language. In the centuries, even decades before Shakespeare, English was considered a common language, unfit for civilized discourse. Latin was still the language of choice for official business and cultivated communication. Now, of course, English is the richest language on earth. It has a vocabulary many times that of any other language and a literary tradition without parallel.

Just as popular music grew out of the intermixing of two dissimilar musical traditions, so did English develop from two dissimilar language families, the Germanic languages of northern Europe and Latinate languages of southern Europe. This dual heritage is in large part responsible for the enormous quantity of English words and the subtlety of meaning that they can express.

The history of popular music in this century suggests a parallel with the development of English. Both began as languages one verbal, the other musical, not fit for people of taste and breeding. Both developed a rich vocabulary by drawing on disparate sources.

If the parallel between English and popular music held true in every respect, then we would have every right to expect a Shakespeare of popular music. But it does not. Aside from the obvious differences in language forms (verbal vs. musical), there are crucial differences in the structure of society, the role of the artist, the creative process, and the prospects for financial gain, along with the enormous pressure from those who sponsor popular music—the media, the recording industry, those who promote live performance—to achieve commercial success.

One of the most discouraging features of the popular music of the eighties was the absence of a great innovator—a Louis Armstrong or Charlie Parker, a John Lennon or James Brown, someone who could open the door to an entirely new artistic experience. One wonders whether it is an inherent shortcoming in the music of the period, the result of commercial pressure, bad luck in geniuses, or something else.

There should be no question that popular music style has the expressive capacity to produce monumental music. In chapter after chapter, we have encountered music of real emotional power and directness. There have been moments of profound intensity. The primary unanswered questions are: can such moments be incorporated into a larger structure; can they be sustained longer than three or four minutes?

In the last decade or so, popular music seems to have turned in on itself. The rise of country music, always the most traditional popular style, the broad appeal of oldies stations and anthologies of earlier music, and the extensive use of sampling: These and other signs suggest that popular music is, more than before, seeking inspiration from the past rather than looking forward to the future. Hopefully, the current creative lull is a prelude to an even richer future rather than a sign of evolutionary exhaustion. We'll check back in a few years.

Glossary

a cappella singing, usually by a group, without instrumental accompaniment.

AAB form a three-part form in which the first two sections (A) are, more or less, identical and the third (B) is different. AAB form was used extensively by *rock*-era songwriters.

AABA form a four-part form in which the first, second, and fourth sections (A) are identical and the third (B) is different. AABA form was the most widely used song form between 1920 and 1955.

accent a musical event that stands out from its neighbors because of a change in one or more musical elements. The most common sources of accent are *intensity* (the event is louder), *duration* (longer), *density* (the event contains more parts), or *pitch* (higher or lower).

acoustic bass see *string bass*. The term came into use after the invention of the *electric bass*.

acoustic recording an early recording process in which sound vibrations were transferred directly to the recording medium (cylinder or disc) by means of a large horn or cone. In 1925, it was replaced by *electric recording*.

African-American romantic music a term used here to describe *rock*- and *jam*-based love ballads sung by African-American artists.

Afro-Brazilian music created by Brazilians of African descent. Also, the influence of their creations.

Afro-Cuban music created by Cubans of African descent

amplification the process of increasing the *intensity* of a performer's sound by external means.

amplifier a piece of equipment that can increase the strength of an electrical signal.

Anglo-American an American of English, Scottish, Welsh, or Irish ancestry.

AOR (album-oriented radio) a type of FM radio format that emphasized a restricted playlist.

aria an independent vocal solo that is part of a larger work, such as an *opera* or oratorio.

arpeggio a *chord* whose pitches are performed one after the other, instead of simultaneously.

art music music created strictly for concert listening. Art music serves no functional purpose; its value lies solely in its inherent musical worth. *Classical* music is, by and large, art music; so is much *jazz*, and some *musical theater* and *rock*.

art rock a *rock* substyle that sought to elevate rock from teen entertainment to artistic statement, often by drawing on or reworking *classical* compositions (e.g., Emerson, Lake, and Palmer's version of Mussorgsky's *Pictures at an Exhibition*). Art rock was often distinguished by the use of electronic effects and mood–music-like textures far removed from the propulsive rhythms of early rock.

asymmetrical melody an irregular, fast-moving stream of notes commonly heard in *bop*-era *jazz* performances.

backbeat a percussive accent occurring regularly on the second beat of beat pairs: 1 **2** 1 **2** or 1 **2** 3 **4**.

banjo a four (or five) stringed instrument, with a skin head stretched over a wooden or metal hoop, that is strummed or plucked. The banjo has been used principally in minstrel show music; early *jazz* and *syncopated dance music*; and *old time music* and *bluegrass*

bass the generic term for the lowest pitched instrument in a popular music ensemble.

beat 1. the rhythmic quality of a piece of music that invites a physical response ("that song has a good beat"); 2. the (usually) regular marking of time at walking/dancing/moving speed (usually between seventy-two and 144 beats per second); 3. the rhythmic foundation of a style or substyle, distinguished by the consistent use of regular rhythms and rhythmic patterns: a *two-beat*, a *rock* beat, a *shuffle* beat.

bebop See *bop*

big band the large *jazz* ensemble of the *swing* era that typically contains a complete *rhythm section* and three *horn* sections: three to five *trumpets*, three to five *trombones*, and four to five *saxophones*.

Billboard a prominent music business magazine, *Billboard* is the primary source for *chart* information for a variety of musical styles.

blue note notes from the African *pentatonic scale* that are interpolated into a song using a *diatonic scale* for expressive purposes. The end of the first phrase of Jerome Kern's "Can't Help Lovin' Dat Man" features a striking "blue note" on the word "man."

bluegrass an updated version of country's *old-time string band* music. Bluegrass developed in the late forties under the guidance of mandolinist Bill Monroe.

blues 1. a melancholy mood or feeling ("I've got the blues"); 2. a style characterized principally by highly inflected, often speech-like melodic lines; 3. a song in *blues form*. See also *country blues; electric blues*

blues form a standard blues form consists of a rhymed couplet, with the first line repeated. Each line lasts four measures, so each couplet is matched to 12 measures of music. Each 12-measure unit forms one *chorus*; a typical blues song contains several choruses.

boogie woogie a *blues* piano style characterized by repetitive bass figures, usually in a *shuffle* rhythm.

bop a *jazz* style that developed in the forties characterized by fast tempos, irregular streams of notes, and considerable rhythmic conflict.

bossa nova a *samba*-based, jazz-influenced Brazilian popular song style that became popular in the United States in the early 1960s.

bottleneck originally the neck of a beer bottle worn over a finger of a guitarist's left hand; when placed in contact with the strings, it produced a sliding or whining sound, ideally suited to accompanying the *blues*. Later, narrow metal cylinders replaced bottlenecks. Also, used generally to describe a *guitar* played using a bottleneck or bottleneck-like device.

brass bass See *tuba*.

bridge 1. a wooden arch that conducts the vibrations of a string instrument to the resonating cavity; 2. the B, or contrasting, section of a song in *AABA form*.

brushes two groups of thin wires bound together to make narrow fans. Brushes are used by percussionists in lieu of sticks when a more delicate sound is desired.

cadence a conventional harmonic progression whose goal chord marks the end of a musical section.

cakewalk a dance fad of the 1890s; music to accompany the dance.

call and response a rapid exchange, usually of *riffs*, between two different *timbres*: solo voice/*guitar*; solo voice/choir; *saxophones/trumpets*; etc.

canto the verse-like section of a *salsa* song.

cha-cha-cha a Latin dance that became popular in the 1950s. Its name comes from the signature rhythm that ends each phrase.

chart a listing of the most popular songs during a given time period. Charts have been compiled from sheet music and record sales, as well as radio airplay. There are separate charts for different types of music.

chop-chord style in *bluegrass*, a *mandolin* accompaniment characterized by a heavy *backbeat*.

chord a group of *pitches* considered as a single unit. The notes of a chord may be played simultaneously, or they may be played in a series as an *arpeggio*.

chord progression a series of *chords*. Many of the chord progressions in popular music follow well-used patterns: e.g., the chord progressions for "Heart and Soul" or "La Bamba."

choreographer a person who designs dances and dance routines.

chorus 1. a large singing group; 2. in *verse-chorus* and *rock* songs, that part of a song in which both melody and lyrics are repeated; 3. in *blues* and *Tin Pan Alley* songs, one statement of the melody.

clarinet a mid- to high-range woodwind instrument. It was the high *front line* instrument in *New Orleans jazz* and a solo instrument in thirties jazz.

classical music *art music* by European composers like Bach, Mozart,

Beethoven, and Stravinsky, or music by any composer in the European tradition of music for concert performance.

clave   the characteristic rhythm of *Afro-Cuban* music. It can be represented as: ‖**x** x x **x** x x **x** x ‖ x x **x** x **x** x x x ‖ "Xs" indicate an *eight-beat rhythm*; "*x*s" are accented notes. To create a reverse clave rhythm, switch the two measures.

claves   two cylindrical sticks about 1″ in diameter used to tap out the *clave* rhythm.

collective improvisation   an improvisational context in which more than one performer is improvising a *melody*-like line. Collective improvisation is standard practice in *New Orleans jazz*, *free jazz*, and much *rock*-era *jazz fusion*.

comping   in *bop jazz* style, chordal accompaniment played in rhythmically irregular or unpredictable patterns.

conga drum   a large (2.5′ high), cigar-shaped drum, which is open at the bottom and covered by a drum head on top. It is one of the essential instruments of *Afro-Cuban* music, and has been used in addition to or in place of *drum sets* during the *rock* era.

contour   the pattern of rise and fall in a melodic line, or any other part (e.g., a walking bass) considered melodically.

cool jazz   a *bop*-derived *jazz* style that developed around 1950. Cool jazz retained the harmonic complexity of bop but operated within a much more restrained emotional range: softer *timbres*, lower *dynamic* levels, less rhythmic conflict.

cornet   a *trumpet*-like instrument that was widely used in military bands and early *jazz*. It is stockier, and the sound is not as brilliant as that of the trumpet.

coro   the refrain section of a *salsa* performance. The coro may feature one or more recurrent *riff*-like melodic ideas, improvised solos on pitched instruments, and a *montuno* section.

country blues   a family of African-American folk *blues* styles that flourished in the rural South. Country blues differs from commercial blues mainly in its accompanying instrument—usually *acoustic guitar*—and its tendency toward less regular forms.

country   a commercial form of the music of white Southerners, which began with the advent of commercial radio in the early twenties. The different styles of country music mix elements of the traditional folk music of the South with other popular styles, such as *jazz*, pop-song, and *rock*.

country rock   a hybrid style that merged *country* music and *rock*. Country rock developed in the late sixties, chiefly through the efforts of Gram Parsons.

countrypolitan   the *country*/pop/*soft rock* combination popularized by Kenny Rogers and others in the seventies.

crash cymbal   a *cymbal* used primarily for accents.

crooner   a male singer who sings with a *sweet* sound in a conversational, low-key manner. *Amplification* made crooning possible. Bing Crosby was the most successful of the early crooners.

cross-pollination   the stylistic interchange between different musical styles, such as European-derived and African-inspired music.

crossover a term used to identify a song or artist associated with one popularity *chart* (e.g., *rhythm and blues*) who attains popularity on another chart. Early in his career, Elvis was the ultimate crossover artist, placing songs on pop, rhythm and blues, and *country* charts.

cubop a fusion of *bop* and Latin rhythms. Cubop developed in the late forties, primarily under the guidance of trumpeter Dizzy Gillespie.

cymbal a metal, circular plate, with a slightly raised indentation, often mounted on a pole, that, when struck, makes a ringing or bell-like sound.

delineator a minstrel performer who purported to portray African-Americans in an authentic manner.

density the measure of the amount of musical activity occurring simultaneously in a composition.

diatonic scale a scale made up of seven different *pitches*. The opening of "Joy to the World" uses a descending form of one of the diatonic scales. (There are eight notes in the opening; the first and last belong to the same pitch family.) There are three kinds of diatonic scales commonly used in popular music: *major* ("Joy to the World"), *minor* ("My Funny Valentine"), and *modal* ("Eleanor Rigby" uses one kind of modal scale).

disco a dance music that rose to popularity in the mid-seventies. Disco songs typically had a relentless *beat*, a complex rhythmic *texture*, usually with a *16-beat rhythm*, and rich orchestration, typically an augmented rhythm section, horns, and strings.

distortion electronic timbral alteration. In some *rock* styles, distortion is intentional; intense distortion is the most immediately identifiable feature of *heavy metal*.

Dixieland jazz. See *New Orleans jazz*

dobro an instrument associated with *country* music, with the body of an acoustic guitar and a resonating device placed in the sound hole. Like the *steel guitar*, the dobro is played horizontally and the strings are stopped with a metal bar.

drum kit See *drum set*

drum set a group of percussion instruments set up so they can be played by a single performer. The standard drum set includes a bass drum, struck by a pedal operated by the drummer's right foot; a *snare drum*; two or more *tom-toms*; a *hi-hat* operated by the drummer's left foot; and two or more suspended *cymbals*.

duration the length in time of a musical event.

dynamics levels or changes in *intensity*. The dynamic level of a Ramones song is very loud.

eight-beat rhythm a rhythm that divides each beat of a four beat measure into two equal parts. It is the characteristic rhythmic foundation of *rock*.

electric bass a solid body, *guitar*-shaped bass instrument. It is tuned like a *string bass*. The electric bass came into widespread use in popular music around 1960.

electric blues a post-World War II *blues* style characterized by the use of a full *rhythm section,* including *electric guitar.* It is the most popular form of contemporary blues.

electric guitar an electrically amplified *guitar.* The first electric guitars retained the hollow body of an acoustic guitar and added a *pickup* to convert the string vibration into an electrical signal. By 1960, the solid-body guitar, with no resonating cavity, had emerged as the primary design for electric instruments.

electric piano a *keyboard* instrument popular in the sixties and seventies that combines electronic sound generation with a piano-like action. The most popular model was the Fender Rhodes. With the application of microchip technology, electric pianos have largely been replaced by digital keyboards.

electric recording a recording procedure developed in the twenties that converts sound into an electrical signal before recording and converts the electrical signal back into sound for playback. Electric recording, with its far superior sound quality, immediately made *acoustic recording* obsolete.

endless loop form a form in which one section flows into another without a *cadence* to emphatically divide them.

endman a comic in a minstrel troupe. Minstrel performers sat in a semicircle onstage; an endman sat at one end or the other.

fiddle the informal name given to the *violin* by folk musicians. Fiddle tunes are the traditional dance tunes played primarily in the Southern Appalachians.

flute a metal wind instrument in the shape of a cylindrical tube. It is open at one end and has an opening at the other that the performer blows across.

folk music music made by a group of people (e.g., Cajuns, Navahos, or whites from rural Appalachia), mostly without formal musical training, primarily for their own amusement or for the amusement of others in the group. Within the group, folk music is transmitted orally. Within the popular tradition, folk music has also referred to folk songs sung by commercial musicians (e.g., the Kingston Trio) or music with elements of folk style (e.g., the folk rock of the late sixties).

form the organization of a musical work in time.

four-beat rhythm a rhythmic foundation in which each beat receives equal emphasis; the common rhythmic basis for *jazz.*

fox-trot a popular dance created in the teens by Irene and Vernon Castle. Also, a song with a *two-beat* rhythmic foundation suitable for dancing the fox-trot.

free jazz a *jazz* style that developed in the late fifties that abandoned the rhythmic, harmonic, and formal conventions of '50s jazz.

front line the horns (or other *melody*-line instruments, like the *vibraphone*) in a *jazz* combo. The term comes from the position of the horn players on the bandstand: they stand in a line in front of the rhythm instruments.

functional music music created to support some other activity. Dance music, marching music, and exercise music are all functional.

funk a *rhythm and blues*-derived style that developed in the seventies, primarily under the guidance of George Clinton. It is characterized mainly by dense *textures* (bands may include eight or more musicians) and complex, often *16-beat* rhythms.

fusion a term applied to much of the *jazz-rock* interactions since the seventies. Fusion often combined the improvisational fluency and harmonic interest of jazz with an *eight-* or *sixteen-beat* rhythmic foundation and a group-oriented, rather than solo-oriented, approach.

glam rock a *rock* style of the early seventies in which theatrical elements–make-up, outlandish dress, etc.–were prominent. David Bowie, in his various incarnations, is considered by many as the major figure in glam rock.

gospel a family of religious music styles: there is white and black gospel music. Black gospel music has had the more profound influence on popular music, by far. Created around 1930 by Thomas Dorsey and others, gospel has influenced popular singing, especially *rhythm and blues,* since the early fifties.

griot a member of an African tribe who serves as tribe historian, doctor, and leading musician.

guitar a six-stringed instrument that is either strummed or plucked. In popular music, guitars come in many forms, both acoustic and electric.

habanera a dance created in Cuba during the early nineteenth century. It became popular in both Europe and South America. Its characteristic rhythm resurfaced in the Argentine *tango* and the *cakewalk.*

Hammond organ a brand of electric organ invented in the thirties. It became a fixture in African-American *gospel* music, and has been used occasionally as a *jazz* and *rock* *keyboard* instrument.

hard country an updated version of honky tonk style popular since the late '60s.

hard rock a family of rock styles characterized by loud dynamic levels; a strong beat; aggressive, blues-influenced vocal styles; and prominent guitar lines, often with distortion and other modifications of the basic sound.

harmony *chords,* and the study of *chord progressions.*

head in *jazz* performance, the statement of the *melody.*

heavy metal a *hard rock* style that developed in the early seventies. Heavy metal rock features often ear-splitting volume, heavy use of *distortion,* simplified chord progressions and melodies, lyrics that reflect adolescent, often male preoccupations, and elaborate stage shows.

hi-hat a pair of *cymbals* attached to a vertical stand. A pedal operated by the drummer's left foot brings the cymbals together, then apart.

hierarchical form a *form* in which small units coalesce into larger units, which can form still larger units. The *verse-chorus songs* of the 19th century are excellent examples of hierarchical form.

hillbilly a derogatory term for white rural southerners. Hillbilly also identified early *country* music.

honky-tonk 1. a rough bar; 2. *country* music associated with honky-tonks. Honky-tonk, which developed around 1940, was distinguished from other country music of the period in its use of drums, a heavy *backbeat,* and *electric guitar.*

hook a catchy melodic idea in a *rock*-era song. It usually comes in the *chorus,* where it can be repeated frequently.

horn a generic term for wind instruments. The horn section of a *funk* band, for example, may contain *saxophones, trumpets,* and *trombones.*

improvisation the act of creating music spontaneously, rather than performing a previously learned song the same way every time. Improvisation is one of the key elements in *jazz.*

inflection moment-to-moment changes in *dynamic* level. Aretha Franklin sings in a highly inflected style.

instrumentation literally, the instruments chosen to perform a particular score; broadly, the instrumental and vocal accompaniment for a recording.

intensity the degree of loudness of a musical sound.

interlocutor the straight man in a minstrel show. The interlocutor would sit in the middle of the semicircle and ask questions of the *endmen,* who would give comic replies.

interpolation the insertion of a song into a *musical comedy* for which it was not written. Interpolation was common in the early years of musical comedy, when producers would insert a song into a show simply because it was a hit.

interval the distance between two *pitches.*

jam 1. to perform *jazz* without rehearsal. Such performances are called jam sessions; 2. a term used in this book to identify the family of styles based on a *16-beat rhythm.*

jazz a group of popular-related styles primarily for listening. Jazz is usally distinguished from the other popular music of an era by greater rhythmic freedom (more syncopation and/or less insistent beatkeeping), extensive improvisation, and more adventurous harmony. There are two families of jazz styles: those based on a *four-beat rhythm,* and those based on a *rock* or *sixteen-beat rhythm*

jazz rock a sixties style that mixed *jazz* and *rock* in varying proportions. By the early seventies, jazz rock was more commonly known as *fusion.*

jump band in the late forties, a small band—*rhythm* section plus a few *horns*—that played a *rhythm and blues* style influenced by *big band swing* and *electric blues.* Saxophonist/vocalist Louis Jordan was a key performer in this style.

keyboard a generic term for an instrument–piano, organ, *synthesizer*, etc.– played by depressing keys. It also refers specifically to electronic keyboard instruments, especially synthesizers.

libretto the text of an *opera*, musical, or other sung dramatic work.

looping electronically sustaining a note well beyond its normal duration; a technique commonly used by electric guitarists.

mambo a Latin dance fad of the late forties and fifties that combined the rhythms of the *Afro-Cuban son* with the horn sounds of *big band jazz*.

mandolin a small plucked string instrument of European origin. It is used chiefly in *bluegrass*.

march music for marching, or a composition in the style of march music.

marimba a pitched *percussion* instrument. It has wooden bars laid out like a piano keyboard, with resonators under each bar. The bars are struck with mallets.

measure a consistent grouping of *beats*. A *waltz* has measures containing three beats; a *march* has measures with two beats.

melisma several *pitches* sung to a single syllable. In popular music, melisma has been most widely used by African-American musicians, especially *blues* and *gospel*-influenced artists.

melody the most musically interesting part of a musical *texture*. The melody is typically distinguished from other parts by the interest and individuality of its *contour* and rhythm.

microphone a device that converts soundwaves into an electrical signal. The microphone has been in use in popular music since the twenties.

minstrelsy a form of stage entertainment distinguished by cruel parodies of African-Americans. Minstrelsy was popular from the early 1840s to the end of the nineteenth century.

mixing the process of integrating the many tracks from a multitrack recording into a finished recording.

montuno in *Afro-Cuban* music: 1. a syncopated accompanying figure, usually played on the piano, that is repeated indefinitely; 2. another term for the *coro* section of a song.

Motown slang for Detroit. Also the music produced there in the sixties and early seventies, chiefly by Berry Gordy, for his record label of the same name.

multitrack recording the process of recording each part of a performance separately, then *mixing* them into a complete performance. The Beatles, along with their producer George Martin, were among the first to take full advantage of multitrack recording techniques.

multisectional form compositions (usually instrumental) with three or more sections. *Marches* and rags typically use multisectional form.

musical comedy a form of sung dramatic stage entertainment characterized by a loosely organized, lighthearted plot, generally about a contemporary situation familiar to its audience, e.g., *A Trip to Chinatown*.

musical theater drama enriched by popular song. Musical theater generally refers to musicals that make a serious effort to integrate drama and music, such as *Showboat* and *Oklahoma!*

Nashville sound a pop-oriented *country* style that enjoyed a vogue in the late fifties and early sixties featuring sumptuous orchestrations and sweet-voiced singers in place of *fiddles* and other identifiably country sounds.

New Orleans jazz Style of *jazz* performance based on the early bands that performed in and around New Orleans; revived in the late forties, it is based on *collective improvisation* and quick *tempos*. The *front-line* instruments usually include *cornet* or *trumpet*, *clarinet*, and *trombone*, with a *rhythm section* usually including *banjo*, *tuba*, and sometimes piano. Also referred to as Dixieland jazz.

new wave the "back to basics" movement within *rock* beginning in the late seventies featuring simplified instrumentation and basic chords and melodies. An early new-wave band was Talking Heads.

Newyorican New Yorkers of Puerto Rican descent; something related to or created by them.

octave the *interval* between two *pitches* that vibrate in a 2:1 ratio. Pitches that vibrate in such a simple ratio to each other share the same letter name.

old time music the earliest recorded *country* music of the twenties and thirties; refers in general to the style and repertory of older country musicians.

olio the variety section of a minstrel show. Generally, an olio would feature a series of unrelated acts, much like the later *vaudeville* shows.

opera a music drama in which the entire *libretto* (text) is sung.

operetta originally a kind of European music drama that was less serious than *opera*, with speech instead of singing between songs, but with more dramatic integrity than *musical comedy*. Generally plots told a fairy tale-like story of princes and princesses, gypsies, etc., in a far-away place and/or in a long-ago time. European operettas were popular in the United States through World War II. *Showboat* began an American operetta tradition.

oral tradition aspects of a group's culture—songs, stories, etc.—that are passed from generation to generation by singing, talking, or playing, rather than in written form.

outlaw a term that came into use in the seventies to describe the music of Willie Nelson, Waylon Jennings, and other like-minded *country* artists. Outlaw artists rejected Nashville and its slick production style.

overdubbing the process of recording an additional part onto an existing recording.

parlor song a song to be sung at home in the parlor, like Stephen Foster's "Beautiful Dreamer," popular through most of the nineteenth century.

part one strand in the musical texture. A *rock* power trio has four parts: vocal line, *guitar*, bass, and drums. A single part can be performed by more than one musician, as in the string parts in *Motown* recordings.

pentatonic scale a scale with five notes per octave. Two pentatonic scales are used widely in popular music: the Anglo-American pentatonic scale, heard in minstrel songs (Foster's "Oh, Susanna!" begins with such a scale) and some *country* music; and the African-American pentatonic scale, heard in *blues* and blues-influenced styles. (Henry Ratcliff's unaccompanied blues "Louisiana" makes extensive use of the African-American pentatonic scale.)

percussion a family of instruments whose sounds are produced primarily by striking some kind of vibrating medium. There are two branches of the percussion instrument family: instruments with indefinite *pitch*, like drums and *cymbals*; and instruments with definite pitch, like *marimbas* and *vibraphones*.

pickup a device that connects an acoustic string instrument to an *amplifier*, allowing the instrument to be amplified directly instead of through a *microphone*.

pitch the relative highness or lowness of a musical sound. The pitch of a sound is determined by the frequency with which it vibrates.

plantation song a minstrel show song that mixed the subject of a minstrel song with the slower, more melodious, and more sentimental *parlor song*.

punk a *rock* style that emerged in the late seventies characterized musically by relatively simple instrumentation, rhythms, and production. The Ramones were one of the best-known punk bands.

punk/funk fusion music from the eighties (e.g., much of Prince's music) that combines the hard edge and drive of *punk* with the greater rhythmic and textural complexity of *funk*.

race record a term that came into use in the early twenties to describe recordings by African-American artists intended for sale primarily in the African-American community.

ragtime a popular style at the turn of the twentieth century, ragtime mixed European *forms*, *harmony*, and *textures* with African-inspired *syncopation*. Ragtime began as a piano music, but soon the term was applied to any music–song and dance as well as piano music–that had some syncopation.

rap a musical style of the eighties and nineties characterized by a rhymed text spoken in a heightened voice over a repetitive, mostly rhythmic accompaniment.

refrain See *chorus*

revue a type of stage entertainment popular in the first third of the century. Revues were topical; they often lampooned prominent public figures. They had a flimsy plot, designed to link–however loosely–a series of songs, dance numbers, and comedy routines.

rhymed couplet two lines of poetry that rhyme.

rhythm and blues a term used since the midforties to describe African-American popular styles, especially those influenced by *blues* and/or dance music.

rhythm section that part of a musical group that supplies the rhythmic and harmonic foundation of a performance. A rhythm section usually includes at least one chord instrument (*guitar,* piano, *keyboard,* etc.), a bass instrument, and a *percussion* instrument (typically the *drum set*).

rhythm song a *Tin Pan Alley* song in which a catchy, syncopated melodic rhythm is the most noteworthy musical feature. The Gershwins' "Fascinating Rhythm" is an excellent early example of a rhythm song.

ride cymbal the *cymbal* on which a *bop* or post-bop *jazz* drummer plays a ride pattern, most commonly "dummmmm, dump a dummmm. . ."

riff a short (two to seven pitches), rhythmically interesting melodic idea.

rock 1. an umbrella term to describe the family of styles that share an eight-beat rhythmic foundation; 2. music made by musicians associated with rock. (Many of the Beatles' songs, for example, do not use a rock beat, but they are classified as rock because they are by the Beatles.)

rock 'n' roll a transitional style that emerged in the midfifties as the precursor of *rock.*

rock musical a musical that uses *rock* rhythms and generally incorporates some of its ideas and attitudes; *Hair* was a prototypical rock musical.

rockabilly a fifties style, performed mainly by white Southerners, that combined elements of *country* music with *rock 'n' roll.*

rumba an *Afro-Cuban* inspired dance popularized in this country during the early thirties.

salsa the term that came into use in the sixties and seventies to describe an updated form of the *mambo.* It is (now) the most popular traditional form of *Afro-Cuban* music in both the United States and Cuba.

samba the most popular *Afro-Brazilian* dance music of the century, both in Brazil and elsewhere. The samba has been popular inthe United States since the early 1930s. The *sixteen-beat rhythms* of samba influenced the new *jazz* and African-American popular styles of the 1970s and 1980s.

sampling a recording technique used since the early eighties, in which a short excerpt from an earlier recorded performance is recorded ("sampled") and interpolated into a new recording. Sampling has become a common technique in African-American dance music and *rap.*

saxophone a family of keyed brass instruments with *clarinet*-like mouthpieces. The tenor or alto saxophone has been one of the lead melody instruments in *jazz* since the thirties.

scale a conventional arrangement of *pitches* in a series separated by small *intervals.* The two most widely used families of scales in popular music are *dia-*

tonic scales, with seven pitches per octave, and *pentatonic* scales, with five pitches per octave.

scratching a sound produced by rotating an LP record back and forth on a turntable while the needle is in a groove. the tone arm picks up the vibration as if the record were spinning. The performer can control both the pitch and the rhythm of the sound produced in this way by the speed and duration of the movement. Scratching is part of the sound world of *rap* and other African-American popular styles of the eighties and nineties.

sequencing a recording technique in which an excerpt of music, e.g., a rhythm track, is recorded several times in succession. When it is played back, it gives an unvarying *texture* to the accompaniment.

sheet music music in notated form. Popular songs were sold exclusively in sheet music until the advent of recording in the 1890s.

shuffle a *four-beat rhythm* in which each beat is reinforced with a long/short pattern. Shuffle rhythms were most common in post-World War II *jump* styles and *rhythm and blues.*

singer/songwriter a term that came into use around 1970 to describe songwriters who performed their own music. The music of singer/songwriters was generally characterized by an emphasis on *melody,* a folk-like accompaniment, and a relatively low *dynamic* level.

sixteen-beat rhythm a division of the four-beat measure into four equal parts; the rhythmic basis for contemporary styles such as *disco* and *funk.*

slap bass a technique used by electric bassists in which the strings are slapped, usually with the right thumb, instead of plucked, producing a more percussive sound. Slapping is a common technique in *funk* and funk-influenced music.

snare drum a shallow, two-headed drum with rattling wires placed underneath the lower head.

sock cymbal See *hi-hat*

soft rock a family of *rock* styles characterized mainly by sweeter singing styles, more melodious, even *Tin Pan Alley*-ish vocal lines, richer instrumentation, and a gentle *dynamic* level.

son the most characteristic style of *Afro-Cuban* music. The *son* was popular in Cuba during the early part of the century. Some of the Cuban musicians who migrated to New York in the thirties and forties blended *son* with *big band swing* to produce the *mambo.*

song interpreter singers, like Billie Holiday and Frank Sinatra, who transform popular song into personal statements, often thoroughly altering the *contour* and rhythm of the *melody.*

soul a term used widely in the sixties by both African-Americans and whites to describe popular music by African-Americans, particularly music, like that of James Brown, marginally influenced by pop or white rock styles.

spiritual a kind of African-American, religious folksong that flourished in the nineteenth century. Spirituals were introduced to white audiences after the Civil War by groups like the Fisk Jubilee Singers.

standard a *Tin Pan Alley* song of enduring popularity.

steel guitar an electric version of the Hawaiian guitar that has been a popular instrument in *country* music since the mid-1930s. The steel guitar rests on the performer's knees, or on a stand just above the knees. The strings are stopped with a metal bar held in one hand and plucked with the other hand. A more modern and complex version of this instrument is the pedal steel guitar, which may have several necks, as well as foot-activated pedals and knee-operated levers that allow for changing the *pitch* or *volume*.

string band a small group in early *country* music consisting mainly of string instruments of various types: *fiddle, banjo,* and *guitar* were the most widely used.

strophic a song form in which two or more verses of text are sung to the same melody. A hymn is strophic.

sweet As opposed to *swing,* so-called sweet bands played songs in a *two-beat rhythm,* with little syncopation, *slow* tempos, and flowing *melodies.*

swing 1. the sense of rhythmic play, the result of various kinds of rhythmic conflict, that characterizes good *jazz* performance; 2. music, often jazz or jazz-influenced, based on a clearly marked *four-beat rhythm;* 3. an era in popular music extending from about 1935 to 1945 that featured *big bands* playing swing-based songs.

syncopated dance music a post-ragtime orchestral dance music popular in the teens and early twenties. It was characterized by the use of syncopated rhythms over a *two-beat rhythm.*

syncopation accents that come between the *beats* of a regular rhythm, rather than with them.

synthesizer a family of electronic instruments in which sounds are produced electronically, either by generating a wave form within the machine or by recording acoustic sounds (e.g., the tones of a piano) digitally. Most, but not all, synthesizers are operated by a keyboard.

tambo and bones nicknames for the *endmen* in a minstrel show, so called because one usually played a tambourine and the other a pair of bones.

tango an Argentine dance seemingly based on the *habanera* that has been popular in Europe and the United States since the teens. In the United States, it was the first of the Latin dance fads.

tempo the speed of the *beat.*

texture the relationship of the *parts* in a musical performance.

timbales a pair of shallow, single-headed drums tuned to different pitches. Timbales are a customary component of the *percussion* section of an *Afro-Cuban* band.

timbre the distinctive tone quality of a voice or instrument.

Tin Pan Alley a nickname for a section of East 28th street in New York where many music publishers had their offices. Also, the styles of the songs created in the first half of the century for these publishers: a Tin Pan Alley song refers to songs by Irving Berlin, George Gershwin, et al.

tom-tom a two-headed drum of varying depth that has become an integral part of the *drum set*. Most drummers use at least two tom-toms, which they play with drumsticks. The smallest is still larger (and lower in pitch) than a *snare drum*, while the largest is smaller than a bass drum.

trio 1. a group of three musicians; 2. the second half of a *march*, rag, and other compositions in *multisectional form*. In marches, the melody of the trio is often lyrical.

trombone the tenor and baritone voices in the brass section. Trombones use slides (instead of valves) for changes in *pitch*. The trombone was a staple of the marching band, early *jazz* bands, and pre-*rock* dance orchestras. It appears occasionally in contemporary *horn* sections.

trumpet the high voice in the brass section. The trumpet consists of a mouthpiece, a long, slightly conical tube that bends back on itself and then out in the original version, where it ends in a flared bell. Valves permit a trumpeter to make adjustments in *pitch*.

tuba the bass voice of the brass section. The tuba contains a long, wide bored tube, which gives it a mellow sound. It has been used infrequently in popular music, most importantly as the bass instrument of the *rhythm section* during the twenties. By 1930, it had been replaced by the *string bass*.

tumbao a syncopated bass pattern characteristic of *Afro-Cuban* music.

turkey trot a popular animal dance of the early twentieth century. Like many of the other animal dances of the period, the turkey trot was considered scandalous because it encouraged "lingering close contact" between the dancers.

twelve-bar blues See *blues form*

two-beat rhythm The division of the measure into two primary *beats* or *accents;* the rhythmic basis of the *fox-trot* and other early syncopated instrumental styles.

vaudeville a form of stage entertainment popular from the 1880s to about 1930. A vaudeville consisted of a series of acts: singers, dancers, novelty performers, comics, etc. Vaudeville differed from the *revue* and *musical comedy* in that there was no attempt to link vaudeville acts into a dramatically coherent whole.

vernacular speech common everyday speech, usually rich in slang.

verse-chorus song the most popular song form of the late nineteenth century. The verse tells a story in several stages (this section is *strophic,* i.e., different words are set to the same melody), while the *chorus*, which comes at the end of each verse, repeats both words and *melody* to reinforce the main message of the song. In early verse-chorus songs, the chorus was often sung by a small group, usually a quartet.

vibraphone a pitched *percussion* instrument. The vibraphone consists of a group of metal bars arranged like a piano keyboard, with tubular resonators underneath. Dampers, activated by a foot pedal, allow the player to control how long each note sounds. The vibraphone has been used mainly in *jazz* as an alternative to *horns* in the *front line*.

vibrato a slight oscillation in the basic *pitch* of a musical sound. Vibrato is used by most popular singers and instrumentalists (except for pianists and percussionists).

violin a high-pitched stringed instrument that is usually played with a bow. In popular music, the violin has been used in several quite different ways. It has been played *fiddle*-style by early minstrels and *country* performers. It is played in the classical manner in *sweet* dance orchestras, film soundtracks, richly orchestrated pop vocal arrangements, and other situations in which a lush, warm sound is desirable. It has also been used as a solo *jazz* instrument.

walking bass a bass line in which the performer plays one note every *beat*.

waltz A dance originally from Eastern Europe featuring a three-beat rhythmic basis, with emphasis on the first beat.

waltz song a type of song popular around 1900 in which a flowing melody is supported by a simple, waltz-time accompaniment.

washboard a "homemade" percussion instrument used in many Southern folk styles—*blues*, Cajun music, etc. The performer strokes the washboard with thimbles on his fingers in a rhythmic pattern.

washtub bass a "homemade" bass instrument consisting of a washtub, piece of cord, and a broomstick; the washtub serves as the resonator, and *pitch* is adjusted by tightening or loosening the cord that is fixed at one end to the tub and the other to the stick.

western swing a Texas *country* style popular in the thirties and early forties. Western swing added drums, *horns*, piano, and *steel guitar* to the instrumentation of the standard country band. This horrified traditionalists but delighted others.

Bibliography

ENCYCLOPEDIAS, DICTIONARIES AND OTHER REFERENCES

Carlin, Richard. *The Big Book of Country Music* (New York: Penguin Books, 1995). [Complete guide to artists and genres in country from the turn of the century to today.]

Clarke, Donald, ed. *The Penguin Encyclopedia of Popular Music* (London: Penguin Books, 1989). [A fine, affordable one-volume reference. Good on contemporary peripheral figures and subjects, e.g., salsa artists; less helpful on nineteenth- and early twentieth-century artists and styles.]

Gänzl, Kurt. *The Encyclopedia of the Musical Theater* (New York: Schirmer Books, 1994). [A massive encyclopedia with worldwide scope, including biographical entries as well as genres and specific shows.]

Kernfeld, Barry, ed. *The New Grove's Dictionary of Jazz* (London: Macmillan, 1988). [Standard two-volume reference work, recently issued in a one-volume version by St. Martins Press for home use.]

Kinkle, Roger D. *The Complete Encyclopedia of Popular Music and Jazz, 1900-1950* (New Rochelle, NY: Arlington House, 1974). [Kinkle's encyclopedia contains biographical entries, lists of popular songs and shows, popularity indices, and catalogs of the major record labels during the first half-century.]

Larkin, Colin, ed. *The Guinness Encyclopedia of Popular Music* (London: Guinness Publishing, 1992). [Not really an encyclopedia; it consists mainly of biographies, weighted toward the contemporary British scene.]

Oliver, Paul, Harrison, Max, and Bolcom, William. *The New Grove Gospel, Blues and Jazz* (New York: W. W. Norton, 1986). [Compiled from entries in *The New Grove's Dictionaries*, available in paperback.]

Sadie, Stanley and Hitchcock, H. Wiley, eds. *The New Grove's Dictionary of American Music* (London: Macmillan, 1986). [Although not devoted exclusively to popular music, *TNGDAM* contains entries on major artists, styles, terms, instruments, recording, and many other related subjects. *New Grove's* dictionary entries have helpful bibliographies as necessary.]

Santelli, Robert. *Big Book of the Blues.* (New York: Penguin Books, 1993). [Biographical dictionary of leading blues players from the twenties to today.]

SURVEYS

Chase, Gilbert. *America's Music,* revised 3rd edition (Urbana, IL: University of Illinois, 1989). [Covers the full range of American music–classical, folk, and popular. It is especially strong in nineteenth-century popular music, although Chase writes with authority and style about all kinds of music.]

Hamm, Charles. *Music in the New World.* (New York: W. W. Norton, 1983). [Hamm's survey, designed to be used with the New World recordings, covers a great variety of American music. It is organized primarily by genres; the book is, in effect, several short books, each covering a style over a fairly extended timespan. The discussions of nineteenth- and early twentieth-century vocal and instrumental music are especially good.]

Hitchcock, H. Wiley. *Music in the United States*, 3rd edition (Englewood Cliffs, NJ: Prentice Hall, 1988). [Like Chase and Hamm, a well-written and informative survey of American music. It is somewhat shorter than the others but rich in information and insight.]

Kingman, Daniel. *American Music: A Panorama*, 2nd edition (New York: Schirmer Books, 1990). [A wide-ranging book covering folk, popular, classical, and jazz styles.]

Southern, Eileen. *The Music of Black Americans*, 2nd edition (New York: W. W. Norton, 1983). [The definitive history of African-American music in the United States. Particularly informative about minstrelsy, ragtime, early jazz, and African-Americans in entertainment around the turn of the century.]

Sanjek, Russell. *American Popular Music and Its Business* (New York: Oxford University Press, 1988). [A history of popular music from its roots in Elizabethan England to the mid-1980s. Written by a former BMI executive, it is especially enlightening about the music industry.]

van der Merwe, Peter. *Origins of the Popular Style: The Antecedents of Twentieth-Century Popular Music* (New York: Oxford, 1989) [A thorough and provocative study of the roots of contemporary popular styles in folk and nineteenth-century popular music.]

CHART INFORMATION

Whitburn, Joel. *The Billboard Book of Top 40 Albums*, 2nd edition (Menomonee Falls, WI: Record Research, 1991).

____. The *Billboard Book of Top 40 Hits*, 4th edition (Menomonee Falls, WI: Record Research, 1989).

[Whitburn's books are the industry source for information about hit songs. He has several other catalogs along the same line, including comprehensive listings for country and rhythm and blues.]

____. *Pop Memories, 1890-1954* (Menomonee Falls, WI: Record Research, 1986). [A listing of the top singles from the beginning of commercial sound recording to 1954. Organized by artist, with song cross-references.]

RAGTIME

Berlin, Edward A. *Ragtime, A Musical and Cultural History* (Berkeley, CA: University of California Press, 1980). [A comprehensive study of the music and the period in which it developed.]

Blesh, Rudi and Harriet Jans. *They All Played Ragtime*, 4th edition (New York: Oak Publications, 1971). [The classic study, first published in 1950, that started the ragtime revival.]

BLUES

Cohn, Lawrence, ed. *Nothing But the Blues*. (New York: Abbeville Press, 1993). [A fine collection of articles by leading scholars on the blues.]

Oliver, Paul. *The Story of the Blues* (Radnor, PA: Chilton Books, 1982). [An excellent account of country blues.]

Roberts, John Storm. *Black Music of Two Worlds,* Revised edition (Tivoli, New York: Original Music, 1992). [Classic study of African and African-American music.]

MUSICAL THEATER

Bordman, Gerald. *American Musical Comedy, From Adonis to Dreamgirls* (New York: Oxford University Press, 1982).

____. *American Musical Theatre* (New York: Oxford University Press, 1979).

____. *American Musical Revue* (New York: Oxford University Press, 1985).

____. *American Operetta; From* H. M. S. Pinafore *to* Sweeney Todd (New York: Oxford University Press, 1981).

[Bordman combines thorough scholarship with real understanding of musical theater as drama and music. *American Musical Theatre* is an exhaustive chronicle of the musical. The three shorter studies offer interpretive surveys of the main subcategories of staged popular music.]

Gänzl, Kurt. *Gänzl's Book of the Broadway Musical* (New York: Schirmer Books, 1995). [Plot summaries, cast lists and production information, and the songs in the seventy-five most popular musicals produced on Broadway from the 1880s to today.]

Mast, Gerald. *Can't Help Singin'* (Woodstock, New York: Overlook Press, 1987). [Mast writes with imagination and insight about the entire history of musical theater. His book also includes discussions of many film musicals.]

POPULAR SONG

Forte, Allen. *The American Popular Ballad of the Golden Era 1924–1950* (Princeton: Princeton University Press, 1995) [A detailed analytical study of the vocabulary and compositional procedures of the Tin Pan Alley songwriters. Demands more musical background than Wilder, but contains unique analytic insights into the songs.]

Hamm, Charles. *Yesterdays: Popular Song in America* (New York: W. W. Norton, 1979). [Hamm traces the history of popular song over the last 200 years. His book is particularly informative about nineteenth-century and early twentieth-century song.]

Wilder, Alec. *American Popular Song* (New York: Oxford University Press, 1972). [The most thorough and authoritative analysis of the work of the great Tin Pan Alley songwriters.]

LATIN MUSIC

Manuel, Peter. *Popular Musics of the Western World* (New York: Oxford University Press, 1988). [This broad survey of popular musics includes helpful discussions of Latin and Caribbean styles.]

Roberts, John Storm. *The Latin Tinge* (New York: Oxford University Press, 1979; reprint Tivoli, New York: Original Music, 1992). [A full-length study of Latin music in the United States.]

COUNTRY MUSIC

Malone, Bill C. *Country Music, USA,* revised and enlarged edition (Austin, TX: University of Texas Press, 1985). [The definitive history of country music. Malone also compiled the Smithsonian country music anthology, for which he wrote extensive commentary.]

ROCK

Belz, Carl. *The Story of Rock,* 2nd edition (New York: Harper and Row, 1973). [Gillett (in *The Sound of the City*) and Belz both tell the story of the early years of rock. Both have strong opinions and convincing points of view about the music and the industry that supported it.]

DeCurtis, Anthony and Henke, James, eds. *The Rolling Stone Illustrated History of Rock and Roll,* 3rd edition (New York: Random House, 1992). [A useful companion to *Rock of Ages,* this book contains profiles of important artists and styles. Discussions focus more on the music. Entries include thorough discographies.]

Gillett, Charlie. *The Sound of the City,* revised and expanded edition (New York: Pantheon Books, 1983).

Ward, Ed, Stokes, Geoffrey, and Tucker, Ken. *Rock of Ages* (New York: Summit Books, 1986). [A history of rock through the early eighties. Mostly an account of the major trends and events; little discussion of the music.]

BLACK GOSPEL

Heilbut, Anthony. *The Gospel Sound* (New York: Limelight Editions, 1985). [The best survey of early black gospel music.]

JAZZ

Gridley, Mark C. *Jazz Styles,* 3rd edition (Englewood Cliffs, NJ: Prentice Hall, 1988). [Gridley combines a comprehensive history of jazz with careful analysis of jazz styles past and present.]

Schuller, Gunther. *Early Jazz: Its Roots and Musical Development* (New York: Oxford University Press, 1968). [The definitive study of jazz through 1930 and a model for the study of any music whose history is documented primarily in recordings.]

Stearns, Marshall. *Jazz* (New York: Oxford University Press, 1955). [One of the first and still best overall surveys of the genre.]

RELATED MATERIAL

Marcus, Greil. *Mystery Train: Images of America in Rock 'n' Roll Music* (New York: E. P. Dutton, 1975). [In portraits of seven artists, some famous, some obscure, Marcus uses rock 'n' roll as a lens to view American culture. One of the best books of its kind.]

Rockwell, John. *All-American Music* (New York: Knopf, 1983). [Rockwell's insightful essays on contemporary American artists include profiles of such disparate musicians as Stephen Sondheim and Eddie Palmieri.]

Stearns, Marshall and Jean. *Jazz Dance* (New York: Schirmer Books, 1979). [An excellent account of black and black-influenced social and stage dancing from the 1890s through the 1960s.]

Discography

Example 2.5, "Isn't She Lovely," can be found on Stevie Wonder's *Songs in the Key of Life* (Tamla 340). It's also on Wonder's anthology *Stevie Wonder's Original Musiquarium I* (Motown 37463-6002-2), the most affordable source for the Stevie Wonder songs discussed in Chapter 20.

Example 3.12, "Tell the Truth," is included on *Ray Charles Live* (Atlantic 7-81732-2). The excerpt discussed in the text begins about 1'50" into the performance.

Examples 10.5 and 10.6, "Here's That Rainy Day" and "I've Got You Under My Skin." The most useful source for these Sinatra recordings is the Smithsonian Collection, *American Popular Song.*

Examples 14.6 and 14.12. "Mystery Train" is probably in your library as part of the original New World set distributed in the 70s. On CD, it is available on the Sun Sessions CD. "Jailhouse Rock" is included on numerous greatest hits collections (e.g., RCA 47-7-35). If you want to splurge, you can buy *Elvis— the King of Rock & Roll: The Complete '50s Masters.*

Examples 14.10 and 14.11. *Ray Charles Live* (Atlantic 7-81732-2) includes "A Fool for You" and a live version of "What'd I Say." The studio version, which is discussed in the text comes from *His Greatest Hits* (DCC D2 33079-2).

Examples 2.13 and 15.1. Both Rolling Stones songs can be found on their *Hot Rocks* (London 606/7), a greatest hits compilation.

Examples 15.2–15.5. The best Beatles' starter albums are *The Beatles 1962-1966* (Capitol SKBO 3403) and *The Beatles 1967–1970* (Capitol SKBO 3404). The tracks are also available on their original albums: *Yesterday . . . And Today, Sgt. Pepper's Lonely Hearts Club Band, Revolver,* and *Rubber Soul,* respectively, and the ultimate box set, which is called *The Ultimate Box Set.*

Example 15.6, Dylan's "Subterranean Homesick Blues," is available on the original album, *Bringing It All Back Home* (Columbia 9128). It is also included on his first album, *Bob Dylan's Greatest Hits,* (Columbia 9463).

Example 15.7, "Purple Haze," has since appeared on numerous greatest hits anthologies. Currently available is *The Ultimate Experience,* MCAD-10829.

Example 19.1, "Tiny Dancer," was originally on John's album, *Madman Across the Water,* which has been reissued on Polydor 825487-2. The song can also be found on several greatest hits compilations, including the current *Your Song,* MCAD-31016.

Example 19.2, "Black Dog," appears on Led Zeppelin's untitled fourth album (Atlantic 19129-2). The album is a classic; it remains available on CD.

Example 19.3, "Born to Run," is the title track from Springsteen's 1975 breakthrough album. It remains available on CD (Columbia CK-33795.)

Example 19.4, "I Don't Wanna Go Down to the Basement," is one of a generous number of cuts on the Ramones' *All the Stuff (and more) v. 1* (Sire. WB 9 26220-2.)

Example 19.5, "What's Your Name," is most easily found on Lynyrd Skynyrd's 2 disc greatest hits set, *Gold and Platinum* (MCAD2-6898).

Example 19.6. *Sweet Baby James*, which included "Fire and Rain" among its cuts, has been reissued on CD (WB 1843-2). For those who want a broader view of Taylor's work, his *Greatest Hits*, (WB 3113-2) is recommended.

Example 19.7. *Clouds*, the Joni Mitchell album that contains "I Don't Know Where I Stand," has been reissued on CD (Reprise 6341-2).

Example 19.8. *Still Crazy After All These Years* has been reissued on CD and is available on Warner Bros (WB 25591-2). The greatest hits compilation, *Negotiations and Love Songs* (WB 25789-2), also includes "Still Crazy After All These Years."

Example 19.9. "You've Got a Friend" can be found on *Tapestry*, reissued on CD on the Ode label (Ode 77009).

Examples 20.4 and 20.5. Both "You Are the Sunshine of My Life" and "Send One Your Love" can be found on Wonder's anthology *Stevie Wonder's Original Musiquarium I* (Motown 37463-6002-2), although there are (for some reason) overdubbed brass and backup vocal lines added to "You Are the Sunshine of My Life." Alternatively, both *Talking Book* (Motown 37463-319-2) and *Journey Through the Secret Life of Plants* (Motown 37463-6127-2) have been re-released on CD.

Examples 20.7, 20.8, 20.9. The original albums for these three songs are still in print. They are, respectively: "Wanna Be Startin' Somethin'"–*Thriller* (Epic 38112); "Sign O The Times" and "It's Gonna Be a Beautiful Night"–*Sign O the Times* (Paisley Park 25577-2).

Index